Brooks Range

Mt McKinley

Alaska Range

Coast Range

Rocky Mountains

Sierra Nevada

Sierra Madre

Cumberland
Peninsula

• Mt Rainier

Yosemite

• Mt. Washington

• Huascaran

• Pumasillo

Andes

• Aconcagua

• FitzRoy

Since this book was prepared for publication the tragic news of the death of Alan Rouse has been received. Caught in a snow storm, he perished after reaching the summit of K2, the second highest, and arguably most challenging, mountain in the world.

CLIMBING

CLIMBING

ROCK Ron Fawcett

ICE Jeff Lowe

ALPINE Paul Nunn

EXPEDITIONS Alan Rouse

Editor: Audrey Salkeld

Bell & Hyman

Published in 1986 by
Bell & Hyman Limited
Denmark House
37–39 Queen Elizabeth Street
London SE1 2QB

First published 1986

ISBN: 0 7135 2620 3

British Library Cataloguing in Publication Data

Climbing
   1.   Mountaineering
   I.   Fawcett, Ron
   796.5'22   GV200

Typeset by August Filmsetting, Haydock, St Helens
Produced in Italy by Motta-Milan

Contents

Introduction

In bringing together four such respected mountaineers to describe the diversity of climbing, the intention has been not only to pass on the wealth of experience they have gathered over long association with the hills, but to convey also something of what climbing means to them. Without doubt, it can be a stimulating sport, but it can be very much more. For our four authors, and for many others like them, climbing is a way of life; it is their life force.

For convenience this book is divided into four sections: rock, ice, alpine and expedition climbing. In a sense, it is an artificial division. Of course they are not separate and unconnected activities; each borrows from each, and it is possible to make of climbing as much or little as you wish. Rock climbing can mean pleasant days with friends on local outcrops, or it can take you around the world seeking out the warm limestone gorges of southern Europe, the sandstone pinnacles of Bohemia, or the great granite sweeps of Yosemite Valley. On a long, multi-day ascent, you are already making an expedition. Ice-climbing can be practised as an individual activity in winter gulleys or on frozen waterfalls, but apply it to alpine ascents and you will require to blend with it rock and snow skills and a good sense of navigation.

The division between alpine and expedition climbing is perhaps the most blurred of all. We have taken alpine climbing to refer to that practised in the relatively accessible snow ranges of the world: the European Alps, the Rockies, Japan, and the Southern Alps of New Zealand. Yet, to organize climbing holidays to any one of these areas, can involve planning every bit as detailed as for a simple expedition. The difference is one of degree. To climb in the higher and remoter mountains of the world—the Himalayas, Karakorum, Alaska, Andes etc.—requires self-sufficiency over extended periods, and this aspect has been dealt with in the expeditions section of the book.

The four authors were chosen for their supremacy in one particular facet of climbing. Ron Fawcett has been a leading technical rock climber over the past decade. It was his good fortune to come young into the sport at a period when it was undergoing great change. Rock climbers were only just becoming aware how dramatically performance could be improved with specialized training. At the same time, there was a swing away from ascents aided by equipment towards free climbing. The scene was wide open for someone of Ron's natural athletic ability, and he was quickly to be seen 'freeing' many of the old, harder aid routes. He climbs with an effortless fluency that is a joy to watch and has made him the subject of a number of television films.

Jeff Lowe was lucky to be born into a climbing and skiing family and was making adventurous trips into wild country from a very young age. His father took him up the Grand Teton in Wyoming when he was only seven, and he made his earliest first ascent at the age of fourteen. He says that although the mountains he climbs now are very much bigger than the East Face of Mount Ogden, they don't get any bigger in his mind. In recent years he has soloed Ama Dablam and Pumori in the Himalayas, and made the first ascent of the extremely difficult North Face of Kwangde with fellow-American Dave Breashears.

A constant, high-performing figure on the national and international mountaineering scene for very many years has been Paul Nunn. Since 1961, he has missed only one 'alpine' season and his climbs have taken him all over the world: to the Alps, the Arctic, the Soviet Union, the Karakorum and Himalaya. He is Associate Editor of the influential magazine *Mountain* and author of a number of guidebooks. Thoughtful and wise, Paul is deeply concerned that traditional skills and ethics are not sacrificed in the current trend towards more specialized and competitive climbing.

From an apprenticeship on rock, Al Rouse has become one of the most experienced all-round mountaineers active today. A nine-month climbing trip to South America during 1976–7 when he and his friends managed 17 major first ascents, convinced him of the workability of small lightweight expeditions, with members climbing independently as pairs, but offering each other back-up in difficulty. It is a system he has since applied to climbs on major Himalayan peaks with great success. He has climbed Jannu, Nuptse and Kongur, been to Everest in winter and twice to K2.

Each author has been asked to set out the techniques of their speciality, and to describe its scope for development. They have examined the history and the way unwritten codes of conduct and fair play have evolved. Above all, they have injected into their testimonies something of the fun and satisfaction climbing gives them. It is noticeable how all have developed an instinctive sympathy with mountain environment and a meditative response to mountaineering. From such teachers, any novice climber, or anybody who knows nothing about mountaineering at all, can obtain from these pages a picture of the essence and ethos of the sport, an overview, which it would be hard to acquire elsewhere. Someone who wants to take up rock climbing, will find here sound advice on how to start.

The real beneficiaries of a book like this, however, will be those who already climb and enjoy their climbing—at whatever grade. Unique practical tips from the acknowledged experts offers them the chance of improving technique and style. Ron Fawcett describes the variety of methods that can be employed to take advantage of even the tiniest holds; Jeff Lowe tells how to negotiate a wide variety of snow and ice features, while Paul Nunn suggests tours of graded difficulty on which accumulated experience can be tested. There is advice from Al Rouse to take the headache out of trip planning—a guide to the paperwork

At the Mönchjoch in the Bernese Oberland.

you need, the jabs, and how to plan your food and medical requirements.

There is emphasis too on safety: sensible advice for avoiding trouble, and for getting out of it if you are unlucky enough to get caught in a potentially dangerous situation. It is no use pretending there is no danger in climbing. Of course it is dangerous. The skill and the fun comes from learning to recognize risk and to exercise a measure of control over it. Experience teaches a climber how to translate natural apprehension into sensible action, but above all to recognize the dividing line between acceptable risk and foolhardiness. The safe climber knows when to back off.

There are no shortcuts to experience; practice is the only way to achieve expertise, but armed with advice such as can be found in these pages, it should be possible to put practise to the very best advantage. Good climbing!

Audrey Salkeld
Clevedon, 1986

Rock Climbing Grades

UK	UIAA*	EAST GERMANY	CZECHO-SLOVAKIA	FRANCE	USA		AUSTRALIA
MODERATE	III				5.0		4
DIFFICULT	III +				5.1		5
HARD DIFFICULT	IV −				5.2		6
VERY DIFFICULT	IV				5.3		7
HARD VERY DIFFICULT	IV +				5.4		8, 9
MILD SEVERE	V −				5.5		10, 11
SEVERE 4a / HARD SEVERE 4a	V			4c	5.6		12, 13
SEVERE 4b / HARD SEVERE 4b / VERY SEVERE 4b	V +	VIIa	VI	5a	5.7		14
HARD SEVERE 4c / VERY SEVERE 4c / HARD VERY SEVERE 4c	VI −	VIIb	VII	5b	5.8		15
5a / VERY SEVERE 5a / HARD VERY SEVERE 5a	VI	VIIc	VIIa	5c	5.9		16, 17
	VI +						
E1 5b / 5b / HARD VERY SEVERE 5b	VII −	VIIIa	VIIb	6a	5.10	− a / b	18, 19
E1 5c / E2 5c / 5c / 5c	VII	VIIIb	VIIc	6b	5.10	c / + d	20, 21
	VII +	VIIIc					
6a / E3 6a / 6a / 6a	VIII −	IXa		6c	5.11	− a / b	22, 23
	VIII	IXb			5.11	c	24
6b / E4 6b / 6b / 6b	VIII +	IXc		7a	5.11	+ d	25
6c / E5 6c / 6c / E6/7 6c	IX −	Xa		7b	5.12	−	26, 27, 28
	IX						
7a	IX +			7c	5.12	+	29
	X −			8a	5.13		30
	X						

*Union Internationale des Associations Alpines

A Comparison of Rock and Ice Technical Ratings

ICE U.S.	Scotland	France	ROCK U.S.	Great Britain	France
AI1	1	F	3rd Class		II
AI2	2	D	4th Class		III
AI3	3	D_{sup}	5.0 to 5.6	4a	IV
AI4	4	TD	5.7 5.8	4b, 4c 5a	IV & V
WI5	5	TD+	5.9	5b	V & VIa
WI6	6	ED	5.10	5b 5c	VIb
WI7	6	ED+	5.11	6a	VIc

According to this adapted Yosemite/Scottish system there is the additional overall grade. For instance, on Ben Nevis, Number 2 Gulley would be graded I, SI1; Comb Gulley would be II, SI3; Green Gulley II, SI4; Pt. 5 Gulley III, SI5; The Chancer II, WI5; Orion Face Direct IV, SI5; Long Climb V, SI5 or 6; Citadel/Sticil Face (on Shelterstone Crag) IV, SI6 if no aid is used.

In France, on Mt. Blanc du Tacul, the regular walk-up would be II, AI1; the Gervasutti Couloir would be III, AI2 or 3; Gabbarrou/Albinoni IV, WI4; Super Couloir V, WI5.

New Hampshire's Repentence is III, WI5; Wyoming's Black Ice Couloir is IV, AI3; Slipstream in Canada is V, WI5; Gimme Shelter is V, WI6.

Only the biggest mixed routes deserved the overall grade of VI, routes such as the Eiger Direct, and the Logan/Stump on the Emperor Face of Mt. Robson. Overall grade VII is reserved for the size, altitude, and difficulties of the hardest Himalayan climbs, done in alpine style. The Spanish route on the South Face of Annapurna would be VII, more for its length, altitude and seriousness than for technical difficulty. The original route on the Hungo Face of Kwangde, on the other hand, should probably be graded VII more for the continuous high-standard technical difficulties, than for the other factors.

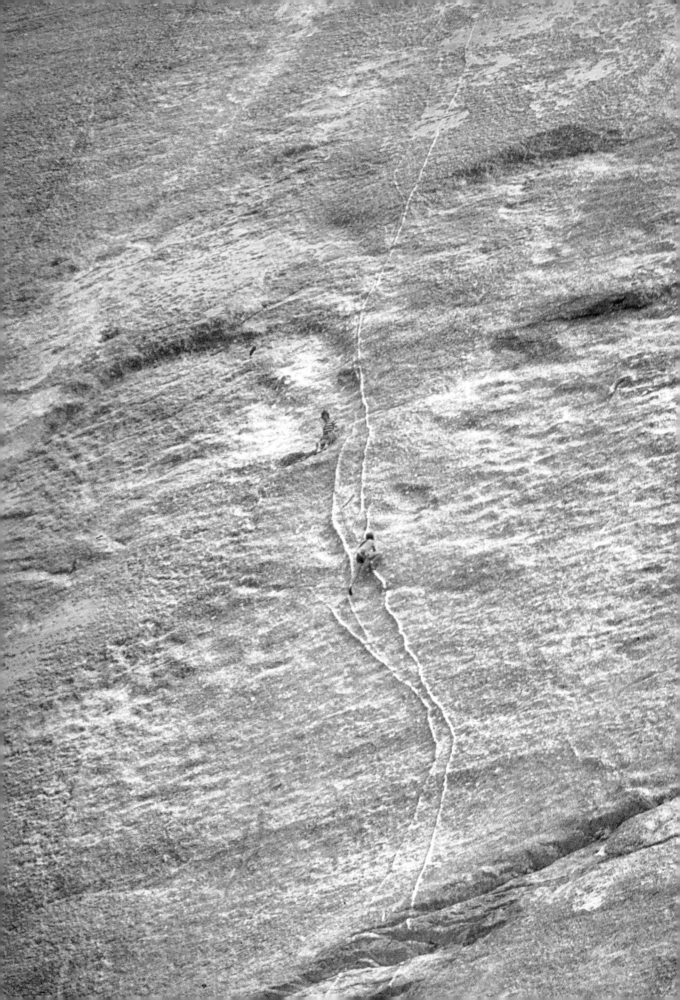

Rock Climbing

Rock climbing in its simplest form could be demonstrated by a youngster scrambling over rocks at the seaside. At the other end of the scale, one of the highest grade performers may take a week to work out a single move on a climb, trying to puzzle out the jigsaw of holds, and then, having technically solved the problem, physically executing the movements required, keeping sufficient energy in hand to complete the rest of the climb. At this level, climbing requires the concentration of a chess player, the power and stamina of an athlete, and the nerve and confidence of a Formula One driver. These are no small demands, but there are plenty of people who are prepared to make the necessary sacrifices to be able to climb the hardest routes.

Slab climbing on the granite domes of Tuolomne Meadows, California.

A Personal View

Of course, not everyone is able, nor indeed wants, to climb the hardest routes, but every climber wants to *enjoy* his or her climbing, which means being competent and in control. I've yet to meet the person who enjoys the prospect of hitting the ground from twenty metres. The whole point about climbing is being in a potentially dangerous situation and yet being in charge of that situation: knowing your limitations, being confident about your abilities, and having faith in your equipment and your climbing partner. The key word is 'fun'. The experience is supposed to be enjoyable, and a better understanding of the techniques involved will enable those involved to get more out of the sport.

Rock climbing is about being out in the fresh air and having fun on rocks. The rocks may vary in size from boulders a metre high to something like the 900 m face of El Capitan in Yosemite, California. A climb may start halfway up a cliff, and often it won't finish on any recognisable summit. Climbing is a sport without set rules or prizes, winners or losers. The game isn't between the participants, but between each climber and his own limitations. A person will have his own set of ethics or rules, which will probably be a minor deviation from the general guidelines which have evolved over the years. Any 'rules' are self-imposed and are there to keep the sport free from misuse. A person is a 'winner' if the climb is done whilst adhering to his rules or ethics.

To some extent, personal freedoms are limited by the wishes of other climbers involved in the sport; there are 'official bodies', but they exist to serve, not govern, climbers. Climbers tend to keep each other in line by peer-group example and by persuasion (gentle or otherwise). However, there is really no way to stop the odd eccentric going his or her own way, and it is this overall principle of anarchy which makes for a relaxed, bureacracy-free atmosphere, at-tracting and producing colourful characters and 'misfits' (in a conventional sense). It is an atmosphere which offers a most attractive antidote to the petty rules and restrictions of today's world. You can't escape totally of course, but it's safe to say, once on your crag, officialdom doesn't have too much power or control over the game.

To a climber, the attractions of climbing are obvious enough: healthy exercise in the open air, nearly always in some of the best countryside there is. For that ever-dwindling group of people known as 'workers', it offers an essential escape. What could be better than spending cool summer evenings swarming over gritstone edges, say, after a day stuck in the office? Then, there is the satisfaction of being in a potentially dangerous

The sea cliff climbs of Mousetrap Zawn, Red Wall and Castell Helen, in the South Stack area of Anglesey.

situation, yet harmonizing mind and body to maximum efficiency to achieve an effect of fluent balletic movement, effortlessly gliding up rock. But the fact remains, that to many non-climbers, it is a totally incomprehensible activity. How often do climbers hear the remarks: 'Oh, I could never do that! I get vertigo standing on a chair', or 'What on earth do they do it for?' and 'Don't they know there's an easy way round the back?' Climbing, like any sport, is about finding out what you can actually do. The initial challenge is an obvious one, offering the reward of surprise and satisfaction at one's achievements, however modest. And, having said all that, it's as well to remember that, as a sport, climbing is relatively cheap. The equipment needed is minimal, and, when starting out, it is often possible to improvize, by wearing pumps, for example, instead of rock boots. Many of today's rock-climbing stars are jobless and on the dole (either intentionally or otherwise), proving that time and dedication are more important in this sport than expensive gear.

Climbing is also a very human and personal experience. There is very little artifical equipment to rely on. (In its 'purest' form, soloing, there is none.) You rely on yourself, on your own abilities; and in climbing partnerships, you extend this reliance to your partner. If you place your life in someone else's hands (in the event of a fall, you rely on your partner to hold you) you quickly build up a rapport, a trust, which enhances normal relationships.

Technique, what it is and why it is important

A good climber quickly realizes that some ways of overcoming problems are much easier than others. This may sound obvious, but judging from the number of people you see climbing who make things harder for themselves, either through fear or ignorance, it is a point that needs stressing. The most economical way of making a move is always the best, and there are techniques

that can be learnt to deal with all the different types of problem encountered on a climb. Many of these are outlined on pp. 38 and 58.

Technique is the ability to execute moves with the minimum of fuss and strain, thus conserving energy for subsequent moves. Lack of technique can only partially be compensated for by brute strength or plain determination, or by a combination of the two. In any case, it is more satisfying to be smooth and in control. It's certainly aesthetically more pleasing to watch a good climber climbing

The Verdon Gorge, an impressive limestone gorge in Provence. Its good weather and 680 m high cliffs make it very popular with both French and international rock climbers.

well, than it is to see someone hesitant and shaking on the rocks, even if the latter does provoke a certain morbid fascination. Much of what we call technique is instinctive to a child who has natural climbing abilities, but has to be re-learnt as a climbing adult.

My own Introduction to Climbing

Having been brought up in a village in the Yorkshire Dales, I was surrounded by moorland and crags. As a youngster my local playground was Haw Bank, a now-forgotten limestone quarry where my friends and I would scramble about on 45 m limestone slabs. No doubt we were a considerable nuisance to the 'proper' climbers there at the time. I was intrigued by the moors and used to spend hours wandering around on my own, getting to know the tracks, peat bogs and crags: Crook-rise, Deer Gallows and Rylestone were always focal points on my walks. I scrambled about and watched men in brightly-coloured anoraks with ropes and helmets. Because I was shy, I never dared approach them, but I studied their routes and when they left, I would often repeat their climbs, solo. This was during my early teens; at secondary school I was introduced to the Lake District and Scotland on walking trips.

Malham Cove in the Yorkshire Dales. The spectacular central walls have only recently been partially free climbed.

When I was fifteen, I heard of a group of climbers who used to congregate in the Venture Scout hut in Skipton Bus Station. Most of them did not themselves belong to the scouts, but found it a useful meeting place. One Friday night I went along and met Paul Trower, Phil Webb, Mick Hillas and the only bona fide member, Arthur Champion. It was Arthur who took me out on my first real day's climbing. I remember managing a few VS's on that first outing, and I was hooked.

For the next year or more, it was a matter of saving money from dinner money, bus fares and any other sources, and hitching off to

The author leading the first pitch of The Gallows, Gordale Scar, Yorkshire (grade E7 6c). On the left is Cave Route, the first free climb on the wall.

Malham for the weekend. We slept in barns and went 'pegging' if the weather was bad. We tried to work our way through the climbs at the Cove. We cut our teeth on Malham VS's and HVS's (some of which are now graded good Extremes), and after six months, started hitching further afield to the Lakes and to Wales. I missed several Mondays at school when I couldn't get a lift home, and no doubt my mother spent some worrying times wondering where I was.

By the time I was seventeen, I was climbing almost every day, usually after school, but sometimes during school hours. I had visited most areas in Britain and managed to repeat some hard climbs and do some new ones. At that time British climbing was entering a renaissance when there was a rejection of artificial climbing and a return to freer methods. A number of the better routes were still, however, climbed with aid points and there were many aid routes crying out be free climbed.

The 1,170 m granite prow of El Capitan, Yosemite Valley, California.

I met Pete Livesey, who was at the forefront of British climbing, and it was his attitude and drive that was to have such an influence on me. By now, my life revolved around climbing: I went to Vercors, the Verdon and to Yosemite, as well as further exploring British routes. I have great memories from this late-teen period of epic hitches across Europe, grappling with the desperate climbs of the day, and also of course of the people I met and the friendships I made. Sharing rope, sharing disasters and laughs, brings people close together and often reveals aspects of character normally hidden. A climbing partnership is something special.

Having now been climbing for 16 years, I feel very lucky to have seen so much of the world through climbing and met so many great people. It was through climbing, in fact, that I met my wife. In return,

I'd like to feel that I've put a little bit back, in the form of new climbs and ideas. As the first British rock climber to make a living from climbing—from sponsorship that is rather than from guiding or instructing, writing, lecturing, or as a retailer—I hope this has made it easier for others to follow. Compared to other sports, climbing is still the poor relation, but times are changing. More and more manufacturers are employing climbers as advisers and to promote their gear. This can only be good for those at the 'top' end of the sport, who must dedicate themselves completely to achieve their goals.

There is one new development, however, which excites bitter controversy, and that is the introduction of organized 'competition' climbing: climbing for points and against the clock. It would doubtless focus more public and media interest onto the sport and thereby bring in more money, but not without considerably affecting its traditional nature. In some countries competition climbing is already being accepted, and it remains to be seen whether or not it will develop in Britain and the United States. That must rest with the next generation.

The Evolution of Rock Climbing

Historical

Though alpine climbing grew steadily in popularity during the middle of the last century, climbing on rock for its own sake held little attraction to the early mountaineers; they were seeking the easiest routes to airy summits, being primarily interested in 'bagging' first ascents. The first of all alpine clubs, the Alpine Club, was founded in London in 1857; its early members did go climbing on native hills, but they regarded this purely as training for the Alps. It took some time before the individual appeal of British rock was recognized although climbing Pillar, a Lakeland pinnacle, was regarded as something of a feat and done frequently from 1826 onwards.

It is debatable who were the very first 'real' British rock climbers, but several memorable deeds stand out. The Reverend James 'Steeple' Jackson is one who could shame many of today's 'rock jocks' with his 'training schedule'. He too climbed Pillar (with the aid of ropes and spikes) in 1874, when he was in his eightieth year, but attempting to repeat the ascent three years later, he fell to his death.

The cliffs of Lliwedd in Wales were climbed in 1883, but on the whole the Lake District appears to have been more popular than

Geoffrey Winthrop Young (seated), photographed with the guide Joseph Knubel in 1911. He was a pioneer of rock climbs as well as the more famous alpine ascents before losing a leg in 1917.

Wales in the formative period of the sport. Walter Parry Haskett Smith discovered Wasdale Head in 1881, and made a number of ascents during that summer and the years following, including a number of highly atmospheric routes on Scafell. Some of these are still graded Difficult, but what is more important is that they were climbed for fun, for the love of moving on rock, and for all the stresses and strains involved. It is not without reason that he is often called 'the father of British rock climbing'. He and his university friends would have been in possession of all the equipment available at the time: a stout staff, leather boots, warm tweeds, and thus equipped, they tackled the obvious lines on the big crags—the gullies—and the north-facing ones in particular were often wet, full of dank vegetation and loose rock. These unpleasant recesses gave the pioneers a sense of security away from exposed buttresses, and also offered the line of least resistance up the crags. Many of these gully climbs are dismissed today because of their unpleasantness, and no doubt the first ascentionists would have preferred better conditions. The irony is, had they been persuaded out onto the cleaner, drier faces in between, they could have achieved climbs of even greater difficulty.

During this period, another cragsman was perfecting his technique on the gritstone edges around the Yorkshire Dales: W Cecil Slingsby may well have been the first climber to train on the gritstone outcrops for exploits on bigger crags. A contemporary was J Norman Collie, who assured his name went into the annals of climbing folklore when he ascended the Collie Exit to Moss Ghyll on Scafell, using an ice-axe to chip a foothold on the crux section. One of the best climbers of the 1890s was Owen Glynne Jones, a Londoner, whose very impressive routes included Kern Knotts Crack, a route he first did with a top rope, using combined tactics and an ice-axe for a foothold, but

later climbed without a rope. It was graded Mild Very Severe and was a considerable achievement for that time.

Great advances were made when climbers did eventually move out of gullies: Siegfried Herford and G S Sansom with H B Gibson and C F Holland climbed the Great Flake on the Central Buttress of Scafell in 1914. The feat was achieved with a rope cradle around the chockstone and combined tactics, but is impressive nonetheless.

During the twenties and thirties, in Britain, gritstone had become a popular testing ground, no doubt due to its proximity to such centres of population as Manchester and Sheffield. The early gritstoners climbed some very advanced

A hand traverse, photographed at the turn of the century. It was not until climbers like Winthrop Young analysed movement that more dynamic techniques evolved.

routes with minimal protection, in some cases with none at all, such as Frankland's Green crack at Almscliff in Yorkshire, which is VS. This would probably stop many of today's good climbers if they were relying on the equipment of the time. The same could be said of some of Harry M Kelly's exploits in the Peak District. The late-twenties saw some very bold efforts on big British crags. One example is Pigott's lead of the route that bears his name on Cloggy (Clogwyn d'ur Arddu) in North

Wales, where he used slings around chockstones, pulled up extra chocks on the rope and even had tension from the rope running over a projecting buttress. Great ethical debates followed and the blame was placed firmly on Morley Wood whose idea it was to place the chockstones. I prefer to think of their efforts as technical advances since the whole idea of modern protection stems from these tentative developments.

Meanwhile, in Europe, there were no such qualms about the use of artificial aid (see p. 50). For many years the fine limestone walls and towers of the Eastern Alps had yielded long routes of sustained difficulty, and a variety of pitons and dynamic rope techniques had been developed and employed to assist their passage. Karabiners, too, made their appearance here. It was a development firmly decried by stalwarts of the Alpine Club. Colonel Strutt, editor of the *Alpine Journal*, dismissed all routes climbed with these new methods as 'perversions' or 'monkey tricks'. There were, too, European climbers who still rejected all use of aid, climbers like Paul Preuss who was one of the great early big wall free climbers, but they were definitely in the minority.

There was an enormous increase in the number of people who went climbing; it was no longer the sport of the privileged few and the professional classes. Between the wars, many young men took off into the mountains, and it was a time of intense development. The great classic routes of the Dolomites were established by such as Riccardo Cassin, Attilio Tissi, Emilio Comici and the Dimai brothers, and rock skills learned in the Eastern Alps were imported to tackle the great North Faces of the Western Alps, particularly by German and Austrian climbers of the so called 'Munich School'.

British rock climbing continued its separate existence. Here, the next climbers to make technical advances were two outstanding cragsmen, Colin Kirkus, who was at his most active between 1930 and 1934, and Menlove Edwards who dominated the scene of the late thirties. Edwards was a highly gifted climber who performed some incredible feats of strength. Unfortunately, like many gifted people, he was also very highly strung, and eventually committed suicide. His routes stand as a fine memorial to the man: Chimney route on Cloggy including the rarely-climbed Rickety Innards, Great Slab on the same cliff, and even some climbs on the sandstone outcrop of Helsby on the Wirral are still strongly rated.

The next wave of development came from working-class climbers, for in Britain too, a working-class invasion was taking place. People took to the hills to escape the grime, poverty and depression of the big industrial cities such as Manchester and Sheffield, and much of the development was on the gritstone crags of the Peak and Pennines, but the higher crags of the Lakes and Wales did not escape attention. During the forties Arthur Dolphin was at the forefront of gritstone climbing and produced some brilliant routes. At Almscliff, he did Great Western, North West Girdle and Birdlime Traverse, which epitomize the best that grit has to offer. Two other outstanding routes he produced at that time were Kipling Grove in the Lake District and Deer Bield Buttress.

The Abraham brothers on Kern Knotts Crack in the Lake District.

During the fifties the climbing world spawned its own legends in the shape of two plumbers from Manchester, Joe Brown and Don Whillans. No-one in the past thirty years, has so touched the climbing public's imagination as much as these two. All their routes have become classics. Whereas the mountain crag routes may have become easier with today's more sophisticated protection devices, their achievements on gritstone are still as ferocious as ever. Goliath on Burbage is a good example, its wide nasty crack being attempted much less than more recent neighbouring routes.

Brown and Whillans were such a dynamic pair that they overshadowed many of their contemporaries. As is typical of human nature, the top practitioners were targets for other climbers to imitate or challenge. Pete Crew was a direct challenger to Brown in particular. Crew stepped in after Brown's failure to produce the classic of the era, Great Wall on Cloggy, using only a smidgen of aid.

The sixties saw a consolidation of standards as more and more people climbed to a relatively high standard. Outcrops were used as training for bigger things at the weekend. The climbing social scene was becoming more frenetic and far-reaching and a host of new clubs sprang up.

It was about this time that British and European climbers began to wake up to what was happening in North America. On the vast granite walls of Yosemite a revolution was taking place similar to that in the Dolomites forty years before. With the advent of new lightweight alloys and the ingenuity of engineers who were themselves climbers, a new range of climbing hardware was produced that permitted direct ascents up the blankest of walls. In the late 1940s the Swiss-born climber John Salathé and Ax Nelson climbed Higher Cathedral Spire, and eventually conquered Lost Arrow Chimney and the south-west face of Half Dome. The north face of Sentinel Rock, and the spires of Spider Rock, Arizona, Totem Pole, Monument Valley, and Cleopatra's Needle, New Mexico were all ascended during the 1950s and Warren Harding and Wayne Merry finally reached the summit of El Capitan in 1957.

During the early 1960s, American big wall climbs multiplied: Yvon Chouinard and Tom Frost achieved the Nose route of El Capitan in 1960; whilst in Colorado, Layton Kor and Bob Culp climbed Chiefshead in 1961 and Naked Edge the following year. A gradual reaction against the placing of bolts set in, characterized by Royal Robbins' and Pat Ament's free ascents of Yellow Spur and Athlete's Feat in 1964. Some solo ascents were also made in the 1960s, amongst them Robbins' ascents of the East Side of Upper Yosemite Fall in 1963 and the Muir Wall in 1968. This opened the way to similar exploration in other places, like Baffin Island and Patagonia.

In 1969, like a prophet in the wilderness, the young Reinhold Messner railed against the poisoning of the pure spring of mountaineering. 'Today's climber,' he said, 'carries his courage in his rucsac.' A murder was being commited, he alleged, the foul murder of the Impossible. This was a sentiment that rang true for an increasing body of young climbers. Throughout the seventies one saw the weakening of dependence on equipment as a means of ascent, allied to a parallel growth in 'protective' devices, designed to minimize the effect of any falls. The great 'artificial' routes began to be climbed with a steady elimination of points of aid. Each generation of climbers likes to think it has seen the limits of what is possible. If the climbers of the early sixties could have had a window into the future, they would have seen a rise in standards so dramatic as to make the efforts of previous generations seem tame by comparison. The reason for this sudden surge was training.

Don Whillans photographed in the 1970s on one of his favourite climbs, Heptonstall Moor.

The Modern Scene: the Advent of Training

Up until the late sixties, training for rock climbing was virtually non-existent. In fact the traditional image of climbers as hard-drinking, permissive and generally unwashed, fitted in well with the general mood of rebellion of the swinging sixties. The climbers' uniform (of collective rebellion) consisted of tight scruffy jeans and tatty woollen sweaters. For an active climber this is a fairly restricting outfit. Lifting and stretching legs in tight jeans is almost impossible. Ed Drummond, a radical climber of this period, started wearing shorts, even on cold days. It's hard now to believe that he was strongly mocked by the 'old guard'.

Pete Livesey came relatively late to climbing, bringing with him a fresh and positive approach. Having been a runner, caver and canoeist, he knew the value of specific training for a particular sport, and applied the same principle to climbing. He also took care to maintain his fitness throughout the winter instead of 'festering', as was the norm. Coincidentally, the first indoor climbing walls were appearing at this time, and one in particular, that at Leeds University (which was designed by Don Robinson) has since become legendary for the number of top-class boulderers it produced, the most outstanding being Al Manson and John Syrett. Climbing came gradually to be regarded as an athletic activity, rather than just 'having a laugh on the rocks' and climbers started to present themselves as athletes, adopting athletic vests and shorts. Livesey started systematic 'gear-racking' and had a completely professional—some might say soulless—approach in that he would deliberately seek new routes for their newsworthiness or spectacular qualities. He had an eye to the magazines and the climbing public.

There has been a large expansion in the number of people climbing regularly. A natural increase in the sport's popularity has been one factor in this, but there have been other significant contributions. An important one must be the economic situation. With over three million unemployed in Britain at present, and with a similar situation throughout the world, living on welfare is a permanent way of life for many. As people have an increase in leisure time and a decrease in money, then a relatively cheap sport like climbing will have its attractions. By its nature, climbing seems to attract

Peter Crew on the Great Wall or Master's Wall on the east buttress of Clogwyn D'Ur Arddu, the big black cliff on the northern flank of Snowdon, North Wales.

non-conformists who find it relatively easy to live on the dole or off successive temporary jobs.

The advent of climbing walls has played its part. It is now possible to maintain fitness and stamina gained through the summer over the winter, and technical standards can be pushed higher as single moves are practised in safety a few metres above the ground. Walls also provide a competitive focus where climbers can 'burn off' each other, where talents can be praised or derided within a group. Climbing walls are now widely spread throughout Britain, and are spreading rapidly throughout Europe and the United States. They provide handy training places if crags are out of reach. As with rock climbing areas, the walls have their own devotees and specialists, who may climb to 7a on their local patch but be unable to perform away from it.

Now that climbing walls have been accepted, the next logical progression is specific gym training. Most top climbers today do weight training, either in gyms or sports centres. At the present time this aspect of training isn't fully understood or correctly applied. Most exercises are done *ad hoc* and not as part of an overall weight training programme, and without due re-

gard for the end result: which parts of the body *need* training for climbing, and what exactly the exercises do to help. This amateurish approach is proved when looking at the number of injuries sustained during training, or exacerbated by the wrong sort of training. One example is the infamous 'dead hang', where a climber hangs by the fingertips from small holds for various lengths of time. All the weight is taken on the fingers, the idea being to strengthen them. This may sound like a good idea, but since it isn't a recognized athletic training method, no-one yet knows what the long term effect might be. Continuously hanging from fingers for several minutes could easily affect shoulder joints, tendons etc. No doubt as more people become interested in training methods, then more knowledge will be gained and eventually recognized exercises will emerge and fewer injuries will happen.

In keeping with the general interest in healthy living today, and

as an extension of training, diets have come under scrutiny. I know several climbers who pay attention, almost obsessively, to what they eat, counting calories religiously, avoiding alcohol and living an austere lifestyle. I have my doubts as to how much better a climber will perform on lentils and hot water rather than pie and chips, since an active person will quickly burn off the carbohydrates present in a normal balanced diet.

Another area of climbing which has changed in recent years is clothing. Where once you wore thick polar wear in winter and shorts in summer, now the emphasis is on 'outrage', with climbers wearing pink shiny dance tights, brightly coloured shirts, dyed hair, earrings etc. How long this post-punk influence will last remains to be seen,

The Acker's Trust outdoor climbing wall in Birmingham, designed by Don Robinson. All rock climbing techniques can be practised on this wall.

but dance tights will probably catch on more and more, since they are ideal for keeping muscles warm while climbing, stretch perfectly for climbing movements—and reflect the individualism of the sport's participants.

Today's rock climber is not progressing towards 'bigger things' in the Alps or Himalayas in the same way as his predecessors were, where overcoming such objective dangers as stonefall or storms played a major part in success. It is the 'move' which interests him, whether it be on a 3 metre boulder or a steep limestone wall, but that is not to say he is not interested in challenges abroad. Today's rock climbers consistently travel to out-of-the-way locations; with widespread information available through books, films and magazines, and with cheaper and easier travel, today's 'rock jocks' go to the South of France, Germany, Poland, Japan, Korea, Australia and all over North America, often making two or three trips in one year. The one major drawback is that when a climber returns from a new area, full of enthusiasm which is then amplified through the climbing media, often a cliff will suddenly become *in vogue* and then be swamped by visitors. The most recent and highly-publicized example of this is the crag at Buoux in the South of France which became internationally popular almost overnight, causing so much friction between the local populace and visiting climbers that the result was to restrict all climbing there.

There have been women active on the climbing scene from the very beginning, some to a very high level. Several women were early members of the prestigious Groupe du Haute Montagne which made many fine alpine first ascents between the wars; Gwen Moffat was the first woman to become a British mountain guide, but it has to be said these were exceptions to the general rule. It was far more common for women to find themselves playing a supporting role, cooking back at base, or at best, climbing permanently second. This is all now changing; with women finding a new consciousness and demanding equality and independence generally, they have approached climbing on an equal footing. Today there are many women who lead climbs and a few who lead very hard routes; there are some like American Lynn Hill who lead the very hardest routes of all. As more women commit themselves to leading, it is only a matter of time before we shall see many more climbing at the top end of the sport.

Competition

The competitive element plays its part today, as it has always done. Competition between climbers is usually a healthy thing and often spurs people on to try harder, either to catch up with or to outshine their peers. There is usually a competitive tinge in every level from V. Diff-leaders to E7-leaders. More often than not, rivalry will be friendly, even though quite intense. It helps stop complacency or apathy. I suppose there is a danger that for fear of losing face, a climber might feel obliged to attempt some 'feat' beyond his abilities at that particular time, but I rather hope that faced with that temptation, his urge for self-preservation would outweigh any feeling of need to 'prove his bottle'.

One of the more controversial developments seems to be the trend of climbing, not for experience alone, but for the resulting media-hype. Climbing magazines exert influence here and amplify the achievements of a few people performing in the 'upper echelons'. I myself have benefited from this attention and have been able to translate media interest into

A French climber leading at Buoux in southern France, a sensitive area, but one of the best limestone crags in the world.

some kind of a living. However, there is now a suspicion creeping in that newsworthy climbs are done for that reason alone, with people deliberately seeking publicity, rather than letting publicity find them. Hopefully the 'pretenders' will be quickly weeded out by their contemporaries.

There is a growing trend towards speed climbing events, which originated in the Soviet Bloc countries, where they are now well-established. Climbers are top-roped and judged on the speed of ascent. Visiting climbers from other countries have taken part by invitation, usually coming second to the Russians, and have been influenced. The Italians recently held a similar event, but judging both speed and style, and the French are preparing to follow suit. Time will tell how long the British and American scenes hold out, but it seems inevitable that some sort of competition climbing will emerge also.

Starting Out

On your own

Many people will start rock climbing after an apprenticeship served as a hillwalker, and will therefore already have an appreciation of the outdoors. I think myself this is the best way to start—going out into the hills with like-minded friends, climbing when you're ready—but I realize it's not possible for everyone, and luckily there are alternatives available for those people.

The chief advantage of 'doing it yourself', working things out from scratch, is that a person will become self-reliant and confident, and will progressively gain experience by making mistakes and learning from them. Some common sense is necessary to build up slowly and surely. The vast majority of climbers start this way, with a friend who knows a little (possibly a risky situation) or nothing at all. Learning by this method, it may be more difficult, initially, to meet other climbers, although by being out on the crags, the ones you do meet will be the active ones. The social aspect of clubs etc. will be missed—which may not be such a bad thing—but younger climbers could have travel problems.

Arranged courses

Sometimes young people can start through their school or an outdoor pursuits club. There are a number of outdoor centres run by local education authorities or other bodies, and some that are privately operated. Adventure holidays and courses for rock climbing (either on its own or combined with other activities) are advertised—you can

Lynn Hill, one of the best American free climbers, on the first pitch of Naked Edge, a classic climb on Eldorado Canyon, Colorado (grade 5.11).

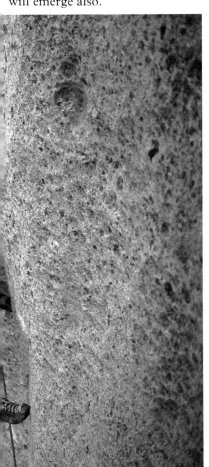

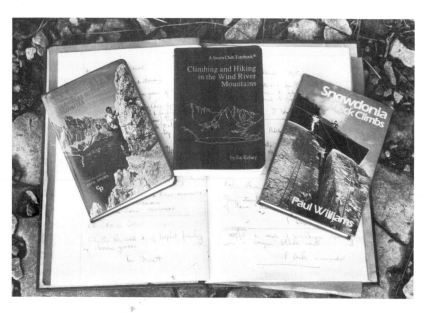

Guidebooks exist to most climbing areas. Recently climbed routes are described in new route books, found in cafes, pubs and shops in the vicinity.

find out about these from recognized climbing centres or by reading the climbing magazines. Qualified guides can be hired for private tuition.

Organized courses offer a convenient and quick way to discover if the sport is for you, without buying all the gear first. You receive concentrated instruction in a short space of time, usually learning with other novices at an outdoor centre. There will be the minimum of risk because the instructors will be well-qualified and will make all the decisions. There is the disadvantage that by being totally looked after, the sense of self-reliance which is an integral part of climbing, may not fully develop. Minimizing the sense of risk may present a distorted view of the sport. Rock climbing is an inherently high-risk sport, compared to, say, tennis; and it is as well to appreciate the fact.

Climbing Clubs

Joining a club is a cheap way of getting started. The main advantage is the cameraderie clubs offer and a usually active social diary. Meeting other climbers for discussion and encouragement is an integral part of a climber's life. A climbing club will often look after its novice members until they can stand on their own feet. Clubs, unlike outdoor centres, provide a continuity of regular meetings for people living in the same area. It is useful to be able to share transport to the crags, and activities like slide shows can be both enjoyable and informative. At local club level there is an in-built restraint and concern for the ethics or unwritten rules of the sport. Being usually conservative and traditional in outlook means a novice soon learns the 'acceptable' way of climbing.

The disadvantage of learning through a club is that climbing is usually limited to weekends. A club climber may not have the time to show a novice correct technique, and there is a consequent danger that the beginner could pick up the bad habits of older climbers, since not all climbers are competent. There is also the possibility that the social activities could take precedence over the climbing, though this can be avoided.

Finding out

Information about climbing and climbing opportunities is available from several sources:

Official outlets

Every country where climbing is well-established has a national organization for safeguarding and furthering the interests of climbers. World alpine organizations are listed at the back of the book. Most will provide information on training courses and compile lists of affiliated climbing clubs, besides holding up-to-date information on access difficulties, etc.

Magazines and Books

Specialist outdoor magazines have advertising sections containing information on courses available, guides offering private tuition, climbing shops, etc. It may even be possible to find a regular climbing partner by placing an advertisement, although caution is advised—a novice would be foolish to embark on a climb with an unknown partner who was similarly inexperienced.

Feature articles offer advice on areas and routes, and on the latest developments in equipment technique. Some clubs and libraries will keep back numbers of national and international climbing periodicals as well as a wide range of books.

Crags and Gathering Places

Of course a lot of useful information and advice can be picked up whilst actually out on a crag (or a climbing wall). Indeed you may well find yourself proferred advice you don't want from self-appointed local experts. Certain cafes in climbing areas are well-known as climbers' haunts. They may have notice-boards advertising useful local contacts, but in any case, generally hanging around can often produce results—try and look enthusiastic and competent. The same applies to pubs, although beware of plans laid in pubs with new friends! Local climbing shops are usually owned by, or employ climbers and will often give advice and information.

The Grading of Climbs

Rock climbs are graded according to their difficulties. A pitch is the length between belays. Sometimes, particularly on outcrops,

Crowden, Great Brook Gorge. Climbers traversing above water level. It is fun and useful to learn in a group like this, with help on hand when needed.

Rock Features

Arête	A steep ridge
Chimney	A vertical crack, wide enough to get inside
Chock	Chockstone. A natural chockstone is a pebble or rock wedged into a crack or chimney
Choss	Loose, unreliable rock
Corner	Vertical junction of two planes of rock, approximately at right-angles
Crack	A crack is not wide enough to get inside
Crux	The hardest part/move on any climb
Dièdre/	The French word for wide-angled 'open' corner.
Dihedral	American word for the same
Flake	A thin, partly detached leaf of rock
Groove	Shallow, vertical crack. As the name suggests, narrower than a corner
Gully	Steep-sided rift/watercourse, wide enough to walk inside
Jug	A large indented hold
Open-book	Angled corner, dièdre
Overhang	A rock face of more than 90° overhanging obviously
Slab(s)	Large smooth rock face between 30° and 60°
V-Chimney	The widest angled corner
Wall	A rock face of between 60° and 90°

this might be between the ground and the top of a crag, but it is obviously never longer than the average rope length which is 50 metres or 150 ft. Each pitch on a climb is given a grade, the main reason being so that a climber will know roughly what to expect. No-one wants to come unstuck, and forewarned is forearmed.

As with any sport, humans like to measure their progress and a grading system allows this. The grades are not absolute and are always subject to discussion. Usually the first person to make a climb grades it and this is either corroborated or corrected by subsequent ascents. The more ascents a climb has, the more accurate the grade will be. Although we talk about a climb being graded, it would be more accurate to say that the moves required to make that climb are graded, which ultimately depends on the person making those moves. A tall man will find it easier to reach a high hold than a small person, so to him, the move will seem easier. On the other hand, if the only available foot and hand holds are very close together, then a short person will find the move easier, so one expects a certain amount of discrepancy.

Different countries have developed their own grading systems, and a comparative table of these is found on p 13. Thus a British Grade 6a is roughly equivalent to a French 6c or an American 5.11. Lower US grades than those listed in the table cover hiking and scrambling over rock, with class 4 for steep rock, and requiring ropes. All US gradings listed are for free climbing, but require some protection. Occasionally you will also find a Roman numeral for the overall climb, with individual pitches graded according to this table.

Ethics and their importance

Having said that there are no

Rock Features
Left: Ron Fawcett at the belay with Jerry Peel seconding on Necronomicon (French grade 6c) in the limestone Verdon Gorge, Provence.
Below: The author on Thin Air, a Derbyshire gritstone slab.
Bottom: Climbing on the sandstone faces of Eldorado Canyon, Colorado

restrictions, there are ethical codes that we follow, unwritten rules which climbers try to adhere to. These ethics vary slightly from area to area, for example, in Britain chalk is frowned upon at Bowles Rocks, say, and used liberally in the Peak District. Basically, there are two types of climbing:

Free climbing
Aid climbing

These days, free climbing is the most popular by far and involves using one's hands and feet on natural holds on the rock. Where runners, pegs, 'Friends' etc. are used, they are for protection and not assistance. Aid climbing involves utilizing artificial means to surmount rock, putting your weight on artificial 'holds'. 'Artificial' covers anything that doesn't occur naturally on the rock—it may be a peg, or nut, or drilling a hole in blank rock to accommodate an expansion bolt.

These two types of climbing are quite distinct, and ethics play a major part in keeping them separate, but some climbers do adopt 'dubious' or 'unethical' practices by blurring the distinctions between them, for instance by resting on equipment during the course of a free climb.

Most countries have developed their own set of ethics according to tradition and a respect for their predecessors' achievements, although it has to be said that most significant advances have flown in the face of past practices. In Great Britain there is a strong tradition of free climbing, no doubt originating from the fact that there are no alpine peaks to scale, a dense population, and large numbers of small crags. Our ethics have developed to try to maintain a sense of adventure despite the lack of major objectives. The sense of trying to attain a summit is minimal and, in case of bad weather, retreat by abseil is nearly always possible. This means that, since there is no absolute commitment as in the Alps, what adventure and risk there is must be preserved. This attitude is best illustrated by the refusal to place bolts on gritstone, thus giving serious climbing on relatively small cliffs.

Ethics vary from country to country. In France, the end-product justifies the method of achievement, which includes prior top-roping, pre-placed bolts and resting on equipment in order finally to make a 'flash' ascent, which means leading from bottom to top without falls or resting. This style of climbing seems to defeat the British objectives of climbing which are risk and adventure. However, the French open attitude of 'anything goes' means by definition that there are no underhand methods and everyone is aware of the method of ascent. British ethics have given rise to several dubious tactics, such as surreptitious top-roping, practising runner placements and so on. The French have maintained a degree of risk by placing protection bolts well apart, usually below the crux of a climb, so it is necessary to 'go for it' before reaching the next bolt. It seems to me that the main difference between the French and British styles is that the French do not regard the possibility of serious injury as part of the sport, whereas it is an inherent risk to the British.

In a country as large as the United States of America, many variations exist: some areas have all their protection bolts placed on the lead, while others don't. Overall, American ethics would be nearer to the British than the French.

Germany has developed only recently as a free climbing nation, from 1976, and this is reflected in their 'ethics' which have not kept place with the advance of climbing standards. This is illustrated by the number of 'doctored' hard routes with manufactured holds, which effectively negate the challenges for subsequent generations. The best possible ascent in Germany is called a 'Red Point', which is similar to a 'flash' or 'no-falls ascent', but for one subtle difference. If a climber manages during his ascent to climb down unaided to a stance to rest, then in all subsequent attempts it is allowable to lower off from the gear and still

Mr Hinotani soloing on Ogowayama Layback in Japan.

achieve a 'Red Point' ascent.

Just over the border in East Germany and Czechoslovakia, rock climbing has been practised on sandstone towers to a very high standard since the turn of the century. It is not possible to use nut protection in these areas as repeated use would wear away the fragile rock. Chalk is not allowed as it would look bad on the dark rock (they are in conservation areas). Climbing in the rain is also not done as the rock becomes even more fragile when wet. To overcome the problem of protecting their climbs, the local climbers have devised an expanding knot, a type of prehistoric 'Friend', which does not damage the rock. For belays and runners on blank walls, huge ring bolts are used, often 10 or 15 metres apart since they are placed while leading and it isn't always possible to stop to place them. Serious falls are often taken straight onto the belay, or be-layer (some climbers go through a number of seconds in this way!).

It is important to be sympathetic to the local traditions, particularly in those areas like East Germany where the ethics are enforced by the Park Authorities. In other areas it is pointless harassing a climber for resting on equipment, when, in his eyes, lowering off protection after a fall and not pulling the ropes down, may be considered equally bad practice. The obvious thing to do is to observe any area's ethics and traditions, in the interests of climbing goodwill.

The Basic Equipment to Start

1. Climbing boots. These should be comfortable and durable, rather than the latest in high technology. They are fairly expensive and often pumps will do to start with.
2. Rope. A single 45-metre 11 mm is sufficient and easiest to handle.
3. A harness (a waist-belt will do to start with). Choose one that is comfortable and hardwearing from a reputable manufacturer. Read all the instructions carefully.
4. Nuts. Initially you will need the larger ones since the easier climbs have larger cracks to take protection. If they are not already wired or threaded, they should be threaded with the largest possible diameter cord that will go through the holes. Don't make the length too long – it's dangerous when climbing as it is easy to trip over them, and it's also pointless as the extra length would only increase the potential fall. Shorter runners also avoid bruised shins from long swinging runners (ankle-bashers!)

Frantisek Cepellza climbing the sandstone Lahvicky inkóustu (small ink bottles) in Czechoslovakia, an area with a tradition of very hard free climbing and strict control over footwear and equipment in order to avoid damage to the rock.

5. Helmet. This is a good idea when starting out. On easy climbs the inconvenience is outweighed by the safety factor. With experience, a climber will develop crag sense and be less likely to bang his head or sit under a loose rock. A helmet will always be handy for aid or winter climbing.
6. Clothing. It is advisable to wear long bottoms, not shorts, since scrapes and bruises are inevitable when learning, but choose something that doesn't restrict your movements. Gritstone in particular is an unforgiving teacher. A gritstone 'rash' is part of a climber's apprenticeship. Waterproofs are advisable since beginners are often very keen and will even climb in the rain!
7. Guidebook. You need the guidebook to the area you are climbing in; often there will be a 'selected climbs' guidebook to an area otherwise covered by several volumes. This will give only the better quality routes and is probably best value for money.
8. Snack Box. This is essential for climbers who want to stay out all day or visit mountain crags.
9. Basic First Aid Kit. This will come in handy for minor cuts and bruises.

KNOW WHAT TO DO IN AN EMERGENCY. KNOW WHERE THE NEAREST TELEPHONE IS.
(Much of this information will be in the guide book to the area.)

The Climber's Equipment

For climbing some vast granite monolith you may need a mountain of equipment and a few weeks of effort, but for an afternoon's bouldering on gritstone, say, a pair of rock boots will suffice. The first thing is to decide exactly what you are going to do and then choose the equipment for the job.

Boots

A pair of boots is probably the most important item in a climber's 'wardrobe'. Rock climbing footwear has evolved over the years from stout walking boots to the lightweight boots of today. A variety of nailing patterns were tried (using 'clinkers', 'hobs' and 'tricounis') in attempts to get the best bite and grip, and these were followed with the imitation nailing patterns of vibram rubber soled boots. When intricate footwork was required, the climber shed his boots in favour of plimsolls or 'rubbers', putting socks over the top in wet or slimy conditions. The first purpose-built rock boot, the PA, was made by Pierre Alain for climbing at Fontainebleau near Paris (and appeared in the late-fifties). Today there are hundreds of different boots to choose from, the best being tight-fitting models with smooth rubber soles (the idea being the same as that for a racing car tyre, to get as much rubber as possible in contact with the ground—hence a smooth sole in preference to a tread).

When beginning, it is as well to choose a pair of hard-wearing, comfortable boots that are affordable, regardless of the manufacturer's high technical precision. Alternatively you can start off with gym shoes or trainers for early bouldering problems. As a climber's career progresses through the grades, then design details have to be more precise to cope with the thin-edging and friction moves the harder climbs require. The latest development in rock boots has been on the friction of the sole, with super-sticky rubbers being used. Although this kind of rubber is softer and wears out more quickly, most climbers feel it is worth it in terms of increased performance.

Ropes

The early pioneers relied on very basic rope. Hemp was preferred by the discerning climbers of the 1900s. Its major faults were that it was very heavy, relatively weak, hard to knot and difficult to handle when wet. During the Second World War, considerable development work went into climbing equipment and 'nylon' ropes were one offshoot.

Basically nylon ropes are interwoven or plaited strands of thin

The beginner can start climbing in trainers (bottom left) or in leather boots (top centre). Tight fitting friction boots (bottom right) are popular with more advanced climbers.

A typical gear rack for a day's climbing, laid out in an anorak taken in case of rain or cold. Clockwise from bottom left: 45 m of 11 mm rope coiled ready for use(see over, p. 35); runners for protection; nuts threaded on to coils of rope; a harness; friction boots with soles of specially developed rubber which give extra friction when in contact with the rock; a chalk bag—chalk is light magnesium carbonate, used to improve finger and hand holds on the rock; and karabiners attached to tape slings.

strands are twisted together to make a core which forms the basic strength of the rope. It is protected by a sheath, which is a woven outer layer of hard wearing, colourful nylon which is forced over the core to form a very strong durable unit. Kernmantel ropes come in varying lengths and diameters and are either static, which means the rope has no stretch, or they are dynamic which means that the rope has a shock absorbing capacity. In a climbing situation it is important that the rope absorbs as much 'shock' as necessary, thus protecting the climber in a fall. Dynamic rope is used for climbing situations although static rope is sometimes used for roped runners or as accessory cord.

Static rope does have its uses in specific situations such as abseiling or prusiking or, for example, when cleaning new routes, when it can be important not to have a stretchy rope which will rub over sharp edges in a swing motion, and can easily cut through. However, whilst static ropes do not stretch as a climber bounces during abseiling, they do vibrate from side to side which can cause fraying.

Today's ropes have progressed a long way since the 1900s and rope techniques have advanced. When climbers use ropes they will either climb on a single rope or use two together for double rope technique.

Ropes are now classified according to their diameters, ranging from 8.7 mm to 12 mm. The most usual single rope is 11 mm wide, and for double-rope technique, a pair of 8.8 mm or 9 mm ropes are used. The most common lengths are 45 m and 50 m, and are a matter for individual preference, although there is a move towards the longer rope. Some ropes have a quick-drying finish which is useful in damp climates, although the finish does have a certain waxiness which sometimes makes handling more difficult.

(For rope technique, see p. 42.)

Harness

Climbing harnesses are made from

nylon strands. The original ones were hawser-laid and were categorized according to thickness, Nos. 1. 2. 3. or 4. The thinnest was a No. 1 and little more than boot-lace, whereas the thickest No. 4 was used as a single climbing rope. Nylon ropes were a great improvement on the old hemp ropes but tended to kink very badly and a climber abseiling or prusiking would often spin uncontrollably when hanging free.

Over the last fifteen years the kernmantel rope has taken over from the hawser-laid for climbing purposes. In these ropes nylon

nylon tapes stitched together. Don Whillans designed one of the first sit harnesses, which is still widely used. The function of a harness is important. In the event of a fall, the harness relays the impact force to the climber's body; since this can be anything up to 1200 kg, the parts of the body directly related to the force can obviously suffer severe injury. A harness has to be designed to ensure that the force or shock is distributed as evenly and gently as possible, preferably onto that part most able to withstand it—the bottom, since it is a strong area and able to absorb high forces. A well-designed harness will have a wide surface area to spread the impact.

Most rock climbers today use only a sit harness although the combination of a sit and chest harness has been very popular on the Continent. Whichever style of harness is used, one important factor is that in the event of a fall, a climber will stay in an upright position, i.e. head up. There is less likelihood of hitting the head during the fall and no chance of falling out of the harness, and it is easier to effect a rescue from this position, if necessary.

Karabiners

These metal snap-links are an integral part of a climber's gear collection, serving a variety of purposes, such as clipping the rope through the runners, as part of the belaying system, or for attaching all sorts of equipment to a harness. The best karabiners are made from aluminium alloy and should be strong and reliable, and reasonably light since a climber may have to carry up to thirty of them; they should have a smooth gate-action for easy opening and handling; there should be no unfinished sharp edges on which gear could snag; and it must be possible to open the gate under body-weight for aid climbing and for rescues. The two main types of karabiner are the simple snap type and the screw-gate, which can be 'locked' by means of a barrel on a screw-thread. The latest development is

When you finish climbing, coil the rope loosely around your neck (top left). Make a bight across the top with one end of the rope, then wrap the other around it several times before tucking the end through the loop and pulling tight (above) to carry (top right).

the 'Twistlock' karabiner, which is self-locking, so there is no possibility of forgetting to lock it.

Runners

Runners are the climber's way of protecting himself while climbing. A point of attachment is made to the rock, whether it be a peg knocked into a thin crack to which a karabiner can be clipped, or a metal wedge placed in a crack, usually with a length of tape and a karabiner attached. The climbing rope can then be clipped into the karabiner, and this means that should the climber fall, then the distance he falls is only twice the height that he is above his runner, instead of twice the distance to his last belay.

Before the development of purpose-made runners, pebbles of various sizes were sometimes carried on a climb, placed in a crack and a length of cord threaded over them. During the sixties mechanical nuts were drilled out and threaded to make crude runners. Modern protection has come a long way since then and the choice of runners for a climber is vast, although they can be broadly classified into wedging nuts and camming devices.

Wedging nuts are usually tapered or curved, and work by wedging on irregularities in cracks. Camming devices are designed so that as pressure is exerted, the device expands, or cams into a crack or pocket and thus 'holds'. Nut runners vary in size from a few millimetres to several centimetres and are available either loose (just the head part) or already threaded with cord or wire. Whereas nuts are fabricated from a single blob of metal, the latest camming devices can utilize several moving parts and the very latest in design technology.

An extension sling reduces the risk of the wired nut lifting out of the crack as the rope moves.

The first such devices were invented by Greg Lowe in the early 1970s and are now known as 'Friends'. They each have four independent cams which expand and grip the inside of a crack when pressure is exerted in the event of a fall, and they represent a big step forward since they made parallel and flared cracks protectable.

Apart from new camming devices on the market, the most important recent developments have been towards lighter and stronger tiny nuts. Austalian Roland Polig designed and gave his initials to one of the most popular sets of such small nuts, RPs.

Tape slings

These are loops of strong nylon tape, either knotted or sewn, in various lengths. They are used in many situations such as threading natural chockstones, lengthening nut runners, placing over protruding spikes or around trees for protection, plus many more. Sewn slings are bought as such and are stronger than knotted ones. They also have the advantage that there is no bulky knot to get caught or jam, but they are less versatile since they are permanently of one

A tape threaded round the back of a rock pillar to form a natural thread runner.

length. The shorter slings, about 15 cm are known as 'quick draws'. It is usual for a climber to have four or five of these on a rack.

Descendeurs

This name applies to any device that is used for descending down the ropes (usually called *abseiling*). The basic principle is one of friction, i.e. by wrapping the rope around a particular shape of metal, the friction thus produced allows a controlled descent. The most common descendeur is the Figure of Eight shape, which is made from high strength aluminium and has one 'eye' smaller than the other. The rope is threaded around the body of the Figure of Eight and the device is clipped into a karabiner attached to the climber's harness.

A mechanical descending device. Keep your hand on the bottom rope and let the rope slide through to belay.

Belay Devices

When a climber falls off, it is up to the second person—the belayer—to hold the ropes and prevent him hitting the gound. Since a fall often produces a high shock, it is sometimes difficult to hold the rope. It has to be held in a particular way (see Belaying p. 40) but it is the friction produced between the rope and the belayer's hands, arms and

Belaying with a belay plate and double ropes. If the climber falls the rope jams in the belay plate.

upper body, which holds a fall. This can produce rope burns, and if there is a large difference in body-weight between the climber and the belayer, it may prove hard to hold a fall.

Belay devices are usually flat pieces of metal with either one or two holes, for one or two ropes to be used. A bend in the rope is pushed through a hole and a karabiner—screwgate or 'Twist-lock'—clipped in and attached to the specific part of the harness. The friction generated by the rope against the belay plate is controlled by the belayer by drawing back the inactive rope opposite to the direction of the fall. Some belay plates have a spring attached to prevent possible inadvertent jamming.

Ascendeurs
As the name suggests, ascendeurs (or jumars) are mechanical devices to enable a climber to ascend the rope. They are usually metal clamps placed on the rope which, while able to be pushed upwards, jam when a downward force is exerted. A climber will use two of these clamps resting the weight alternately on one while the free one is pushed higher up the rope.

A well placed kingpin peg in a vertical crack, with most of the peg inside the crack.

Pegs
These are purpose-made metal pins or flakes, which are placed or hammered into cracks for protection or aid. (See Aid climbing p. 50.)

Bolts
These are purpose-made metal devices, which are used on blank walls (like rawlplugs) when no other protection can be found. Used in free and aid climbing.

Helmets
Helmets are made from a mixture of fibreglass and resin and form a

Top: A protection or aid bolt, with the back of the hanger flush against the rock so that it cannot work loose. A karabiner clips into the eye.
Above: A ring bolt for aid or protection, well hammered into the rock.

protective shell for the head in case of stonefall, or against hitting the head on rock in the event of a fall. Many climbers complain of a 'numb' feeling when wearing helmets and find the weight cumbersome so prefer not to use them, but they are used a lot in aid climbing, in winter climbing and by beginners. They should always be considered where there is high objective danger.

Equipment Techniques

Basic Knots

Knots have one big advantage over permanent methods of joining ropes and cords together (like sewn slings): they can be rapidly and easily tied and untied. Their disadvantage is that they significantly weaken the rope in which they are tied. Knots should really be regarded as a temporary method of joining ropes together. If the correct knot has been selected for a particular job, then it won't untie itself.

In a knot, the rope often turns about a very tight radius. Looking at the Figure of Eight Knot below, or at those illustrated opposite, it is clear that the line which travels the greatest distance in any knot is that around the outside. Crimping a rope into tight bends causes great stretching around the outside of the bend and noticeable compression on the inside. The fibres within the rope do compensate for this to a degree by shifting within the structure of the rope, which itself flattens to cope with the tension as much as possible. However, tying and using knots repeatedly

on a rope will produce an uneven strain, so ropes should be regularly checked for signs of weakening.

Although it is virtually impossible, due to the complexities involved, to take into account all factors relating to knot strength, it helps to understand the general principles involved, so that a climber knows what to expect from various kinds of knots in different types of ropes.

Fibre elasticity must be the most important factor influencing knot strength. A very elastic fibre under strain will elongate to accommodate the strain, so that part of the load is transferred to other fibres initially untouched. If the fibres were not elastic, the first fibres to come under strain would break before the load could be shared with other fibres. Today's climbing ropes and cords, being nylon, are all 'elastic' to a degree, and so knots in climbing usage are operating under optimum situations. The strongest knots are found in nylon ropes. (Ropes have knot strengths roughly proportional to their elasticity.)

All knots are weak, some more so than others. Knots such as the bowline and clove hitch are popular because they are relatively strong, due to the way the load is distributed. The bowline, for example, is often said to be 60 per cent as strong as the rope it is tied in. This is an optimum figure, sometimes a bowline can weaken a rope to as little as 10 per cent of its strength, depending on the type of rope used.

Types of knot
Stopper knots
There are many situations where it is useful to have a knot on the end

Tying a Figure of Eight Knot
(1) Make a bight (bend in the end of the rope), passing the end under the standing part.
(2) Pass the end over the near side and through the loop.
(3) The knot is drawn up.
(4) Finish off with a half hitch knot.
Use the Figure of Eight Knot as a stopper knot or for tying into your harness.

Figure of Eight

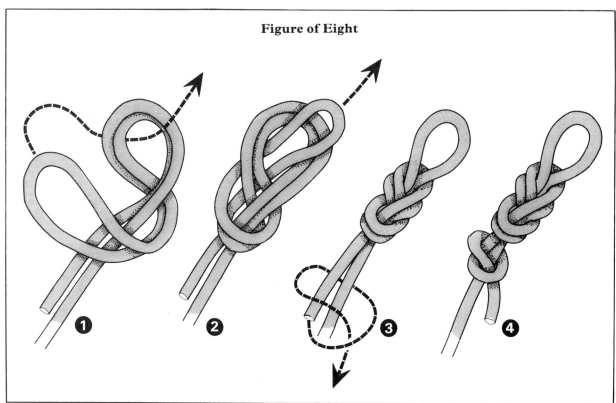

Bowline

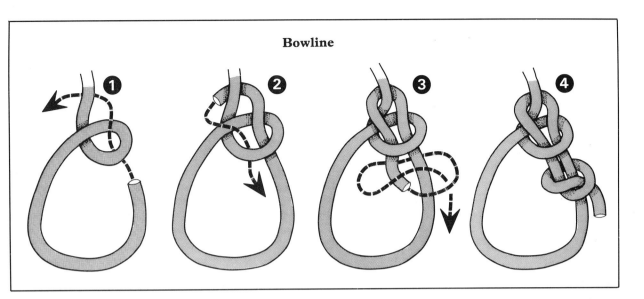

of a piece of rope to stop it pulling through. One is in abseiling in dramatic situations or in the dark when there is a very real possibility of going off the end of the rope. It may be useful to have a knot on the end of a rope to make it easier to grip, as a rope can easily slip through your hands. The Figure of Eight Knot is the standard stopper knot, and in many ways, the best. It is easily tied and untied, and it increases the diameter of the rope by three.

Double Fisherman's Knot
This is used for joining ropes when abseiling, and also for forming slings.

Half Hitch
The standard method of finishing off any knot is to loop the loose end round the rope and back through itself.

Tape knot
This is the only knot suitable for tying tape loops.

Tying a Bowline
(1) Make a loop in the rope.
(2) Pass the tail through the loop while presenting the loop.
(3) Pass the tail around the back of the static rope and back into the loop.
(4) Finish off with a half hitch to prevent any slipping.

NB The way a bowline is subsequently loaded is important, and a 3-way pull should not be applied as this may untie the knot.

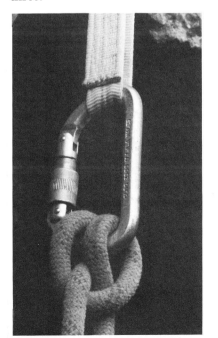

A clove hitch using a screwgate karabiner which can be used for belaying.

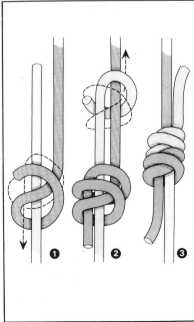

Double Fisherman's Knot
When forming rope slings, tighten knot with body weight.

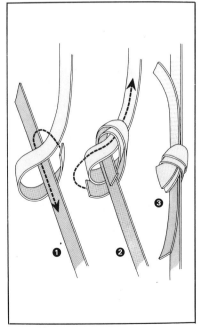

Tape Knot
Tighten the knot with body weight to prevent it working loose.

Bowline

This is the most versatile knot in climbing. It is the best knot for putting a fixed loop in the end of a rope because it never slips or unties itself—which makes it invaluable as a harness knot—yet it is easily untied afterwards, regardless of the load it has sustained. The only limiting factor—the one that applies to all knots—is that the bowline is weaker than the rope it is tied in.

Tying On

The usual method of tying onto the end of a rope is with a bowline. For tying on in the middle of a rope (e.g. when climbing in a threesome) a Figure of Eight Knot is used.

It is important to read the harness manufacturer's instructions for tying into harnesses, as this varies from one make to another.

Belaying

Belaying is the name given to the technique of 'managing' the rope with the object of checking a fall, should one occur; and a belay (or belay point) is the name given to the safe stance from which this takes place—be it from the ground, after every pitch, or on the top of the crag. Belays may be made on a large ledge with substantial trees for anchors, or there may be no such luxuries—maybe all you have are two tiny footholds and an *in situ* bolt to hang from. Whatever the situation, the important thing is that the belay is safe, either using natural resources such as trees or rock spikes, or by placing anchor points such as nut runners or pegs. The directional pull from a potential fall must be considered when placing anchors—an outward pull may rip out runners. The belayer is tied to the anchors by his climbing rope, the length of which depends on the situation. If the only suitable anchors are well back from the top of the crag, or from the front of the ledge, then there will be a lot of rope between the anchor point and the climber, so an extra subsidiary belay can sometimes be placed nearer the edge. On a hang-ing bolt belay there may be only a few centimetres of rope out. Wherever possible, a belayer should be able to see the moving climber and be ready for a fall.

When the leader is climbing, it is the second's job to belay him, either from the ground or from the last belay stance. When he has completed his pitch or reached the top of the crag, the leader then must belay the second climber. In either situation there are a variety of methods used, with or without equipment specially designed for belaying.

Using a single rope, or double ropes as such, the most common method without purpose-designed equipment is where the rope runs around the belayer's body and the inactive part is twisted around the hand for extra control. The friction caused between body and rope is usually enough to hold a climber's weight unless there is a great discrepancy between the weights of the two climbers. In this case, most climbers use a belay plate (see p. 37). A loop of climbing rope is fed through and clipped into a karabiner which is attached either directly to the belayer's harness, or to a rock belay. Obviously the belayer must be tied on to a belay also. As the climber progresses, the rope is paid out through the plate and if a fall occurs, the 'dead' rope is pulled back to form an S-shape, thus effecting a braking system. A Figure of Eight descendeur can also be used instead of a belay plate.

If a waist belay is used to stop a fall, a belayer simply clasps both arms in front of his body, providing greater friction between the rope and his body. Since the strain placed is quite considerable, it is important to place a runner between the climber and the belayer as soon as possible, particularly with the waist belay in order to reduce the length of a potential fall.

Once a fall has been held, the belayer must lower the climber to the ground, or belay stance, as gently as possible. Friction generated can be intense, and a slow, steady lower will reduce any pain.

Rope Calls

When visual contact is lost, climbers rely on communicating by a code of shouted instructions, such as:

'I'm there!' – the climber has finished a pitch and arrived at a belay stance.

'Taking in!' – the belayer pulls up all the rope until it becomes tight against the second man.

'That's me!' – indicates that the rope is taut on the climber (and not just snagged on a spike or tree).

'Come on!' – the belayed person is ready for the other climber to start climbing.

'Climbing!' – the second is starting to climb.

'OK' – signals that the belayer is ready for the second to climb.

'Tight!' – means that the climber requires the rope to be taken in tightly.

'Slack!' – the opposite, pay out more rope.

'Take in!' – the belayer should take up any slack rope that has occurred.

'Take me!!' – means the climber is about to fall off and warns the belayer.

There are other calls, such as 'Twenty feet', when a leader only has twenty feet of rope left to be paid out. Using a universally-understood code like this is useful when climbing with different or unaccustomed partners, but regular climbing partnerships will usually develop their own call systems. Some may use a series of gentle pulls on the rope (especially useful if wind-noise makes shouting difficult to hear); some may devise private codes if they don't wish to broadcast their intentions to the world at large.

Runners

Runners are devices which the rope runs through to prevent a climber falling to the ground. If a runner is sound, the climber will fall twice the distance of his position above the runner, plus a little extra when the rope stretches. There are various forms of runners, such as nylon slings, metal wedges, *in situ* pegs and bolts, etc. The leader sets up the runners and the job of the second (or last man on the rope) is to remove all the equipment inserted. A beginner will usually only have to know how to remove nut runners from cracks. It's fairly obvious how to unthread a sling from around a tree or chockstone in a crack. Nut runners are designed to wedge into cracks with a downward pull, so pushing from below, or flicking, will usually remove them. Always keep one hand on the rock when removing runners and use gentle persuasion rather than force.

The rope will be running through a karabiner which is attached to the runner. The rope is first unclipped from the runner, then the runner removed from the crack, before being clipped onto the gear loop on the harness, or onto a sling worn across the shoulders (called a bandolier).

When leading and placing runners, look for V-shaped slots. It may be necessary to try several sizes of nut before finding the correct one. Seat it into the crack by pulling it down into the 'V'. Always keep one hand on the rock and never 'test' a runner by tugging on it with both hands. Before leading climbs, it is a good idea to be familiar with runners and their uses by practising placing them while standing on the ground.

Good runner technique is high on a climber's list of priorities. Everyone falls off at some stage in their climbing career, and the runners decide whether the fall results in injury or merely hurt pride. A good climber will be able to tell what runner is needed from a few moves below; he will know exactly where that particular runner is on his harness, will unclip, place the runner first time, and clip the rope into it in a matter of seconds. It will be a smooth process without

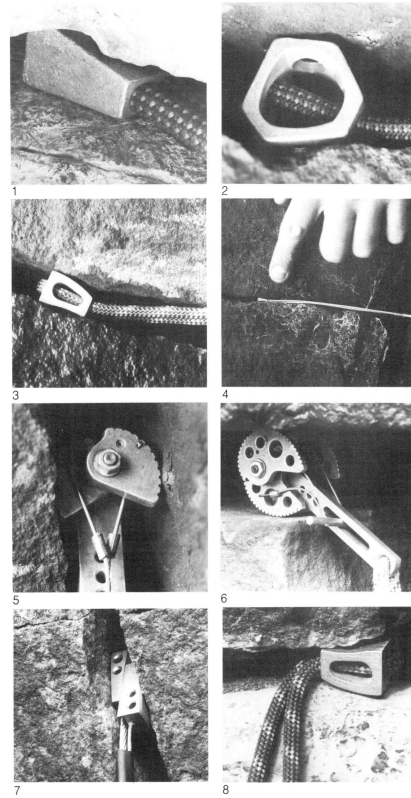

(1) A nut well seated into the crack and biting into the irregularity in the rock. (2) A Hexentric nut. (3) A curved nut, kept in position by pressure on the rope. (4) A tiny brass nut for protection when running a belay. (5) A Friend – the bar should be in line with the direction of pull. (6) A badly placed Friend. (7) A slider nut. (8) A badly placed nut.

fumbling, dropping the runner or taking several tries to clip the rope in. Much of this efficiency will have come with experience, but there are ways to make things easier for yourself.

When climbing a multi-pitch route, it is imperative to put a runner in as soon as possible to prevent a fall coming directly onto the belay or belayer.

Runners are available in several forms (see p. 41). First of all decide what protection equipment you will need. This is done by reading the guidebook to find out what sort of route it is, by looking at the climb itself, and by talking to other climbers who may have done the climb already. There may well be a crucial runner that is missing from your rack. On harder climbs, the protection is more and more scarce by definition, so knowledge of a climb becomes important. However, just by looking at a climb and the length of the route, will tell a climber roughly what sort of gear to take. If there are wide parallel cracks, then 'Friends' may be needed; if there are trees or bushes on the route, then long slings are necessary to place around them; if a chockstone is visible in a crack, then a sling will be needed to thread it; if there are pegs on the climb, then take 'quick draws'; if the climb wanders around through overhangs, then you'll want long slings again to reduce the 'drag'.

Karabiners through bolts or pegs should be turned so that the gate faces outwards, otherwise a shock load may force the gate against protruding rock and flick it open.

'Friends' were designed to work in parallel-sided cracks and flared cracks, and having discovered that they work, the beginner's first reaction is to place them all over the place, pushing them as far as possible into the back of the crack in the belief that it's safer. Wherever it is practicable to use a nut, it's still usually best to do so—they are easier to remove, cheaper to lose, and safer. Always place a 'Friend' with the bar facing downwards, so that the bars are easily reached. If

using them in a horizontal crack it's best to use a small sling to 'tie-off' the 'Friend' so that the weight—in the event of a fall—will come onto the 'Friend' as close to the edge of the crack as possible.

Another common fault when using 'Friends', is to choose the largest size that will fit. This often means inverting the cams to make the gear fit the crack. If the bar is swivelled excessively within an irregular crack, the cams can become very offset which can also lead to them being inverted. Inverting the cams invalidates their use. At the other extreme, you should also avoid having the cams wide open, and only just gripping. If the cams are as closed as they can go, the 'Friend' can sometimes get stuck; the best method of removal is to place two loops—one either side—of the trigger and pull, or wire nuts can be used effectively. A purpose-made device is now available for this.

'Racking' Gear

Before starting out on your route, it is a good idea to spy out all its pitches and decide the equipment necessary (see p. 41). It is quite common to see climbers on an obvious handjam pitch encumbered by RPs (see p. 36) and a whole rack of tiny nuts which are obviously going to be useless. The other extreme is possibly more stupid—carrying 'Friends' on a slab-climb.

Having decided what you need, you must then rack it in a system that you know well. It doesn't matter if you use a bandolier (useful for swapping leads and gear on a multi-pitch climb), or rack on the gear loops of your harness. I rack my gear in increasing size. On the right-hand side I have several karabiners, then RPS up to size Rock 5, and on the other side, Rock 6 upwards. It doesn't matter what system you use as long as you've got one and are familiar with it—clipping on runners higgledy-piggledy really isn't on. It can be gripping to snatch desperately for a runner, only to find it's on the other side of your harness! If you can pick your runners off without

looking, then you will save a lot of time messing about and may even avoid a serious fall.

Rope Technique

Having chosen your route and your gear, having racked up and psyched up, have one last mental check that your harness is fastened properly, clean your boots on a towel before you get on the rock (it may be off-route to you, but the place you smear your muddy boots may well be someone else's bouldering circuit), and finally, check that your second stands well into the rock at the foot of the crag. I have seen several leader falls which should have been no problem, but with the belayer standing too far out, the runners flick out. I have even heard of a belayer being dragged across the ground and breaking his ankle.

Single rope technique
In this situation the leading clim-

ber ties onto one end of a 45–50 metre rope, usually 10.5–11 mm diameter. The rope is tied into his harness using either a bowline or Figure of Eight knot. As he climbs the second (or belayer) pays out the rope, leaving enough slack rope for the climber to clip into runners but not too much so that he may fall and hit the ground. When the leader reaches the belay or runs out of rope then he takes a belay, (makes himself safe) and takes in all the loose slack ready for the second to follow up.

Single rope technique has become a widely accepted practice where climbs follow direct lines, for example on the soaring cracks of Yosemite Valley. The climbs here do not wander from side to side, making belaying and runner placements much simpler. There is only one rope to worry about and clip in to karabiners. On the Southern French limestone of Buoux, for example, where the routes are

Above: Seconding at Buoux on a single rope. The climber is unclipping a karabiner from a bolt and retrieving gear placed by the leader.
Left: Paul Williams leading Fern Hill, Derbyshire, using double ropes. As he moves upwards there will be no awkward pull on the ropes, so the runners will stay in position.

often under 50 metres in length with well spaced bolts, the local climbers have perfected the 'art' of clipping a single rope into bolts, taking one or two seconds. Often a row of 'quickdraws' (see p. 36), are clipped to the rope in readiness for a quick clip. With single rope a belayer must be particularly alert to pay out slack rope when needed since there is no 'back-up' of a second rope. If the rope snags as a leader pulls up rope to clip a piece of protection and he comes off, then he will fall much further than with two ropes.

Originally the single ropes used were heavy and inflexible and consequently stiff and hard to handle. Today's high-tech modern cords are light, flexible and very strong. Preference amongst top climbers has shifted away from the 11 mm diameter ropes a lighter 10.5 mm rope.

The obvious advantage single technique has over double, is that there is less weight to carry up the climb. There is also less to worry about; there is no dithering about which rope to clip into the runner. Its simplicity means it is the preferred method for beginners. Cost comes into it too, of course; it is cheaper to buy one rope than two.

Double rope technique
Double rope usage differs from single rope in that instead of one thicker rope being used, two thinner ropes are used in parallel. There are various reasons for preferring one to the other but mostly double ropes are used in more advanced climbing situations where a few centimetres of slack rope may mean hitting a ledge or the ground.

In Britain, two 9 or 8.7 mm ropes are used for double rope technique. The British preference for double ropes has evolved because many of our climbs tend to wander around quite a bit and, if the ropes are used correctly, two ropes will help stop rope-drag and prevent runners lifting out. Another advantage is when you come to abseil, it's useful to be able to abseil a full rope length (rock pitch) each time. In some countries where climbers used a single rope, they drag another up behind for abseiling. This seems pretty pointless to me.

In the unlikely event of a rope breaking, or snapping over a sharp edge, then with double ropes, there is always the second rope to back it up.

Imagine the situation: you have a good runner two metres below your feet and a poor one above your head. With a single rope you have no option but to clip that rope into the poor runner. If for any reason you fall off, or lower off, onto the poor runner which rips (out), then you will fall much further, increasing the possibility of hitting the ground or protruding rock. With

double rope it is possible to pay out one rope whilst taking in on the other.

With dubious protection, it is possible to place two runners in parallel (one rope on each), so that if a fall happens, the shock is taken on two runners. Also, two 9 or 8.7 mm ropes will stretch more than a single 11 mm one, thus lessening the shock on the body if a fall occurs.

The ropes must be kept separately if they are to be used correctly. It is bad practice for the ropes to twist around each other. This causes drag and will lift runners out.

Abseiling (Roping down)
If the popular press were to be believed, then abseiling (or rappeling) would be a sport in its own right; sponsored abseils seem almost as popular as sponsored parachute jumps. The fact that many children on outdoor education courses seem to regard abseiling as the most exciting part of their climbing course is to be deplored. It may be cheap thrills, but it's also very dangerous and should be done as little as possible. Several people are killed every year in abseiling accidents.

Abseiling is most definitely not a sport, it is a method of retreat or of gaining the bottom of a sea-cliff or gorge, or of inspecting a new route. You abseil if it becomes too difficult or dangerous to carry on with a climb, or if, on the larger crags, bad weather forces a change of plans. If you wander off route and have to retreat, then abseiling may be necessary.

The most important element of abseiling is to have a safe belay anchor to abseil from. A poor belay equates with death. Two belays should be used wherever possible.

Setting up an abseil
Suitable belay anchors for abseiling might be pinnacles, chockstones, pegs, bolts, trees, flakes or nut runners. If an abseil anchor is already in place, then it should be checked, particularly old or worn slings, or old pegs and runners.

Trees should be strong and large. Rock formations, such as spikes and flakes, must be solid. The rock around the 'placements' must be solid. If in doubt, back up any existing equipment by placing more.

Never hammer pegs in further to make them 'safer' as this will loosen them; gentle tapping will indicate their condition somewhat. Old slings can be replaced with the largest available tape or rope slings, not less than 7 mm. It's best to thread the rope through a karabiner or a belay ring because it is easier to pull the rope down over metal rather than through other nylon.

When several belay points are used, it is best to use separate slings for each one in case they pull out. Make sure the belay anchors are pulling in the correct direction of the abseil. If two ropes are used they should be tied together by a Double Fisherman's Knot (See p. 39) and the ends further secured with half-hitches.

The Abseiling Process
The most common method is using a Figure of Eight descendeur (see p. 36). The speed of descent is controlled by allowing the trailing rope to run slowly through the hand. The other hand is often held against the active rope to keep a steady position. If the abseil is too fast, it is possible to wrap the trailing rope around the leg for extra friction. If it becomes necessary to stop completely, then the trail rope can be locked across the active rope between the descendeur. If a very slow descent is required, or if one very thin rope is used, it is possible to wrap the rope around the small hole rather than the large hole.

Other abseil methods include the Classic (or Dülfer) Method, which acts on friction caused between the rope and the climber's body; it is not much used nowadays, or it is possible to abseil on a belay plate. A Karabiner Brake relies on karabiners being arranged in such a way that as the rope runs over them, the friction produced gives a controlled

Above: Abseiling in the Verdon Gorge, Provence.

Left: Jan Beatty abseiling down a sea cliff using gloves to prevent burning her hands. Her right hand is on the live wire at the bottom.

descent. The advantage of the latter is that a descendeur may not always be available, but karabiners usually are. It is important to remember that the rope must run over the backs of the karabiners, otherwise as soon as pressure is put onto the rope, the arrangement will fall apart.

When abseiling, it is best to be even and consistent in movement as sudden strain on the anchors is not advisable. Also, sudden friction translates to heat and the device gets hot; the heat generated by fast abseiling will damage a rope and melting can occur. If the rope runs over sharp edges, bouncing on the rope will cause wear and can cut it through.

Having said that abseiling is dangerous, you *do* need to know how to do it, and it is best to learn to set one up in safe, controlled conditions. When learning to abseil, a top rope is advisable. Practise well away from the climbing environment where falling rope or stones won't annoy other climbers (such as off bridges or climbing walls.) Never smear muddy boots on the rock when abseiling.

Prusiking

Prusiking is a method of ascending a fixed rope, either by alternately pushing up two friction knots, which jam as weight comes onto them, or by using mechanical clamps which will slide up the rope but have cams which, under pressure, will grip the rope tightly to prevent them sliding the other way.

There are many situations where prusiking is a useful technique to use:
- When suspended freely after a fall or accident.
- In some aid climbing situations, a third man follows by prusiking up the rope.
- Inspecting and clearing a new route.

Abseiling amid the dramatic scenery of Yosemite Valley, California. Abseiling should be used as a means of retreat or speedy descent in rock climbing.

Safety Rules for Abseiling

1. Always be tied into the belay when sorting out the ropes.
2. Make sure anchors are safe.
3. Make sure other climbers know when ropes are going to be thrown over.
4. Lower the rope-end gently over the edge to avoid knocking down rocks and to avoid tangling the rope.
5. Make sure the ropes reach the bottom, or the next belay stance. In multi-pitch abseils, it may be necessary to tie a knot in the ends of the rope, so as not to slide off the end.
6. Try to abseil evenly without swinging from side to side, otherwise the rope may knock rocks onto your head or cut through on a sharp edge.

   On the ground (or at end of abseil pitch):
7. When two ropes are used, remember which rope end has to be pulled to retrieve the ropes, otherwise the knot will jam.
8. Give clear calls when untied from the rope.
9. Keep out of the line of fire as a second climber abseils down.

Prusik knots

Prusik knots use the principle of winding a loop of thinner rope around the fixed rope in such a way as to provide enough friction not to slip under a climber's body weight. There are a wide number of knots to choose from, depending on the job required and the materials used. The most common knot used is simply called a Prusik Knot (diagram below).

The thinner rope is wrapped around the main rope and threaded through itself twice, making sure that the second 'wrap' is inside the first. It is important that the knot is symmetrical and that no overlapping occurs, otherwise the knot might slip under loading. It's a good idea to practise prusiking in a safe, controlled environment to discover its limitations and to find the best slings to use.

Mechanical Ascending Devices

These have several advantages over knots: they are purpose-built, easier to use, and generally safer. However, some disadvantages do exist. They are expensive and much heavier than prusik knot slings. They only serve one purpose, whereas slings are useful in other climbing techniques. Also, as with any metal, they may be subject to some fatigue or malfunction.

The most popular type consists of a shaped metal handle with a semi-circular sleeve, through which the rope runs. As it does so it

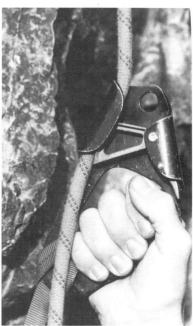

Above: A mechanical ascendeur for prusiking or jumaring – the cams jam against the climbing rope if any weight is applied.
Below: A Prusik Knot. Loop the prusik rope twice around climbing rope, and pass the other end through. Pull tight.

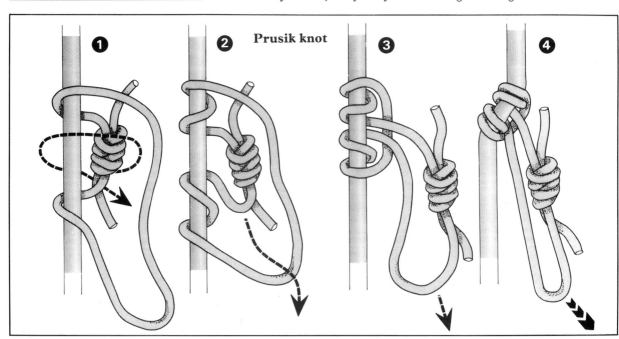

Prusik knot

is kept in position by a spring-loaded clamp with small teeth which bite into it. When a weight is placed on the device, a camming action forces the teeth into the rope and they hold it firm.

These clamps are used in pairs, so that one is holding the climber's body-weight as the other is pushed up the rope.

Top Roping

Top roping is a system of running the rope through a belay at the top of the route or pitch (frequently held from the ground), so that the climber is totally protected from above. Although it is by no means a new technique, particularly on lesser crags, it is certainly becoming more widespread. It helps build up stamina out on the crag rather than in a climbing wall indoors, and it is useful as a training method during the winter.

There is also the practice of top roping a climb in preparation for a lead. My personal ethics disagree with this, but so long as the tactics are declared after an ascent, it is generally accepted.

If you are top roping, then make sure the belay is backed up. Use a long sling to put over the edge of the top of the route so that the rope isn't running over a sharp edge. It doesn't take very much to cut a rope through.

As with leader climbing, make sure the belayer stands reasonably close to the crag, since there is less shock absorbed with just one 'runner' and more likelihood of his being pulled off his feet if the climber comes off.

Self Belaying For Soloing

There are two systems available for protecting a solo climber. The first is known as a short loop system, and the second as the 'z' system.

Short loop system

This method involves climbing on a continuous short loop of rope which is always clipped through three or more runners. As the climber moves up he has to clip into another runner then descent to unclip the bottom one. Since the

climber has to place his faith on just a few runners all the time, it is not such a reliable method as

The 'Z' system

which involves having a static belay as in a usual climbing partnership. One end of the rope is tied off to a belay and a Figure of Eight Knot is tied about six metres from it. The climber clips into this knot and proceeds to climb. As he climbs he places runners until he reaches the end of the six metres, or at some convenient place before, he will tie into a further six metres of rope and proceed. At a belay point the climber fixes the rope and then descends on a second rope to the first belay. It may have been necessary to fix the end of this second or 'trail' rope to the belay to reach it. Then he prusiks up the fixed

climbing rope, retrieving his gear as he goes.

Clothing

The type of clothing required depends on the weather mainly. For summer rock climbing, you need something on your legs that doesn't restrict your movements, such as shorts, track suit bottoms, or leotard bottoms (dance tights). An athletics vest or cotton t-shirt is usually enough for your top. It may be possible to climb shirtless between showers. It is often useful to have some warmer clothes (track-

Mark Wilford self-belaying on the Colorado Diamond, using a rope loop passed through the protection bolt clipped to his harness.

suit tops and bottoms) to wear before your climb and to put on after a climb to keep your muscles warm. It's much easier to climb when your muscles have warmed up properly.

During the winter, it's best to wear thermal or polar clothing to climb in. Polyprop underwear will 'wick' the moisture away and keep you dry. It's pretty horrible climbing if you feel cold and clammy. I find the best wear for cold climbing is a pair of salopettes since they exclude draughts around the kidneys as you reach above your head. Failing this, a really long shirt to tuck into your bottoms will do.

Aid Climbing

Aid climbing is the art of progressing up a rock face by the means of artificial tools. These tools may be hammered, jammed or hooked into natural features in the rock, or, when there is nothing natural like a crack to make use of, it may be necessary to drill a hole and insert an expansion bolt. Bolts are very controversial, since they effectively make all rock faces accessible, thus reducing the challenges. As in free climbing, they are placed only if there is nothing else, and after deliberation.

Today there are more climbers than ever .there were, and with more leisure time, more climbers are climbing at the highest standards. Through the widespread use of climbing walls and training methods, many young climbers progress rapidly through the grades, bypassing the long apprenticeship that used to be the norm. Whereas aid climbing was once accepted as good exercise and fun during the winter months, now the climbing walls and gyms have replaced this function.

Aid climbing has also become more and more unfashionable. This means that many good free climbers are pretty ignorant as regards aid techniques, and more importantly, don't have (and are not conversant with) the gear and equipment it requires. There are, however, numerous situations, such as retreating from a climb, injury, accidents at crags, and the general 'epic', when basic knowledge of aid climbing skills would make life easier. Aid climbing also makes it feasible for climbers of any free climbing standard to reach and enjoy spectacular positions, such as Kilnsey Main Overhang.

The aid climbing process starts when the climber places an aid point, such as a nut or a peg, as high as possible, usually by standing in étriers (portable tape or metal ladders). He can then place another aid point higher. The other étrier is clipped into the highest point, climbed up, and then the lower étrier retrieved for further use. Most aid climbers have a short sling about 20 cm long (a Cow's Tail) attached to the harness, which is clipped into the aid point in order to be able to sit back and rest while sorting out the gear.

An aid climber standing on étriers on an overhanging wall.

During the climb the aid points are used as runners where necessary.

The first thing to remember is that areas where traditionally 'free' climbing is practised are *not* the places to go aid climbing. It is considered totally unacceptable to hammer pegs into a climb that is done free. Sometimes peg scars or smashed nuts do mysteriously appear on free climbs, and one assumes they are the work of some misinformed novice. Places like old buildings, railway cuttings, even trees, are useful places to practise aid techniques. At one time aid climbers in Britain haunted loose limestone crags, such as Raven's Tor in Derbyshire or Gordale Scar in Yorkshire, and disused gritstone quarries, such as Millstone near Sheffield. These places are now well-established free climbing areas, and aid climbing at these or other free areas would be considered a retrograde step these days.

As with free climbing, aid climbers practised their skills on the smaller crags to transfer their techniques to more exciting and remote areas of the world. The free climbers mecca of Yosemite Valley in California is just as famous for its big walls, sporting some of the world's best aid climbing, particularly El Capitan and Half Dome. For more remote aid climbing, Baffin Island in the North East Arctic area of Canada offers adventurous climbing. At the other end of the American continent, Patagonia contains some of the most exciting aid climbing areas in FitzRoy and Cerro Torre where the battle with the elements takes as much energy as that with the climbs.

In a softer setting the European Dolomites have been a breeding ground for the mountaineers and rock climbers of the Continent for generations. Indeed their famous *via ferratas* make the limestone rockfaces and summits accessible for climbers and walkers of all standards.

It's worth saying that many classic free climbs would not exist unless the aid men had been there first. Several cracks would not be physically possible unless pegs had been repeatedly bashed in and removed, thus widening the crack sufficiently to get fingers in. Equally, several of the existing climbs would be devoid of protection if pegs and bolts left by the aid men were not there. However, there are still plenty of places for new aid climbs to be done if you know where to look. The accepted practice in Britain seems to be that none should be done on gritstone, nor on existing free climbs, and that once an aid route is free-climbed, then it should be subsequently climbed free, or at the least, should not be further damaged with pegs. Instead nuts should be used for aid or free climbing protection.

Equipment for Aid Climbing

In general, aid climbing is more complex than free climbing and an aid climber will usually have served a free-climbing apprenticeship and own the basic free-climbing equipment, such as sit harness, ropes and runners. A helmet is often worn in aid climbing since much aid climbing is done on loose rock, and a chest harness may be used in conjunction with a waist harness (necessary for climbing under large overhangs since it gives more support to the body in an upright position). Extra equipment required will include a peg hammer, pegs, étriers, also extra karabiners, extra slings and 'tie-offs' (which are short slings for tying off dubious pegs), bolt kit, bolts etc. The list is almost endless without such specialized items as haul sacs, hammocks, porta-ledges, etc.

Mike Weis reaching down to unclip étriers on the big wall of Moose's Tooth, Alaska. He has a white trail rope to pull up haul bags.

necessary for multi-pitch big wall routes, such as those in Yosemite.

Étriers

In their simplest form, étriers are small ladders made from tape with a shorter loop at the top for attaching to an aid point, via a karabiner. The usual style has three 'rungs' or stirrup loops, and most climbers will carry two, sometimes three, étriers. The idea is for a climber to stand in the top rung of the étrier and place another aid point (be it nut or peg), to which he will then clip the next étrier. Manufactured étriers are stitched together. It is possible to make your own by knotting the tapes together, but it is advisable to test a home-made one in a safe position first. Originally, étriers were made like little ladders—wooden rungs threaded onto rope. Later, aluminium replaced the wood, and these are still used widely. Tape has certain advantages over aluminium: it means the étrier can double up as a sling if needed, so a climber isn't carrying extra equipment, an important consideration on a long route. Tapes are also more flexible and easier to carry than metal, which is prone to jam in cracks; and although it might appear easier to place a boot or thigh quickly on the permanent rung of a metal étrier, with a little practice and the correct-size loop, it is just as easy to place feet into tape.

Cow's Tail

As the climber moves up the étrier he can rest by clipping this short sling from his harness onto the aid point. About 20 cm is the usual length.

Fifi Hooks

Occasionally, it is more convenient to attach a fifi hook onto the top of an étrier. A fifi hook is tied to the waist by a thin cord in case it gets dropped.

Belay Seat

A belay seat is a small hammock which is made from rip-stop nylon and tapes. This can take the pain out of long hanging belays, but a

comfortable harness invalidates this. Experience of hanging belays will tell you whether you need one.

Belay Devices

The friction devices used with free climbing usually apply.

Karabiners

Exactly the same type as used in free climbing are applicable. More will be needed, so lightweight ones are more practical, as you will be carrying up to fifty at once. Extra requirements are that a karabiner should be big enough to let a rope and two other karabiners (with étriers on) pass through. It is essential that it should fit into the eyes of the pegs and bolts easily. Make sure it will open under bodyweight, since it is more usual to be hanging on one in aid climbing than it is in free climbing. It is a good idea to carry a couple of screwgate karabiners, one for the haul bag (if one is carried), and one for the descendeur. If no screwgates are available, you can use two ordinary ones facing opposite directions.

Nuts

As in free climbing ethics exist in aid climbing and the current trend away from pegs and bolts towards nuts must be a good thing. In terms of damaging and scarring the rock, nuts are positively gentle. Other advantages of nuts are that they can quickly be placed and removed. It is also possible to see whether a placement is good, since a nut is usually visible, whereas a peg is buried in the rock.

A fifi hook, which is sometimes used as a quick means of attaching étriers to karabiners.

However, the distinction between nuts and pegs is not so obvious when considering placements such as 'Bashies' and 'Mashies'. These are blobs of soft metal that are tapped or hammered into shallow or flared cracks until the metal bites onto the surface of the rock. 'Copper Heads' are a refinement of the same principle.

Slings

A variety of slings are needed, particularly the short 'tie-offs' which are useful in conjunction with dubious pegs, or pegs that stick out a long way. Placing a 'tie-off' over the peg as near to the rock as possible, instead of through the eye, places a lot less leverage upon it.

Hammers

One of the most essential items in the climber's kit. There are several types for sale and it is important that somewhere in the design, the hammer has a hole for attaching to a harness. A hammer holster is useful for storing a hammer when not needed.

Pegs

Pegs are used when nuts cannot be, in cracks and seams. Some can be placed by hand, but most need to be hammered in. Practice is needed to develop an eye for a potential placement, and experience tells when a peg is safe. As a peg is driven into the rock, a ringing noise is heard. This becomes more and more high pitched in tone, indicating a good placement. When the tone stays consistent, then the peg is 'home', or as far home as it is going to go. Further hammering will then only loosen the peg, and it may spring out suddenly. It is a good idea periodically to inspect pegs for cracks or fractures and rusting.

Most pegs are made from chrome-molybdenum steel and come in several lengths and thicknesses. The predominant shapes for pegs are shown opposite.

Bolts

As with free climbing, bolts are considered a last resort and cause some controversy. They are used when nut placements and peg cracks are not possible. The basic principle is that a cylindrical hole is made in the rock and a piece of metal with a head is inserted. The two main types of bolt are the expansion bolt and the contraction bolt. The former works on the principle of the metal inside the hole expanding to exert pressure on the rock around it, and the contraction bolt works on the basis that a bolt stem is a bit too big for the hole drilled, but can be smashed in.

If a climber wants to keep moving upwards, and no other placements are possible, then a bolt is the only answer. Sometimes it may be necessary to place a small number of bolts to reach vast areas of good climbing, such as on Salathé Wall, El Capitan. It would be a shame that that route was not done merely for the sake of 13 bolts. Then, there are cases where the constant hammering and removal of pegs destroys the rock completely so that good placements are no longer possible; one bolt before then may preserve the rock intact. Bolts are becoming acceptable on belay stances and in bivouac and abseil situations. Whether or not this is good or bad, is up to the individual to decide.

The major argument against bolts is that they take away the sense of adventure since the outcome is known in advance.

	There are several types of peg available:			
Bugaboos and Knifeblades	The characteristic of this shape is that the eye is offset on the edge of the blade. (Bugaboos are the smaller of the two)			bongs have holes drilled in them for lightness.
Lost Arrows	A Lost Arrow peg is tapered in two planes, and is available in several sizes.	Leepers		In cross section these have a Z-shape.
Angles	These have a V-shaped cross-section. Originally, the older type of mild steel channel pegs were U-shaped.	'Rurps' (Realised Ultimate Reality Pitons)		These are similar to a razor blade, and may be flat or bent. Used in very thin situations.
Bongs	These are metal pieces that appear to have been folded in half; they are a logical progression from angles. Some	Sky Hooks		These are devices which are merely hooked over a flake or edge of a pocket. They are used when nothing else is available unless a bolt is drilled. By nature they are precarious, since a climber's body-weight is what holds them in place.

 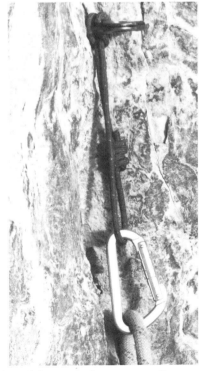

Left: A badly placed peg which could work loose under pressure. It should be hammered further into the rock and tied off with tape in a half hitch to reduce leverage (**Right**).

Physical Techniques

Many climbing techniques are natural—pulling up on holds and placing feet for balance is obvious; to a child, mantelling is a natural move – but some, such as jamming, are quite artificial. An understandable reaction to a crack problem would be to layback up it; jamming has to be demonstrated before being put into practice.

It is possible to classify the main climbing techniques under the following headings:

Balance climbing	– the most obvious useful situation being on slabs.
Jamming	– used for climbing cracks of all sizes.
Pressure climbing	– pressure is exerted in two directions to maintain equilibrium and, hopefully, upward momentum.
Power climbing	– used in places where it is physically impossible to stay in one position, such as roofs and overhanging walls.
Gimmicks	– this takes in those specialized techniques, such as knee bars, heel hooks etc, which are 'one-off' and not needed in a normal climbing day. May be called trick techniques.
Face climbing	– a synthesis of these and other techniques.

Balance climbing
Balance means being in control of one's centre of gravity by keeping your weight over your feet as much as possible, in line with natural gravity.

A climber will need his sense of balance whether he is on a low-angled slab climb or on an overhanging wall. A climber's 'sense' of balance tells him which foot and hand holds to use in order to stay in control. As a climber gains experience, there will be less need for deliberation. It will become more instinctive as he gains a feel for the rock and develops his sense of balance. A

climber can further develop this sense by doing more climbing, but simple balance exercises will help as well. Good balance will only come with experience, but some people have a natural advantage.

Slab climbing
A slab is usually defined as any smoothish rock tilted at between 15 and 75 degrees. In Britain, most climbers get their first slab experience on gritstone, although there are some notable examples on

A climber on a slab climb using her hands to push off from the rock in order to keep her weight over her feet.

other sorts of rock, like The Devil's Slide on Lundy, and the Etive Slabs in Scotland (both granite). Slabs are not so common on limestone, where cliffs are more usually vertical.

Gritstone is a very compact and

hard rock and since its natural protection only exists in the cracks, slab climbing on grit can be very bold, and is technically some of the hardest. A few pegs still exist on quarried gritstone, but long tradition has resisted the placing of unnatural protection on the natural gritstone 'edges', and this has maintained the seriousness of many of the harder routes.

Classic harder slab climbs may see several ascents in a weekend using a top rope, but only one or two leads, since (as with many grit climbs) leading means soloing.

The most important asset for balance climbing on slabs is confidence. Placing feet must be done positively and moves should be made surely and steadily. Dithering while you worry about whether or not your boot will 'stick', is a major factor in failure. Today's high friction boots will stick in the most ludicrous situations, and believing this, is halfway there. It helps to test friction on boulder problems in safety. That way you know exactly what your boot soles will stick on.

The most common bad habit is to lean into the rock under the false illusion that it is more secure, rather than trying to maintain an upright position.

Jamming

The art of jamming is the most unnatural form of rock climbing, and the methods for overcoming crack problems are not obvious. It is an essential part of a climber's repertoire and most climbers have served a painful jamming apprenticeship (with scars to prove it, as skin and flesh have been left behind on hard crystalline cracks when jams have slipped). Having mastered the art, a climber quickly realizes that a 'solid' jam is one of the best holds to have. It is secure, safe, and allows the other hand or arm to be rested, or to arrange protection.

Having learnt the various techniques for jamming, it is necessary to learn when and where to use them and to promote the stamina and power needed to execute the moves. Stamina and power will come with with training and climbing. Economy of effort comes with

experience. Other problems associated with jamming might be lack of 'bottle' or courage, or over-enthusiastic jamming—usually a by-product of fear—resulting in too much energy wasted.

Cracks are found face-on in walls (vertical and horizontal), or in corners. There are several basic techniques for climbing them. Alternating the leading jam hand works well on wall cracks, but a shuffling method, keeping the same leading hand, is better for cracks in corners, since it is awkward twisting the body in confined spaces. Whichever hand is the 'leader' depends on which way the climber faces. If his right shoulder is up against the rock, then his left hand will lead, and vice versa.

Jams are classified as to their size in relation to a climber's hands, fingers etc. A hand jam for one climber may be a fist jam for another, so a climber has to

Space Babble, a face climb on the Middle Cathedral Rock in Yosemite Valley, California.

A thin finger jam, with stacked fingers. The middle finger on top of the forefinger exerts pressure.

recognize jam placements for himself.

Finger cracks

Fingers are the smallest part of a climber's body that can be wedged into a crack. Place the fingers in a crack and wedge the knuckles against any irregularities in the crack (rather like placing a runner). Choosing the right knuckle to wedge depends on the size of the crack. Finger cracks often seem to be halfway between face climbing and crack climbing. Shallow peg pockets dotted up a hairline crack call for both techniques.

The most common type of finger jam is the thumbs-down position. Here the fingers are placed in up to the first or second knuckle, with the thumb pointing down. Twisting the wrist in a downward motion gives a secure torquing effect. For a slightly wider jam, the thumb can be placed (stacked) under the jammed fingertips, using the wrist as above for torque. This jam, needs practice before it feels secure

but can be very useful.

For cracks that won't take even the first knuckle, it may be possible to use a thumbs-up technique. This means that the little finger can be used by pulling straight down on it like a nut. It's possible to reach further from this position than from the thumbs-down position.

When climbing a crack in a corner, a mixture of the two types is necessary. A mild layback motion helps to decrease the effort needed to get little finger jams into a corner. When moving up it is important to keep the wrist low to keep the jam stable. As a crack widens, make an effort to jam more knuckles in.

As mentioned, finger crack climbing can depend on a mixture of face and crack climbing, and the feet mustn't be forgotten. There will often be footholds on the faces either side of the crack which are easily overlooked since there is a tendency to develop tunnel vision—only looking into the crack for foot jams.

Always place jams positively and carefully for efficient technique. Small fingers and feet are an advantage for finger crack climbing.

A solid hand jam. The thumb is crossed over the palm and the fingers are extended with locked joints.

Off hand jamming (between finger and hand jamming)

This is the size just too big for fingers and not wide enough for a hand. It is a particularly hard size to jam and when to use this technique obviously depends on the size of a climber's hand. If the crack accepts the fingers, but not the hand, then there is a choice of solutions. The first is to torque the fingers; this is strenuous. Place the hand, as in finger locks, wrist low, thumb down, with the fleshy part of the forefinger wedged in. The arm is used for leverage as the fingers twist in the crack. The more fingers in the crack the better, as it spreads the strain. The second method is to thumb-lock, which is more difficult to place than the first, but less strenuous. The thumb is put vertically into the crack and then the forefinger is placed over the thumb's first knuckle, letting the other fingers find their natural position. Using the combined pull-down leverage

A fist jam, again with the thumb crossed over the palm for increased strength.

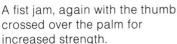

of the forearm and fingers keeps this jam in place. The next solution is to knuckle-jam whenever there is an irregularity in the crack. Stacking two or three knuckles horizontally just above the kink, and curling the fingers into a little fist, will make the knuckles expand and grip the side of the crack. It is better to keep the fingers tucked into the hand, rather than poking out into the crack.

In a corner or awkward position, it will be necessary to jam thumbs-up. The quickest way, and most precarious, is to layback up (see p. 60). Another way is to place the hand in as far as possible, using the fingers like a lever between the tips and the back of the hand. This is extremely powerful. A variation on this is to wedge the fleshy part below the little finger in the crack, so that as the pressure is applied, the hand wedge takes some strain. None of these techniques will work once the hand fits in beyond the biggest knuckle, often referred to as the 'dreaded inch and a quarter'.

Handjams

A handjamming possibility exists when the crack will just allow the hand in with the minimum of slipping. On the smaller hand cracks, it is useful to think of the hand as a nut, wedging it in at the wrist. If the crack is wide enough for the hand to fit comfortably, wedging the thumb against the palm gives security. If the crack is wider still, then twisting or torquing will help. It may be necessary to use a wide handjam which is done by pressing against the crack with the fingertips, the back of the knuckles and the fleshy part of the palm. This makes a bridge which can be made more secure by placing the thumb over the index finger.

Fist Jams

This is the most famous jam, reputed to have originated with Joe Brown and Don Whillans in the fifties. It is also the most secure jam. The three variations depend on where the thumb is put. The first type is where a usual 'fist' is made and wedged in either vertically or horizontally, palm up or down. As the crack widens, it is

A toe jam in a vertical crack. The camming action of the foot locks the boot into position.

best to move the thumb out to the side, pressing on the side of the forefinger. This makes the fist about 2 cm wider. The second type is when a very tight fist is required. These jams are 'bombproof' but some people find them difficult to do because of their bone structure. To make a tight fist jam, put the hand in the crack, usually thumbs-down, and put the thumb between the little finger and the third finger, making a small fist.

Feet

The upper body is only half the story. Footwork is just as important. When climbing any sort of crack, an experienced climber will look for footholds on walls and corners, but failing any footholds, then footjams may be necessary.

On the smallest, thinnest cracks (finger cracks), it will be necessary to look for pockets or irregularities in the crack. In wide pockets, the toe is placed in with the outside ankle downwards. Twisting the outside ankle presses the inside of

Foot jamming – the lower foot twists over to get better leverage and camming in the crack.

With all his weight on the left foot, fully jammed into a constriction, Ron can raise the right foot.

the toe further into the pocket. This is often useful for 'smearing' on the shallowest indentation, giving some friction. If the crack is too thin for toe jamming, then more smearing is called for. A crack that is face-on in a low-angled wall is best attempted by pointing the toe downwards and smearing the inside edges of the rock boot. If a crack is face-on in a steep wall, it's best to keep the foot toe-up and try to jam the front part of the outside edge in. It's important not to lift the heel up when moving up. This position may hurt when done correctly.

For a foot jam, cracks must be large enough to accept some part of the boot, whether it is the merest hint of rubber, as above, or the whole boot. If it is possible to put the boot in, then keep the heel low when standing up. As the foot torques, then body-weight keeps it twisting and the jam is very easy to do and maintain. This twisting foot jam is good for cracks up to hand-sized jams.

If a crack is diagonal, offset, or leaning, then the natural tendency is to adopt a layback position with the heels pointing down as much as possible. One common fault is to move the feet too close to the

hands. This puts an inordinate strain on the arms and fingers. It is important to keep the hands and feet as far apart as possible. The exceptions to this are flared or very steep cracks. Here the leading hand goes in thumbs-down, and the trailing hand palms the rock near the feet.

If a crack is fist-sized, then the foot will fit across horizontally, and it is possible to jam the foot in like climbing a ladder rung. If the crack is a wide fist-jam size, then bending the ankle allows a jam to be made against the inside edge of the boot.

Off-widths

The next crack-size up from a wide fist jam is known as an 'off-width'. Off-width techniques have been perfected by American climbers since they have a great variety of off-width cracks. Apart from a few notable horrors on gritstone, there are very few off-width climbs in Britain. Most are avoided as much as possible since the climbing is difficult, awkward and strenuous, often resulting in one long painful 'thrutch'.

There are some basic rules to follow when climbing off-widths. The body will be sideways to the crack. If one edge is offset, then try to have the back against it. For leaning cracks, it is best to face downwards. With straight cracks it doesn't matter, but facing the best

edge will help as it may be possible to pinch the edge, or layback occasionally. It is easiest to palm a flared edge, if one exists.

Off-widths are almost full body jams, but the arm and leg inside the crack work together, pressing in opposite directions to maintain the body position. As the arm holds a suitable jam, then the jammed leg or foot moves up to take the weight. The thinnest arm jam is called an arm bar. This is done by inserting the arm as far into the crack as possible, with the shoulder also in. Bending the elbow and pressing the palm of the hand on one side of the crack whilst the shoulder presses against the other, makes this jam, albeit a particularly strenuous one. A second jam is the forearm lock, which is less useful, but less strenuous in a suitable placement. This is made by placing the arm in the crack, palm up, then drawing the forearm back towards the shoulder, making a wedge.

For climbing wider cracks (but not as wide as chimney), two more techniques are available. The first is a variation on the arm bar where the arm is fully bent at the elbow and the hand is almost opposite the shoulder. Leaning out will wedge the lock further. The second tech-

Fist jamming up a wide, awkward crack. His weight is on both fists and the right leg, so the other leg can be raised.

nique is another variation where the elbow points upwards and the fingers downward. This jam is useful for resting as it needs little energy if done properly.

Generally, in off-width climbing, the 'trailing' arm is used for holding the outside edge with the elbow almost horizontal at shoulder level. If the arm is too high it is very tiring.

Off-width – The lower body
The inside leg can take some strain by bending at the knee, twisting the ankle and calf into the crack. It may be possible to do a knee-lock by bending the calf further back instead of twisting it. This expands the muscles around the knee and wedges it.

The outside leg does a lot of 'thrutching' and gives upward motion by doing a heel-toe jam across the crack. It's easy to waste energy here with bad placements and rushing, so it is better to place feet carefully and positively, keeping the toe lower than the heel, and twisting the foot inwards to maintain stiffness. In the off-width situation it is often difficult to see what the outside foot is doing, and a feel for the rock helps. On overhanging

rock it may be unbalancing to keep the outside foot in the crack and it is often better to place feet on small holds on the walls.

After heel-toe jams, wider cracks call for a particularly specialized technique called T-stacking. This is when the feet are placed inside the crack so as to form a T-shape.

The most important part of climbing these types of crack is to maintain a rhythm with the method chosen, resting where possible (a heel-toe jam or knee-lock work well), trying to conserve energy.

Resting
Crack climbing is often strenuous, so mastering the art of resting is crucial. Resting while jamming is done by jamming one hand and then straightening the whole arm so that the weight is taken by the bones. Keeping the arm bent merely lets the muscles take the strain, making the exercise pointless. Try to keep the resting arm as low as possible to maximize blood circulation. Shaking the arm, or wiggling the fingers, helps promote blood flow. This is in order to get oxygen to tired muscles as quickly as possible. Alternate the arms until they are sufficiently recovered. It is important to remember that a climber won't recover 100 per cent, and only experience will tell the difference between

Ron uses a narrow finger crack for further balance, whilst keeping his feet and one fist in the larger crack.

being as far rested as possible and dithering.

Before setting off on a climb, try to decide beforehand where it will be possible to rest—look for a good foothold, or kinks in a crack which may give good jams. The best for resting are hand jams and finger-locks.

Pressure climbing

Chimneys
A chimney is a wide crack large enough for a climber to get inside. It may be a tight squeeze or it may be as much as a metre wide. The usual technique for dealing with chimneys is to 'back-and-foot!' The climber puts his back against one side of the wall and places his feet on the other side, forming a bridge. The hands are kept pressing palms down, on the same wall as the back. By bending and straightening the legs it is possible to 'walk' up the chimney. It may be necessary to straddle the legs across the gap, one hand on either wall alternately pressing and pushing with feet and palms. Whilst chimneys are usually easy to climb, though often unpleasant, they are frequently difficult to protect as there may be no cracks inside the main crack.

1

2

3

4

5

6

Chimneying
(1) Ron palms off with his right hand while exerting pressure with the back and the ball of the right foot. (2) Raising the left foot, he can then use the balls of both feet to push upwards. (3) Using the back and right foot and the ball of the left to create opposing pressures, Ron palms off the arête of the chimney. (4) He transfers his right foot to the other side of the chimney and uses opposing pressure to push upwards with the right hand. (5) He palms upwards with both hands. (6) He stands on small footholds, using opposing pressure from back and feet.

Laybacking
Laybacking is used for climbing arêtes, corners with cracks in, or offset cracks in walls. It is a quick efficient way of climbing but care is needed since it can be precarious, it may be difficult to stop and place protection on a long layback pitch, it is quite strenuous and it is easy to get into an awkward position and then pump out.

Laybacking an edge means placing the hands to grip the edge, gripping the edge between the fingers and the fleshy part of the palm, thumbs pointing upwards or gripping some small indentation. As the hands and arms pull in one

direction, so the feet and legs push in the other against the edge lower down. The legs and feet should be kept as low as possible for minimum strain. A common fault with inexperienced climbers is to move the feet too close to the hands.

Laywaying
This is the same principle as laybacking, but the edge is not an arête but a single hold or small edge maybe just large enough to curl fingertips around. Sometimes referred to as a side pull which aptly describes the motion. The arm is kept as straight as possible to 'layway' on it.

Laybacking a hairline crack, Ron keeps hands and feet close together, making use of the balls of his feet for pressure.

Mantelshelfing on a thin ledge, Ron keeps his bodyweight over the left hand until he can raise a foot.

Mantelling

The technique of mantelling is used when there is a blank section of rock above a decent ledge or hold. Depending on the angle of the rock above it may not be necessary for another hold to exist for several metres. The principle depends on the body-weight (centre of gravity) being placed directly over a climber's hand which is pressing palm down, fingers pointing downwards. This position is maintained as the feet are placed onto the same hold as the hands and then a rocking over move is made to let the feet take the weight, push up and stand up. Variations on this theme exist with the rock being very steep above the hand hold or the holds being very small or sloping. Fingertip mantelling is used on the tiniest finger holds and is self explanatory with the palm pointing away from the rock. (The crux of Down hill Racer is a food example.)

Often the start of a mantelshelf move is the most awkward as it requires a good impetus to push up and get the weight over the hand. It is necessary to keep the arm straight to lock it in position as bending at the elbow increases strain on the arm muscles.

In Britain the mantel technique is associated with gritstone since one of the features of this rock is that it often has rounded ledges with blank sections between. Many gritstone climbs require the mantel technique at the finish, as the top is often flat with rounded edges. Climbers may often execute the rest of their climbs reasonably, only to have a struggle thrutching over the top, as their intended mantelshelf move flounders, through lack of strenth or impetus.

Bridging

Bridging is self explanatory. By straddling the legs across a gap to form a bridge, a climber's weight is taken on the legs rather than the arms. The distance able to be bridged depends entirely on a climber's flexibility and length of legs, varying from one to two or three metres. The technique is obvious for climbing corners and chimneys where it not only gives upward motion but is invaluable for resting. Even if there are no footholds, the pressure exerted by the legs pushing against the sides of a groove will be enough to maintain equilibrium, depending on the angle and nature of the rock. It is possible to bridge up an overhanging gritstone groove but almost impossible to bridge up a low angled frictionless groove on rock such as slate.

As the feet are pushing against the rock so the hands play their part. If there is no crack in the back of a crack or groove for jamming or laybacking, then there may be small holds on the walls. If not however then it is necessary to use the palms of the hands to press up, fingers pointing down, thus bridging with the arms as well. If there are small holds one can pull away from the centre of the groove on these.

Bridging using pressure holds, relying on the diagonal of left foot and right hand.

Placing the thumb over the finger joints helps keep them in position on the tiny razor-sharp edge.

On a sloping edge, more of the surface of the hand is used, giving a crimping action.

On smaller edges the forearm muscles are used to keep the fingers in position.

Power climbing

I use the term 'power' climbing to describe the technique needed to climb overhanging walls and roofs, situations where rests are not feasible and some degree of dynamism is required. Almost all of the harder routes today come into the category, and no doubt tomorrow's 'desperates' will call for more and more of the same.

Power is defined as the ratio of strength to weight, so massive muscles are not essential since more muscle just means more weight to drag around. The most important muscles used are around the shoulders, forearms and fingers, with biceps marginally second. Legs are important here for pushing, since feet smearing on the tiniest edge are better than legs dangling in space. It's important to be able to make use of any available footholds, to be flexible enough in the hips to use out-of-the-way footholds and to be strong enough in the legs to maintain the position whilst the arms and upper body are sorting out the next moves.

Power climbing requires the basic ability to lock off on a hand hold especially when holds are far and few between. Locking off on one arm means holding a hand and pushing up with the legs, or pulling down on the holding arm in order to gain enough height, usually when the head is level with the hand is the maximum on overhanging rock. The holding arm is locked in that position where the elbow is fully bent and then reaching with the other hand to the next hold. If the holds are large enough, i.e. jugs, or a climber is strong enough he can 'rest' by hanging off one arm, fully extended and shaking the other arm. This kind of 'rest' is really relative to the type of climbing already done.

Good balance is important here since spreading the strain through the legs can relieve much weight on the arms. The legs are much stronger than the arms, so any opportunity to put the load onto them is infinitely preferable.

Roofs

A roof is an obvious climbing term and relates to a cap of rock jutting out at right angles to the rock below. They vary in size from a few centimetres to several hundred metres. If a climber is lucky, there will be a crack running the length of the roof providing jamming opportunities and protection within. If there is no crack, hopefully there will be large holes and

Roof climbing. **Left:** Reach up for a good hold round the roof and raise feet against the back wall.

This will give extra impetus when pulling up (**Centre**). **Right:** Transfer weight over right foot and

pockets in the roof—particular kinds of rock, such as limestone, lend themselves to holes in the rock. Large jugs often just require physical strength, and the courage to keep going, to swing baboon-like from one to another. Arm strength can be saved by hooking the feet over the edge of pockets or jamming toes into them. It is often possible, depending on the size of the roof, to use the back wall for foot support and reaching as far as possible before 'cutting loose' with the legs and maybe relying totally on the arms.

If a roof is seemingly bald then a combination of upside down palming and laywaying on tiny edges must be used.

Dynamos

'Dynamos' are an integral part of hard and power climbing but an average weekend climber will probably not be proficient with the technique. The word 'dynamo' comes from the term 'dynamic' and implies an explosive movement. Basically a 'dynamo' is a jump from one hold to another with everything off the rock in between. Depending on the distance between holds, a mixture of

reach over rock with left, moving up above the rock as quickly as possible.

crouching, pushing off with feet and springing is used. It is best to practise these moves on climbing walls, or bouldering in relatively safe conditions, before transferring them onto a climb. It is possible to cover considerable distances between holds by dynamos, up to one and a half metres in some cases.

Gimmicks

Several specialized techniques have evolved which may be used very occasionally – the average weekend climber is unlikely to ever have recourse to them – but in certain situations they are useful.

Knee Bar

A knee bar is made by wedging foot and knee across a gap. If secure then it's possible to take both hands off to rest on overhanging rock. However it's not advisable to do this with shorts as it can be painful on the knees.

Heel Hooks

As the name suggests, this move involves hooking the heel in a variety of situations such as over the edge of a pocket, around an arête or around a roof. It is useful in strenuous climbing situations such as roofs for helping relieve the weight on the arms even for just a few seconds while another hold is reached for. If the edge of a pocket is good enough, i.e. sharp not rounded, then it is possible to hang upside down from a double heel hook to 'rest' the arms.

Toe Hooks

This technique is similar to heel hooking except it is more secure since it is easier to hook the toe over the lip of a pocket than the heel.

Figure of Four

This is a technique for gaining extra height using a method of treating one's own arm as a hold and hooking a leg over. Having found a good jug to hang on, then, by pulling up and threading a leg over the holding arm, a position is achieved whereby a climber seems to be sitting on his own arm. This will give a few centimetres extra

reach which could be crucial. However, due to its strenuous and awkward nature, it is usually only seen on climbing walls.

Face Climbing

Face climbing refers to a steep rock face over 60 degrees which lacks cracks or grooves which usually offer the line of weakness up a crag. Because of this lack of features, face climbing has a feeling of exposure and seriousness. There is a scarcity of natural protection, and the harder face climbs are usually bolt-protected.

To the untrained eye a face will seem 'impossible'—how do you climb on seemingly blank rock? However most rock faces lend themselves to climbing by their superficial texture. The very rough monzonite rock of Joshua Tree, for example, gives good friction and is covered in tiny incut holds where thin flakes have broken off. The Verdon Gorge in France is famous for its seemingly blank faces which are often easily climbed on large jugs, formed by rain wearing away at the soluble limestone, known as 'gouttes d'eau'. Where the crags contain different types of stone, some harder than others, then natural weathering by the elements has worn away the softer rock leaving protruding knobs and crystals; the 'chickenheads' of Yosemite are one example of this.

Protection on wall climbs is much more subtle than crack climbs for example. Tiny nuts fiddled into pockets, slings over spikes and even skyhooks taped over edges can be used (see Equipment Techniques section).

To climb a face a variety of methods and techniques are adapted: bridging—not against the walls of a groove, but on crystals, knobs and tiny edges; laywaying—rather than continuous movement on an arête or the edge of a crack, an occasional layway move on small vertical edges of sloping holds. So rather than making a series of similar moves, as when crack climbing, face climbing requires the use of several techniques giving interesting and varied climbing.

Whilst it is impossible to describe fully face climbing as a single technique, there are several important points to notice. Balance is very important to keep as much weight as possible on the stronger leg muscles. Leaning sideways, laywaying off holds to get bodyweight over a single foothold helps. Most footwork concentrates on the front inside edge of the boot, 'edging' on small footholds varying in size to the tiniest 'razorblades'. On small edges the usual position is where both feet are 'turned out', similar to a ballet dancer, to accommodate both inside edges on small footholds. If a climb has pockets the foot is placed straight to jam the toe of the boot in.

Bridging techniques are adapted so that instead of using the soles of the boot to push against the walls of a groove, the 'pushing off' movements are done against sloping footholds, edges or the sides of pockets.

High step-ups are usual, making use of footholds at waistlevel for example, so flexibility in the lower body is necessary.

Depending on their size, pockets can be used in a variety of ways—pulling up on one-finger pockets or jugs, laywaying off the sides, undercutting off the top edge and so on.

'Chickenheads' or other types of protruding knobs can be used as handholds, footholds and for mantelling on.

The harder face climbs call for some dynamism as the holds become further apart. This involves holding the upper body close to the rock, getting feet as high as possible, and pushing off to reach high with the free hand, in a springing movement.

Training

During the last decade, the sport of rock climbing has advanced quite considerably, particularly in terms of technical difficulties. There are several reasons for this, including lighter, more refined equipment, more climbers becoming more committed, and the training methods employed.

The concept of doing specific exercises for climbing was almost unheard of until twenty years ago. Most climbers thought that by climbing routes, they would be doing enough. Up to a certain level this is valid, but training for climbing has certain advantages over just going climbing. Particularly in Britain, it is not possible to climb every day even if a climber is totally dedicated, so gym training or indoor climbing walls are necessary.

Even when it is possible to climb continuously, training plays a major part in an individual's progress. Some climbs require tremendous amounts of stamina, while others call for short intense bursts of energy. Aspects which can be significantly improved by training include: finger strength, suppleness, balance, muscle power, and technique, as well as attitude of mind and confidence.

The first sort of training was bouldering. Nowadays bouldering is so far advanced as to be considered a sport in its own right (See p. 66). A 'boulderer' may never venture more than 3 m off the ground, may never use a rope, but perform the most gymnastic feats in relative safety. However, without going to these extremes, most climbers will have bouldering sessions. Hard technical moves can be practised close to the ground and rehearsed for use on particular climbs.

Once the validity of bouldering had been established as a training tool, the next advance came with the advent of the climbing wall. The first climbing walls (in France, Germany and Japan) were built out-of-doors, but it was the concept of an indoor climbing ground that was seized upon by climbers in Britain, where the weather prohibited an all-year round climbing programme. (See p. 25.)

Since then, the idea has flourished. Climbing walls have been incorporated into existing buildings (by chipping holds or cementing pieces of natural rock into brick walls). Many have been purpose-built and are housed separately from other sporting facilities (such as that at Plas Menai, where the climbing wall is in its own room). Walls exist now in Britain in nearly all the major cities, being found in colleges, schools, sports halls and outdoor education centres. They have been slower to develop elsewhere, although some are now springing up abroad (and many are designed by Don Robinson). Climbing walls serve a variety of purposes and are used by both experienced and novice climbers.

Experienced climbers use the climbing wall in order to train throughout the year, regardless of weather. It is useful for perfecting climbing skills and techniques, and to try out new ones in a safe place, as well as for maintaining fitness and stamina away from the crags. If you live in a large city where it isn't possible to get to climbing areas regularly, climbing walls will be used during good weather also. They provide an active social focal point where climbers can meet and talk and examine each other's skills, not always kindly, but usually a healthy competitive spirit exists with climbers encouraging each other.

Climbing walls are also used by inexperienced climbers to get them started, somewhere where they can learn the basic techniques before applying them outdoors. Outdoor centres and schools often use the walls for climbing courses.

Climbing walls must definitely now be considered a major influence and are accepted as part of the climbing scene. Their only drawbacks are in the way many of them are run: being governed by petty rules and regulations which are out of step with climbing traditions, but are imposed by the administering authorities fearful of their liability in the event of an accident. Some walls in Sports Centres are only available at certain times because of other sports taking place nearby. Some walls are now so popular that it is difficult even to find a space to train on. But all in all, it is generally agreed that the advantages far out-weigh the disadvantages.

Since the advent of the climbing wall, technical standards in climbing have risen dramatically. The success of any method of training—whether it be running or weight-training—depends on how closely it simulates actual climbing movements. At first, press-ups and pull-ups were practised, but more specialized techniques are now rehearsed.

Climbers do not train merely to increase muscle size, but to develop a range of skills from balance to power, stamina to flexibility, and just as importantly, for concentration and mental preparation. Training may be applied for an overall increase in ability, or it may be done with a specific objective in mind such as a particular climb. Balance training may be undertaken for delicate slab climbing; biceps may be built up for explosive power moves.

The most obvious form of training is weight training for developing bigger muscles. However, it is as well to remember that bigger muscles mean more weight to carry.

Power

Power is defined as a short intense burst of effort, often necessary to do the crux moves on a hard climb, or for the harder strenuous boulder problems. This type of activity is encouraged by small numbers of repetitions with high resistance (i.e. large weights. Pull-ups with hanging weights are also useful.) This type of exercise is known as anaerobic, i.e. done without oxygen, using glycogen. Muscles should be properly warmed up before attempting them to avoid damage to joints and tendons.

Stamina

Stamina is the ability to carry out work continuously, whether it is running long distances, or strenuous climbing on overhanging rock. Stamina, or 'staying power', is necessary on easier multi-pitch climbs. Energy for stamina is found by aerobic means

Three illustrations of typical warming up exercises for rock climbing. With careful stretching and exercising before you start to climb, routes will be both easier and less dangerous, as warmed muscles are more efficient, more flexible and stronger. Take care to keep warm both before and after a climb to ensure continued suppleness.

(i.e. with oxygen), and although unable to be sustained at a high intense level, can be kept going for longer periods.

Exercises for promoting stamina include:

1. Circuit training, whereby a series of exercises are carried out non-stop.
2. Traversing on low-level boulder problems.
3. Top-roping strenuous climbs which are comfortably within your ability range, down-climbing and repeating as much as possible.
4. Gym exercises, such as push-ups, pull-ups and sit-ups.
5. Purpose-made rope ladders have been used extensively, but an increase in injuries to

shoulder and elbow joints has been seen and attributed to their use. Use with care and moderation.

6. Activities such as running or swimming long distances will also help.

Balance

Good balance will come with experience and time but can be encouraged by activities such as rope walking and simple balancing exercises, for example, balancing on one leg and lowering down and then pushing up again. This also helps strengthen leg muscles. There is really no good substitute for climbing and bouldering. Many women climbers do tend to have a better sense of balance to start with.

Flexibility or suppleness

This is one area where the majority of climbers can improve their performance by training. Again women tend to be naturally more supple than men and can capitalize on this. As part of a climber's routine before climbing, stretching exercises should be done to help warm up muscles and lessen the chances of an injury. These can easily be adapted from school P.E. routines, ballet related movements or yoga.

Co-ordination

Bringing together all the physical and mental aspects of the sport results in a well co-ordinated climber, one who is good to watch, relaxed and in control of the situation. A badly co-ordinated climber will be tense, frightened, possibly shaking and only marginally 'in control'.

Having mastered the various physical techniques and gained the energy necessary to make the moves then it's just as important to make the most of any opportunity to relax whilst climbing. This may take the form of a massive ledge, or a small foot hold where a climber can lean into the rock to shake both hands out, or it may be a jug on an overhanging wall where a climber can relax only one hand at a time, The important thing is not to waste energy unnecessarily. An inexperienced or frightened climber will grip the holds too hard, thus expending too much energy. The art lies in knowing how much effort is required and doing just enough to make each sequence of moves. There is no point in straining on tiny fingerholds if a simple bridging move will relieve the strain on the arms, even if this means moving into a slightly more precarious position.

Bouldering and Soloing

Bouldering

Bouldering can be the most expressive part of climbing. Unencumbered by the restrictions of equipment and rope in a relatively safe position, it's possible to wander at will over the rock, climbing at an individual standard, pushing oneself to the limit of one's technical abilities or flowing over the rock using large holds. Bouldering usually refers to solo climbing on boulders of varying sizes but can also be practised at the foot of a large crag. There is no definition as to when a boulder problem becomes a route—it isn't possible to say categorically that above 5 m a boulder problem becomes a climb or vice versa. Bouldering is about trying to link together some desperate series of moves, maybe only two or three, armed only with rock boots, chalk bag, a towel to dry off boots and maybe a toothbrush to clean excess chalk or dirt off small edges. It doesn't matter if another climber finds the chosen 'de-

Bouldering in Joshua Tree, California.

Chris Gore bouldering on Inaudible Vaudeville on the famous Bowderstone, Borrowdale, Cumbria.

sperate' problem very easy since bouldering, unlike roped climbing, is a uniquely personal experience. Today bouldering is considered as a game in its own right with its devotees. There are boulderers who can execute the hardest technical moves a few metres from the ground but are unable, or uninterested in performing with a rope and runners.

Bouldering offers freedom and convenience. It is easy to go out and have a good training session without having to make arrangements with a partner. Very little equipment is needed and, if a suitable circuit is picked, it is possible to push one's body to the absolute limits. This may be done by repeatedly trying one very hard move, working out the jigsaw of holds for the correct sequence, and perfecting the art that lies in learning how to use a particular tiny edge or pocket to gain those few extra centimetres which may be crucial to success. Or the limits of achievement may be reached by making repetitive traverses or circuits on large holds until 'pumped'. To the layman it may seem ridiculous to spend hours, sometimes days, on one facet of a measly lump of rock to work out a sequence, but when accomplished, it becomes an individual's equivalent of Bob Beamon's classic long jump record.

I personally think that the best exercise for climbing is climbing itself, so if it is possible to get to a crag and boulder it will help improve your 'feel' for the rock.

Specific areas that will be helped by bouldering include:

Finger Strength
This is useful for all climbers but essential to hard climbing. The best way to develop muscle and tendon finger strength is through bouldering. Fingertip pull ups are good but must come second to actually climbing. By pushing oneself on hard problems and trying harder moves on smaller holds, fingers will get stronger. The best holds to work on are small incut edges to make the fingers work rather than the arms. It is important not to overdo it at first and to build up slowly especially if not fit since it is easy to strain tendons.

Endurance
This can be developed by non-climbing training such as weights, running, circuit training etc. but being outside in a climbing environment is more enjoyable. A good way to improve endurance is to find a strenuous traverse, preferably incorporating a variety of moves on overhanging rock, so that different muscles are used. Once the traverse is mastered the next step is to do several traverses continuously.

Flexibility
This is a very important but often overlooked asset for a climber. An active young person will be reasonably supple already but harder routes demand a degree of flexibility normally found in gymnasts.

problems are ideal for getting the feel of boots and testing their friction and edging properties. Using footholds in different ways, e.g. using the inside edge rather than the toe, enables a climber to assess the potential of his tools in a relaxed situation. The other aspect that easy bouldering allows to be examined is the climber's own assets. These will be different for everyone, one person will have small fingers which are good for finger cracks . . . another may have long legs which will be good for power.

Hard problems

These require much effort and

Above: A low level traverse. Laywaying off the right arm and smears his left toe in the crack.
Right: Laybacking on an arête to raise the right foot.

Flexibility can be improved by specialized activities (see Training) but technical bouldering includes dynamic moves, long bridging and high step-up moves which are especially beneficial.

Power

Power is defined as strength to weight ratio, and thus is not totally dependent on the size of muscles. Power climbing is linked to endurance, strength and flexibility but the power required to perform a short explosive move can be practised and perfected through bouldering. It's much better to discover body potential in safe conditions.

Boulder problems

Easy problems

These can be achieved at the first attempt. These are good for getting the feel of the rock after a long lay off or winter stagnation. They are good for beginners to get a 'taste' of the rock, to learn how to move on the rock with the least effort, to learn not to pull viciously on the holds with the arms but to use the legs, shoulders and upper arms which are stronger. A boulderer's 'tools' are his boots and these easy

concentration for success. These problems are usually small and a good soft landing below such as sand or grass helps because of the repeated jumping or falling off involved. These give the proficient climber great technical exercise and also help to improve the ability to solve the problem of which holds to use and how to use them to their best advantage as well as how to rest in awkward positions to conserve energy and strength. Having found a problem and failed, then if success is a long time coming the achievement will be so much greater when it does happen.

Sustained Strenuous Problems
These are good for both cardiovascular exercise and muscle building 'endurance work. These problems are often in the form of traverses near the ground or in very safe situations. I think they are particularly good training for actual roped climbing since, although there is no danger of falling off, it is

possible to link traversing sequences together to make several hundred metres of climbing. Once the initial problem of solving the moves is done then the useful training begins, repeating the traverse or overhanging problem several times, climbing back across or down to stay off the ground, thus avoiding a good rest. It's best to keep going until the arms seize up.

High Bouldering
Once again these problems could be described as mini-routes. Often the problem is one of mental control. This sort of climbing is not for the cowardly. Everybody gets 'gripped' occasionally when climbing but this sort of climbing goes to an extreme and will pump the adrenalin around. Although bouldering is supposed to be safe, many problems of this type do qualify as extended boulder problems and are very bold and dangerous. Many gritstone 'routes' fall under this heading. Climbs such as Desperate

Dan, and Linden and those in Joshua Tree, California, are extended versions of such problems and are the next step up. However the question arises of where does one draw the line? The border between being bold and being foolish is an individual thing which every climber decides for himself. The fitter one is, mentally and physically, the higher one should be able to push and still be in control with something in reserve for a controlled retreat. On a detrimental note, one could obviously top-rope such problems. This type of climbing however is in keeping with the 'bold is beautiful' tradition and top-roping routes is anathema to me because the leading spirit isn't there.

Climbing an overhang on Derbyshire gritstone. Overcoming problems such as this while bouldering near ground level is excellent training for the kinds of difficulties you may encounter on larger climbs.

Worldwide Bouldering Possibilities

Although bouldering exists wherever there is rock, some places are more suitable than others. Whilst its perfectly possible to boulder at the foot of El Capitan, it makes more sense to use the hundreds of boulders scattered on the valley floor. Obviously there are thousands of areas suitable for bouldering, too numerous to mention. However one or two are internationally renowned. Fontainebleau outside Paris is one such area, providing Parisian climbers and visitors with endless opportunities with its colour coded circuits for varying degrees of difficulty.

Today the USA has more specialist bouldering areas than any other country with many climbers travelling to the granite mecca of Yosemite with its 1000 m walls, to sample the bouldering delights, or spending the winter in the Sonoran Desert searching out the thousands of possible boulder problems at Joshua Tree National Monument.

Several boulderers have achieved worldwide acclaim by raising standards or pushing the limits in their particular area. One of the first was the American John Gill who has gained legendary status with the execution of his incredible problems performed in the Central and Western States of America during the sixties. He adapted gymnastic training techniques which brought him to a level of fitness and flexibility never previously attained in the climbing world.

In Britain certain areas are noted for their potential. Yorkshire and Lancashire offer such gritstone challenges as Almscliff Crag and the Cow and Calf at Ilkley, whilst in the Peak District there is the limestone of Rheinstor and Cressbrook Dale. The small roadside boulder called the Bowderstone in the Lake District has been highly developed, with most of the problems situated on a 45 degree overhanging wall. The best known place for bouldering in Merseyside is Pex Hill, a hole in the ground some 200 m across contained within 12 m high vertical sandstone walls on which some particularly desperate problems have been worked out.

Tools of the Bouldering Trade

Boots
The new high friction boots are the best and most popular. Different rock favours different boots.

Towel or Cloth
This is very important for drying wiping off dirt from the boots.

Mat
If the ground is damp or muddy placing a mat at the foot of the problem gives a clean dry base to start from. It also gives something to aim for when jumping off.

Chalk bag
A small bag containing chalk which is bought either in block form or in powder.

Fontainebleau, in France, is one of the best bouldering areas in the world, with a variety of climbing at all levels.

Toothbrush
This is used for brushing the foot and hand holds which often become caked in chalk.

Wirebrush
This is used in the same way as a toothbrush but with more effect. Footholds on popular problems may become polished and a wirebrush will take the shine off them, giving better friction.

Resin bag
This is not common in Britain although very popular in the rest of Europe, particularly at the highly developed bouldering area of Fontainebleau near Paris. It is a large cloth with powdered resin placed in the middle, tied with string and used for 'thwacking' against holds for extra adhesion.

Renzine
This is a brown liquid used on the fingers to help chalk stick longer. It also has some healing properties for cuts.

Clothing
The usual uniform for bouldering is either stretchy track-suit bottoms, shorts or, more recently, dance-tights. (T-shirts optional.)

Tape

Soloing
Soloing is the art of moving on rock alone. It is usually practised without the 'inconvenience' of ropes and a partner, though in this aspect the difference between high bouldering and soloing is vague. I would define pure rock soloing as when a fall would result in a serious injury. However soloing also covers any aspect when a person climbs alone—it may be solo aid climbing or a long route which may involve using a rope for protection and specialized techniques to self belay when climbing.

Soloing is the ultimate personal climbing activity—you're on your own and have to be able to sort out any situation that might arise. Climbers tend to have very strong views about soloing, being either

Soloing on gritstone on Browns Eliminate, Derbyshire.

firmly opposed to a 'foolish dangerous trend' or being quite addicted to the adrenalin buzz. The dangers are obvious and people are killed soloing but proportionately no more so than, say, abseiling.

Climbers who do solo will usually climb well within their limits and be confident of the ability to retreat from a tricky position. There are a few people who will solo at the same standard as they lead which perhaps means that they don't trust equipment to hold them so leading falls don't occur, or they don't push themselves hard

enough when leading, or it could mean they have incredible mind control and exclude the possibility of a fall, or they are merely daft. It is very easy to become committed when soloing a climb having made a hard irreversible move. I myself have had my fair share of the jitters when soloing. Several years ago I decided to solo the classic crack line of the Demande in the Verdon gorge, a 400 m limestone cliff in Southern France. It is a twelve pitch route up a vast overhanging wall. I'd never done the climb before but thought the route finding would be simple, just following the obvious crack and chimney line. After three quarters of an hour I was two-thirds of the way up and staring at an evil, overhanging off-width which, although unpleasant, looked the obvious route. This was very nearly my undoing as I become totally stuck in this orifice. But I was committed to this route and couldn't retreat, so somehow I managed to find a sequence of moves to get out of the predicament. I discovered later that I had wandered off route and it was one lesson I have remembered well. If you solo you should know where you're going.

Mental Preparation

In the preceding chapters concerning physical and equipment techniques, I have looked at two of the three areas which make up the climbing experience. Physical techniques are necessary to be able to execute the moves on a climb. Equipment techniques are necessary for safety and convenience. But these two by themselves are not enough. The missing link, and certainly the most important for hard climbing, is the mental approach—attitude, commitment and preparation, all adding up to confidence. As a climber progresses through the grades, whether it be from V Diff to MVS or from E1 to E5, it will become apparent, usually with hindsight, that confidence is the key to progress. Believing that it is possible is half the battle, and certainly it sometimes feels like a battle, as climbers not only have to grapple with the physical problems of the climb, but also their own resistance and self-doubt. A climber may adopt a whole range of handy excuses for not wanting to, or not being able to climb a route.

Confidence comes with experience, and having solved the problems of one climb, a climber is better equipped to deal with any of those problems next time he meets them on a different climb. And with confidence, comes control, even in the most frightening situations. A confident climber looks perfectly at ease in precarious places.

Confidence is rather like money: the man who doesn't have it envies the one who does, but cannot imagine how to attain it quickly. Of course it can't be gained quickly. Confidence is acquired steadily, over time, with the more climbs that are successfully completed and a progression through the grades. There are several ways to help the process along and a few simple guidelines a climber can follow to give himself every chance of success:

– He should be competent in the physical techniques, either by practising on easier climbs, or at a climbing wall, or bouldering.
– He should have good equipment management (and only take what he might sensibly need. Taking large 'hexentrics' (nuts) on a slab climb offers nothing but unnecessary weight to tote up and extra equipment to trip over.)
– He should find out as much information about a climb beforehand as he can, either by reading from magazines and guidebooks, or by asking other climbers. He should certainly familiarize himself with the route description so as not to wander off into difficulty.
– He should choose an easy climb with every chance of success to warm up on first, thus get the feel of the rock. Muscles can be warmed up by bouldering or stretching exercises.
– It is wise to match climbs to personal talents. Women often have better balance than men and are good on slab routes. Unless overhanging walls are your speciality, avoid them—there's no law that says every climber has to be able to climb a roof or an overhang. Many people hate wide chimneys—if you do, avoid them. Remember, climbing is for fun.
– He should be satisfied his sec-ond can hold a fall in a controlled situation. This will ensure confidence in the second's ability to manage the ropes correctly. Many injuries occur when the second fails to hold the leader, and this is inexcusable.
– Have a plan of action for the day's climbing to make the most efficient use of time and energy. Have an aim for the day. It may be to climb 4 VSs; or it may be to try and climb a classic 'Severe' on several different crags in Wales, hiking between; it may be just one E6 at Malham Cove.
– He should not be afraid of losing face by retreating. Boldness and stupidity are two different things. There is much to be learnt from 'tactical retreats', and the sense of accomplishment when a 'defeat' is wiped out at a later date, will be that much greater. As the old saw goes: 'He who turns and walks away, lives to climb another day.'
– He should develop climbing skills at his own pace. Nobody can do everything straight away, and a climber's apprenticeship should teach sense for the future.
– He should not go climbing with a hangover or after an all-night party. A good night's sleep beforehand is essential—it's always possible to celebrate *after* the day's climbing.
– Smoking immediately before a climb won't help. A cigarette on the stance, if you need one, would be the lesser evil.
– Do warm up properly before attempting a hard climb. Cold muscles use up much more energy than warmed ones, and

the risk of injury through tearing or straining is much greater.
– There is no law as to when the first runner should be placed. If a runner two metres off the ground helps your confidence, then so be it, but DO place runners sensibly. It won't help your peace of mind if you have used them all up ten metres below the belay stance!
– Crowds can often put people off. The feeling of being 'on show' doesn't suit everyone. Go to a quiet crag if necessary.

There will be any number of methods and routines an individual develops that will help him or her calm nerves or 'hype-up' before a particular climb. If it works, then that's the method to stick with.

The need for 'psyching-up' before a big climb should not be underestimated. It's a bit like the way a boxer behaves in the ring before the big fight starts. He is oblivious to the noise and the crowds, and is concentrating merely on the job in hand. All his mental energy is being focused on one thought— get out and hit the other chap! Fortunately, climbing is a lot more laid-back and relaxed than a big-business sport like boxing, but the same kind of single-mindedness may be needed. The psyching-up process may only take a few minutes as a climber decides which route to try, or it may be spread over a period of days, even weeks, as the idea of a climb is nurtured in the mind. The desired climb may be several grades too hard at the time it is first thought of, but by continuing to push his standards up until he is ready to try it, the climber will have been preparing himself for the 'big one'. Consider the case of a person going on a Himalayan expedition: the planning and mental preparation may take years.

A climber competent at a particular standard will not spend hours psyching up for a climb at that grade. He will be able to arrive at a crag, choose a route and climb it without any hesitation or prevar-ication. The more out of depth a climber is, the longer it will take him to psyche up. It all comes back to confidence, again. Confidence in one's own abilities is the key.

Fear

Every climber knows the meaning of the word 'fear'. The climbing term for a frightened climber is 'gripped'. This is a particularly apt word to describe the situation as a person will grip the holds far more enthusiastically than necessary through panic. Another term used in this context is 'wobble' which describes the physical, and possibly mental, condition of a frightened climber as he shakes and wobbles on the rock. He will probably also be swearing and/or calling for help. If a climber reaches this stage and is unable to calm down then he will usually fall off. Shaking legs are indicative of a degree of fear although a climber can get the shakes in his legs without being frightened through strain in the muscles giving rise to involuntary muscular spasms or cramps.

The latter state can be sorted by resting each leg alternately or banging feet against the rock can help.

Fear is of course a necessary element. Without it there would be many more accidents and deaths. Fear is a natural temper to fool-hardiness. Apart from acting as a caution against dangerous courses, fear can be used constructively through the adrenalin surge it produces. Adrenalin is produced in the body in times of stress to give a boost to get out of the situation as quickly as possible. Adrenalin can be effectively channelled to give a person a boost. In climbing situations it can be used to make more of an effort rather than retreating. In this context, 'getting out of the stressful situation' means making the moves and getting higher up the climb to a good runner or a resting place.

You are more likely to succeed in a climb if you are calm and confident. Think over the route and your equipment before you start.

Minimizing the Risks

Climbing is inherently a risky sport in that the positions achieved are spectacular and, to the layman, dangerous. However, many of the dangers that do exist can be kept to a minimum by common sense, knowledge of equipment and its limitations, developing a crag sense (which includes behaving sensibly), and following a few simple rules:

Before you set out:
1. Be prepared for the day's undertakings:
   Check that you have the correct equipment for the job. If it is a cold day and plans include climbing on a high mountain crag, take sufficient warm clothing, and food and hot drinks.
2. Have the necessary guidebook and information to the area.
3. If climbing in an out-of-the-way location, leave details of your plans with someone in case of failure to return.

At Yankee Doodle, Lands End, Cornwall. Whilst clearly climbing in such dramatic locations is inherently dangerous, there is much you can do to reduce the risks.

Basic Climbing Rules

1. A suitable partner is the first step. It is sensible to discover each other's capabilities on easy climbs first.
2. Select a route to suit your capabilities; always keep to easy climbs when starting to lead.
3. Read the guidebook properly before starting out and, if the route-finding looks tricky, carry the book with you.
4. Make sure you and your partner understand each other's calls properly. Know the calls. (See p. 40.)
5. Develop a routine gear check before starting every climb: Always check harness knots and buckles. Check rope for cuts and abrasions. If the rock is loose, wear a helmet.
6. Don't stand directly under a climber, a rock (or a climber) may fall on you.
7. Tie in with care, and don't interrupt someone else tying into a harness. It's possible to stop and forget to finish the job.
8. Don't stand on ropes or gear. Grit and wear cause abrasions and damage.
9. Always clean your feet well before climbing, especially on wet rock.
10. When you start to climb, don't be afraid to put runners in. There's no such thing as too many runners. It's your neck—so don't worry what others say. If in doubt, put a runner in. Take care to place runners correctly.
11. Never be afraid of turning back, climbing down, lowering off or abseiling if a climb becomes too difficult. The route will still be there tomorrow.
12. Don't ever throw rocks or stones. If you happen to knock rocks off, always shout 'Below!' at once. Also call 'Below!' when dropping ropes for abseiling.
13. If someone shouts 'Below!' then act on it by looking to see where the danger is coming from. If it's coming for you, crouch into the rock and protect your head.
14. If you are belaying the leader always pay the rope out smoothly without jerking. It is easy to pull a leader off balance.
15. Don't stand too far away from the bottom of the crag—it might pull out the runners if he does fall.
16. On stances, always use two belays if at all possible.
17. Check your screwgate karabiners are done up properly each time you use them.
18. Don't fool around at the top of the crag. Accidents often happen when climbers relax after having completed the climb. Pay attention to the wet or muddy rock.
19. Take as much care over the descent as the ascent. The climb is only 'over' when you are safely on the ground again.
20. Know what to do in an emergency, where the nearest telephone is etc. (Much information will be in the guidebook of the area.)
21. Don't become too confident after completing a few routes.

ABOVE ALL, CONCENTRATE, STAY ALERT, AND USE YOUR COMMON SENSE.

Accidents

Sooner or later, everyone who climbs or spends much time in the outdoors, will be confronted with an accident. Accidents occur for a variety of reasons – lack of the correct equipment, equipment failure, a rapid change in the weather, losing the way; plus a host of subjective reasons such as incompetence, inexperience, stupidity or overstepping one's ability. Very often they are caused by a combination of factors or a build-up of wrong decisions. The belief tends to exist that accidents can only happen to the very inexperienced or very incompetent. This is a dangerous way of thinking. Accidents can happen to anyone – even the most proficient climbers.

Due to the increasing numbers of people climbing—particularly young people on outdoor education courses—accidents will occur with more and more frequency. It is essential to know what action to take in such a situation. A delay in acting correctly can prove fatal.

In most countries where climbing is practised, a mountain rescue system operates to help cope with accidents and emergencies. In Britain this is the responsibility of the Mountain Rescue Committee (MRC), a voluntary body which operates a network of rescue teams and rescue posts; the police (or HM Coastguard, if accident is on a sea cliff) usualy act as co-ordinators in all search and rescue exercises, calling out teams and public services as needed.

In North America, as in Britain, rescues are largely carried out by volunteer teams. In most areas responsibility for rescue rests with the County Sheriff, the National Park Service, or some comparable governmental department. By contrast, in the Alpine countries in Europe, rescues are generally undertaken by professional guides of the area, usually employing helicopter assistance, and can consequently be very expensive. It is always worth taking out mountain rescue (and hospitalization) insurance when climbing abroad.

IMMEDIATE ACTION IN CASE OF ACCIDENT

1. Note state of consciousness.
2. If a person is unconscious, make sure that the air passages are not blocked by the tongue or vomit. Try to keep the patient on his/her side, or front.
3. Safeguard the patient against further fall or injury and ensure your own safety. If the patient is unconcious he/she may start moving vigorously or become violent on regaining consciousness.
4. Stop any bleeding by pressure with handkerchief or First Aid dressing, etc. Cover open wounds with clean light dressing.
5. Make the injured person as comfortable as you can. Keep

him/her dry, insulated from the ground, and move as little as necessary. But don't touch the injured person before deciding, by asking and observing, whether the spine is injured. (One indication in pain in the back, another is inability to use the legs, but neither is conclusive.) If spinal injury is suspected, don't attempt to move the person.

6. Use a temporary splint or some other means of immobilization in the case of broken limbs.

7. Keep the patient warm with extra clothing, survival bag etc. Unless internal damage is suspected, hot drinks can be given, but remember, in cases of exposure, warming a person too quickly can also be dangerous.

8. Try to attract help by shouting, whistle blasts, torch-flashing, etc.

Use the Alpine Distress Signal (Six long blasts, or six flashes, a minute, repeated after a minute's interval.)

9. Send for help by telephone. The message should be written down at the other end with the exact location, time of accident, and nature of injuries. Give name and address of casualty if known. STAY AT TELEPHONE.

If the injured person has to be left alone while summoning help, two actions should first be taken:

a) Mark the spot well for the return, and

b) put a belay on the injured person in case they stagger off semi-conscious.

10. Ensure the safety of the rest of the party (if any).

Accidents are always a possibility when climbing. Properly tied into your harness and well belayed, you should avoid serious injury.

1. If the wait for rescue is likely to be long, then a shelter of some sort should be made. If it has proved impossible to fetch help, then continue methods of attracting attention (8 above). Flashing a mirror at the sun can be used if you have no torch or whistle; or a distress flare.

Choosing and Caring for your Equipment

Great care is taken in the manufacture of the majority of climbing equipment. There are several rigorous tests which are carried out to show what shock loading and strain equipment can take before failing. As in most things, you get what you pay for, and it is obvious that a very high quality of hi-tech piece of equipment is going to cost you more than a dated piece.

When buying equipment, find out what it will do and how to use it properly. If there are no manufacturer's instructions with it, then ask the local specialist retailer—you will usually find people in the shop who are climbers themselves and quite happy to explain the subtleties of the latest gadgets.

Most manufacturers will give clear instructions as to how their gear should be used and looked after. If there is any doubt, contact the company for advice.

Having bought the necessary gear, it is important to look after it properly:

Ropes:

(A rope is your lifeline, and should be treated as such.)

Never stand on it—there may be a sharp edge underneath, or you may press small bits of grit into it which will increase the wear rate. Never store a rope in direct sunlight as ultraviolet radiation weakens nylon. When travelling with gear in a car, make sure it is away from battery acid, oil and other like substances, since this will eat away the nylon. Rope can be occasionally washed in warm water with a mild soap.

Know your rope's history and how many falls it has taken. Inspect it regularly for damage.

Harness:

Keep away from such substances as battery acid. Inspect regularly for signs of damage.

Karabiners:

Keep alloy karabiners away from alkali, as this will quickly attack them. If karabiners come into contact with sea-water, wash them thoroughly, and dry. It may be necessary to lubricate the gates occasionally or the action may become rough. Don't drop or throw karabiners around, it may cause fracturing. Don't put a 3-way pull on karabiners, they are designed for a 2-way pull only.

Runners:

Runners on rope or tape should be checked to make sure the knots haven't loosened. Wired nuts should be checked to see if any strands of the wire have broken.

Rock boots:

The soles of rock boots should be regularly wiped clean with a damp cloth, since gritty particles will wear away the rubber more quickly. Rock boots shouldn't be worn for walking to the crag. They are not designed for this and will only wear out more quickly. On routes with difficult descents, it is often practical to carry a pair of training-shoes for a comfortable descent. Avoid sitting on boots in a sac, or cramming them into a sac, as this will cause the shape to deform. If boots have become wet through rain or sweat, don't dry them in direct heat, as this may cause the sole to peel. Airing them gently and slowly is the best way.

Friends, camming devices:

If the movement becomes stiff or sticky, then spraying the moving parts with a lubricating agent, such as WD40 (NOT oil) will work. Try to keep them away from the ground to prevent dirt particles getting in.

Behaviour on the crags

Much of the following should be common sense but judging by the numbers of people who regard climbing as an escape not only from everyday life, but also as an escape from decent behaviour, it needs stressing that climbers should:

a) Respect other people's rights to use the outdoors—climbers are not a special case.
b) Follow the country code.
c) Not leave litter such as chalk wrappings and old slings.
d) Try not to use offensive language in 'sensitive' areas such as where access may be threatened or where members of the public visit. Extra aggravation for climbers is not needed.
e) Try not to be loud and raucous. Other climbers might want a quiet day out.
f) Respect other climbers' intentions. Climbing is done on a 'first come, first served' basis, so pushing in ahead of other climbers waiting to do a climb is not done. Abseiling down where people are climbing or about to climb is not appreciated. It's best to ask first.
g) Try not to use chalk too liberally. Even chalk has its limitations.
h) Don't wipe mud off boots on to the rock. It may not be an obvious hold to you, but it might be a crucial hold on someone else's boulder problems.
i) Respect local regulations. Some crags are off bounds due to nesting birds, rare plants or the danger to the public from falling rocks.
j) Respect an area's ethics and traditions.
k) Warn other climbers of imminent dangers such as poor belays instead of waiting for the inevitable accident.
l) Perform 'necessary duties' away from crags.

Ice Climbing

The rock climber moving freely over good rock is like an ape swinging unencumbered through the forest. Even shoes and clothing can be dispensed with by the fanatic seeking an ultimately 'pure' experience. However, the person who looks for enjoyment and challenge on frozen waterfalls or alpine ice slopes must first be equipped with a certain minimum of clothing and specialized hardware that would seem to dictate a less direct encounter with the environment. Yet we have evolved beyond the simple joy of the ape. Today most of our knowledge of our world and universe comes to us indirectly through extensions of mind and body, i.e. through tools. Just as a powerful hand glass allows us to see clearly that the flakes of falling snow are far more intricate and beautiful than they appear to the naked eye, an ice-axe and crampons, wielded with skill and concentration, can magnify our appreciation of existence. The ice climber's being is amplified by the tools. A new animal is created that lives a special version of life amidst awesomely beautiful, seemingly impossible terrain.

Rick Wyatt climbing in Provo Canyon, Utah.

Introduction

By carefully selecting simple, well-designed, and versatile tools; combining them with the proper skills and experience; and matching them to an appropriate climb, it's possible for the ice climber to drink deeply of a heady wine. The surreal beauty of a belay situated in a cave with translucent blue walls and a ceiling of a hundred icicles is more other-worldly than anything in the rock climber's experience, and ice climbing has always appealed to the person who loves adventure more than gymnastic exercise. Yet there are similarities in the rewards offered by the two types of climbing. The weekend recreational rock climber, for instance, on a winter icefall, can achieve the same relief from the ennui of everyday life as on a summer crag. And for the extremist, in these times of vertical waterfalls and thinly iced mixed climbs, it's possible to push technical and physical limits as far as imagination and vision allows. Another benefit to the rock climber who learns ice technique is that some of the finest rock in the world is thus opened to him, for instance the great granite free climbs of Mont Blanc, or the big walls of the Karakorum.

Joe Brown maintained that if a climb is easier with crampons than without, it could rightly be considered an ice climb. This is the only definition that is comprehensive enough to account for the entire spectrum of activities that are generally included under the heading of ice climbing. In the Alps and Canadian Rockies people are climbing the iced-up chimneys of winter and spring as well as the classic faces of alpine ice. In Colorado they're venturing out onto steep faces and buttresses of verglassed rock. In places as diverse as Scotland, Vancouver Island, New Zealand, and Patagonia the attraction is rime-ice and snow-ice. Mount Kenya's Diamond Couloir has a frozen waterfall headwall that provides an African parallel of an experience

The skills learned on rock will make you a better ice climber. Jeff Lowe on the first ascent of Icarus, Colorado 6b or 5.11d.

that can be replicated in the Caucusus, Norway, Italy, Peru, Japan, Korea, the Tatra—in fact anywhere in the world where cold temperatures, steep hillsides, and running water are found in conjunction. But on the soft cliffs of Dover a few demented souls have stretched Brown's definition to ridiculous lengths by climbing the bare chalk walls in full ice gear!

Ice climbing is a member of a small family of sports, such as white-water kayaking or windsurfing, that use highly developed but basically simple tools in a subtle interplay of man and a wild environment. Because they both deal with movement over slopes of snow and ice, skiing and ice climbing seem the most closely related to me. The balance, intimacy with the medium, and open-minded attitude of the best practitioners are shared by both activities. It is for this reason that in the ice climbing section of this book I have made use of an instructional method that in the last ten years has yielded excellent results with skiing. The basic process involves first helping the student to free his or her mind of preconceptions about the sport and to let go of the attendant expectations and/or fears which are blocks to learning and moving freely. Once this is done it is possible to extract the most information from each suggested exercise. Along with an open mind, the 'inner', or 'centred' climber, which

I am trying to foster, develops an awareness of a physical, mental, emotional, and spiritual balance point that enables him or her to remain relaxed but alert in a stressful situation. This optimum state-of-being best enables the climber to envisage and execute the exact sequence of movements that represent the most efficient, elegant, and therefore enjoyable response to any piece of ice.

This section has been written with the inherent assumption that before the reader attempts to utilize the techniques described, he or she will first become familiar with rock climbing as described by Ron Fawcett in the preceding section. Thus, we can avoid repetition of certain basics, but more importantly, rock is generally a less fickle and dangerous training ground, and the best place for absorbing the essence of the ethics and traditions of ascent. It is also true that the more proficient you become on rock, the more potential you have as an ice climber, assuming you take the time and effort to accumulate the necessary additional skills and intuition required by ice. Also, that most elusive of attributes, personal *style* is nurtured more by the direct contact with rock than purely on ice.

A Short History

Shepherds and Englishmen

The first real evidence of ice climbing comes from the sixteenth century. Alpine shepherds would attach spiked horseshoe devices to their feet which, along with iron-tipped 'alpine sticks', allowed them to 'counteract the slipperiness of the ice' on steep slopes they crossed while controlling their flocks in high alpine valleys. These same shepherds must have challenged medieval superstitions that held there were demons on summits and that glaciers were dragons that would steal down at night to drain the udders of sleeping peasants' cows!

In the early 1800s, tourists from England began to holiday in the alpine villages. The Victorian sensibilities of these wealthy gentry were piqued by the spectacle of inaccessible mountain tops, and they hired the peasants to guide them amongst the peaks. By mid-century a symbiotic relationship had been established whereby shepherds earned a living and were exposed to the English culture while their employers were educated to the mysteries of life in the mountains. Such combined interest led to improvements in equipment and ascents of classic snow and ice routes. The shepherd's three-pronged 'crampon' was replaced by nailed boots; the 'alpine sticks' which had been taller than a man were shortened; and an adze was added for chopping steps to climb steep slopes of ice.

The latter half of the nineteenth century—the Golden Age of mountaineering—saw all the summits of the Alps climbed. Then new and harder routes were tackled. The first ice climbs were almost always led by one of the great step-chopping guides such as Melchior Anderegg, who led the first ascent of the Brenva Spur on Mont Blanc in 1865, or Christian Klucker, who climbed the North Face of the Lyskamm and loved to climb with or without clients.

In the final decades of the century some of the alpine guides travelled to other countries as far away as Canada, New Zealand, Russia, and Argentina along with their employers to help establish their sport in those places. In their own mountains, the German, Swiss, Austrians, and French continued to range over ever steeper and icier ridges and faces. Some of these Europeans were guides, but an increasing number were amateurs who were climbing simply for their own pleasure, following the example of British climbers who were setting new standards on rock.

An old lantern slide of ice climbing in the Alps.

Scottish Gullies and North Walls

The Scottish Mountaineering Club was formed in 1889. Although the general trend in the Alps was towards rock climbing, by 1920, Scotsmen had extended the art of pure ice and snow climbing in gullies and introduced climbing difficult summer rock climbs under a coating of ice and snow. Harold Raeburn, the outstanding practitioner, led Green

Gully on Ben Nevis in 1906, cutting steps with a long axe and wearing nailed boots as in the Alps. In 1976, on a pilgrimage to Scotland, I made an ascent of Green Gully as one of my first climbs there. Even with the latest 'revolutionary' ice technology adorning my hands and feet, I was impressed by the steep initial pitch and the beauty of the final runout to the summit plateau. In 1920 Raeburn made the first winter ascent of Observatory Ridge, an iced-up rock route which retains the respect of modern climbers for, when the ice is thin, insubstantial, or rotten over rock, technological advances are less important than the skill and spirit of the climber. In Scotland the difficulties of Raeburn's climbs were not surpassed until the 1950s.

In 1908, a technological advance was made that wouldn't be wholeheartedly adopted by the recalcitrant Scots for forty years and yet it changed the nature of climbing on the ice and snow faces of the Alps. Oscar Eckenstein, an experienced English climber, created a ten-point crampon, and invented a 'flat foot' climbing technique that allowed many climbs to be done with few or no cut steps. This Eckenstein technique was quickly adopted by the French who found it excellent for the névé of the western Alps.

With the new crampons and an axe shorter than the old shoulder-high style, alpine ice climbing entered what has been called its most productive era. The great guide Hans Lauper capped his brilliant career in 1932 with the first ascent of the North-East Face of the Eiger, the well-known Lauper route, seldom climbed and highly respected today. In 1924 special pitons for ice designed by Fritz Riegele were used by Willo Welzenbach on the North-west Face of the Gross Wiesbachhorn. Between the wars Welzenbach distinguished himself as the best of a bold new generation of ice enthusiasts. Climbs such as the north faces of the Gross Fiescherhorn, the Grand Charmoz, the Gletscherhorn, and the Lauterbrunnen

Breithorn remained even into the 1960s as some of the most difficult in the Alps.

Following Welzenbach in the classic north wall era, Jacques Lagarde and Henry de Ségnone maximized the Eckenstein technique on the North Face of the Plan in 1924. Perhaps the finest exponent of this technique, Armand Charlet, climbed the Nant Blanc Face of the Aiguille Verte in 1928 with Camille Dévouassoux. Greloz and Roch climbed the classic North Face of the Triolet in 1931. The Schmid brothers from

Gardyloo Buttress was one of a trio of fine climbs made by Robin Smith and Jimmy Marshall in 1960 during one week of intense activity. Harder climbs were not made in Scotland until the mid 1970s.

Munich climbed the North Face of the Matterhorn in 1931, the first of the three most famous north walls in the Alps to be climbed. The next to fall of the trio was the Croz Spur on the Grand Jorasses in 1935. The remaining and greatest wall, the Eigerwand, was finally climbed in 1938 by Anderl Heckmair, Ludwig

Vörg, Fritz Kasparek and Heinrich Harrer. On this most controversial and heralded alpine climb of all time, Heckmair was the natural leader. He used twelve-point crampons, designed by Laurent Grivel in 1932, to front-point up the icefields in a fraction of the time it would take to cut steps. Heckmair's performance defined the frontiers of the art until the late 1950s.

Routes climbed on the classic north faces in the Alps and in gullies of snow-ice and buttresses of snow, rock, and verglas in Scotland were not improved upon until after World War II. Existing equipment had already been pushed to near its absolute limits, and most of the obvious and attractive lines had been done.

In other ranges of the world during this period, standards were not being set on ice, yet many good climbs were made in New Zealand and the Canadian Rockies. Both of these ranges offer scope for ice as great as the Alps, but they were slower in being developed and their contribution to the sport would come later. The next advances would occur once again in the crucibles of the Alps and the Scottish highlands.

Post War and into the Sixties
Scottish winter climbing was taken a step beyond Raeburn's most difficult climbs in the Fifties mainly by Tom Patey, Jimmy Marshall, and Hamish MacInnes. Utilizing axe and crampons, cunning and craft to their fullest in a uniquely electric Scottish blend of step-cutting, front-pointing, flat-footing, and mixed climbing, these climbers, along with a few others, established most of the best climbs of the day. The most impressive climbs were MacInnes' ascent of Raven's Gully in 1953, Brooker's ascent of Eagle Ridge on Lochnagar, and Patey and MacInnes' climb of Zero Gully along with Graeme Nicol; their climbs left a future generation of climbers to struggle in their footsteps. Jimmy Marshall's climbs of Parallel Gully B in 1959; and the next year, with

The North Face of the Triolet, first climbed in 1932, is typical of the great climbs of the classic era of alpine ice climbing.

the brightest of his apprentices, Robin Smith, his climbs of Gardyloo Buttress and Orion Face Direct were other landmarks from this adventurous era. Harder climbs were not made until the seventies, with the aid of new technology.

In the Alps during the first two post war decades, most climbers were challenged enough by repeating the great routes of the Thirties. A few harder climbs were made, such as Walter Bonatti and Cosimo Zapelli's climb on the Eckpfeiler buttress of Mont Blanc in 1962, the North Face of Les Droites by the Cornau/Devaille in 1955, and Robert Flematti and René Desmaison's climb of the Shroud on the Grandes Jorasses in 1968. These were all major events at their first ascents, accomplished only by some of the best climbers of the day pulling out all the stops, facing terrifying objective hazards, and launching whole-heartedly into the unknown.

Jeff Lowe on the Squid, a grade 6 Colorado ice climb. Such climbs would not be possible without the century of development of equipment, techniques and attitudes of ice climbing.

During the Fifties and Sixties different nationalities still clung to their own preferences in regards to the techniques used to climb ice. In Scotland step-cutting was the standard, in France the Eckenstein flat-foot method had been so completely adopted that it had also come to be known as 'French Technique',

while the Austrians and Germans had for quite some time favoured front-pointing in almost every instance. During this time the small numbers of ice climbers in the rest of the world had to sort out for themselves which of the techniques was best, usually coming to the conclusion that front-pointing with short axes and daggers on hard ice required football-sized calves, step chopping for more than a rope length required the arms of a gorilla, and flat-foot or French technique is totally unsuited to the human anatomy.

The new ice age

Of all the early pioneers of alpine north walls, Anderl Heckmair is probably the most well known for his brilliant leadership of the first ascent of the Eigerwand. In a virtuoso display of talent he front-pointed the icefields with such confidence that years later Heinrich Harrer still wrote with amazement about the performance in his classic book *The White Spider*. But Heckmair's technique was not the only thing he had going for him. There is an old black and white photograph taken during the Eiger climb that shows that Heckmair was using a short axe with a distinct down-curve to the pick. This simple curve increases the security of an axe placement many times over, thus allowing faster *and* safer climbing. In the late Sixties the 're-volutionary curve' was discovered once again by Yvon Chouinard, and with the popularization of its use, ice climbing was changed for all time, with even the greatest of the existing routes now open to the average climber. Heckmair was merely 30 years ahead of his time!

The North American Contribution

Mountain climbing in all its forms was slower to develop in Canada and America than in the UK and Europe. By the early 1960s, however, Americans had developed new equipment and techniques for rock climbing that allowed them to make the first ascents of some of the world's greatest rock walls in the Yosemite Valley of California. In the mid-years of the decade some of the Yosemite climbers travelled to the Alps and made the hardest rock climbs of the day utilizing the hardware and techniques they'd brought from home. At the same time, these Americans were introduced to ice and snow climbing, and Yvon Chouinard in particular, who had been one of the main innovators of rock climbing hardware, now directed his energies to the creation of more functional ice gear. In 1967 he rediscovered the advantages of the curved pick as well as another old idea, the rigid crampon. In his typical creative fashion Chouinard was soon offering beautifully designed curved-pick axes and rigid crampons to the climbing public.

Apart from in Alaska, the opportunities for alpine type climbs on glaciers and icefields is limited to only a few areas in the high mountains of the US. In winter, however, frozen waterfalls and ice-filled chimneys are plentiful throughout the northern states, particularly in the north east, and Intermountain region of Colorado, Utah, and Montana.

In the early years of the 1970s the standards of the hardest Alpine and Scottish climbs were equalled in the north east with such climbs as John Bouchard's solo first winter ascent of the 200 m Black Dike on Cannon Mountain, and the climb of Repentance on Cathedral Ledge by John Bragg and Rick Wilcox, which consists of four pitches of hard ice climbing on a route that is 5.9 as a summer rock climb. These eastern climbs were impressive enough and provided the impetus for a ten year growth in the popularity of eastern ice climbing. But it was in Utah and Colorado that new standards were set for free climbing on ice.

By 1971 my brother, Greg Lowe, had already utilized the new ice gear on the first ascent of an obscure but for the time phenomenally difficult climb on Mahlen's Peak Waterfall in Northern Utah. The 3rd pitch, under the conditions of the first ascent, is 25 m of vertical and overhanging ice which Greg led entirely free with almost no protection. In one bold stroke ice climbing had been brought up to par with rock standards. In the mid-sixties, Greg had been the first to lead 5.12 on rock in classic completely free style. The same strength and abilities had now been shown to be applicable to ice, opening up a vast and exciting new arena for adventure.

Mike Weis and I were introduced to the beauty and challenge of frozen waterfalls by Greg Lowe in the winter of 1972, and found it much to our liking, complimenting

the other three seasons of rock climbing and mountaineering that constituted the focus of our existence. On January 2, 1974, we completed the first ascent of Colorado's Bridalveil Falls. We found 130 metres of near vertical, vertical, and overhanging ice spiced with cauliflower and chandelier-like formations. We discovered that the tube screws and ice pitons commercially available at that time would only fracture the extremely cold and brittle ice into large plates and chunks, but Greg had lent us half-a-dozen homemade chrome-

Jeff Lowe on the second pitch of Bridalveil Falls during the first ascent on January 2, 1974. Later in the season the ice fenestrations usually fill in and the climb becomes somewhat easier.

molly tubes with tips bevelled to the inside. These could be driven in without destroying the ice, allowing us to make the climb with some protection, and were later developed into Snarg ice pitons.

At the same time as Americans were making their initial explorations of winter icefalls, a group of

Two climbers in the centre of
Colorado's Bird Brain Boulevard.

ex-patriot Britishers, led by Bugs
McKeith, along with local Canadian climbers, were busy searching
out the best of the frozen waterfalls
to be found in the Canadian
Rockies. Although the first ascents
made by this group tended to be
done with the use of fixed ropes
and aid climbing techniques, such
as aid slings attached to the tools, it
wasn't long before all the Canadian
routes were free climbed. These
free ascents were at first the work of

visiting Americans, but soon the
locals resumed the lead role. In the
late Seventies the Canadians John
Lauchlan and Jim Elzinga put up
what, at the time, was probably the
hardest high-mountain waterfall
climb in the world: the 850m
Slipstream on the Snowdome at
the Columbia Icefields. Slipstream
was surpassed only in 1984 by the
ascent of Gimme Shelter on
Mount Quadra by Kevin Doyle
and Barry Blanchard.

Amalgamation
Although technical standards were

being set by American and Canadian climbers during the last decade, climbers in the Alps and New
Zealand were only slightly behind
on waterfalls, and equal on the
mountain ice routes being done in
North America. The north east
Couloir of the Dru was climbed in
winter 1972–3 by Walter Cecchinel
and Claude Jager in four days. In
1974–5 Rab Carrington and Al
Rouse introduced Scottish grade V
to the Alps with their winter ascent
of the thinly-iced slabs of the
North Face of the Pélerins. Jean-
Marc Boivin and Patrick Gabarrou
climbed the strikingly beautiful
Super Couloir on Mont Blanc du
Tacul in 1975; the Balfour Face of
Mount Tasman in New Zealand
was done as early as 1971 by Bill
Denz and Brian Pooley.

All these climbs are roughly
equivalent to Canada's Grand
Central Couloir, which Mike Weis
and I climbed in 1975. Al Rouse
and Rab Carrington climbed one of
the most difficult Scottish routes in
1975: the Citadel/Sticil Face combination on Shelter Stone Crag.
Also of similar difficulty was Mike
Covington and Yvon Choiunard's
direct climb of the Diamond
Couloir in Kenya in 1975, and the
Breach wall (Laide Route) of
Kilimanjaro, done by Reinhold
Messner and Konrad Renzler in
1978.

In the winter of 1977 Henry
Barber and Rob Taylor introduced
American waterfall techniques to
Norway, making the first ascent
of the Wettifossen, 300m of
Bridalveil-type intricate climbing.
By the late 1970s and early 1980s
waterfall climbing was well estab-
lished throughout the Alps. In the
Cirque de Gavarnie many excep-
tional climbs were made, mainly by
Dominique Julien with the 470m
Voie de l'Overdose being every
bit the equal of the big North
American waterfalls.

The Super Couloir rising to the left
of the Gervasutti Pillar on Mt.
Blanc du Tacul, first climbed in
1975 by the great French climbers
Gabarron and Boivin, has become
a latter-day classic.

Coming of Age

Within ten years, equipment evolved drastically. Simple curved or angled picks gave way to reverse-curve or tubular and interchangeable picks which now had graphite shafts and tubular adzes. Footfang crampons and Snarg ice pitons made their appearance. The number of participants had swelled worldwide, and climbs that were the ultimate in the previous decade were now being done within the first few outings by aspirant ice climbers. Ice climbing, however, was to take a back seat in the early Eighties to free rock climbing, which seems more appealing to the young masses.

But the general trend to rock did not halt the expansion of the ice climber's horizons, and the first half of the current decade has seen harder and steeper mixed climbs and the introduction of the highest standards to the world's greatest ranges. The mountains of Alaska, the Andes, and the Himalaya are now fair game for lightning fast ascents by experienced and adventurous climbers.

The earliest of these 'Ice Climbs of the Eighties' actually occurred at the end of the previous decade. In 1978 Nicholas Jaeger made a series of solo climbs in Peru that were technically as hard as anything in the Alps, at elevations around 6,000 m. Perhaps his finest routes were the South Face of Taulliraju, an 840 m alpine ED + route done in 8 hours, and the South Face of the East Peak of Chacraraju.

After working during 1979 on a television film of the second ascent of the South West Ridge of Ama Dablam in Nepal, I made the first ascent of the 1,500 m South Face of this 6,800 m peak in 10 hours. The difficulties were similar to those found on the hard alpine climbs. These climbs set the stage for the coming years of alpine style ice climbs of technically demanding Himalayan faces.

The best Himalayan alpine style ice climbs have included the East Face of Dhaulagiri by Alex MacIntyre, René Ghilini, and the Poles, Wojciech Kurtyka and

Ludwik Wilczyczynsk, in 1980, with technical difficulties similar to some of the 1930s alpine routes, but done on an 8,000 metre peak; a new route on the South Face of Annapurna in 1984 by another moderately technical line by the Spaniards, Enric Lucas and Nil Bohigas; a solo winter ascent of the South East Spur of Pumori 7,100 m, which I made in three days in December of 1983; the West Face of Gasherbrum IV 5,900 m, one of the most attractive of all the great Himalayan walls, by Robert Schauer and Wojciech Kurtyka in 1985; the North Ridge

Canada's Weeping Pillar is approached by a grade 5 climb of 150 m and is itself 200 m of vertical ice, giving an overall grade 6. First climbed in 1978.

of Rakaposhi, also in 1985 by Dave Cheesemond, Kevin Doyle, Barry Blanchard, and the Hungo Face of Kwangde in 1982 by Dave Breashears and myself. The 1,500 m of climbing on this relatively low (6,000 m) mountain maintains itself at an amazingly high standard for the entire climb, and is an indication of the great climbs now available.

The Necessary Technology

While ice climbing is not about the gear that is used in its practice, there is indeed much to admire and learn from in the materials, design, construction, and function of modern ice tools and clothing. Understanding the technology is the first step to being able to make enlightened choices that will enhance your ice climbing experience. Climbers who refuse to educate themselves as to the strengths, weaknesses, and functional characteristics of the equipment, and who treat it shoddily, seem to have more than their share of epics and accidents. There is no need to buy every new thing that comes along.

Clothing and Accessories

Dressing for warmth and comfort in an activity such as ice climbing, that can take place under conditions as varied as those found at the dry frigid poles in winter to a near-freezing rain on Ben Nevis in a thaw, is an art in itself. Although new fabrics and insulations have greatly increased the comfort and survival probability for any ice climber, there are as yet no true 'miracle' solutions to the age old problems of wet and cold and the accompanying possibility of hypothermia and frostbite. Until the advent of synthetic fibres and their use in long underwear and pile garments, wool was the most efficient material for everything from socks to sweaters to trousers, mittens, hats, and underwear. Unlike other natural fibres such as cotton, wool does not lose all its insulating characteristics when wet. For all basic garments wool is still an acceptable material, with the advantage that it is often possible to find good second-hand or surplus garments at a modest price. However, ever since Chris Bonington kitted out his 1970 expedition to the South Face of Annapurna with synthetic underwear and fibrepile jackets, the superior characteristics of these man-made substitutes has been known. Synthetics are much lighter, 'wick' body moisture away from the body, provide superior insulation, and dry very quickly. When used in a 'layering' system, synthetic clothes can comfortably see you through a day of widely varying temperatures and activity levels. Layering with synthetics might be accomplished in the following way.

Feet
A thin polypropelene or other 'wicking' sock is desirable to transport moisture away from the skin and should be covered by a heavier synthetic or wool sock for insulation. Terry-knit provides more cushioning and makes blisters less likely. To inhibit perspiration, an antiperspirant may be used on the feet. Then one should add the boots and high gaitors with overboots or supergaitors for colder conditions.

Duncan Ferguson front-pointing on Mt. Lady Washington, Colorado.

Boots

Boots specifically designed for ice climbing are quite specialized. They may be made of plastic or leather and be one-piece or double construction with a removable innerboot. (Plastic is used generically here as a catch-all term for the wide variety of polymeric compounds, some not plastic at all, of which boots are moulded.) Plastic boots, which today are the most popular due to their low-maintenance waterproof characteristics, are commonly of double construction. As yet, no manufacturer has offered a plastic boot with sufficient ankle flexibility to suit my taste, nor are most of the standard innerboots very well made or very warm. Expensive Alveolite foam inners are available for some models; these are indeed very warm, but the foam breaks down quickly. Many plastic boots also suffer from an ill-fitting shape that sacrifices control, and an overall rigidity that makes graceful movement on ice about as easy as dancing in ski boots.

On the other side of the coin, many leather boots are nearly as stiff in the ankles, and there has never been a leather boot that has maintained its water-repellence without frequent treatment. I have found a double leather boot from one manufacturer that seems to have been designed by someone whose ideas are sympathetic to mine. Right off the shelf, the Asolo 8000 has the features I look for in an ice boot: a very stiff but not rigid sole; a rigid, roomy toe that will stand up to step-kicking in hard snow; a flexible ankle that allows full range of motion with little resistance or irritation at the boot top; light weight; an innerboot of durable and crush-resistant neoprene foam; and a fit that holds the heel firmly in place. I mention this boot by name merely to give a concrete example. There are certain to be others equally as good on the market. I should also confess to having done a lot of climbing in plastic boots.

A good single leather boot allows better feel on pure rock sections of mixed routes. A single boot is warm enough for most people under normal ice climbing conditions, with an overboot that can be removed anytime crampons are not being worn, or with a 'super-gaiter' (an overboot which leaves the vibram sole exposed). A good fit, with no pressure points and plenty of room in the toe area, is crucial to maintaining good circulation, and the key to warm feet in single *or* double boots.

For your first season of ice climbing, it's possible to get by cheaply by purchasing an old pair of leather ski boots and having a cobbler remove the stiffening material from the ankle and add a vibram sole.

Concepts, Theories, and Suggestions

Inherent in the system of dressing for cold weather outlined here are several theories and concepts that deserve explanation, and knowledge of which will allow you to make better choices in developing your own systems.

Gear laid out at basecamp in preparation for a climb on Ama Dablam's South Face.

Whether leather or plastic, ice climbing boots are designed to stop wet from getting into the boot. This effectively creates a barrier to the natural moisture of the foot escaping the boot, thus the socks may eventually become moist and lose some of their insulating value. However, the use of a plastic bag or commercially available waterproof nylon sock, placed between a thin inner sock and a thick outer sock, creates a barrier to foot moisture and keeps the outer sock dry. Surprisingly enough, the foot does not end up drenched in sweat, since the body regulates perspiration according to the humidity of its immediate environment. This is the Vapour Barrier Liner (V.B.L.) theory. The idea has been used extensively in clothing for the body, as well as the feet. The idea is that a waterproof layer over long underwear limits the cooling effect of perspiration evaporating into the atmosphere. In practice, I find this technique to be uncomfortable, but others have used it successfully.

Another barrier idea, this one utilizing high-tech metalized fabrics, helps to limit the escape of body heat through radiation. Such a Radiant Heat Barrier (R.H.B.) does add some warmth when used as a lining in parkas, sleeping bags, and other insulated garments.

Lower Body
A layer of polypropelene or similar underwear will help to keep the skin dry and should be covered by stretch trousers or salopettes of ski-pant type material which allows excellent mobility, sheds snow quite well, and offers reasonable protection from wind while at the same time allowing moisture to pass freely into the atmosphere thus keeping you dry.

A wind-proof panel in the underwear crotch extends the viability of this combination in high winds before it becomes necessary to add a wind-proof over-layer. For very cold conditions, or for standing around while on belay, pile trousers with full side zips allows a final insulating layer to be easily donned or doffed. For long

routes, a crotch zip in all layers extending from the front down around and up to the small of the back greatly facilitates the answering of nature's call, even while wearing a harness. Windproof and/or waterproof (Goretex) salopettes or pants with full side zips are the final layer. Overpants insulated with down or Qualofil might be necessary for alpine winters or Himalayan climbs.

Upper Body
My preference is to wear a Farmer-

In the layering system of dressing for ice climbing, it helps if zips and vents in the various garments match up, and good overlaps and seals are achieved at neck, wrists, waist, ankles and other openings.

John type underwear suit which automatically gives the same initial polypropelene layer on the upper body as the legs. Over this several layers are used as required for warmth. First is a medium-weight wool or synthetic turtleneck shirt with a zip in the neck for ventilation. This can be covered by a light wind-shirt, a stretch jacket, or pile jacket, both with high zip collars, depending on conditions. Windproof, waterproof or Goretex are layered over this with a down or Quallofil parka for extreme cold.

Hands

A good combination is polypropelene gloves inside wool or pile mitts, covered by windproof/waterproof or 'miracle' shell mitt. Neoprene 'wet suit' gloves work well in extremely wet conditions, while ski gloves offer decent protection and good dexterity in dry conditions. Down or synthetic insulated mitts are used on the coldest climbs.

Head and Face

As much as 40 per cent of heat loss is through the head. The shell parka should have a secure neck-closure/hood combination that allows a complete seal around the face without restricting vision either straight ahead or when looking to either side or up and down. A good hood has a visor that helps to protect the eyes from wind, snow, or rain but does not interfere with vision. A visor, cotton golfer's cap or baseball cap shades the eyes on sunny days, while a balaclava of synthetic or wool is the traditional and still appropriate insulation for the head. If it's cold enough for a down or fibrefill parka, it's cold enough for a hood of the same insulation. Windproof or Goretex hats lined with pile or insulated with fibrefill, complete with ear flaps, cheek protection, and visor, are perhaps the most appropriate and versatile of all head coverings. An insulated mask of windproof material that covers the entire face, with holes for breathing and the eyes, prevents frostbite in high winds and is very light.

Dark Glasses and Goggles

On glaciers and snowfields it is necessary to wear dark glasses when the sun shines to avoid snow-blindness and other damage to the eyes from ultraviolet and infra-red rays. Even on a cloudy day, infra-red rays will still penetrate and blind you almost without any discomfort until it's too late. All good dark glasses come with literature explaining their effectiveness in filtering ultraviolet and infra-red. To be adequate for high mountain use, glasses must filter 100 per cent, or nearly 100 per cent, of these rays. The best glasses usually come with leather sideguards and sometimes nose guards. If you wear prescription glasses you will want to fully explain the need for ultraviolet and infra-red protection to your optician.

In very stormy weather and high winds, goggles are sometimes necessary to maintain any sight at all. However, fogging up often renders goggles useless, especially for those who must wear glasses under them. Various methods of ventilation have been devised to help alleviate the problem. The most successful to date are those goggles that are equipped with a small battery operated fan—admittedly quite a technocratic solution! Alternatively, lenses may be treated with anti-fog cream. Goggles or dark glasses should be worn at all times when climbing brittle alpine ice or frozen waterfalls to protect the eyes from flying chips of ice.

Accessories

In addition to the clothing for ice climbing, there are a number of items that are essential at various times.

A headlamp is often useful on short winter days or pre-dawn alpine starts. Lithium-powered lights shine many times longer than those powered by regular batteries, but they are expensive and several extra bulbs must be carried as they burn out quickly. Alkaline batteries are next best, and cheaper. Batteries kept warm under the parka or sweater will last much longer than those exposed directly to the cold air.

A water bottle insulated with closed-cell foam, or a thermos, will keep liquids from becoming undrinkable solids. A map and compass, and at least rudimentary knowledge of their use, will help you to navigate in a white-out. An altimeter can tell you how high you've climbed, or warn you of a change in weather. A thermometer can tell you just *how* cold you really are, while an inclinometer will tell you just how steep the ice really isn't! Finally, a first aid kit, the contents of which will be suggested in the next chapter, is always advisable to carry along, and a helmet with a 'U.I.A.A.' certification label may forestall use of the first aid kit.

Hardware

Axes and Hammers

Ice-axes are available in countless variations of two basic types: with a one-piece head, or with interchangeable picks and (in some cases) adzes. The one-piece head means there is no possibility that the pick will vibrate loose. On a well-designed interchangeable-pick tool, pick loosening is not a serious problem and the picks may be replaced if damaged or worn out, which is a major advantage.

Picks on either type of axe are available in numerous configurations, some useful, others less so. The traditional ice-axe has a pick that sticks out at 90° from the shaft, but many of the techniques described in this book are not possible with such an axe. We are concerned only with those picks that have a drooped curve, reverse curve, or are steeply angled. A not too radical drooped curve allows a natural swing and is best for all-around use, while a reverse curve also uses a natural swing but is more suitable in shorter shaft lengths and on steeper ice. An angled pick has good 'hooking' ability on rotten or 'chandeliered' ice. Other factors affecting the function of the pick are the shape of the tip, the shape and depth of the teeth, and the overall cross-sectional shape and dimensions. A pick may exhibit 'positive' or 'negative' clearance. Positive clearance gives smoother performance in self-arrest, while negative clearance is more secure in thin ice and requires less penetration to hold well in thick ice.

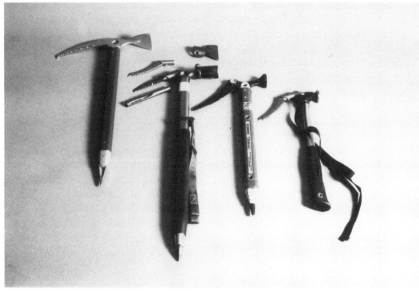

Positive clearance pick on left, negative clearance pick on right.

Teeth along the entire underside of the pick help the pick to stick in the ice, but if they are too deep (more than about 4 mm) the pick will be hard to remove. A thin cross-section displaces less ice and therefore causes less fracturing.

Most good axes have an adze almost perpendicular to the shaft. The adze should have sharp corners for cutting. Exotic, wavy edges add nothing to function.

In addition to standard-type picks and adzes, Lowe Big Bird axes offer tube picks and adzes as accessories. The special uses of these are discussed in the technique chapters.

Although some climbers use one, a leash from the tool to the harness provides no extra margin of safety that I can think of, and I've watched climbers become so entangled in one that minutes have been wasted and strength squandered while they sorted themselves out. I don't recommend using a leash.

On steep and vertical ice, two tools are used, one in each hand. In the mountains on the classic routes, the best combination is an alpine hammer used in conjunction with the axe. On short stretches of very steep ice, a quick wrist loop

can be fashioned by wrapping a prusik loop around the handle or a short runner through the karabiner hole in the tool's head, if there is one.

The strongest and best shafts are aluminium-alloy, fibreglass, or carbon-fibre wrapped thin-wall alloy. Metal shafts should be covered with smooth soft rubber for insulation and good grip, while carbon fibre and fibreglass shafts are warm enough as they are, yet they too are easier to hang onto if they are equipped with a rubber grip. For all round use the best shaft length is between 60–70 cm, depending on personal style, preference, body size, and whether the primary use is general alpine climbing or steep frozen waterfalls. If you plan to do only extreme climbs, you can get by with a shorter axe, but tools less than 60 cm length are increasingly difficult to self-arrest with. The spike and ferrule at the bottom of the shaft should be smooth and gradually tapered so that it will penetrate snow easily.

For general low-angle and moderate use, a wrist loop is not necessary or even desirable. For steep and vertical ice, however, you'll need to use one. There are some commercially available wrist loops that attach through the hole in the head of the axe, or you can

A selection of modern ice tools, left to right: Classic Chouinard curved piolet, Lowe Alpine Systems interchangeable pick Hummingbird model, Chacal reverse curve north wall hammer, Terrordactyl, Hummingbird Alpine Hammer.

make your own. Make it easily removable, so it can be dispensed with when it's not needed. The Big Bird axe is equipped with a cam action wrist loop that provides support at any position on the shaft.

Most people like to carry a north wall hammer as a second tool on modern extreme climbs. These are similar to an ice-axe in most respects. However, the head has a pounding anvil in place of the adze, and the curve or angle of the pick is more radical. The spike and ferrule should be stubbier than on the axe, so that a full grip is allowed at the bottom of the shaft and not much spike sticks out to get in the way when swinging the tool on steep ice or in tight places. North wall hammers vary in length from about 45 cm to 55 cm. Once again, the choice of length is dependent on personal climbing style, strength, size, and type of climbing normally done.

A number of manufacturers offer matched sets of short tools, one with an adze and the other with an anvil. Climbing on extreme ground with this combination is balanced and symmetrical, but there are occasional drawbacks to this system which will be discussed in the technique chapter.

Your tools are best carried in holsters on your harness or a separate belt. Most leather or nylon webbing holsters make withdrawing or inserting the tools an awkward task. Carpenter's holsters with wire loops are easiest to work with although they sometimes hang up in chimneys and other tight situations.

Crampons
Crampons come in these basic configurations with endless variations: rigid with 12 points (2 projecting forward and 10 downward under the boot), hinged in the middle with either 10 or 12 points, or ultralight with 8 or fewer points. Lowe Footfangs fall outside the standard categories, being rigid crampons with 20 points and parallel side rails.

The best crampons are adjustable to fit a very wide range of boots, and a pair of adjustable rigid 12-point crampons, or Footfangs, will serve you well on summer alpine climbs, winter icefalls, rime-coated rock, or frozen névé.

Before the universal adoption of front-point technique, 10-point crampons, which have no front points, were used by climbers favouring flat-foot techniques. Now, however, such crampons are outdated and should not be purchased by anyone who wishes not to limit his or her progress on ice. 8-point, ultralight crampons *are* very useful though, for snow approaches to rock climbs, where the difficulties are moderate but where lightweight mountain boots or rock shoes alone are dangerous. These crampons are limited on serious ice and will not be discussed further.

Crampon straps used to be the only method of attaching the crampon to the boot. The best straps are made of neoprene-covered nylon which remains flexible in wet freezing conditions, but beware of any straps that rely on a single rivet to attach them to the body of the crampon, as rivets quite often fail. Whatever the strap system, the crampon must fit the boot very snugly, and the straps should buckle with a pin through a hole in the strap. Friction-type buckles can slip, allowing the crampon to come loose or fall off the boot.

Although Footfangs were not the first to use a ski-binding type of approach to anchoring the crampon on the boot, the toe-bale and heel-clamp binding, which was developed for Footfangs, has proved itself to be more positive and secure than earlier bindings. Copies of this binding are now available on other types of crampons. Bindings have numerous advantages over straps: greater speed of application and removal; more positive hold on the boot; no pressure over the toe or foot to restrict circulation, and less breakage. I highly recommend that you choose a crampon with a toe-bale/heel-clamp binding. To ensure secure attachment, your boot must have a welt (lip) of 4 mm at the toe and heel for the binding to grab. Do not attempt to use this type of binding on a boot with less purchase than this.

Care of Gear
Sharp tools penetrate the ice easily, fracture it less, and add greatly to your security. Don't use a power grinder, as it may ruin the temper of the steel. File all points in the same configuration as they came from the factory, whether it's crampons or axe. On long mixed climbs I carry a small mill file in an accessible place.

Cross-country ski waxes can be used on bare shafts to increase grip. Dry and lightly oil metal parts after use to inhibit rust. Before each climb, check all crampon straps, wrist loops, hammers, and axes for hairline fractures and fatigue cracks; also check screws and bolts for tightness. Locktite or other liquid compound will help to keep bolts tight.

Protection Hardware
The reliability of protection on snow and ice is as variable as the medium itself.

Tubular Ice Screws
These can provide excellent protection. Depending on the quality of the ice, a well-placed tubular screw will hold from 680–2,040 kg. In rotten ice, screws hold very little.

The core of ice in tube screws tends to freeze to the inside walls. An ice-filled tube cannot be placed again until the core has been re-

A selection of crampons (top to bottom): Lowe Footfangs, Chouinard rigids, Salewa hinged.

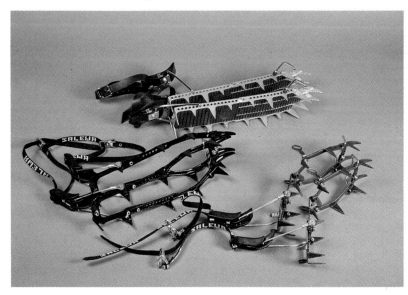

moved, and removal of the core is extremely difficult unless the design of the screw has specifically dealt with the problem. Two effective solutions have been discovered: differential inside diameter allows the ice to be forced through a slightly smaller opening at the tip, allowing it to be shaken out the back. A full-length slot, from the rear of the tube to 13 mm from the tip, on the other hand, allows mechanical clearing of the ice core using the pick of a hand tool. Tube screws or tube pitons with partial slots are hard to clear and not much better than solid tubes.

Ice Pitons

Ice pitons, or protection that is pounded in, come in two main styles. Those with a solid cross-section, such as the 'wart hog', tend to fracture brittle ice quite badly, and they must be chopped out. They do work quite well in certain softer ice conditions, however. The Lowe Snarg was the original pound-in, screw-out tube piton, although now there are many copies. For hard ice conditions the Snarg is far superior to solid-shafted designs.

In relatively soft snow the best protection can be arranged with the use of cabled aluminium plates anywhere from about 15 cm × 20 cm to 25 cm × 30 cm. These *deadmen* are buried in the snow and under a load tend to 'sail', or 'fluke' deeper into the snow, providing variable security. On harder snow, in particular the walls of bergschrunds, cornices, and the like, snow stakes of tubular, V-shaped, or T cross-section are useful. Snow stakes vary from about 45 cm to 90 cm long, for different snow conditions.

Energy-Absorbing Devices

The reliability of a questionable ice or snow anchor can be enhanced with the use of such a device deployed between the piton and the rope. Such devices limit the force that can be applied to the anchor to around 300 kg. They are either a friction plate and web arrange-ment, or more simply, the 'Air Voyager' is a strip of webbing that relies on a series of bar tacks ripping to absorb the force.

Ropes

'Dry', or water-repellent ropes are a major improvement for the ice climber as they tend to freeze up much less than untreated ropes. Most treatments wear off with use, however, so the advantage is eventually lost. For easy snow and glacier tours an 8 or 8.5 mm dynamic rope is probably adequate, while on long hard routes a doubled 8.5 or 9 mm rope gives insurance against cutting and may be used single strand for long rapid leads on easier terrain.

Further Equipment

Other items that have particular advantages to the ice climber, are a harness with adjustable leg loops to accommodate varied clothing; a chest-harness to be used along with the sit harness for glacier travel (or a full-body harness as is popular in the Alps); mechanical belay and rappel devices for consistent control; a U.I.A.A. approved helmet for obvious reasons; a shovel for digging snow pits, freeing avalanche victims and digging snow caves. Snow shoes or skis for approach and/or descent in deep snow; a repair kit containing enough spare parts and materials to allow you to deal with broken or damaged equipment; ascending devices, such as the 'Gibbs Ascender' or 'Bonatti' ascendeur, that positively grip icy ropes; and a first aid kit with contents appropriate to the seriousness of the intended venture.

To carry your clothing, equipment, food, and drink, you'll need a pack or sac. You probably already own a small pack from rock climbing, which will do fine for starting. But if you have to (or want to) buy a pack for ice climbing it should have these features: padded adjustable shoulder straps and waist belt, load stabilizing straps (compression straps on sides) at waist belt and top of shoulder straps, convenient attachment points for axes, crampons, skis, etc., and a removable foam pad (small packs) or internal frame (larger packs suitable for extended trips of 3 or more days).

After all this talk of exotic equipment and clothing, it is well to re-emphasize that owning the latest and greatest ice climbing paraphernalia is not the goal. To get started, you and a friend can use army-surplus woollies or old ski clothes, hire axes and crampons from a local shop, and take off for the snowy hills.

Protection devices for ice and snow: Chouinard tube screw (top right), Lowe Snarg ice piton (bottom right), Clog deadman (top centre), MSR snow stake.

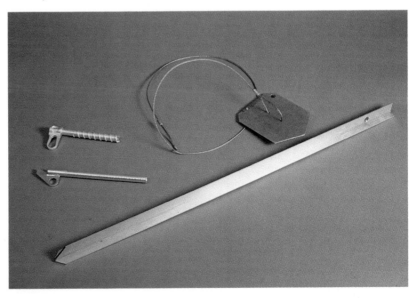

Important basics

It is possible for the aspiring ice climber to advance rapidly through the ranks of difficulty and accomplish some very impressive climbs within the first season. But technical ability on hard ice is only a secondary measure of a good ice climber. Far more important is the depth of a climber's experience with, and knowledge of, a host of related concerns. The climber must understand the phenomena of avalanches and mountain weather; have a knowledge of snow conditions and the ability to navigate successfully and travel safely on snow and glaciers; and know how to avoid the hazards of falling rock and ice, collapsing cornices, and altitude illness. If an accident occurs, a good climber is fully prepared to effect a self-rescue and administer appropriate first aid. The best ice climbers are equally at home travelling on foot, skis, or snowshoes. They have developed an unconscious rapport with the mountains and are constantly filtering information from the environment through a screen of intuition and hard-won knowledge. This provides the appropriate response to any set of circumstances almost without thinking.

Weather
A little-praised side benefit of learning to ice climb is that we begin to recognize the beauty of savage weather. Such weather is responsible for the arc of a cornice, the spreading wings of icicles on a frozen waterfall, the sharp-edged clarity of the atmosphere when a cold-front pushes out the storm, and the quickening of the blood and brain on frosty pre-dawn starts. Sleet, snow, sun, wind, wet, thaw, gust, gale, blow, freeze, whiteout, haze, mist, fog, clouds: the ice climber is treated to a kaleidoscopic experience of high and wild places. Gradually learning to cope with ever more harsh conditions is as rewarding as learning to climb steeper and harder ice. Successfully interpreting the meaning of high cirrus clouds turning red in the sunset, or a sudden rise in temperature— accompanied by a cessation of wind and lowering of clouds—not only allows retreat to be made in time to avoid an epic, but offers the satisfaction of being intimate with one of the most fascinating aspects of nature. We learn to face the storm with a grin, and the sun with dark glasses and an adequate sunscreen to protect nose and lips!

Frank Sarnquist on Mt. Rainier.

Snow and Ice Features

The chart below may help to explain the main types of ice and terrain with which an ice climber is concerned. Of course there are infinite variations on these themes.

TYPES OF ICE

Alpine Ice	Water Ice	Rime Ice
snow	verglas	atmospheric ice
névé	laminated flow ice	snow ice
glacier	cauliflower ice	frost feathers
north wall	chandelier ice	
winter gully	rotten ice	

TERRAIN

Alpine Ice	Water Ice	Rime Ice
glaciers	frozen waterfalls	can be found on any
a) icefalls	& drainages	rock surface exposed to
b) séracs	verglassed rock	the necessary conditions
c) crevasses	of any configuration	of wind, precipitation
faces		and/or humidity, and
gullies and couloirs		temperature

Snow Climbing

Snow climbing may not be as exciting to do or watch as hard ice climbing, since it lacks the 'fly on a pane of glass' quality, but snow can often require a more refined understanding and technique. On a double-corniced Alaskan Ridge or a steep face of Andean 'cheese ice' insecurity reaches a zenith never matched in other types of ascent.

Timing and Route Finding

More than any other consideration, *when*, and under what conditions, you do a snow climb, determines how difficult and/or insecure the ascent will be. For instance, a prolonged warm spell followed by a hard frost will turn a hillside of bottomless mush into a delightful slope of crisp névé, which may be too hard in the morning to climb without crampons, but which will yield perfect steps at 10 am after an hour's exposure to the morning sun. In another hour the snow may rapidly regress to its former sloppy state, requiring three or four times the effort and time. You will want to learn to predict when such 'windows of opportunity' exist in the mountains, and develop your skill at prediction through thoughtful observation. Capitalizing on mistakes promotes the deepest knowledge.

Just as important as *when* you climb, is *where* you climb. On any given day conditions will vary greatly from one aspect of a mountain to another. You may travel on good windpack on the lower East Ridge, flounder through a metre of dangerous sugar snow as you traverse out beneath the North Face, which may offer a path up the edges of spindrift—gouged avalanche runnels, and finally reach the consolidated 'summer snow' on the southern slopes which may be softened just enough to allow a wonderful sliding 1 pm descent back to camp.

In a less obvious fashion, each

This detail of a pillar of water ice shows a nicely welded icicle configuration.

facet of the mountain also contains a multitude of conditions, less dramatically variable than those found on opposite sides of the hill, but just as important to the climber. You'll learn to identify the slight difference in the opacity of the thicker wind crust, that will just bear your weight, or sport the firm avalanche debris under its mantle of new snow.

Self-Arrest

Using the ice-axe self-belay and kicking good steps, you'll rarely find yourself in an uncontrolled fall on snow. But such falls do happen, and the technique of self-arresting with the pick of the ice-axe, was developed to stop them. For practice you must find a slope with snow firm enough to slide on, and a good runout. Do *not* wear crampons. Quite obviously a slope above a drop-off or one that ends in a field of boulders, is not the right place to learn. Although a fall can leave you in any position, even upside-down and backwards (about which more later), begin with trying to stop yourself from a position where your feet are pointing downhill and you are lying on your back. Grasp the axe with one hand very near the spike, the shaft diagonally across your chest, and the fingers of the other hand curled over the head of the axe and the thumb wrapped around between the adze and the shaft. If your left hand is near the spike and the right hand is holding the head, let yourself slide a little and roll to your right, *toward the pick of the axe*, and as you roll over onto the pick, gradually insert it into the snow to stop your slide. If the pick of the axe is in your left hand, then you'll roll to the left. If you roll toward the spike, there is a danger it will catch in the snow as you roll, which will almost certainly wrench the axe from your hands. Also, to keep the spike from catching as you apply braking force, pull up on the spike as you hunch your weight onto the pick. You can also dig the toes of your boots in for extra stopping power.

Once you have the skill to stop yourself at greater speeds from this

(A) (B)

Self arrest: breaking (above), turning (above right), stopping (right).

(C)

basic position, try ever more exotic falls, always remembering the basic principles of rolling toward the pick and controlling the spike. The illustrations show the sequence for stopping an upside-down and backward fall. First it is necessary to try to sit up a bit and drag the pick into the snow at about waist level (A). This begins to act as a pivot around which your feet can swing away from the pick (B), at the same time you begin to roll toward the pick with your upper body. This finally puts you in a position to effect a classic arrest (C).

Step Kicking

In both hard and soft snow it is often necessary to kick steps. In hard snow a small platform on which to stand is 'sawed' into the slope with a forward thrust of the edge of the boot. In soft snow kicking directly into the snow— sometimes accompanied by a 'tamping' motion, or two, or six or

Holding the head of the axe with both hands in order to push the shaft in deeper, a hold called *piolet manche*.

eight in very soft snow—will yield a big step that shouldn't give way under body weight.

Self-Belay with Ice-Axe

Much snow climbing is safely done unroped with the expectation that the support of the ice-axe shaft, which is shoved as deeply as possible into the snow before each step, will be adequate to catch a slip before it turns into a fall.

Some people are adamant that the pick should point away from the body, thus making injury in a slip less likely and giving a more comfortable grip with the wide adze in the palm of the hand. Others insist the correct way is exactly the opposite with the adze pointing forward. Their reasoning is that a self-arrest (see below) can more quickly be applied if the self-belay should fail. I don't feel strongly either way, but tend most often to point the pick forward, finding the adze provides a more comfortable support.

Belays and Protection on Snow

Snow belays and protection are less reliable and require more skill than those on rock or hard ice. Luckily, the forces to be controlled are usually not as large, however, and with experience roped climbing on snow can be safe enough. We've already discussed the first two lines of defence in snow climbing, i.e. self-belay and self-arrest. Ninety per cent of the time these techniques will be effective even in a roped party. But if the axe is lost, or in a fall through a cornice or into a crevasse, an adequate belay must be arranged.

While the party is moving simultaneously over moderate terrain, the members, who each carry a few coils of the rope, should be prepared to stop another's fall with a potential belay. A potential belay is applied at the instant of need. A loop is tied in the rope a metre or so in front of each climber, passed up the shaft of the axe and held in the hand that holds the axe head. When a fall occurs, the belayer instantly drops his coils, giving time to ram the shaft into the snow with all his weight, at the same time allowing the pre-tied loop to drop to the surface of the snow to keep

Climbing snow using the axe as a self-belay.

leverage on the shaft to a minimum. With practice, moderate falls can be held this way, but it's best not to expect the technique to hold anything very severe. The *boot/axe* belay is more reliable, though still only effective against relatively low forces. After a platform has been stamped in the snow, the rope is passed over the boot and around the shaft of the axe. The belayer's weight is kept on both the boot, and the head of the axe through a nearly straight arm, while a dynamic breaking force is applied by pulling the rope

back around the ankle with the other hand.

Still more secure is the *sitting hip belay*, backed up by the axe which is inserted horizontally into the snow, perpendicular to the force of a fall. Pass a runner around the middle of the shaft and cut an exit groove in the snow for the belayer to clip into for the runner. If a U-shaped channel is stamped into the snow in which to sit, this belay can be quite strong.

Snow stakes, or *deadmen*, are used both to anchor belays and to provide protection on the lead. In certain hard snow conditions, snow stakes pounded vertically into the snow are quite strong. More often, however, a well-placed deadman is best. Pound the deadman at a 45° angle into the slope, and make certain to cut a groove for the cable so that when the cable is loaded, there is no upward force on the deadman.

A boot/axe belay in snow.

Use of Crampons in Snow Climbing

In soft snow crampons may be more of a hindrance than an aid in climbing. The snow will often form a clump between the points, making a heavy, rounded mass that is slippery and awkward to walk on. When crampons must be worn in soft snow, a shuffling gait will keep clumping to a minimum. In the worst conditions, however, you'll find it necessary to knock the clumps off with the spike of your axe, sometimes with each step. When the snow is firm or overlays ice or rock, crampons become more necessary. In frozen névé you'll find your points sinking all the way in under body weight, but your feet will stay on the surface. This condition is an ice climber's dream, and very steep slopes can be ascended with ease and security. On the other hand, sloppy wet snow over ice, or powder snow

over rock can make even gentle terrain quite hair-raising. In these conditions it's often best to front point even on moderate angles, kicking hard to get through the slush, or compacting snow into a platform, taking some support from the underlying rock or ice.

Descending Snow

If there is no safe runout, the slope is overly steep, or the snow is very hard, it's best to back down the hill, facing in and kicking the toes directly in. The shaft of the axe should be shoved deeply into the snow as low down as is comfortable before each step, thus providing a self-belay if your feet should slip. When the slope is long enough, the snow is good, and you feel confident that you can effect a self-arrest, it is faster to turn and face the valley, using the *plunge step* to go down. Lean far forward and transfer your weight completely with each step, digging your heels in deeply. Descent at a slight diagonal allows the spike and shaft of the axe to be planted low before each step as a balance and safeguard against a slip, but when that isn't necessary, just walk down the slope with the axe in one or both hands, ready to arrest a fall. On spring and summer snow with a surface of sun-softened corn, moderate and lower angled slopes may be 'skated' down in great diagonal strides, eating up distance in very little time. This is actually a modified glissade, which is the art of 'skiing' down a slope on your boot soles, and this enjoyable technique deserves a complete treatment.

Glissading

Actually, the most basic glissade is not made on your feet at all, but rather inelegantly on your rump in the same manner you used to slide down snowbanks in your snowsuit as a child. This *sitting glissade* (A) is used on snow that is too soft to allow sliding on the boot soles. A sitting glissade should not be used on harder snow, however, because there is a loss of control in comparison to a crouching or standing glissade, although from the lower

position a faster self-arrest can be made.

Much drier and more enjoyable though still somewhat awkward is the *crouching glissade* (B). Hold the axe across your body in the self-arrest grip and apply weight to the spike to control your speed. You'll find that turns are difficult, but note that it is easier to turn to the side on which you are dragging the spike. Obviously, then, if you want to turn right but the spike is in your left hand, you'll need to switch hands first. You must practise doing this quickly so unwanted speed does not build up during the switch. To stop, turn to the side with the spike and apply greater force while simultaneously edging your boots and weighting them equally.

The most controlled glissade of all, and with the most potential for fun, is the *standing glissade* (C). An expert skier will take to this technique like a duck to water, but even the newcomer will be able to link turns and have a good time the first day out. Although the standing glissade is closely related to skiing, it is much easier and more natural since there are no long boards strapped to your feet. Like skiing, however, you'll find it necessary to bend your knees quite deeply in order to develop control in turns and to be able to 'swallow' bumps and other irregularities in the snow without upsetting your balance. With your back nearly vertical and your knees relaxed and bent, just point your knees in the direction you want to go, edging your boots into the snow at the same time. Keep your upper body quiet—the action should occur from the hips down. Hold the axe in either hand with a pick pointing forward to lessen the chance of stabbing yourself in a fall. The usual mistake is leaning back, which will cause your feet to scoot out from under you, depositing you on your backside in a flurry of arms and legs. If you feel your weight more on the balls of your feet than the heels, you are properly balanced. Also, during standing glissades you will want to feel your weight equally on both

Glissading

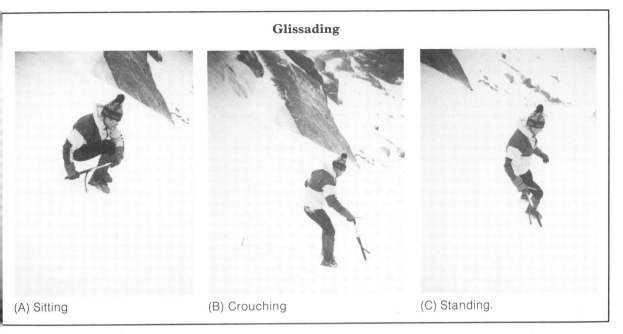

(A) Sitting   (B) Crouching   (C) Standing.

feet at all times. This will help to counter the tendency to lean into the slopes while turning, which also causes your feet to skate out from under you.

To come to a stop from a standing glissade, exaggerate the bend in your knees, at the same time reaching forward with spike of your axe (reach downhill more than across the slope), turn your knees and edge your boots to the side holding the axe (but keep your upper body looking more directly down the slope), and once you've slowed down enough, plunge your axe into the snow with a nearly straight arm and give an extra emphasis to your edge set. On many slopes it's not necessary to ram the axe in to stop, because proper edging with bent knees will eventually bring you to a halt.

Step Cutting

Since the advent of curved picks and rigid crampons few climbers have bothered to become expert at chopping steps which is a time-consuming process. However, the technique is useful for those climbs when just an occasional step will obviate the need to carry crampons on mountain rock routes, or when a crampon is broken or dropped.

In cutting belay and bivouac stances, a great deal of energy can

be saved by employing proper technique. Mentally outline the step before you make the first swing using the adze, make a chop at the closest point to your body on the outlined step and make successive cuts moving farther away. You will find that the ice behind the first chop is easier to remove. In hard snow the adze may enter the snow at an acute angle. A flick of the wrist at the end of the swing will pop out a large chunk. On hard ice, the adze should strike more obliquely in an effort to shave the ice away. If one pass leaves a step that

is too small, make successive passes starting just below the first. On steep ice once the basic step has been fashioned, the overhanging lip above the step can be quickly removed with a couple of blows of the pick. A basic step is one that accepts the entire boot sole and slopes into the mountain slightly. A series of these would ascend in a diagonal line up the slope, though this may be modified in any number of ways to suit various situations.

Water ice terrain

Glacier Travel and Crevasse Rescue

While it is true that some climbers manage to get away for years with unroped travel on snow-covered glaciers, far too many others less fortunate have been fatally surprised when an apparently safe expanse of snow collapsed and dropped them into the depths of an icy slot. Experience *will* help you to detect the subtle shadings and depressions that may indicate a hidden crevasse, but no one I know has climbed for long in an alpine environment and not fallen into a hole or two. Where the ice is bare of course the crevasses may be seen and unroped travel is often justifiable, otherwise, use the rope.

For the rope to be a true safeguard, it must be properly employed. This means you must be prepared to stop a fall and to extricate yourself or another from a crevasse. The basic two-man party should tie into the ends of the rope normally, and then each climber should take up $\frac{1}{3}$ of the rope in coils and clip into the shortened rope with a Figure-of-Eight and locking karabiner. The extra coils may be carried over the shoulder, or as I like to do, stuffed into a bag that is clipped to the harness. This extra rope is thus available, once a fall has been held and anchored, to be thrown down into the crevasse to the fallen climber. A prusik and foot loop of 7 mm cord is tied just in front of the Figure-of-Eight knot or ascending device if it is available. If you have successfully held your partner's fall, the axe shaft may be rammed through this loop into the snow and backed up as needed, and the load of the fallen climber can then be taken by the prusik or ascendeur, freeing the belayer to extract himself from the rope, and further assist the victim.

First removing his pack and hanging it from the rope, the person in the crevasse stands in the foot sling and rights himself. For glacier travel a chest harness used in conjunction with the sit harness will reduce the chance of a broken back caused by a heavy pack. Once the pack is hung and the extra rope from the person on the surface has been lowered, the ropes padded with a pack or ice-axe to keep them from burying themselves in the edge of the crevasse, the victim can then alternately slide up and stand in the foot sling and be held on belay on the other rope until he's worked his way out of the crevasse.

If the victim is injured or unconscious, mechanical pulley systems can be arranged, but these seldom allow one unaided person to hoist another.

Careful route finding will make a fall into a crevasse less likely. Travel against the general grain will lessen the chances of all members falling into the same crevasse, and a tight rope as you walk will keep the fall to a safe minimum. Remember that there are generally fewer crevasses where the ice is under compression, such as in dips and the inside of bends in the glacier. Where the ice flows over a hump, or on the outside of corners, you'll find more crevasses.

If you must cross a suspect snow bridge it's best to set a boot/axe or

Glacial features and alpine terrain.

other appropriate belay in advance while the leader gingerly probes with his axe to ascertain the strength of the snow before lightly walking or crawling (to distribute the weight better) over the bridge. The other members should be belayed across as well. Snow-shoes and skis effectively spread body weight over a large area and often make such crossing safer.

The huge masses of ice in séracs and icefalls are unpredictable, since the movement is affected more by the glacier's continuous downward motion than by superficial freeze and thaw. Therefore whenever possible avoid routes that require travel through icefalls or exposure to séracs. In those rare instances when for whatever reason you choose to accept these risks, remember that speed is the most important safety factor.

Water ice terrain

A) High summits
B) Feeder Slopes
C) High Avalanche Hazard
D) Ice Wall or Frozen Waterfall
E) Ice Chimney
F) Approach Gully Avalanche potential
G) Safer Free-covered Slopes
H) Valley Bottom

Alpine ice terrain

A) Snow Ridge Cornice
B) Ice Arête
C) Ice Face
D) Snow Flutes Avalanche runnels
E) Couloir
F) Bergschrund
G) Catchment Basin
H) Crevasses
I) Icefall
J) Sérac
K) Hanging Glacier
L) Accumulation Zone—Snow does not melt completely above this line every year

Navigation

Normally the mountaineer can find his way using the many landmarks that are a part of the alpine scene.

Climbing a corniced ridge on Latok 1 in Pakistan.

During storms and whiteout conditions, however, landmarks disappear and skills in the use of map and compass become essential: the ability to take a bearing from the map and follow it through the mountains, or vice-versa; the art of finding your current location on the map through triangulating two sightings; and the skillful avoidance of hazardous terrain and dead-ends through knowledgeable scrutiny of the contour lines on the map. But total reliance on map and compass is not necessary or even desirable. If one has no map, or has lost the compass, then a finely-honed 'sixth sense' such as that which allows the Polynesians to navigate unaided from island to island across large expanses of open water comes into its own. We are all born with this instinctive sense of where we are and how to get from here to there, but it is a long process learning to use it. This sense is buried by the technology used in everyday travel but can be rediscovered with practice.

The crevassed surface of a glacier. With experience you come to detect lines of navigation and potentially safe routes.

Bivouacs

There is an old adage that says if you carry bivouac gear, you'll use it. The extra weight of the gear will cause you to go so slowly that you'll certainly be caught out at day's end. If an unplanned bivouac is a possibility, there's a point to be made for limiting equipment to the absolute minimum required for survival. A water bottle and bivouac sack, in conjunction with climbing clothing and a pack to sit on should suffice.

A slight extra degree of comfort might be allowed for planned nights out. A $\frac{3}{4}$ length pad of 13 mm closed-cell foam, cooking pot and stove, food, and ultralight sleeping bag will improve things.

When the snow is deep enough, a snow cave is always better shelter than a tent or bivouac sac, but to make one you will need to carry a shovel.

Skiing and Snowshoeing

Some winter ice climbs can be approached only by ski or snowshoe. Deep soft snow can render foot travel impossible. The advantages of snowshoes are that anyone who can walk can learn to use them immediately; they are more compact

Skis have the advantage over snow shoes in that not only are they utilitarian on the approach, but they can make the descent as exciting as the climb. Jeff Lowe on the first ski descent of McHenry's Notch Couloir in the Rocky Mountain National Park, Colorado.

when they must be carried; and snowshoes usually cost less than skis. Some snowshoes are only about twice the size of a bootsole, and while these are not of much use in fresh powder, they may be carried in the pack on technical ground, ready to be pulled out for use on easier sections of snow.

Skis, on the other hand, allow faster uphill travel, and, going downhill, there is no comparison. Not everyone has an easy time mastering the skills of skiing, but persistence along with some instruction from a friend or professional will soon pay dividends of more than a simple utilitarian nature. The skier playing with gravity learns to identify a sort of internal gyroscope that plays a more subtle but equally important role in ice climbing. It is neither necessary nor appropriate to deal here with all the varieties of ski equipment. Suffice it to say that for approaching ice climbs the ski/boot/binding combination must allow the heel to move freely up-and-down so that a motion similar to walking is achieved.

Avalanches

Avalanches of various kinds are perhaps the biggest threat to an ice climber. On the approach to a climb a new snow or slab avalanche may be a possibility. Slopes above may release and funnel onto you while you're on an ice face or in a gully or couloir. Under thaw conditions, an entire winter's snowpack may slide on a gentle slope of water-lubricated granite slabs with an incautious or unknowledgeable climber clinging to it. Knowledge of the basic phenomena associated with avalanches can help you avoid exposure in the first place, and lessen the chances of being caught in an avalanche if you must travel or climb in dangerous conditions. The information presented here is enough to give you a basic understanding of the factors involved in avalanche prediction and avoidance, but it is not enough to make you an 'expert'.

Always err on the side of cau-

tion. Even the most acknowledged authorities take this approach when they are in the field. The variables are simply too many to gamble your life on. However, with time and sensitive awareness, you'll eventually develop a 'feel' for conditions that will serve you well. Snow avalanches are of two main types: loose snow avalanches, which start at a point and gather mass in fan-shape as they fall, or cohesive slab avalanches that start sliding over a large area all at once, creating a well-defined fracture line. Either type of avalanche re-

Approaching an ice climb on skis or snow shoes is often the only feasible way.

quires a 'trigger', which may be the weight of a climber, a falling rock or cornice, the collapse of a weak layer in the snowpack, a sudden change in barometric pressure or temperature, wind, the tug of gravity, new snowfall, a combination of the above, or something else! Of the two types, slab avalanches are often the most damaging and deadly, and often are triggered by the victim's weight on a stressed slab that is weakly bonded to the ground or other layers within the snowpack. An avalanche of either type need travel only a short distance to gain deadly force and mass. People have been buried at the bottom of a 10 m slope.

Steepness is one of the factors that influences whether the introduction of a 'trigger' will release the slope. Slopes of 30 to 45 degrees are low-angle enough to allow snow to accumulate significant depths with poor bonds. Avalanches most often occur on these slopes, but in unstable conditions may occur at angles greater or less than this.

Slope configuration is a determinant also. Slab avalanches most often occur on convex slopes, breaking at the crest, but they may also break on a concave slope, if other factors overcome the natural compression on such slopes.

Snow on north-facing slopes (south-facing slopes in the Southern Hemisphere) receives little or no sun and often is slower to stabilize than on other aspects. South-facing slopes exposed directly to the sun are especially dangerous in the spring and summer. Slopes of other aspects to the sun are variously affected. Slight changes in this aspect can have dramatic effects on slope stability. Snow tends to be removed from windward slopes and deposited as slabs on leeward slopes, which are often unstable. If surface features such as rocks, trees, or brush are present sticking up through the snowpack, in significant quantity, they help to anchor the snow. Once these features are buried, avalanche hazard increases.

If the rate of new snowfall during a storm is more than 25 mm per hour, avalanches are quite likely to occur. If wind is present the danger increases rapidly. New snow is not necessarily deposited evenly on every slope, so be alert for variations in depth. When 15 cm or more of new snow builds up on a slope without sloughing, avalanche conditions are dangerous. In the absence of new snowfall, wind alone is a major contributor to

instability. Sustained winds will transport loose snow into gullies and slopes on the leeward sides, forming slabs.

Snow crystals are not all the same. Star-shaped, angular crystals interlock better than needles or pellets, creating a more cohesive snowpack. After falling, however, snow crystals begin to change as wind rolls them along on the surface, or with time, under the force of gravity, new snow on top or the effect of atmospheric conditions.

Storms starting with low temperatures, and dry snow, followed by rising temperatures, are likely to cause avalanches. The dry snow at the start forms a poor bond to the old snow or ice surface. However, if a storm starts warm and gets colder, the new snow bonds well to old snow or freezes to ice, and is more stable. Continued cold temperatures hinder slope stabilization, while warm weather aids settling and stability.

In prolonged cold, clear winter weather, Temperature Gradient (TG) snow, commonly called depth hoar, forms from the ground up whenever the snowpack is thin (60 cm–120 cm). The ground is warmer than the upper snowpack, and moisture is leached from the bottom up through sublimation, creating large, weak, angular grains. Under the weight of new snow or in the presence of another trigger, a layer of depth hoar can collapse, causing an avalanche. In the Rocky Mountains this condition is all too prevalent.

Wet snow avalanches occur most often during the first prolonged spring thaw, but in the high mountains wet snow avalanche hazard may exist throughout the summer, although it generally subsides later in the season.

The art of avalanche avoidance requires a combination of observations to be made, in addition to understanding the factors that predispose a slope to avalanche. As you travel through the mountains watch for old avalanche paths, in particular those that show signs of having slid earlier in the winter or season, as these slopes will be most

likely to slide again. Fresh avalanches indicate conditions are hazardous, at least on slopes of the same aspect, elevation, and snowpack history. If the snow settles with a 'whoomp' around you, and especially if the snow cracks and the fractures travel for some distance, do not cross the slope, avalanche danger is high! In warm weather, snowballs or 'cartwheels' that roll down the slope also indicate danger.

If a slope is suspect, or if you simply have no idea of the stability of a slope, a snow pit dug through the snowpack to the ground will provide much valuable information. After digging the pit, lightly brush the strata to expose the cross-section of the snowpack clearly. Ice crusts, weak bonds between snow layers, and particularly depth hoar will show up. Take a handful of snow from each of the layers and try to form a snowball. If it holds together well then that layer is probably stable. If the entire snowpack exhibits this cohesive tendency, then, in the absence of poor bonds between layers or an underlying surface of ice or depth hoar it is probably quite stable. The snow pit must be dug on the actual slope under question, or on a slope of similar aspect and other characteristics, to be meaningful.

The safest routes follow ridge-crests on the windward side below the potential fracture line of a cornice. On dangerous open slopes or wide couloirs climb up or down the edges in a straight line: switch-backs in the middle of the slop are likely to cause an unstable slope to slide. Traverse dangerous slopes or couloirs at the top, above the release zone if possible. If you can't cross above the release zone, it is worth making even a longer detour below

A new snow spindrift avalanche in Colorado's Blue Ribbon Gully. Such slides are not as dangerous as wet snow or slab avalanches, but if sufficient volume is funnelled onto a climber the force can easily be great enough to wipe him off the ice.

the slope to cross on a flat well away from the bottom of the slope if possible.

If you must cross a suspect slope, only one person should cross at a time, the others waiting their turn in a safe location, keeping a careful eye out for the exposed individual. Roped belays are only useful on small slopes. The force of a major avalanche makes it impossible to hold a victim. Do not assume that a slope is stable simply because one person crossed it safely; each per-son must be watched carefully as they cross. Pick your line to take advantage of rock outcrops, ridges, or other havens. While travelling in dangerous areas unhook the waistbelt of your pack, remove ice-axe or ski-pole straps, safety straps to ski bindings, and ensure that you can quickly drop your pack if necessary. Beware of gear slings and runners over pack straps that make it impossible to rid yourself of this very effective 'snow anchor'. Wear your gloves and hat and secure all openings in your clo-thing to avoid frostbite and hypo-thermia if you're caught and trapped in an avalanche.

If you are caught in an avalanche get rid of all equipment and your pack, and try to stay near the surface of the tumbling snow by 'swimming'. Direct your efforts to making your way to the side of the avalanche. As the snow slows down, keep your hands in front of your face, trying to create an air pocket when the snow stops. You

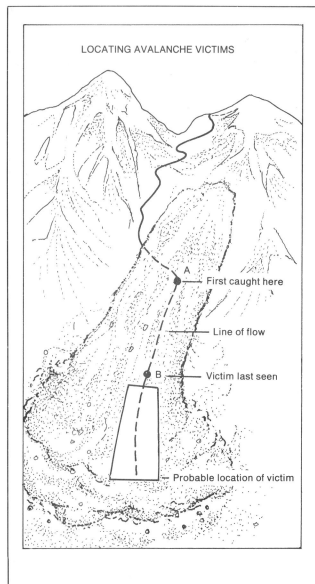

LOCATING AVALANCHE VICTIMS

A — First caught here

Line of flow

B — Victim last seen

Probable location of victim

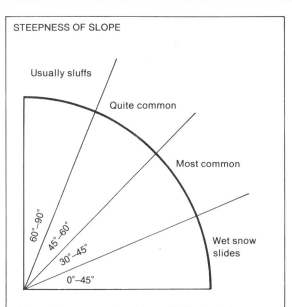

STEEPNESS OF SLOPE

Usually sluffs

Quite common

Most common

Wet snow slides

60°–90°
45°–60°
30°–45°
0°–45°

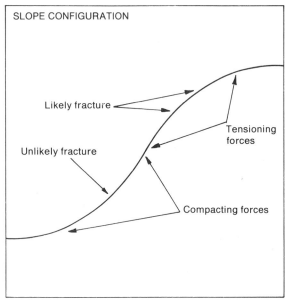

SLOPE CONFIGURATION

Likely fracture

Tensioning forces

Unlikely fracture

Compacting forces

will survive longer when you're buried if you don't panic, giving your partner(s) time to find you.

The members of the party who are not involved in the avalanche should mentally mark the spot where the victim was first caught, and also the place last seen. A fan-shaped area bisected by an imaginary line drawn between the first and last places seen, is the most likely area for the victim to be found. Articles of clothing or equipment may indicate the location of the victim and should be quickly checked by probing with a special probe, ski pole, or ice-axe in the immediate vicinity. If this fails to locate the victim quickly, probe and scuff the snow in the fan-shaped area, especially the places you somehow feel might be most likely to yield results. You are the victim's most likely saviour, and if the hasty search does not locate him, do a grid search, probing the area first at metre intervals, and finally at half-metre intervals. Go for help only if all this fails. Chances of survival diminish rapidly after the first $\frac{1}{2}$ hour, but people have been known to survive for 24 hours.

After successfully locating and freeing the victim, treat for suffocation, shock, any traumatic injuries, and finally for hypothermia and frostbite, if appropriate. Do not remain any longer than necessary in an area exposed to further avalanche danger.

Miscellaneous Hazards

Falling rock, collapsing cornices and séracs, storms, loose rock, hidden crevasses, weak snow bridges, and avalanches are often termed 'objective' hazards, since there is apparently little the climber can do to alter them. But such hazards, as well as cold and altitude, are often used to excuse accident or tragedy. However, haven't we *chosen* to expose ourselves to these possibilities in our decision to travel and spend time in the mountains? Should we not accept the responsibility for our decisions and their resulting consequences? If we do admit that a skull broken by a fall-ing rock, or a life smothered by an avalanche, *is* our fault, then aren't we more likely to be extra cautious, scrupulously avoiding times of excessive danger, doing our utmost to learn all we can about the rhythm of the mountains and inserting ourselves into that rhythm only at appropriate times and places? Shouldn't we have the patience to wait if necessary and never to go in those places that are always unsafe?

We should cross the zones of rockfall only when the rocks are frozen solidly in place, avoiding the morning thaw and evening freeze. We should allow enough time for new snow to settle and stabilize before we commit ourselves to the avalanche slope. We should rope up when snow hides the crevasses, unrope to move faster when that is appropriate, be prepared for freezing temperatures and storm, allow time to acclimatize adequately, test our holds before weighting them; listening to and trusting both our intuition and intellect, never gambling recklessly.

First Aid

Even the most careful and experienced climber will at some point be required to provide emergency medical assistance to a member of his own party, or another, or himself. The alpinist who does not take the time to become proficient at least to the advanced first aid level is negligent, in the moral sense, of accepting a duty to him-self and others. A thorough understanding of basic bodily processes and anatomy also serves the climber well when it is time to choose the clothing and food that will go with him into the mountains. Most clubs and organizations host first aid courses and medical seminars specially tailored to the needs of climbers. You should seek to attend these.

Absorbing the Mountain Essence

'Ambition feeds on itself, it can never be satisfied; you can only let go of it.'
Doug Scott

Success in ice climbing depends as much on attitude as the mastery of individual skills. Whether you can gain the maximum enjoyment of the sport by advancing as rapidly as possible depends to a large extent on how you view yourself. Leave preconceptions behind, open up all your senses and feel, try and do something new without passing judgement on your own or others' efforts to learn.

An aerial photograph of Ben Nevis in a clearing storm. The ice climber should be thankful for bad weather; without cold and storm there would be no ice to climb.

The Coldest Dance

'To the extent that a person loses his ability to concentrate, he himself becomes powerless to accomplish, to enjoy, and above all, to love.'
—Timothy Gallwey
Inner skiing

We are possessed of bicameral minds. Our left brains function analytically, our right brains are more creative. Western culture favours logic and reason over emotion and feeling. This tendency to live in our heads has divorced us somewhat from our senses. In ice climbing it is best when we re-inhabit our bodies. The centre or balance point from which all movement and all awareness originates is located in the lower abdomen. Functioning from the centre allows one to remain calm in the midst of external confusion. Through re-sensitized hands, feet, eyes, ears, and noses real information can go straight to this source of power, where a balanced response is automatic, by passing the mental screen of ideas, values, beliefs, and conditioning that can put a 90° bend in reality. Anyone who has turned a somersault knows his centre, and so, for that matter, does anyone who has 'rolled out of bed'. The exercises below are designed to help you to find your centre and get clearer input from your senses. This will allow you to get more out of ice climbing.

The mechanics are important, too, however, and here you'll find each technique broken down into its component parts. Movements are isolated for discussion as if they were complete in themselves. It's up to you as you read to visualize the flow. Imagine yourself in the pictures, but go further and make a movie out of the stills. Run through the sequences until they are smooth mentally, and when you actually try them on the ice they'll be much more comfortable.

When you do go to the ice, go with an experienced friend or an instructor, and after you've donned crampons, insist on taking

Even overhangs can sometimes be climbed utilizing rock climbing techniques such as the layback without resorting to hand tools.

a little time before you start to climb, and do these things:

1) Open up and start feeling, seeing, hearing, and smelling. Replace expectations with an awareness of the cold seeping up through your boots into the balls of your feet—wriggle your toes to warm them. In a similar fashion check out the rest of your senses and extremities.

2) Determine the true angle of the ice you've come to practise on. Take 2 ski poles or ice-axes of equal length and hold one vertically with the point on the slope and make a right angle pointing toward the slope by holding the other pole or axe horizontally at the top. If the horizontal pole or axe fully outstretched just touches the slope,

then it's 45°. If the appendage doesn't reach, then the angle is less than 45°, and if the horizontal member forms a T with the vertical brace when the point touches the slope, then the angle is greater than 45°. Study the detailed structure of the ice.

3) Isolate as many muscle groups as you can and alternately tense and relax each one, starting with your head and working down, concentrate especially on the calf muscles.

4) Breathe slowly and deeply until your breathing is smooth and relaxed.

5) Still breathing evenly do some stretching exercises.

6) Recall the last time you felt real confidence. Hold that feeling.

7) With both knees slightly bent and feet at shoulder width, take a

Alex Lowe on *Sky Pilot*, a grade 6 climb in the Canadian Rockies.

step forward, but just before transferring your weight, step back. Do this with both feet and feel your centre of gravity.

Now you're ready to climb.

Climbing Low Angle Ice

Depending on the quality of the ice, up to about 45° a natural progression is as follows:

On flat ground walk normally but with a stance that is slightly wider than usual to avoid crampons snagging the other foot or trouser leg. Hold the axe in one hand by the head like a cane with the pick pointing forward. On slight inclines splay your feet like a duck and follow a straight line. As the slope steepens make a diagonal ascent, and bend your ankles to allow all except the front crampon points to penetrate. Up to 35° or so it's most convenient to keep the axe in the uphill hand as a walking stick, but above that angle, with a reasonably long axe it's best to hold the axe diagonally across your body with the inside hand near the spike and the other hand on the head with the pick pointing forward. Whichever way you hold the axe, keep your feet flat to the slope with toes horizontal or pointing slightly downhill as it gets steeper. As you take each step, alternately crossing the feet over each other, you'll be moving from a position of balance (A) to one that's out-of-balance (B). Move your axe before making each step, not during the step. When it's time to change direction, make a step with the toes pointing uphill a bit as if you were stepping into the out-of-balance position (C). But now instead of crossing the trailing foot over the lead foot, simply splay the hind foot in the new direction. Now switch hands on the axe and you're ready to head off in the new direction (D). If because of very hard ice or a steeper angle you find it awkward to make the full direction change by splaying the feet, you will find it more comfortable to make an intermediate front point move with both crampons, between the two splayed-foot moves. Always while climbing ice, move

Climbing Low Angle Ice

(A)

(B)

(C)

(D)

Climbing Low Angle Ice. The arm gripping the head of the axe across the body, a hold known as piolet ramasse. (A) In balance. (B) Cross over. (C) Turn. (D) New direction.

only one point of contact at a time, and in a precise sequence. Avoid the tendency to rush in the beginning and make certain each move is correctly executed and feels secure.

Descending Low Angle Ice

Using an axe with a classically curved or slightly drooped pick, it's possible to descend securely facing out on slopes of up to 45°, once again depending on the type and quality of the ice. Squat down and plant the pick as low as possible. As you step down, a slight outward force on the shaft will lock the pick into the ice and allow you to make aggressive and positive steps

down. Sliding your hand down the shaft will allow you to to make two or three steps without replanting the tool. The axe can be quickly removed by popping the shaft back against the ice, grasping the head, and pulling out along the smooth top surface of the pick. Descent straight down the fall line in this manner is the most secure, with the toes splayed and the feet about shoulder width (E). However, a diagonal descent may also be accomplished when required, with toes pointing across the slope and ankles bent to allow penetration of all but the front points (F).

On very low angle terrain, simply

Descending Low Angle Ice

(E)
Using the shaft of the axe as a rail, a technique known as *piolet*

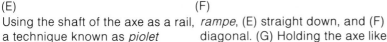

(F)
rampe, (E) straight down, and (F) diagonal. (G) Holding the axe like

(G)
a cane, in descent, known as *piolet canne*.

face the valley and hold the axe as a cane (G). Positive weight transfer with each step in all these techniques is an essential element of security. The type and quality of the ice, and the skill of the climber will determine at which angles and under what conditions these classical 'French' techniques may be employed.

Climbing Moderate to Steep Ice

On most types of ice above 45° flexing your ankles enough to get all the points in is quite difficult. Here it is more natural to front point. Depending on the type of ice and your own preference and skill, up to angles of about 60° or so one of two basic techniques will be found useful. (See p. 114 for photographs.) Either use pure front pointing combined with one or two tools held in the palm(s) (A), or alternate front pointing with one foot and using the other foot sideways, in conjunction with the axe placed every second step as an anchor (B). Generally, the pure front-point and palm technique is faster, while one-foot sideways with ice-axe anchor is more secure and reduces strain on the calves. In practice on a long climb you may find yourself switching between these methods.

Above 60° on most ice you'll find the technique named by the French *piolet traction* to be the swiftest and most secure (C). This involves front-pointing with both feet and use of a tool in each hand that is planted with each step for balance and use as a hand hold on which to pull. up. *Piolet traction* is often abused by beginners and even experienced climbers. On ice under angles of 50° it forces one to 'crawl' inelegantly and waste energy by virtue of being out of balance, so it is better to use this method only when it's truly required by the angle or condition of the ice.

When front-pointing, your heels should never be higher than your toes. Contrary to what might at first seem to be the case, standing straight-up in balance over the front points, with calves relaxed and heels low, you'll actually achieve a more secure stance than if you are tensely poised on tip-toe. Similarly, on any but the steepest ice (or on rotten ice where the surface needs clearing) repeated fierce kicking of the front points does little toward promoting security, while a gentle but carefully aimed and weighted kick preserves the integrity of the ice and promotes conservation of energy.

Traversing and Descending Steep Ice

Photographs (on p. 114.)
If a traverse must be made on steep ice, you'll get the most out of each tool placement if you place your tool diagonally as close to your body as possible, just above shoulder height (D). Then lean as far as possible in the direction of the traverse and place the other tool diagonally at a comfortable arm's reach. You can either take small sideways steps, or, if you're feeling confident, you may cross one foot in front of the other (E).

Descending steep ice is best done in a similar manner. Place one tool off to the side and as low down and close to your body as you find comfortable (F). A slight layaway off of this tool will allow you to take several steps down, at which time you are ready to place the other tool low down and diagonally off to the other side, ready to repeat the procedure (G). A more secure descent on thin or rotten ice is made by simply backing straight down with small steps and short placements of the tools at about head level or just above. Placing the tools off to the side allows a better swing and firmer placements, while going straight down gives greater control and allows both tools to remain planted while you step down.

Climbing Moderate to Steep Ice

(A) Front pointing with the feet and holding the axe like a cane but sticking the spike into the ice (*piolet panne*). (B) Flat foot technique (*pied a'plat*) using the axe as an anchor (*piolet ancre*). (C) Front pointings with the feet and using two axes, so that all extremities become tools (*piolet traction*). (D) and (E) Traverse. (F) Descent by laywaying. (G) Descent by placing the other tool.

Climbing Extreme Ice

As you approach the vertical there will come a time when you'll no longer be able to stand in balance over your front points. Although it's possible by brute strength to hold yourself vertically up against the ice, there is a far more efficient method, which I have termed The Monkey Hang.

Beginning at the bottom of a near-vertical, vertical, or gently overhanging section of ice, the correct sequence is as follows:

1) Plant both hand tools comfortably high and far enough apart so that there is no danger of fracturing out the ice between them. Now, hanging straight armed from the tools and letting the wrist loops do their intended job of holding the heel of the hand, so as to allow a light grip on the shafts, walk your feet up the ice until you're in a mild crouch (A). Since your buttocks are away from the ice in this position, your weight will be pushing your front-points into the ice rather than applying a sheer force.

2) Now look ahead and choose the exact spot where you'll make your next placement. Still hanging straight-armed, loosen the appropriate tool in preparation for easy removal and replacement (B).

3) With one tool merely hooked in its hole, keep your eyes glued to the exact spot you've chosen for replanting the loosened tool, and in one smooth sequence stand up, remove the loose tool, and positively replant it in the spot chosen (C).

4) In the instant of penetration you will ascertain that (hopefully) the placement is solid and trustworthy, and you will instantly weight the tool with a straight arm (D). This leaves you in position to replant the other tool and repeat the sequence, or to remove an ice screw or piton from your rack (E), and place protection for continuing the lead (F). This one-handed method of placing protection is the simplest and purest on steep ice, but a deep and narrow starting hole for the screw or piton must be clipped. This technique conserves energy and allows the climber to ascend long vertical stretches cleanly.

Climbing Extreme Ice

(A) Squat.

(B) Loosen.

(C) Swing.

(D) Hang.

(E) Grab screw.

(F) Place protection.

John Cunningham on a bulge of water ice on Ben Nevis.

Clearing a Bulge

Very often the most difficult moves on a pitch are at the top or where you must clear a bulge. The normal tendency is to reach far over and plant the tools as far back from the lip as possible. However, doing this, make it impossible to see your feet as you come over the bulge. What's more, you won't be able to keep your heels low enough as your tendons simply won't stretch that far, and you'll find your front points shearing out. It's better to plant your tools just over the bulge and climb and mantel on them until your feet are above the lip. Then replant your tools higher.

Belays and Protection

It would be difficult to attempt to describe all the possible ways of dealing with all the potential belay or protection situations you'll encounter as you climb ice. But a few basics will give you the tools to begin to safely acquire your own experience. Eventually there will be times when you will make a belay off one screw only or even just two tools, but you won't understand enough of the variables and forces involved to do this sort of thing safely in the beginning!

A Standard Belay Set-up

One of the safest and most logical belays, and one that I use at least 90 per cent of the time on technical grounds is arranged like this:

1) Chop a step wide enough to accept both feet. Stand in the step.

2) At a comfortable arm's reach above the ledge, on the side on which the second will follow the lead, place a drive-in or screw and clip into it with a clove-hitch. You may now give the off-belay call to your belayer. This anchor will become the first point of protection for the second as he or she leads through onto the next pitch.

3) Place a second anchor below the first and at the opposite side of the ledge. Also clip into this anchor with a clove hitch and adjust the slack as necessary.

4) Clip the rope that leads to the second through the higher anchor with a separate karabiner and run the rope around your waist or into a belay device in the normal fashion. Running the tail of the rope around your body and through a karabiner at your harness tie-in point will ensure control of the belay, and works smoothly even with an iced-up rope.

Placing a Piton or Screw

Whether you're placing a piton or screw, the angle at which it should be driven varies between perpendicular to the surface and a 45° upward angle. This angle is affected primarily by the type and quality of ice, but the angle of the slope and other factors are also important.

Generally speaking, on sound, cold, vertical water ice, you might drive a Snarg directly in at near right angles. On soft glacier ice, on the other hand, you'd want to chop a step and place a screw vertically down at the back of the step. On any ice, however, any poor surface material must be removed before placing a screw or piton. As the device is driven, more surface ice will

e disturbed; this, too, must be removed and the screw or piton
driven until the eye is flush against
good, unfractured ice.

Particularly while leading, a
deep, narrow starting hole will
make placement easier and keep
surface fracturing to a minimum.
Make the hole as deep as possible
while maintaining a diameter that
is slightly less than that of the
screw or piton. A properly placed
screw or piton will stand any force
to which you are likely to subject it
(see photo right).

Hanging to Place Protection

Although it feels like aid climbing
to me, a common and useful technique that frees both hands for
placing a screw on steep ice is to
clip into one or both hand tools
with a karabiner (or a skyhook)
attached to a cow's tail that is tied
to your harness. This technique
also is useful in certain emergency
situations such as when the pick of
one tool breaks, or a crampon goes
askew on a boot.

Aiding on Ice

Piolet traction, skill, and boldness
will eliminate the need for aiding ice
99.9 per cent of the time. Once in a
while, however, an overhanging
serac wall or some other horror will
tumble you into using aid. The
fastest way is to clip étriers into
small loops of cord that are tied
through the holes in the spikes of
your tools. Simply place the tool
and stand in the sling. Ice screws or
pitons may also be placed and progress made by climbing étriers
which have been clipped into
them, but this is much slower and
usually not necessary.

Climbing Mixed, Thin, and Rotten Ice

Ice climbing as defined in this book
includes climbing half on rock as
well as ice, snow-up rock climbed
with crampons and/or hand tools,
and the occasional move on dry
rock that may be necessary to con-
nect bits of ice.

Such 'mixed' climbing, as well
as climbing on thinly iced rock and
rotten ice, tends to defy efforts to

A properly placed Snarg.

analyse carefully the techniques required for success, since virtually
every move is different and in fact
you are inventing the best technique as you go. But this sort of
climbing provides the greatest
challenge and intrigue, and a few
generalizations can be made.

Use of rock holds with crampons
is often more secure using the front
points. Whether you've placed
front points or side points on a
hold, any movement of your foot
will tend to make the points 'walk'
off the hold. On very low-angle
smooth slabs, keeping all points in

contact with the rock will yield better results than efforts at edging or
front-pointing. On slightly steeper
slabs the opposite is true, and a
single point on a tiny crystal may
provide all the purchase you're
going to get.

Ice-axes or hammers with
steeply-drooped picks hook well
on rock holds, but if too steeply
drooped you'll have difficulty getting them into corner crooks and
'torquing' them there. A moderate
droop or curve with a sharp hook

Duncan Ferguson, master of thin ice, climbing in the Rocky Mountain National Park.

shafted axes. These tools give more options for placements, and more force can be generated when they are swung, to penetrate through surface layers. Rotten ice is ready to collapse, so beware.

Beyond Technique

The techniques described here will do the job for you. Yet mastering these methods need not be the final goal. With the skills discussed here as your basic repertoire, you can go further, modifying and expanding according to your own instincts. The creative ice climber is a sculptor, but rather than carving the ice to suit his vision, the climber's vision is fashioned in a beautiful adaptation to the medium.

Suggested Exercises

'Embrace Tiger, return to mountain'
—Tai-chi lesson

Good crampon technique comes as a result of confidence. Confidence is gained through experience. Slow movement allows time for fear. Fear interferes with pure experience. So, to maximize experience, short-circuit fear and foster good crampon technique, set up a top rope on low-angle ice. Then, with an alert belayer, *run*, as fast as you can, up and down the slope. Try this with an upright posture, and again from a light crouch with your back straight and knees bent, and yet again any way you want. Now consider what you've experienced.

When cramponning with one or both feet sideways, it is important that all side points be equally weighted and penetrate the ice to an equal depth. It's also important that the points of the trailing foot remain equally weighted as you step up. If you try to edge the upper points or if you allow your lower foot to torque in the ice as you move up, you may fracture the ice in a 'dinner plate', losing your purchase. To illustrate this effect, try it out on hard ice. Experiment

configuration at the very tip of the pick will allow the best torquing, slotting and camming in cracks and still hook well. The adze may also be used for these manoeuvres, which are often combined with layback technique to effect upward progress. In wider cracks, the axe shaft can be advantageously brought into use. Especially if it is rubber coated it may provide a good hold in a constriction or when

laybacking a wide vertical crack. Since the shaft is oval shaped, a securing camming effect is achieved in cracks only slightly wider than the narrow profile of the shaft by inserting the axe nearly to the head and levering sideways on the pick.

On thin ice always apply only a downward force on the shafts of the tools, and use several very light taps to chip small holds for the picks and front points. This ice must be treated gently.

Thick but rotten ice is often easier to deal with using two long-

Jeff Lowe on a thinly-iced overhang.

with different angles of ankle bend and slope steepness. Assuming you are cramponning flat-footed on a 30° slope, close your eyes and back off 15° in your ankle bend, then allow your points to drop down again into the proper position. Concentrate on the information travelling from the ice up through your crampons, boots, feet, ankles, and legs to your brain. Feel what's happening to your foothold as you torque the points. Be alert for this feeling as you climb, and seek to avoid it.

Think of your front points (all your crampon points, for that matter) as your claws, rooted deep in your feet. Obviously you'll not want to slam, wedge, and otherwise abuse yourself any more than necessary. Even on very hard ice a good climber will gently tap his front points in on ice up to 60° or 70°, preferring to stand upright in balance and with heels low to let gravity pull his points deeper into the ice. On even steeper ice finesse is still possible as slight wrinkles nearly always exist in the ice surface, and these can be used as small but adequate foot holds. Try top roping pitches of various angles using front points only and no hand tools. Search for footholds, and use as little force as possible while kicking in. Try 'pressing' and weighting your points on 50° ice, with no kicking. What happens when you point your toes down a little and try to kick the points in? Also on a top rope try a very steep pitch of waterfall ice using natural handholds only. Finally, climb a pitch of 60° to 70° ice blind-folded. As you climb quantify the degree of tension in your calves, fully tensed, 50%, 10% etc. At what level of tension do you feel you are getting the most security from your front points?

Breakthrough Experiences
We have all known those times when a skill we've been attempting very hard with no success to master, suddenly comes to us, often when we were not even trying. If we don't recognize such break-throughs immediately and allow

the lesson to sink in at the very moment it occurs, we are in danger of losing much of what has been gained. An example all first time ice climbers can appreciate is the first experience of a properly swung and planted ice-axe. The first several swings will most likely cause more shattering of the ice than penetration, with a wobbly hold resulting. But that first swing when forces are properly aligned through shoulders, arm, shaft, and pick, and the resulting thunk provide an unmistakable feeling of security and satisfaction. Such feelings, once recognized, are available for use later on, precipitating the correct sequence and execution of actions that will yield the desired results again and again.

Leaving the discussion of breakthrough experiences, but to further elaborate on the use of the axe and other hand tools, it is well to recognize exactly what was meant by the statement '... when forces are properly aligned...' Hold your ice-axe vertically at arm's length in front of you. Point the pick directly

forward. Put the pick against the ice (or a wall). Any force travelling from your shoulder, arm, and through the shaft and pick will be aligned on one plane and will therefore cause the greatest possible penetration of the pick. Now turn the pick 10° out of this alignment and it's easy to visualize the confusion of forces which results in shattered ice. But the shaft also must be properly oriented with the ice. Again holding your axe in front of you, allow the pick to rest on the surface of the ice (or the wall), and hold the shaft roughly parallel to the surface. It can be seen that all forces are now converging closely on the pick. They will converge exactly if you are using a tool with a pick curved to match the arc of the swing, but will be slightly conflicting on very steeply drooped picks.

Mike Weis in the Indian Peaks, Colorado. Many winter crag climbs require the use of picks stuck in frozen turf. Especially in Scotland this is prevalent on the buttress routes.

This accounts for the need for a downard flick of the wrist at the end of the swing when using Terrordactyls, for instance. Keep the pick against the ice and pull the spike away. Note the glancing blow that would result. Try this information out on the ice. Identify exactly the degree of misorientation with each swing that is less than perfect. Pick the spot you want to hit and keep your eyes on it as you swing (glasses or goggles are recommended to avoid injury from ice chips). Again pick the spot, and holding it in your mind, close your eyes and swing. Try concentrating on a spot a few centimetres under the surface of the ice that is where you want your pick to end up.

On a top rope, climb the same pitch twice using hand tools and crampons. The first time up, attack the ice with all the rage you can muster, and allow yourself to be lowered down. The second time climb with as much style and finesse as you have at your command, and climb back down. Note how you feel after each ascent. Climb the same pitch blindfolded.

Climb a pure rock pitch (an obscure and ugly one), and experiment with all your tools. Try various combinations of tools in different conditions.

Mentally climb a route you've just done, recreating it in as much detail as possible. Concentrate especially on the things you felt as you climbed. Try not to *watch* yourself do the climb, but *do* it in your head. Before starting up a new climb, imagine yourself in as much detail as possible making the ascent. After you've made the climb, was your imagination equal to the challenge, or are there gaps in your mental abilities? Work on those gaps—they are the only true limits of what is possible for you.

When you're out with climbers who are more skilled than you, turn off your analytical mind when you watch them climb. Let the performance flow directly into your subconscious. Like a young child don't reduce what you are seeing into words. Just let yourself learn by good example.

'*Above us, grey rock showed here and there, with only thin streaks of ice. Time for gloves off and a bit of the bare knuckle stuff, groping for rock holds in the powder and under verglass. It was painfully slow, with the hot aches to be endured, and it was an hour before I could traverse round a little corner back to where the gully re-asserted itself. Here, there was a cave of sorts and a bulging section beyond, where a chockstone barred the way. We had arrived at the famous crux pitch. A crack over on the right seemed to offer the best hope. One crampon scraped its way up this whilst the other scratched at a slab on the left as a mittened hand fumbled for rockholds. Sometimes a mittened handjam worked best, at other times a quick lob of the pick into a dribble of ice or a frozen sod. It was a style of climbing typical of the cliff's harder routes.*'

Paul Nunn describing
the Western Gully in
Cold Climbs, Diadem, London

Duncan Ferguson and Mark Wilford on Englishman's Route, Hallet's Peak, Colorado.

Advanced Considerations

In addition to the techniques and exercises discussed in the previous chapter, there are a number of other considerations that may aid the aspirant ice climber to progress to higher levels of safety, performance, and enjoyment. Once the basic skills of ice climbing have been acquired specialized physical and mental training, and new perspectives on the choice and use of equipment will shorten your apprenticeship and allow you more quickly to begin to lead those routes that you desire.

Special Training
It has often been said that climbing itself is the best training for climbing. But this is not always true. Sometimes the very practice of climbing itself gets in the way of advancement. For instance, it has been stressed here that one of the goals of an ice climber should be to achieve nearly effortless upward movement. Ironically, however, if you come too close to realizing this goal, your future progress may stagnate due to lack of strength. On the other hand, if you rely on muscle alone, but climb enough, you may still be able to get up most hard, strenuous routes, but remain unprepared for delicate climbs.

Co-ordination between eye and hand or foot and tool is enhanced by the practice of other sports and activities that utilize tools in their play. Soccer, cricket, baseball, and tennis, for example, all involve the dynamic manipulation of a tool through space and time with either hands or feet. Once again, skiing is the best parallel sport for ice climbing, as it involves both hands *and* feet in precise, simultaneous, balanced movements, co-ordinated through sight and feel. Rough carpentry definitely helps in learning to swing tools accurately and with subtle power, while cabinet making and fine woodworking are excellent introductions to the subtle qualities of well-designed tools, and their interface with the medium that is being worked.

Modern and classical dance, the martial arts, and certain eastern practices, especially Tai-chi, which is directly concerned with centring and movement, can bring you in closer touch with your body and improve its quality of motion. Meditation or self-hypnosis may be an aid in concentration and preparing the mind to face new problems, while stretching or hatha yoga will make you more supple and teach you better breathing. All of the foregoing are helpful in increasing strength, but gymnastics and weight training are best for

Alex Lowe on Hot Doggies, a class 7 Colorado climb.

developing climbing muscles, and running, biking, or other aerobic exercise is required for endurance.

In short, imbued with the right spirit, there are numerous opportunities to 'train' for ice climbing even if you live a thousand kilometres from the nearest frozen water! This explains why some

David Breashears high bouldering on Class 7 ground, equivalent to 5.11 or 6a rock.

do little lead climbing but are satisfied with very short technical problems.

Friendly competition among a small group of climbers will sometimes yield surprising results as each individual's imagination, creativity, strength, and motivation is gently pushed, prodded, and inspired by others. Any kind of 'score-keeping' attitude among the group is usually counter-productive for all except the 'top dog' who makes the hardest moves of the day and who is in a position to reap temporary ego benefits at the others' expense. It is better when everyone is let in on the secret of just how a move was done – what it felt like to accomplish it – not in the sense of good/bad or easy/hard, but more along these lines: 'As I was laybacking around the lip I found that my left crampon held better when I placed it out onto the thin ice and just sort of shifted my weight onto it without kicking it in; I just sort of pushed and stood up; it felt like the points melted their way in.'

Although ice bouldering is relatively less dangerous than lead climbing on ice, it should be remembered that in even a very short fall crampon points can snag in the ice or your own leg, snapping an ankle or tearing a calf muscle. A top rope reduces the chance of such occurrences. The constant use of a top rope may also lessen the degree of concentration applied to each move, and the climber consequently learns more slowly, so ice bouldering definitely has a place.

Food
Although I'm not an expert nutritionist, it does seem safe to make a couple of observations regarding diet for the ice climber:

1) Although carbohydrates provide the best source of energy for most sports activity, the special demands of ice climbing, i.e. cold and long-term output of effort, would seem to indicate greater proportions of protein and fat.

2) Caffeine is a vaso-constrictor, which cuts off blood to extremities. Therefore, tea and coffee cannot be

The purpose of bouldering, on ice as well as rock, is to push your strength and technique as far as it will go, thus expanding your limits and knowledge.

people can come off an extended lay-off and climb better than others who climb every day.

Bouldering on Ice
Ice bouldering is practised unroped at the base of frozen waterfalls or on glacial séracs in those areas where a fall poses no threat or serious injury. The reasons for ice bouldering are the same as those for bouldering on rock. Here it is possible to really push your technical ability without the distractions of exposure and high risk. New, very specialized techniques can be worked out. Strengths to deal with specific problems can be developed, and on ice in particular, the limitations, potential, and strength of each tool, and the ice itself, can be expanded upon, realized, and discovered in a relatively safe manner. And although they are extremely rare, there are even a few ice bouldering specialists, who

recommended, since they increase the likelihood of cold injury.

Obviously there are few climbers who will practise all that has been preached here, but the point to be made is that anyone's climbing can benefit both from a holistic approach to physical and mental balance, as well as a specific programme of strength, endurance, and agility training, and that this training can be varied and enjoyable.

Plateaus

Sooner or later every climber's progression seems to halt, no matter how ardently improvement is sought. The first thing to remember is that this is natural, and that one of the causes for the plateau you've reached may very well be that you're trying too hard. These cycles in performance may be due to a stagnation in our acceptance of the experience; our senses sometimes become dulled by what we think we know about our oft-repeated activity. This is the time to back off, get loose, and remember it's all a game and should be *fun*.

Planning

The common idea of planning is to draw up lists of equipment, food, and so forth in the hopes that some important item or detail will not be overlooked. This is great as far as it goes, but such paperwork should be supplemented (it can eventually be almost entirely replaced) by what I call 'long-range imaging' or taking the skills of visualization you've learned to use in dealing with technical problems, and applying them to an entire climb, trip, or even a three-month expedition. It's simple, really. You just do the climb, imagine the trip, or run the expedition in your head a few times, letting all the possible scenarios run their course. Actually it's only controlled daydreaming, but it's a powerful and effective tool.

Packing Light and Right

Excess weight in the pack or on the body is the killer of the aspirations of many over-prepared climbers.

You'll never move fast if you go by the book (even this book!) and always carry the famous 'ten essentials', which in any case seem to vary from one authority to the next. For a given climb there may in fact be only three essentials: an axe, crampons, and your skill. Headlamps, waterbottles, helmets, harnesses, extra clothes, first aid kit, avalanche beepers, stoves, sleeping bags, tents, spare matches, toilet paper, great literature, jumars, ladders, and the kitchen sink all have their place in the scheme of things, but if you put them all in your pack each time you go, you won't be going far, believe me, I've tried it more than once. Be bold, leave something behind, see if you miss it.

Moving Fast and Conserving Energy

You don't necessarily move fast in the mountains by running. A thoughtful choice of route and careful timing, along with a light pack and good pacing, will save $\frac{1}{2}$ hour when you don't have to backtrack through the icefall to find a way out of the cul-de-sac you've blindly wandered into; cut the time of ascending a slope in the late morning slush by three-quarters simply by being there two hours earlier; save energy, effort, *and* time by not having your home on your back; and eliminate the need for long rests to 'catch your breath' which you never would have lost if you'd adopted the right pace from the beginning.

Another thing to consider is that when it comes to equipment, light is not always right. For instance, I have found it less tiring to use a pair of 'old fashioned' heavy leather boots for mountain routes simply because the flexible leather ankle is not constantly trying to throw me off balance when I step up onto a boulder, or forcing me to front-point on long slopes of moderate ice, as do modern plastic boots. In the same way, a pair of Footfangs, although heavier than other rigid crampons, are also more rigid, allowing use with lighter boots and effectively ex-

tending the 'platform effect' farther back under the foot on terrain of all angles, thereby conserving energy and placing less strain on the calf muscles. Remember, total effort expended is equal to the weight of equipment multiplied by the efficiency of that equipment as utilized by the skill of the climber.

Staying Warm

Staying warm while ice climbing is often quite easy. The climbing itself is strenuous enough, so you'll probably err on the side of being overdressed while you're moving. In very cold weather it's especially important not to overheat and drench your clothes in sweat, which will cause an instant chill when you stop to belay or rest. Learn to anticipate the exact clothing you'll need to wear and adjust things accordingly *before* committing to a pitch. If the climbing is so difficult that you're leading without a pack, a light parka in a stuff sack can be clipped to your harness, ready to put on at the end of the lead, *before* you start to cool down. When you feel your hands or feet getting too cold, stop *now* and warm them up. Vigorous swinging in a wide arc is the quickest way to force warm blood to the extremities. Keep a constant bit of awareness focussed on the temperature of all extremities including the exposed and delicate nose, cheeks, ears and chin—these are often frostbitten without the victim even being aware of a problem. Protect your core temperature with an adequate intake of the right foods and liquids, and try not to exhaust yourself. Take pride in never succumbing to cold injuries, a more subtle accomplishment than climbing itself, but equally satisfying, and more difficult in the long run.

Intuitive Avoidance of Danger

Mountain hazards can be avoided by two methods. The first is the scientific, or 'text book' approach that monitors conditions through the use of thermometers, hydrometers, barometers, wind meters, inclinometers, snow pits, shear

David Breashears and Jeff Lowe using covered single-point hammocks on the four bivouacs on the North Face of Kwangde, a grade VII climb.

tests, and other carefully plotted observations. This approach is very appropriate and should be carefully studied and adapted by the ice climber. But the scientific approach to avoiding hazards should be viewed as an adjunct to, rather than a replacement for, an intuitive rapport with the mountain environment. No matter what your instruments and rational observations say, if you have a deep-seated feeling that conditions just aren't right, then don't go on. At times you'll find you've misinterpreted your feelings and turned back for the wrong reasons, but eventually you'll learn to separate those unfounded feelings of dread from the genuine subconscious, computer-like accumulation and evaluation of all the data bombarding your senses from all angles and perspectives.

Going Solo

Alone on ice is a wonderful place to be. At times, soloing exposes the climber to greater danger, but very often the experienced person is safer on his own. The soloist leaves behind doubt, fear, and competitive urges, and strikes out on a journey of self-discovery, vulnerable to new insight and experience. Every move takes on added significance as in Willy Unsoeld's words you are 'walking the edge of imminent dissolution'. Without question the most dangerous terrain for a single climber is traversing snow-covered glaciers with hidden crevasses. Most people avoid this situation, which leaves a little too much to chance. On the other hand the solo climber's speed can turn many rockfall-and-avalanche-prone alpine routes into reasonable ventures. Even the steepest frozen waterfalls can be safely ascended by the experienced soloist who treats each axe placement as a portable belay, never making a move until he 'knows' the placement is absolutely reliable.

Rating Ice Climbs

Many climbers feel that rating ice climbs is an undesirable and even futile activity, given that a large part of the beauty of ice climbing lies in its appeal to the adventurous spirit, and that conditions, and therefore exact difficulties, vary constantly. But on well-known climbs the adventure of discovery is already gone, and after years of climbing all over the world, repeat-ing climbs in the same and different seasons, I have found that rating a climb for the conditions under which it is normally climbed can provide a very good guideline for interested parties as to what can be expected. This is especially useful for climbers with limited time who are travelling to a new area and who want to do climbs commensurate with their abilities.

In 1979 I introduced a rating system for ice climbing which has been widely adopted in America, and which is designed such that it can be used to describe climbs throughout the world. Basically this system uses a grading that was developed to describe the overall difficulties of rock climbs in Yosemite Valley. Length, continuity, most difficult pitch, seriousness, and commitment are all taken into account in a scale of Roman numerals I to VI, with most grade VI's requiring two or more days and 680 metres or more of hard climbing, although today's best climbers can often complete such routes in one day. To this six-grade scale I have added a seventh which is necessary to describe the biggest and hardest Himalayan alpine style climbs with their greater size, altitude, and commitment.

In addition to the overall grade, there is another useful rating that describes the hardest technical section of the route, thus helping to differentiate between long climbs of moderate difficulty and short climbs of great technical challenge that may merit the same overall grade.

For the technical rating it is convenient to start with the Scottish grades of 1 to 6, which were originally intended only to convey a sense of overall difficulties similar to the Yosemite rating, but for ice climbs. Over the years, however, the Scottish system has sometimes been misused to describe individual move and pitch difficulties. It is this bastardized use that I have found useful in describing the technical problems that one may expect on a given climb under 'average' conditions. Once again, a seventh grade has been added to the technical scale to accommodate today's hardest mixed climbs. There is a rough comparison of rock and ice technical grades on p. 13. It is also useful to designate the type of ice to be found on a climb by the capital letters AI or WI preceding the technical grade, indicating permanent Alpine Ice, or seasonal Winter Ice.

A COMPARISON OF ICE CLIMBS AROUND THE WORLD

Overall Grade	N.A.	Scotland	Alps	N.Z.	Cordillera Blanca	Himalaya
I	Standard Rt. Frankenstein Cliff, N H	Comb Gully, Ben Nevis				Kalar Patar
II	Skyladder, Mt. Andromeda	Green Gully, Ben Nevis	Standard Rt., Mt. Blanc du Tacul		Standard Rt. on Pisco	
III	Repentence, Cathedral Ledge	Point Five Gully, Ben Nevis	Gervasutti Couloir, Mt. Blanc du Tacul	Standard Rt., Mt. Cook	S. Face Artesonraju	Island Peak Standard Rt
IV	Black Ice Couloir, Grand Teton	Orion Face Direct, Ben Nevis	N. Face, Triolet	Balfour Face, Mt. Tasman	S. Face, Ochshapalca	Standard Rt Lobuje Peak
V	Grand Central Couloir, Mt. Kitchener	Vertigo Wall, Cairngorms	N. Face, Le Droit	Hardest Rtes, S. Face of Hicks	Bouchard Rt, Chacraraju	
VI	Logan/Stump Emperor Face, Mt. Robson		1966 Eiger Direct		S.W. Spur Taulliraju	S. Face Ama Dablam
VII						Hungo Face, Kwangde

Technical Grade	N.A.	Scotland	Alps	N.Z.	Cordillera Blanca	Himalaya
1	Muir Rt, Mt. Ranier	#3 Gully, Ben Nevis	Standard Rt, Mt. Blanc du Tacul		Standard Rt. on Pisco	
2	Skyladder, Mt. Andromeda	#2 Gully, Ben Nevis	Gervasutti Couloir, Mt. Blanc du Tacul		S. Face, Artesonraju	Island Peak
3	Black Ice Couloir, Grand Teton	Comb Gully, Ben Nevis	N. Face, Triolet	Caroline Face, Mt. Cook	S.W. Face, Pyramid de Garcilaso	Lobuje Peak
4	Original Rt. Glenwood Icefall	Green Gully, Ben Nevis	Gabbarrou/ Albinoni, Mt. Blanc du Tacul			
5	Repentence, Cathedral Ledge	Point Five Gully & Orion Face Direct	Super Couloir, Mt. Blanc du Tacul	Balfour Face Mt. Tasman	S. Face Chacraraju	S. Face Ama Dablam
6	Bridalveil Falls, Colorado	Citadel/ Sticil Face, Shelter Stone	Voie de l'Overdose, Gavarnie	Sorenson/ Cradock, S. Face Hicks	S. Face, Trapecio	Hungo Face Kwangde
7	Hot Doggies, Rocky Mtn. Nat'l Park	The Needle, Shelter Stone				

The Ice Climber's World

Good ice can be found around the world, often in the most unlikely places. In a cold year there is excellent and challenging though often short-lived ice climbing in a number of unexpected places, for example in Georgia, USA, a state more normally associated with warm southern charm than icy cliffs. The Caucasus Mountains in Russia contain huge mixed routes and pure ice climbs. Circling the globe, the high mountains of equatorial Africa, South America, and New Guinea contain very fine ice. As I've already pointed out, the Himalayas, the greatest range on earth, offer the greatest ice climbs, though at either Pole the mountains are literally buried in glacier ice. There is endless scope for discovery for anyone committing the time, energy and money to research and travel to these places.

In this overview of world ice, I'll touch only lightly on these out-of-the-mainstream or very exotic locations, and deal primarily with the popular, easily accessible, and reasonably economical areas. What general kinds of ice are to be found in a given area? What is the scope and how do the climbs from different areas compare?

The North Face of Mount. Hunter, Alaska, which has many fine ice and snow routes at all levels of difficulty.

The Western Hemisphere

Alaska

Alaska has immense potential for both alpine type and frozen waterfall climbing. Most of the ice climbing that has been done in the high mountains of the state has occurred in the Alaska Range which contains Mount McKinley otherwise known as Denali, North America's highest peak. Denali is like an oversized version of Mont Blanc, a range unto itself, replete with its own versions of the Peuterey Ridge, Brenva Face, and Chamonix Aiguilles. Any climb on Denali is a high-altitude expedition or super-alpine problem. The lower surrounding peaks, however, offer wonderful high-calibre routes from 680–1,670 m high on the many facets of Mount Hunter, Mount Huntington, the Rooster Comb, and others. The Alaska Range, Denali in particular, has some of the worst weather in the world, and approach is either several days by foot, dog-sled, or ski; or half hour by ski-plane from the ramshackle village of Talkeetna, reachable by car or train from Anchorage.

In winter there is very accessible frozen waterfall climbing around Valdez. Since 1975 local and visiting climbers have established nearly one hundred excellent routes of all grades, from low-angle one-pitch introductory climbs, to two hundred metre ascents of grade IV, WI5 and 6, such as Keystone Green Steps, which is only five minutes from the main highway. In December and January the days are very cold and extremely short (five hours of daylight at the turn of the year!). Therefore, the best months for climbing are February and March.

Canada

The entire western half of Canada contains range after range of wilderness peaks, starting with the great massifs of Mount Logan and Mount St. Elias in the north, with their Denali-like climbing and scale, and extending south the the Coast range and Mount Wadding-

Lou Dawson on the last pitch of Ames Fall, one of the best Colorado ice climbs.

ton, 160 km north of Vancouver. All of these remote ranges are heavily glaciated and offer major wilderness ice adventures to those willing to make the discovery on their own. In the winter months the mountains of Vancouver Island provide easier-to-get-to but still very exciting and little-known Scottish-type climbing on the rimed-up 1,000 m cliffs of Mount Colonel Foster and other peaks.

North America's major ice climbing centre is the Canadian Rockies between Banff and Jasper. Here are found the Canadian equivalents of the Eiger or Matterhorn, with correspondingly more problematic faces and ridges. In summer and autumn there are innumerable couloir, gully, and face climbs of hard alpine ice. The Columbia Icefields Campground in particular, on the highway about half-way between Banff and Jasper, is adjacent to a number of excellent ice routes, from the relatively mild north faces of

Alex Lowe on Gimme Shelter,
Canadian Rockies.

Athabasca and Andromeda, to the
great routes of Slipstream and the
Grand Central Couloir. In the har-
sher conditions of winter the climbs
around the Icefields take on added
dimensions of difficulty and seriousness. Large frozen waterfalls
form below the high peaks and are
often climbable from late
November through March.

Although winter temperatures
in the northern Rockies can be very
low (40–50 degrees below zero at
times), and avalanche hazard is
often extremely high, some of the
world's best frozen waterfall
climbing is found in these Canadian locales. The climber may develop his or her skills on routes
such as Cascade Falls and
Professor's Gully, then progress
through Takkakkaw Falls or Bour-
geau Left, and move on to the likes
of the Terminator on Mount
Rundle, or Gimme Shelter on
Mount Quadra, both of which are
among the hardest frozen waterfalls of their length yet accomplished. Hundreds of climbs have
been made of all grades and the
most amazing chunks of ice on the
big faces are yet to be explored.

The USA below Canada

The north eastern USA is well
known for the wide variety of winter ice to be found on such crags
as Cathedral Ledge in North
Conway, New Hampshire, which
harbours dozens of ice climbs
including the famous four-pitch
Repentence, and its harder neigh-
bour, Remission. Not far away,
Frankenstein Cliff gives routes in
all grades up to 100 m, while 200 m

climbs on Cannon Mountain, such as the Black Dike and Fafnir, have a more serious air, and the gullies in Huntington Ravine, (the birthplace of winter ice climbing in the US in the 1920s) are exposed to the renowned Mount Washington winds, which have been measured at over 320 km per hour!

Lake Willowby in Vermont has a wide 130 m high cliff that sports a number of hard climbs, including the Promenade, a climb on good New England ice similar in length and difficulty to Colorado's Bridalveil Falls. Katahdin in Maine gives some of the hardest, longest, and most alpine-like climbing in the region on the walls of its several steep 'Basins' that lead to the 1,700 m summit. However, the approach is long (24 km) and the weather bad, and Katahdin is not as popular as some other areas. The most impressive north eastern ice is not found in New England at all, but north of the border in the Canadian province of Quebec. Deep in the Malbaie Valley are found 330 m waterfall climbs such as L'Equerre and La Pomme d'Or.

There is good summer gully

Camp in the Cordillera Huayhuash.

climbing in the mountains of Wyoming and Montana, climbs in the Tetons such as the Black Ice Couloir, the most famous. The Big Horns and Wind River Range hide some fine climbs for the person not afraid to explore with no certainty of finding anything. Both states also have very good but little publicized winter waterfall climbing.

Colorado and Utah are essentially void of alpine ice, but in winter much frozen waterfall climbing has been done. Some of the best concentrations of climbs are to be found above a highway in Provo Canyon, Utah, with more than a dozen fine lines up to 260 m, and in the Ouray/Silverton/Telluride area in the San Juan Mountains of southwestern Colorado. This latter area includes Bridalveil Falls and Ames Falls, the two best climbs in the state, each having a distinct character. Rocky Mountain National Park, not far from Denver and Boulder, has relatively little ice to offer the many climbers who live in the area, but what there is has been fully exploited, and the term 'mixed climbing' has been extended to include radical techniques on some short but very hard iced-up rocks.

The Sierra Nevada mountains of California are the home of some of the most enjoyable Autumn gullies in the country. The V-Notch, the U-Notch, and the Mendel Couloir are justly popular climbs that are reached by pleasant hikes through John Muir's 'Range of Light'. Further north in Washington are Mount Rainier and the Cascade Mountains. Rainier has been the training ground for generations of Pacific north west expedition climbers, the many glaciers on its flanks closely simulating conditions in the greater ranges. On the other hand, the Cascade mountains, though still glaciated, are considerably steeper than Rainier and contain some good moderate alpine-type routes such as the north faces of Mount Maude, and Mount Redoubt.

South America
Between the southern Rocky Mountains and the beginning of the Andes in Columbia, there is not much for the ice climber, with the exception of the high volcanoes near Mexico City. But, from Columbia to Patagonia, the entire Andean chain is icy in its higher elevations. Peru's Cordillera Blanca is the most popular and accessible of the areas. Routes of all grades, on ice that varies from porridge to good water-ice, can be found at altitudes between 6,000 m–7,340 m. Huaraz, the

main jumping-off point for the Blanca, is a Third World, Spanish speaking Chamonix in June and July, the best climbing months. Even farther south, the Vinson Massif in Antarctica is 5,340 m high with 2,000 m faces.

Great Britain
The Scottish winter hills are the best training ground imaginable for the climber who eventually plans to go to the Alps, Andes, or Himalayas; they are a rewarding field of endeavour in their own right. Spending a day on one of the fine gully or buttress routes of Ben Nevis, occasionally being engulfed in spindrift or buffeted by the storm while grappling with a bulge of snow-ice or trying to delicately front-point up a rock slab that is thinly veneered in verglas, the feeling you get is of bigger, more remote and serious mountains. In the evening, at the pub in Fort William, the day's lessons on the hill are rehashed over a pint, and plans for even greater things on the morrow are made. There is no place in the world more conducive to absorbing the essence of the ice experience than Scotland, with its long history, adventurous traditions, resident masters, and beautifully harsh winter weather.

The huge variety of Scottish winter ice climbing includes the traverse of the Cuillin Ridge on the Isle of Skye, the big walls in remote corries of the Northern Highlands, and the superb climbs of Craig Maigheadh, such as Smith's Gully, South Post, and North Post. Among other gems, the Cairngorms boast Shelter Stone Crag, looking like a mini Dru from below and giving hard 330 m mixed climbs like Sticil Face, Citadel, and Needle. But beware the Cairngorm blizzards; they've proved lethal for several parties. Lochnagar on the east side of Scotland gives climbs from grade 1 to 5 in gullies and buttresses, and it harbours the famous Chimney of Parallel.

If Scotland has more than its share of fantastic winter climbing, in a good season England can

lay claim to a smaller number of equally fine itineraries in the Lake District on Scafell Crag and others, and in North Wales on Craig yr Ysfa, Snowdon, Craig y Rhaeadr, The Black Ladders, Cwm Idwal, Lliwedd, and Clogwyn du'r Arddu. The Black Cleft, Central Gully, Devil's Appendix, Western Gully, and the Somme are names attached to climbs of excellent character. Furthermore, as Rob Collister said, 'The essence of Welsh winter climbing is glinting frozen water against a backdrop of blue sky; axes wobbling in improbable pockets on booming icicles ... It's too bad winter here is so short and inconsistent!'

The Irish winter scene, by comparison to Scotland, Wales, and the Lakes, is very limited. However, there are routes up to grade 4, mainly on fleetingly frozen waterfalls. The Mourne Mountains provide some of the most consistent conditions, along with the Wicklow Hills.

The Alps and Norway
It is hard to say enough here about the Alps, since hundreds of books have been written with the Alps as their subject, so what follows is a sample of what is available.

The Mont Blanc Massif is perhaps the finest mountaineering playground on the planet. Ice climbs of all types and levels of difficulty are available here, usually not over-far from a téléphérique station or hut. Year-round it's possible to ascend elegant snow arêtes or climb classic snow and ice faces. During winter, or in cold spring and fall conditions, great frozen 'cascades' form on the Brouillard and Frêney Faces; in cold summers, the north east Couloir of the Dru, and the Super Couloir on Mont Blanc du Tacul are modern grade 5 classics.

On the limestone peaks of the Eastern Alps, there is scope for any type of ice climbing, from serious classic 'Welzenbach' north faces, such as the Fiescherwand, to 400 m frozen waterfalls in Salzburg and near Vienna. Perhaps the densest concentration of high standard, high quality frozen waterfalls in Europe is found in the Cirque de Gavarnie, in the Pyrenees, which has a dozen routes from 160 m to Dominique Julien's 460 m Voie de L'Overdose. But good waterfalls are found throughout the Alps and, in recent years, the valleys below the peaks in Italy, as well as France, Austria, and Germany, have seen intense development.

Although Norway has no alpine ice, it does have some of the best frozen waterfall climbing in the world. The most famous of these 'fossen' are the Vettifossen and Mardalsfossen, in the Romsdal region.

Local and visiting climbers continue to discover wonderful new frozen secrets each season, and a trip to Norway must rank high on the list of priorities for waterfall ice specialists. Norway also has some of the longest, best, and hardest Scottish-type winter climbs yet done. For instance, the 2,000 m East Pillar of the Trollwall provides a multi-day route at a technical standard that must be similar to the Orion Face on Ben Nevis.

New Zealand

Outside of the Himalayas, which we'll leave to Al Rouse to describe in the Expeditions section, and the mountains of the Iron Curtain, such as the Caucasus, which have a long history of ice climbing, the major remaining ice climbing location is New Zealand. As Mont Blanc is to the Alps, and Denali is to Alaska, Mount Cook is to New Zealand.

Mount Cook itself presents classic snow ridges, ice arêtes, ice faces and mixed climbs. Extensively glaciated, the mountain has provided generations of climbers with alpine-type climbs and excellent experience for the greater ranges. On the surrounding lower peaks (3,300 m) of Mount Tasman and Mount Hicks, routes of a very high standard are available, some of the best being the Balfour Face, the Yankee/Kiwi Couloir, and Heaven's Door—all first-rate mixed climbs of about 660 m. In the Haast Range, the Southern Face of Mount Aspiring is one of the great modern ice climbs.

The Darren Mountains are the site of some of the best frozen waterfall climbing in New Zealand. In recent antipodean winters, climbs have been made on some startling ice pillars.

Other areas

In addition, there are a number of good routes on Africa's Mount Kenya, put up over the last twenty years by a small group of local and visiting climbers. The Koreans and Japanese, have begun to develop waterfall climbing in their mountains through they've been doing snowy winter climbs for years. When you stop to think that more ice climbing areas have been left out of this summary than have been included, it might better have been titled 'The World Of Ice'! The adventure is out there waiting for you, whether on your home ground, 100 m icebergs frozen in the Arctic Sea, or the fantastic bulges of rime-ice on Patagonia's Cerro Torre.

The two charts on p. 127 give a rough idea of how well-known climbs from different areas compare. This is a personal view, not meant to be the only word, but rather to help the travelling climber to understand what is in store at a new area and is compiled either from climbs I know personally, or with the aid of close friends who have done them.

The Balfour Face of Mt. Tasman.

Alpine Climbing

From the birth of climbing as a sport, the Alps have been the crucible of endeavour and inspiration of generations of men and women. The attraction of climbing in them, or in other mountains of similar difficulty, is that technical expertise and the rational calculation of goals are never enough to be sure of success. A host of unpredictable factors—the weather, danger of avalanches, sudden crevasses opening up, unplanned bivouacs—all demand an enthusiasm and commitment which make alpine climbing a stimulating and extremely rewarding sport.

The Aiguille Verte and Les Drus in winter.

Origins of Alpinism

Alpinism is a modern invention, a child of the nineteenth century, when it became respectable among gentlemen of the professional middle-classes (particularly from Britain) as an escape from court-room, office or vicarage. In a world rapidly changing under the pressures of industrialization, the mountains of Europe offered a theatre of recreation and the bonus of heroic endeavour. Leading mountaineers achieved a status akin to that of missionaries or explorers in Africa. The greater the hardships, the better the tales they brought back, and the better therefore the sale of books or reception of magic lantern lectures. From the late 1850s there was a rash of first ascents of the major alpine peaks, punctuated by horrific accidents which could not fail to attract public attention and bemused concern.

It was not that climbing moun-tains was in itself new—countless ascents of peaks and passes had taken place as far back as the Middle Ages, despite the hostility of the Church, which considered the activity heretical. In 1336 for example, Francesco and Gerardo Petrarch ascended Mont Ventoux (1,912 m), and in 1492 Charles VIII of France overcame clerical hostility by sending his chamber-laine Antoine de Ville to climb Mont Aiguille (2,068 m) for him, using ladders and siege machinery. Throughout history, the Alps have been home to their people, to hunters and farmers, drovers and even smugglers, who have ranged freely at unrecorded heights, but it can fairly be said that most early alpine ascents were for practical purposes or scientific curiosity. Alpinism was born when people began climbing mountains for pleasure, and this was superimposed upon the prevailing alpine way of life.

In the sixteenth century a naturalist from Zurich, Conrad Gesner, climbed several alpine peaks, both to explore them and it seems for exercise and enjoyment, but he may well have been unique in this. During the eighteenth century climbing expanded considerably. The Delucs of Geneva ascended the Brévent (2,527 m) in 1754 and Buet (3,110 m) in 1770, setting precedents for the future, but scientific exploration was the predominant motive for climbs of the mid-eighteenth century: doctors, botanists, geographers and even clerics rushed to test their theories on alpine peaks. The Scot, Thomas Blaikie, attempted Mont Blanc with Michel Gabriel Paccard in 1775, reaching a point below the summit

An ascent of the Mer de Glace on Mont Blanc in 1886.

via the Aiguille de Goûter.

In 1779 the Abbé Murith, canon of Great St Bernard, climbed Velan (3,734m), and in 1788 J M Clement of Val d'Illiez ascended the Dents du Midi. Elsewhere Willnotzer reached the summit of Triglav (2,864m) in the Julian Alps in 1778, and Robert Townson ascended Lomnica (2,635m) in the Tatra in 1793. By this time the Alps had been discovered by artists and poets of the Romantic School, and tourism, too, was beginning to flourish.

The great alpinistic breakthrough came on 8 August 1786 when Michel Gabriel Paccard and the porter Jacques Balmat made the first successful ascent of Mont Blanc, a climb unlinked to scientific discovery and motivated by the spirit of adventure which is today the major element of the sport. Mountaineering gradually increased in popularity, so that by 1850 Mont Blanc had attracted fifty different parties complete with guides and porters. Count Franz von Salm sponsored and organized mass ascents of the Gross Glockner in 1799 and 1800, and Valentin Stanig reached the summit of the Watzmann at the same time. In 1804 Josef Pichler and two companions from the Zillertal climbed the Ortler, and in 1811 Johann Rudolf Meyer and Hieronymus Meyer of Aarau the Jungfrau. While some climbers were chamois or crystal hunters, and other tough and knowledgeable local men were drawn in to mountaineering as porters or guides for the growing numbers of visitors, most first ascents before 1850 were made by town-dwelling Continentals. By contrast, during the so-called 'Golden Age of Alpinism' between 1854 and 1872 thirty-one of the thirty-nine major peaks climbed were conquered by British mountaineers and their, usually Swiss, guides.

One of these pioneers, Leslie Stephen, wrote of this prolific era of mountain achievements and literature: 'We rushed with delight into that enchanted land, climbed peaks and passes, made proselytes in every direction to the new creed; and ended, alas, by rubbing off the bloom of early romance....'

Mountaineering became an adventure holiday for enterprising nineteenth-century gentlemen, who flooded to the hills and mountains of Europe with their wealth and leisure time, disturbing and enriching the inhabitants' meagre existence, before returning home to lecture and write about their experiences. The ethics of the amateur as opposed to the professional flourished in Britain through the English Alpine Club, as gentleman climbers treated professionals with at best embarassed ambivalence and at worst outright hostility. They disliked the vulgarity, as they saw it, of such lecturers and self-publicists as Albert Smith and Edward Whymper. The predominant role of the British in the 'Golden Age' marked the practice of climbing in the Alps with their values, which perhaps fitted middle class Swiss beliefs too, and tended to undervalue the creative role of the mountain guides from upland villages at the time. Yet Michel Croz led the most difficult sections of the Hörnli Ridge on the first ascent of the Matterhorn in

Mrs Aubrey Le Blond in her face mask developed for glacier travel, photographed on Durmaalstüd.

July 1865, and only died when a less competent climber Hadow lost his footing on easy ground during the descent, pulling Croz behind him. Whilst many clients were great climbers, so too were numerous local guides in this era, unrecognized just as more recently those Sherpa or Hunza climbers who, supposedly acting as porters, have in fact led many recent ascents of the highest peaks in the Himalaya and the Karakorum.

For the successful alpinists the rewards were high—they became heroes, whether amateurs or professionals, selling edition upon edition of their works and seats in their lectures. The sport became more and more popular, almost all the European summits being climbed by 1877 when the Meije was conquered. The Alps even became overcrowded, so that veterans bemoaned the crowded slopes rather than unsophisticated inns.

Once all the major summits had been reached, new trends developed. Climbers both in Britain and in the Eastern Alps became proficient on rock and climbed the rock needles of Chamonix and the limestone towers of the Tyrol and Dolomites. At the same time there was an increase in the interest of winter alpinism which originated in F J Hügi's excursion to the Strahlegg pass in January 1832 and Charles Hudson's activities near Mont Blanc in 1853. Before the first ascent T S Kennedy tried the Matterhorn in January 1862, and in 1867 Miss Stratton, Jean Charlet and two other guides climbed Mont Blanc in January. W A B Coolidge, his aunt Meta Brevoort, and Christian Almer climbed the Jungfrau and the Wetterhorn in winter in 1874 and went on to make a remarkable series of winter ascents. Subsequently Vittorio Sella traversed the Matterhorn in March 1882, Paul Güssfeldt did the Grandes Jorasses and Gran Paradiso in winter in the 1890s and G A Hasler climbed most of the Oberland peaks out of season.

Another main trend was to apply increasing skill and efforts to the unclimbed ridges and faces of the alpine peaks. This developed intensely in the twentieth century, and was connected with the growth of guideless climbing in the last decades of the nineteenth century. In its most extreme form this was personified in Hermann von Barth who climbed the snow peaks and the steep rock of Untersberg near Berchtesgaden and elsewhere in the Eastern Alps solo in the 1880s.

The solo tradition remained strong there into the interwar years, continued by young, student climbers from Salzburg, Vienna and Munich who could not afford guides and learned to climb at a high standard on the vertical limestone near home. These climbers came to look down upon the well-heeled English and their guided system which dominated Zermatt, Chamonix and other major centres with scorn. Simultaneously the great hiking movement which swept through the German speaking intelligentsia before the First World War carried many on into mountaineering, until German-speaking central Europe became the core of the greatest concentration of mountaineers in the world in the mid-twentieth century.

Climbers from most European countries made important contributions in the Alps and in the lower mountain ranges. Even late in the last century A F Mummery and the guide Alexander Burgener were essentially a partnership, akin to the former's guideless group of W C Slingsby, Norman Collie and G Hastings. Guideless climbers and the more creative guides began to innovate on a scale sufficient to outweigh the conservative practices which emerged wherever guiding became established. This produced floods of new routes on the steeper alpine ridges and faces, which also overflowed into smaller European ranges.

British climbers spread their interests through the empire in the late nineteenth century. European climbers turned their eyes to the Canadian Rockies in the late 1880s, making use of the Canadian Pacific Railway after 1888. William Green was a pioneer there and also the founder of mountaineering in New Zealand, only just failing on Mount Cook in 1882. His exploits, and those of Swiss climbers interested Charles Fay and other members of the Appalachian Mountain Club, first in the Selkirks and then in the Canadian Rockies themselves. Then came the invasion by Norman Collie and other members of the British Alpine Club, a number of vital first ascents and by 1902 the foundation of the American Alpine Club, and the Canadian Alpine Club in 1907.

Alpine climbing today can be readily practised, whether in the European Alps, the Pyrenees or Tatra, the Caucasus, the Taurus, the Rockies of North America, and other accessible American ranges, or the mountains of New Zealand. For the best training, however, as General Bruce stated in 1934, 'The training country *par excellence* is the Alps. Every young man who wishes to qualify as a mountaineer will be taught more by a season of a couple of months under first class exponents in the Alps than he would learn in half a dozen years in the Himalaya where he will have to dig out his experience.'

Ways into Alpine Climbing

Most human activities offering high levels of physical, emotional and intellectual satisfaction involve a mixture of specific skills, judgement and a degree of confidence and commitment. Alpine and expedition climbing of necessity bring together such elements in ever more complex combinations. At the same time, having the will to perform satisfactorily involves putting aside over-concern for details and substituting one's own sense of wholeness and control in

the face of problems which are highly unpredictable. Cool performance in the face of risk and uncertainty is at the centre of success and survival in alpinism, though in extreme circumstances sheer doggedness or even furious rage may be necessary to escape from storms or plough through soft deep snow. Many techniques and ideas applicable to mountaineering have already been introduced, and where necessary will be referred to. But this section stresses that even in al-

pinism more than in rock or ice climbing, the situation tends to be complex and fraught not only with calculable risks but also with incalculable uncertainty. Experience should be gained carefully, valued and put to work to solve later problems rather than merely forgotten.

Frequently mishaps occur which are mirror images of previous difficulties from which little has been learned. In undertaking alpine climbs for the first time per-

haps this above all should be kept in mind alongside the healthy wish to enjoy what is often a refreshing revelation. Alpinism appeals to mavericks, and new climbs or other tremendous feats often reflect the high level of individualism among leading climbers. It is as if the mountain environment gives scope for release of massive energies restricted and repressed in everyday existence. Individual first ascentionists create routes in their own images as in the rare ice tracery of the French super-guide Armand Charlet's routes in the Mont Blanc Range, elegant and sophisticated in physical line and in the sense of timing required to minimize danger. The Nant Blanc face of the Aiguille Verte, first done in 1928, typified both the style and the man, and was ascended without using a single rock piton.

Some 1960s climbs were forced up the steepest faces, but only by using large amounts of climbing hardware. These took the 1930s concept of the direct climb up the steepest walls to an over-technical and sometimes bludgeoned conclusion. They were 'black-smithed' climbs, sheer hard hammer and drill work, requiring a dogged thuggery and suspension of the imagination for many days, as in the ascent of the 'Saxonweg' on the Cima Grande. This was climbing as hard work involving great patience. Much the same might be said about the highly publicized Eiger North Wall Direct climb first done in winter 1966 by a combination of German and international mountaineers, where the techniques of the Himalaya were brought back to Europe. It was a feat of great skill and determination, but also a media event put on for public consumption by the international group's leader, John Harlin, who died on the climb when a fixed rope broke.

Good climbers tend towards exaggerated individualism, because they become accustomed to making serious decisions and enjoying or suffering the consequences. Ultimately it is the climber who must decide whether a

John Barker, Reinhard Karl, Patrick Green and John Sheard camping in Chamonix Mont Blanc.

particular climb or course of action is desirable. It is unwise to allow fear of criticism or ridicule to make you undertake something which you would otherwise avoid like the plague. Read your own strengths and skills, assess the possibilities, and go on or retreat accordingly, where possible. Learn to respect your own judgement.

There is no single way into alpine climbing. It offers a multitude of approaches and possibilities. Many people in Britain, Europe and the USA come gently into mountain climbing from a previous interest in hill walking or 'backpacking'. The hill or mountain environment becomes ever more familiar and welcoming, and frequent walking and good health are associated. Some walkers and climbers share a strong appreciation of natural beauty, and interest in animal life and conservation. They can also share similar

Easy alpine climbing in the Bernina Alps during the filming of 'Five Days One Summer'.

patterns of friendship, membership of clubs and use of hut accommodation in mountain districts. They may also share interests in securing access to mountain areas, and join together in lobbing powerful or petty propertied interests in the manner of the Sierra Club in the USA or the British Mountaineering Council in Britain. To the walker who enjoys mountains in winter or summer, and who perhaps has skiing interests, it is natural to move on to the use of crampons and ice-axe, to the ascent of the more straightforward alpine peaks and perhaps from there to become more interested in mountaineering *per se*. Skills of compass and map work, weather judgement and snow conditions can grow gradually in relation to the seriousness of the mountains climbed. Companions often develop their interests together, gradually extending scope and technical demand until an appropriate level of climbing is reached to provide satisfaction. Typical of this style of development is the hardy walker who develops an ambition to ascend Mont Blanc,

Kilimanjaro, or Mexican volcanoes. Given like-minded companions, and the time to make the venture, he is likely to succeed and to extend skills and experience which might be applied on harder routes elsewhere.

Another major route into alpine climbing is to develop rock climbing skills on the smaller cliffs, and to use the background, fitness and friendships of that world as an entrée into alpinism. The climbing press tends in most countries to serve both rock climbers and mountaineers, and provides much information about recent and long past developments. Climbing has a long tradition, and the oldest climbing clubs are a mine of information, as are national organizations promoting climbing (see table at the back of the book).

In Britain rock climbing usually begins on short climbs, on the gritstone of the Peak District or Yorkshire, the sandstones of Kent or Northumberland, or on the smaller cliffs of Scotland, the Lake District, Wales or Cornwall. Shorter climbs here, or on the écoles d'escalades of Fontainebleau or Saussois in France and similar outcrops in other countries, provide an admirable beginning for the climber who wishes to attain high

standards of technical performance early in his or her alpine career. Short rock climbs tend to be gymnastic, and in most countries teach the elements of rope handling, belaying and the safe placing of protection on rock which competent alpinists require. Co-ordination of movement and judgement of difficulty, self control in action, and an eye for a line are also accentuated by hard rock climbing, particularly when climbs have not been described to death and fitted with fixed protection. Short climbs provide valuable experience and are pleasurable in themselves, as well as affording a measure of one's own capacity which can be applied elsewhere. This applies also to climbing walls (see p.64). However the ascent of climbs of less than two rope lengths can often remain very individualist affairs. Leader and second collaborate in choice of route and co-operate in ascent, but only for a limited period. There is not usually the sense of overwhelmingly serious commitment which comes when sharing long and potentially dangerous ventures.

Longer rock climbs, like those on Clogwyn D'ur Arddu on Snowdon, Carn Dearg Buttress on Ben Nevis, Creag an Duhb Loch in the Cairngorms or in the Verdon, Vercors, Handegg, Val de Mello, Kaisergebirge or Yosemite, are closer in ambience to the alpine experience, both environmentally and in feel. It is harder to know every detail about longer routes before starting, it is often harder to find the route, and you are more subject to the vagaries of weather. Physically, very hard short climbs can be as exhausting as long ones, but usually retreat is more feasible and other dangers less, which allows a corresponding concentration on pure performance carried almost everywhere to a high art. A high capability on rock is a great asset in the mountains, but there it must be tempered by the need to have some reserves and an eye for the capacity of the whole party. Longer rock climbs even when not very difficult can develop the judgement about oneself and one's companions, and provide shared experience which might be a good basis for future alpine climbing. So too might shared adventures of other kinds in caving, at sea or in exploration. Of course the seriousness of rock climbing is not solely determined by length, and rock climbs with loose rock or poor protection, and especially those on sea cliffs with difficult approaches, are often as challenging for all the party as a long alpine climb, as are some mountain rock climbs in bad weather.

Though many hard climbs have been done by highly motivated solo performers, alpinism remains essentially a small group activity where success depends upon co-operation. The motivation of the leader of hard rock routes has to be tempered if he cannot find like-minded companions to go into higher mountains. There is no point in his dreaming of the West Face Direct on the Aiguille du Dru unless it is within the capacity of his companions. This seems obvious, but in a less spectacular manner the mistake of attempting routes which are unsuitable for one or more members of the party occurs all the time. Ideally alpine companions should already know something about the strengths, weaknesses and technical capacity of those they accompany. Under duress people vary a great deal. There is no substitute for having previously spent hard times together if you are caught high on Mont Blanc in an electric storm.

Clubs and Companionship

Despite the public images of 'superstar' professional climbers like Reinhold Messner or Christophe Profit, the reality of climbing is different to most people in the sport. This is all to the good as it would be a much less attractive and amusing activity if everyone pursued their goals with such single-minded determination. In fact many climbers are as social as other groups. Indeed often they seem more so, for there is a tendency for people to carry on some aspects of the sport

throughout their lives, adjusting the level of activity to their changing abilities. Though there are inter-generational differences, alpine climbing in particular binds those of very different ages and backgrounds into a wide framework of common interests. Clubs thrive on that inclusiveness. Most young climbers would applaud William Henry Ellis, a director of John Brown Ltd, who took early retirement at 71 years of age in 1931 so that he could pursue his alpine career more effectively. He went on to climb many alpine peaks, including the Jungfrau with his niece in 1935, and walked up Helvellyn each year until his death in 1945. There have been many such old climbers, like Otto Herzog, whose activities extended from the early 1920s until the late 1950s and included several hundred new rock climbs in the eastern Alps. Many were soloed and the Ha-Hee Groove in the Karwendel done in 1921 remains the first VI superior rock climb in the northern area of the Limestone Eastern Alps. His last solo new grade V was done when he was in his late sixties. In Britain Haskett Smith stood on his head on the Napes Needle at 71, and Ivan Waller repeated his route Belle Vue Bastion, first led in 1927, in June 1985 at the age of 83. There have been women climbers too, who have climbed throughout

their lives and continued to a considerable age, and a few like Madame Denise Escond who did not start until after 50 and went on to repeat a great number of technically difficult 'Grandes Courses'. These people illustrate the capacity for enthusiasm which mountaineering develops in individuals, and should that interest ever flag, it is often refired by friends.

Clubs provide a framework for maintaining that process, for meeting others of like mind and interests, hearing of their experience and frequently seeking to emulate it. In Britain many operate on a city level and tend to be relatively small and intimate, with 50 to 200 members, a weekly meeting place in the evenings, an annual dinner and a programme of activity more or less formalized throughout the year. Some have cottages in popular places like Langdale and Llanberis, but in the main ownership of these is confined to the larger regional clubs – the Climbers' Club, the Fell and Rock Climbing Club and the Scottish Mountaineering Club. Many clubs are involved in producing the climbing guide books for their areas and publish journals. These big clubs, foundations which often stretch back to before the First World War, have formalized entry requirements,

A bivouac below the Chamonix Aiguilles.

and applicants should show a proven interest in climbing and personal association with existing members. Keen alpine climbers are members of one of the local clubs and of the august Alpine Club itself, (or its ginger group the Alpine Climbing Group), or of the American Alpine Club.

All clubs are not involved in alpine climbing, but within most there is a small group at least keen to do some routes in bigger mountains. The BMC supports and is supported by the clubs, and can supply lists of its member clubs to those seeking help in this way. One can often find the same information by talking to climbers on crags, climbing walls, in cafes or in the pub.

These clubs have their counterparts in Europe, though the roles of the national organizations tend to appear more pervasive than in Britain with its informal traditions of club autonomy. In practice,

however, similar regional or city-based groups of enthusiasts exist in Grenoble, Brest, Zurich, Frankfurt, Bergamo, Barcelona, and other towns. Often they are under the umbrella of the national organization, forming a section within it, but effectively they perform the same role as the clubs in Britain. Clubs are also based on institutions and particularly universities, colleges and schools. It is a pattern repeated in Japan, South Korea, and sometimes in North America and Australasia, but everywhere there are individualists who belong to no club, needing no such encouragement to enjoy their sport and social lives.

Of course clubs have their drawbacks as a means of promoting activity. Their entry requirements can seem harsh or forbidding, their members antiquated and opinionated. As there are a good number of such organizations it is best to choose what suits one best, with people of like aspirations, similar age or abilities. Above all, there is no substitute for climbing

often. For most people that generates the main companionships required to try something more ambitious.

Time and Alpinism
It is not expensive to reach the Alps by the cheapest means, but it can be expensive to stay there and to achieve personal goals. Of necessity alpine climbs take time, not merely in their execution, but in planning, choosing the correct time to go up and recovering from the exertion required. A lot can be achieved in a two week holiday, with persistence and good luck, but it is barely enough and in a spell of bad weather can be totally abortive. This is probably more true for the first timer. So it may be as well to plan for a stay of three weeks or one month in the European Alps for a first summer visit, and a similar period for equivalent ranges elsewhere. It is not that nothing can be done in a shorter period, but rather that the longer one allows the more enjoyable the actual climbing can become.

Norman Dyhrenfurth and the young guides of Pontresina.

improved familiarity, a greater amount of practice of techniques, greater physical fitness and altitude acclimatization desirable for the higher summits, all contribute to likelihood of greater enjoyment and success.

Of course once some climbs have been done it is even more pleasant to stay for a little longer, and for those who are able that is often a better arrangement, though it can be a mistake to develop a sense of time being limitless, as it can weaken the incentive to climb.

Alpine Resorts

The popularity of the Alps for more than a century has transformed many alpine valleys. Small villages have been swamped by development, sometimes without adequate environmental and architectural safeguards. Skiing has colonized all the Alps, and despite efforts to reduce its visual effects it leaves a legacy of ugly téléphériques, cables and terminals. That is perhaps part of the price of having fine mountains easily accessible to millions of people, and it must be set against the enjoyment and renewal so many seek there.

Overbuilding, suburban sprawl and the unattractive aspects of conventional tourism are most characteristic of the very popular resorts which are busy winter and summer. Chamonix, Zermatt, and Courmayeur fall into this category, as do other big centres. At peak ski season their facilities for skiing are stretched and the towns are extremely crowded. In summer too tourists flock in: Chamonix and Grindelwald each accommodate a vast short-visits trade as well as the large number of longer term holiday makers. Lesser centres can also be very crowded in the summer.

This raises problems for the first time alpine climber of limited means. If he wishes to stay long in summer, he probably cannot afford inside accommodation, so in practice keen climbers camp when possible. That in turn, together with the demand for camping from other holidaymakers, makes camp sites busy in the summer season

and can make it hard to find a decent camping place at a sensible cost, especially if one has no transport. For those with a fixed holiday there is much to be said for booking a site ahead, which is particularly common in France. Local tourist offices can advise on this so long as they are contacted in good time before. Independent-minded and impecunious climbers of all nationalities have always tended to camp on unregulated ground, though this is often illegal (at least in local Commune regulations in France and totally in Switzerland and Austria). Here there is a need to sort out local conventions and to try to avoid inciting community or police action. Great numbers of 'illegal campers', litter or insanitary behaviour almost always invite retaliation whether the campers are climbers, gypsies or tinkers. Where such problems have long existed the local authorities are usually sick of them, and act in a heavy-handed way particularly if their clearly-stated regulations and instructions are ignored. In Switzerland or Austria this usually means on-the-spot fines, and in the USA it can mean both fines and expulsion from the area.

Climbers staying for a shorter time, or who have more money, can often find quite cheap bunkhouse or pension-style accommodation. For example, in Chamonix there usually still exists a certain amount of unlet apartment, pension and hotel space despite the numbers of visitors because of poor publicity. Low cost accommodation of this type can be an advantage to an efficient group. Eating is more easily arranged, equipment can be dried in bad weather and sickness resulting from contaminated water or inadequately cleaned cooking utensils can be avoided. Of course in winter accommodation is a necessity, but becomes more costly because of competition from skiers.

Alternatively one may avoid the biggest resorts, by camping or staying in smaller villages or away from any large settlements. In Switzerland camp sites exist just

outside most centres. Their situations are often pleasant, but they can be under as much pressure as the big resorts. This applies on the Italian side of the Alps also, though the wildness of some south alpine valleys does seem to leave more possibility of low cost camping. There are also very low cost pensions and bunkhouses, for which it is best to enquire locally. Much the same can be said of the Pyrenees.

A problem for alpine climbers is that they spend nights away from the valley, and risk having to pay both for valley accommodation and fees in huts or refuges in the mountains. This is familiar to local people, and there are often specific arrangements to cover the eventuality, but it is best to discuss it with camp site owner or proprietor of the bunkhouse before going up, to avoid a bigger bill than expected later.

In many places the first stage of going to climb involves the added cost of a bus, rail or téléphérique journey. Some of these can dent the pocket, and it is worth keeping in mind that your route of return might involve a similar cost. Note too whether you could be forced to descend to a different valley than at first intended – an enforced descent can require reserved funds and a passport to enable you to get back. Parties often intend to come back to Switzerland by descending the North Ridge of the Piz Badile in the Engadine, after climbing that route or the North East Face and mistakenly descend instead to the Gianetti Hut in Italy, incur hut fees there and then decide not to re-cross to Switzerland by the high passes because of tiredness or bad weather. They are forced into a long descent on foot and a road route of about 110 km.

Huts and Refuges

Hut and sometimes téléphérique costs can be reduced by joining the national organizations which run them, though often one would have to use huts a lot to recoup the fee. British climbers can now buy a special carnet (ticket) from the BMC entitling them to price reductions and similar carnets are negotiated for members of the Alpine Club in some European countries. Huts are expensive in countries with very hard currencies and the cost can be reduced by taking one's own food and a stove. Usually these have to be used either outside or at best in a separate room apart from the other guests, and they are disliked because hut fires are common and partly because poorly paid hut wardens receive less income this way.

The purist may resent the idea of beginning his first or any other alpine ascent by using a cable car or train, and wish to savour the walk up through woods and meadows so characteristic of the alpine region. There can be great pleasure in this, so long as the overall hut walk is not too long. Beware of hut walks which take much longer than guidebook time. The latter has been fixed by people who know the way to the last metre and are very fit. An overladen or unfit party may take far longer and risk being lost in woods or glacier in the dark.

The alpine countries have a very dense network of hut accommodation. These huts can be a great advantage when trying one day climbs, as places of rest and refreshment enabling the climber to carry less from the valley and on the climb. Before they were built, alpine pioneers used porters in much the same way as Himalayan climbers do today. Huts have their own peculiar customs and traditions and sometimes can seem very uncomfortable. Some are terribly overcrowded, like the Goûter Hut on the Bosses Route to Mont Blanc, or the Hörnli Hut below the easiest route up the Matterhorn. This is not conducive to good sleep as almost before the last person has gone to bed others are getting up, shuffling in the dark with torches to gather belongings, hours before dawn. This is made worse if the climbing to come causes tension or the place is dusty or overheated with every window firmly closed and shuttered. As a result huts without sociable and skilled wardens can be bad-tempered places, evoking the opposite of mountaineering brotherly or sisterly love.

A cold bivouac under a boulder is not always a good start either, and may necessitate the carrying of more gear. Routes which usually require bivouac equipment may create the incentive to use it even in the proximity of a hut. When a hut is well run, with the interests of the visitors very much at heart, it can be welcoming and warming place to spend time with climbing companions old and new. It can also be a place to which members of a party without real climbing ambition can accompany their new friends, walk or potter while others climb, and join the descent.

Guiding and Alpinism

Many of the initial hurdles to alpine experience can be overcome by taking part in guided climbs. In the nineteenth century most prominent climbers used guides and still in alpine countries guides are the usual source of instruction for beginners and people of intermediate ability. Guides are usually either local people or good climbers from outside who have trained and passed a rigorous set of tests to qualify. They form guild-like local corporations or corps and do their best to exclude outsiders, though in effect in alpine countries the guides are incorporated into national systems of organization, as they are in Britain. Standards of qualification are laid down by the international mountaineering 'regulating body' the UIAA. Many teach skiing in the winter.

Guides tend to introduce a few basic skills, particularly on snow and ice, and to lead their clients, if they are beginners, up a prescribed itinerary of easier climbs. They also take clients up specific routes for a fee related to the difficulty, size and danger of ascent. One should thus distinguish between courses run by guides, which often have a large membership, and the individual services of a guide to make specific ascents, instigated by the client. For complete novices,

without rock or snow and ice experience, there is much to be said for a guided course in the Alps or the Rockies, or perhaps for British climbers a Scottish winter climb. Many people with intermediate skills prefer to climb guideless, but for those who are doubtful from lack of confidence, infrequent opportunities to climb, or suitable companions, guided climbing can provide an instructive and enjoyable experience, allowing the client to do routes which otherwise he may never achieve.

The disadvantage is that it is expensive, particularly when employing Continental guides on an individual basis, and, as in other professions, not all guides are exemplary. Some tend to be too forceful with clients to the detriment of their enjoyment and self-respect. Nevertheless, having so much experience, they provide a way over the first major hurdle into alpine climbing and can avoid many dangers. Of course, the individualist almost always goes guideless, not least because he usually has some experience of rock and snow before going to the Alps, and he or she no doubt gains greatly in confidence from the successes and mistakes made – so long as the experiences are not too traumatic.

Insurance

Without elaborating upon the dangers, it is foolish not to insure before an alpine holiday, not least against the normal risk of travel and residence abroad, including loss of money or goods, transport disruptions, or conventional forms of illness which can prove expensive. In Europe EEC regulations provide a little help for their citizens, but this is generally insufficient. Climbing is riskier still, and two categories of risk require cover: rescue is costly, requiring helicopter flights in many cases; and hospital treatment, drug fees, maintenance and other expenses altogether can amount to many thousands of pounds in difficult accidents. There are also additional costs for accompanying friends or anxious visiting relatives. Thus

A Swissair helicopter in action on the Col Bernina with Joe Brown and Andrea Florineth.

death or injury, rescue or recovery should be insured, as should the equipment which might disappear from the tent while one is away.

A variety of insurance schemes exist, through national clubs like the Club Alpin Francais or the Swiss Alpine Club, and in Britain through the BMC. In the USA there are no such schemes—in all national parks, however, where the bulk of climbing is done, all mountain rescue is provided free of charge under federal law, so climbers insure for medical treatment and expenses and loss of equipment through their normal insurers. In all cases some estimate has to be made of the total sums which you seek to cover. For rescue costs it is best to consult the insurer about the likely level of claims given recent experience, as these will keep changing. Do not be tempted into the error of under-insurance. In general the record on payments in settlement of such claims seems a good one, and the premiums not outlandish given the high risks involved.

Alpine Features	
Aigulle	Sharp-pointed mountain (French for 'needle'), particularly in Mont Blanc range.
Arête	Well-defined ridge.
Berg-schrund	A large crevasse separating the upper ice of a glacier from the mountain wall behind; often serious obstacle to climbing. (Also *rimaye*)
Brèche	A gap or notch.
Cirque	Enclosing circle of mountains. (Also *cwm* or *corrie*)
Col	A pass or saddle between peaks.
Cornice	A wave-like lip of snow or ice overhanging crest of a ridge or edge, formed by prevailing wind. May overhang.
Couloir	A gully, or furrow, in mountainside. On rock or snow.
Gendarme	A rock tower, or tooth, on a ridge; often blocking easy progress.
Moraine	A bank of loose debris deposited by glacier (can form long stone ridges).
Névé	Upper snow or snow-ice which feeds a glacier, or patch of hardened permanent snow. (Also *firn*)
Penitentes	Columnar snow, formed at altitude where radiation and atmospheric conditions combine to break up snow surface; the pillars are often bent towards the sun to give a 'penitent' attitude. (Also *nieve penitentes*)
Rognon	Large boulder or boss of rock protruding from glacier or ice-field.
Sastrugi	Wave-like sculpting of dry crust formed by wind over open snow-wastes. Where the full blast of the wind is unimpeded, these features can attain considerable relief and be difficult to traverse.
Sérac	A tower or pinnacle of ice, usually breaking away from a cliff of ice and/or found in ice-falls.
Verglas	A thin layer of ice coating rock.

Making the Transition to Alpine Climbing: The Hillwalker

Experienced walkers and backpackers have already developed some of the attributes and skills essential in alpine climbing. Familiarity with the use of maps and the compass for navigation involves skills which must be applied with discrimination to local conditions. There is the need to plan the route, to estimate the likely time it will take, to fit a route to the party's strength, and to equip the group suitably to that objective and the likely conditions. Camping and survival skills of an appropriate kind have often already been developed. These need only a series of marginal adjustments to suit them to the mountaineering environment. One most important consideration is that on mountaineering ventures even the strongest person has limited carrying capacity, so that judgement has to be applied in fitting together party, food and which equipment to take. Though some groups might be castigated for attempting climbs with too little essential equipment, the usual problem in recent times has been the opposite one, of people carrying too much and thereby slowing their progress or making the climbing too difficult.

This is sometimes hard to accept when the walker comes from a background hedged about by bureaucratic rules evolved for school parties which try to protect young people from being taken ill-equipped into mountain country. It can seem foolhardy to set out on Mont Blanc with no more weight of equipment than is obligatory according to the rules for a school-child in the Trossachs or on Snowdon. But the truth of the matter is that mobility is the key factor on high mountains, tempered always by judgements as to when and how to apply it. Even the first ascent of Mount Rainier (see p. 152) illustrates this, for the supposedly most experienced member of the party, Edward Coleman, appears to have

fallen behind largely because he tried to carry too much equipment. As in walking, or any other activity, equipment is merely a means to an end, and 'gear freaks' put stumbling blocks in their own way by taking too much in their rucsacs. The most important skills or attributes, which the experienced walker usually has already, concern the mountain environment and judgements about one's own abilities and those of the rest of the group. Weather problems should be familiar to hardy walkers who go out winter and summer. In Britain, Europe or in the hill country of North America they will have met the hazards. Winds, sudden downpours of rain or snow, dehydration and sunstroke, wet and obscuring fogs and clouds, with their peculiar depressing influence as well as navigational dangers all should be well known. Mountaineers meet the same problems, but in a highly accentuated form and in situations which make them more problematic. Thus a lightning storm on a Bregaglia rock pinnacle is an altogether more alarming prospect than the same storm walking in the Engadine valleys thousands of metres below. One offers high likelihood of injury or death, the other a mere wetting and a spectacular display. There are more similarities than differences nevertheless. Walkers have to measure their own pace, to watch out for their companions, to agree on decisions including changes of plan when conditions change or a mistake is made, and to accept the consequences.

Those who go out in winter conditions should be familiar with the special clothing and equipment needed in mountaineering, and with the conditions likely to be encountered. For mountaineering at the level of 'alpinism' the clothing prescribed for ice climbing (see p. 89) should usually suffice, with perhaps some modifications for

> **Vital Equipment for an easier alpine peak**
> 9 mm rope (40 m minimum for three)
> 7 mm light rope (40 m for three)
> Helmet.
> 1 or 2 light clamps or 2 prusik slings per person.
> 1 or 2 slings for clamps if used (foot length).
> Ice axe per person (on some routes 1 ice hammer per person, or 1 in party, and a very small number of rock pitons, though not usually on the routes described here).
> Body or sit harness per person.
> A few ice screws and possibly 1 deadman.
> Crampons (1 pair per person).
> A few karabiners (as light as possible).
> Screwdriver or Swiss army knife or Allen key (depending on type).
> Headtorch, spare bulb and batteries per person.
> Rucsac, water bottle or flask.
> Map and compass, altimeter if possible.
> Small first aid kit (1 for party).
> Cigarette lighter, sunglasses.
> Description of route and others near it, including descent and alternative descents.
> Money, Alpine Club Card or Carnet as appropriate.
> Food, stove and fuel when required.
> Clothing and other survival gear.

long multi-bivouac routes or winter alpine climbing (see p. 174). Skiers too will be familiar with the temperatures met on the mountains. In summer it can be as cold above 3,000 m as in winter conditions lower down, or in the mountains of coastal North America. Equipment for alpine routes is a combination of that pre-

scribed in the rock and ice sections. For the walker or backpacker moving into alpine climbing via the technically easier routes, little rock climbing equipment is necessary or desirable in the first instance. It might be little used and has to be carried. More importance should be attached to competence in handling the rope, belay techniques and smooth and careful but relatively speedy progress, glacier skills including finding the way through crevassed areas, crevasse self-rescue and the role of the rest of the party.

Strong mountain walkers or people with experience of rock scrambling should find the ascents of the following peaks feasible with care, planning and the good

weather so vital to success in all mountain-related activity. At the same time a certain amount of patience might be required if conditions prove difficult, or if you feel awed by the size and seriousness of the peaks, or more affected by altitude than anticipated. Do not hesitate to ask for advice from other mountaineers, from valley weather centres, park rangers and hut custodians. It is at this stage that many people in the past felt the need for a guide, and in some cases this is still advisable, but the gains made by making your own way, even when the experience may involve misjudgements, are immense.

The routes described are chosen as a few good examples of moun-

Climbers on the summit ridge of the Eiger.

tains accessible to people of reasonable fitness and strong motivation. Great technical skills are not needed, though a degree of steadiness is assumed in all the party. Ideally everyone should be capable of basic movement using crampons and ice-axe (see p. 96) and all should have practised crevasse rescue. Smoothness in handling the rope to allow relatively swift movement over large tracts of glacier and snow ridges is essential. The climbs themselves are not chosen to provide progression in difficulty. Rather they present a series of possibilities at a similar level. All involve little rock climbing.

DAUPHINÉ, FRANCE
Les Bans (3,670 m)
Description by Steph Rowland

Route:	Ascent and descent by ENE Ridge
Grade:	PD
First Ascent:	NE Ridge by W A B Coolidge and Christian Almer and son 14 July 1878
Maps:	ING: 1:50,000 GHM Composite Edition, Dauphiné
Approach:	From La Bérarde take the route to the Pilatte Valley until the split in the path with that to the Temple Ecrins Hut. The hut is situated on the left side of the Pilatte Glacier and built on a rocky lump west of Mont Gioberney. In detail the approach is complicated by rivers and streams and varied according to the season (3½ hours from La Berarde in good conditions).

The ENE Ridge of Les Bans was the middle route of three day routes in the Dauphiné. We came from Pic Coolidge, a fine view point shared by many other people, back to the Temple Ecrins Hut. There we collected our gear and carried onto the Pilatte Hut above the glacier.

At 4 am we had a scanty breakfast and set off in the dark accompanied by quite a number of guided Continental parties down to the glacier below. A slow mindless plod followed up the gradually steepening Pilatte Glacier in the footsteps of the Continentals. It did register that the bridges over some of the rather frequent crevasses in the glacier seemed extremely thin making us vaguely uneasy about the descent in the afternoon sunshine. We slowly overtook a crocodile of people led by a cheery French guide and realized as we got higher that the wind seemed to be increasing. However after three hours we eventually reached the Col des Bans. Great indecision followed: Was the weather going to hold? The wind seemed very cold! The guided party veered off left to a lower snow peak. Did the guide know better than us?

Whilst the others were still thinking I suddenly decided that it was no colder than the majority of Scottish climbing conditions and anyway it was not a point of no return. We should at least investigate and start the climbing from the col

onto the ridge, so I set off attached to the rope. In fact this was possibly the hardest part of the route for all of us as there was neither sight of nor hearing contact with the team, with the wind howling all the time and hands and bodies numb with cold.

Once we were all safely established on the ridge we gained shelter and scrambled pleasantly up polished rock in the sunshine with no real route-finding problems. We used the description from the French publication *One Hundred Best Routes in the Dauphiné*. The route led round into a couloir until it came to a short steep wall which we pitched using two slings as belays. We met a guide and his client about two thirds of the way up as

they were on their descent. They wished 'Les Dames Anglaises' luck. Another party we had noticed who had started climbing some way behind us turned back. We carried on up the ridge and into another easy slabby couloir and across into a final stony couloir then up to the south summit which, in contrast to Pic Coolidge, we had to ourselves. At last there was time to relax for a few moments and enjoy the grandeur of the cirque of mountains around the Pilatte Glacier—a feeling of achievement and pleasure that we had in fact continued. However there was not long to relax and contemplate as we thought of our descent.

We pitched two sections going down—using nuts this time! It was slightly less windy as we arrived back at the col. We took ages descending the glacier with the first person on the rope very wary about crossing the crevasses. We kept to the tracks as we thought this might be safer than trying to find our own way and had to cross two very large crevasses with what seemed to be extremely fragile snow bridges—all appropriate safety precautions we knew were taken!

The meal in the hut was very welcome, eaten with a feeling of contentment and plans for the E Ridge of Gioberney the next day.

Les Bans: the climbers Margaret, Jay and Sheila at Gioberney.

BERNESE OBERLAND, SWITZERLAND
The Mönch (4,099 m)

Route:	Ascent by the NE Ridge and descent by the S Ridge, starting and finishing at the Jungfraujoch station.
Grade:	PD sup in ascent, F-PD in descent
First ascent:	S Porges, C Almer, U Kaufmann and C Kaufmann 15 August 1857.
First ascent of NE Ridge:	G E Foster with H Baumann, father and son and F Teutschmann 31 July 1877
First ascent of SE Ridge:	R J S Macdonald, C Almer and M Anderegg 29 July 1863.
Map:	Swiss Naval Series No. 264.
Approach:	From Grindelwald most climbers now take the train to the Jungfraujoch station (3,454 m).

The Mönch is a fine summit, magnificently placed between the Eiger and the Jungfrau. Its traverse provides an introduction to the high Oberland peaks amid scenery of unparalleled grandeur. It is also a good acclimatization peak or test of a party's capabilities as the route, though high, it not too long. Its glacial ambience does require careful route-finding, especially in mist or bad weather. It is an expensive outing, involving rail and accommodation costs.

The Jungfraujoch station has some low cost communal space in a hotel which is otherwise expensive. Although self catering may not be allowed, it may prove worthwhile to stay here not only for the Mönch traverse, but for other climbs at comparatively high altitude. It avoids the very long approaches otherwise necessary to huts and peaks in the area. With the fitness gained one may then progress to more formidable objectives if desired.

The traverse first requires the crossing of the pass, the Ober Mönch Joch. The long east tunnel leads from the station to the upper part of the Jungfrau snowfield. From there go NE to the Ober Mönch Joch (3,626 m). Go a little way down the other side to the Ewigschneefeld, then climb to point (3,684 m) on the NE spur of the SE Ridge. After a short distance on the ridge, traverse crevassed slopes NW to the South Eigerjoch (3,759 m–2 hours). In a fine position, climb mixed snow and rock on the ridge passing a bergschrund which is followed by rock sections. These are at first not difficult, and where they appear to become so they are avoided on the left. The summit ridge is often icy and requires careful use of crampons and axe, and the top can usually be reached in about 2½ hours from the South Eigerjoch and 4½ from the Jungfraujoch station.

This summit gives tremendous views into the heart of the Bernese Oberland as well as back into the Grindelwald valley and towards the Eiger. The South East Ridge is the ordinary route of ascent. Descent begins with a sharp snow crest to a snow shoulder, and down the ridge to a rock arête. Go down a final snow slope somewhat to the right, to reach the Ober Mönch Joch. The station should be reached from the summit in not more than 2 hours in good conditions, allowing the whole traverse to be completed in less than 7 hours. It is best to start early to ensure completion of the route before conditions deteriorate.

The Mönch. From the Mönch joch (left) traverse the ice to the ridge.

PENNINE ALPS, SWITZERLAND
Grand Combin (4,314 m)

Route:	The 'Mur de la Côte' from the Panoissière Hut (2,617 m) and descent by the same route.
Grade:	PD
First Ascent Combin de Grafeneire:	C St C Deville with D, E and G Balleys and B Dorsaz 30 July 1859.
Map:	Swiss Naval Series No. 283
Approach:	From Fionnay village (1,489 m), Mauvoisin, in the Val de Bagnes, a path leads SW and is signposted for the Panossière hut. Crossing fields, it climbs at first in zigzags, then takes a horizontal section in a westerly direction. At a fork go left, going S and SE, then back right under the shoulder of a spur on the E of the Corbassière Glacier. Beyond the shoulder it reaches a moraine ridge, then a depression between that and the hillside. After a climb the edge of the glacier is attained at 2,644 m. Continue up the moraine edge to the hut (2,671 m)–4 hours.

The area west of Arolla tends to be a little less frequented in the summer than that centre or Zermatt, which is a charm in itself. Though the Italian south side of the Pennine Alps is probably the most peaceful, the ascent of the Grand Combin by its north face can be a fine long expedition, quite well known and frequented but less so than the overcrowded 'voies ordinaries' of Mont Blanc or Zermatt. It thus provides a pleasant and feasible alternative.

From the hut cross the Corbassière glacier SW towards Point 2,726 m on the left bank. Go up the left bank carefully avoiding crevasses, usual here; cut closely under Point 3,155 m and climb direct towards Point 3,310 m near the SE foot of the Combin de Boveyre (2½ hours). Cross the upper plateau of the glacier south, then work east passing within 400–500 m south of Point 3,406 m. Climb a sloping snowramp SE above a crescent of rock, keeping to its outside edge (Plateau du Déjeuner). Pass S of Point 3,555 m and continue SE up the narrow ice corridor which is threatened from above by séracs. At 3,960 m the top of this corridor is attained and a detour E made, followed by a return SE to come out below the Col du Croissant (4,090 m) with the Mur da la Côte on the R. This complicated section usually takes about 2½ hours but can change a lot.

The Mur de la Côte is often an ice slope, and bars the way to the summit plateau. Climb the steep slope from left to right emerging around 4,100 m on the upper plateau. There can be a big cornice here. Either take the snow spur ahead to the fore-peak of the Aiguille du Croissant then go along the main ridge to the summit of the Grafeneire, watching out for the large cornice on the left, or cross the upper plateau SW under the Aiguille du Croissant, descend a little to cross a huge crevasse where it is easier and climb up snow before returning E to the top. In all, this undertaking takes about seven hours' ascent, and a further four to return. A certain complexity combined with objective dangers and a remote 'feel' demand steadiness in the party despite the relatively low level of technical difficulty. The rewards are the sense of achievement and a whole series of unique unstereotyped views both east and west, and an introduction to a fine, less frequented alpine area.

The Grand Combin.

MONT BLANC RANGE, FRANCE AND ITALY
Mont Blanc (4,807 m)

Route:	The Bosses Arête via the Goûter Hut (3,817 m) and the Vallot Hut (4,362 m). Descent either by the same route or via Grandes Mulets Hut to Plan d'Aiguille.
Grade:	Facile (in good conditions)
First ascent:	Dr M G Paccard and J Balmat 8 August 1786.
First ascent of route described:	L Stephen and F F Tuckett with M Anderegg, J J Bennen and P Perren 18 July 1861.
Map:	Carte de France XXXVI–31
Approach:	Chamonix Les Houches is easily reached by bus or train from Chamonix. The first of the two cable cars runs in the summer, and is best reached by bus as the rail station is about a km away from either of the lifts. From the ridge of Belle Vue (1,790 m) it is possible to take the Tramway du Mont Blanc to the cafe at the Nid d'Aigle terminus (2,386 m) or to walk there in about 1 hour.

The highest summit in the Alps is attractive to many who would not consider themselves dedicated mountaineers, as well as to people of greater expertise. It should always be taken seriously, not only because its height is such that altitude sickness is very common, but also because the route can be difficult to follow above the Goûter Ridge where it is exposed to high winds and the bad weather which is common here. Though the Bosses Ridge is straightforward technically, and on a good morning in summer or the ski season has a deeply marked trail from numerous climbers, Mont Blanc is a highly complex mountain. Any departure from the route is likely to have serious implications for a party of limited experience. Care should be taken in noting key features during the climb in case of cloud or storm during the descent, and clothing and food should reflect the serious nature of the undertaking, even on apparently stable days.

A very well marked path, battered by years of ascent and descent, goes southwards and then zig-zags up from the Nid d'Aigle eastwards after 200 m. It soon reaches a stony hollow and continues climbing on the ridge of the Aiguille du Goûter on scree-covered slopes. Whether one is ascending or descending, this section is not very interesting. Even in summer good weather there are sometimes patches of snow on the ridge before the little Tête Rousse glacier. The Tête Rousse Hut (3,167 m CAF) on the right is rarely used in ascent, and many climbers never visit it, unless they wish to climb on the Aiguille du Bionnassey (3 hours from Belle Vue).

Here mountaineering begins in earnest. The slopes of the Aiguille du Goûter above steepen, and the path towards the hut usually crosses a small couloir before going up a rock rib, which in turn separates the Tête Rousse and Bionnassay Glaciers. Since many climbers go up this section rather late in the day intending to climb Mont Blanc next morning, or descend after the ascent, this couloir and even the lower part of the rib can be dangerous from stone fall. Some of this is natural, and some very likely the result of clumsy climbers above. In any event the couloir and lower rocks are not places to picnic at any time of day. Ice can also cause delay in the couloir in good weather. The final climb to the hut is rocky and care should be taken not to knock debris on people below reaching the Goûter Hut (3,863 m). One should not be surprised to feel quite tired after more than 2,000 metres of ascent from Belle Vue, or 1,421 from Nid d'Aigle terminus. From Nid d'Aigle this is likely to take 4–5 hours.

The hut itself tends to be extremely busy, and because of the length of ascent to it and the dangers of the lower section of the slope below, and to secure a place to stay there, it is best to set off early on the first day's climb, so as to reach the hut relatively early, rest and acclimatize a little and thus enjoy the ascent of the mountain more on the second day.

It is especially important to begin the summit day early, when the snow is frozen and the sun not yet tiring to climb in. Many parties

Evening on the Dôme du Goûter.

leave at midnight or soon afterwards, which is well advised. The way begins on a relatively narrow flat ridge, then wends its way up a wide slope with crevasses towards the Dôme du Goûter. All this section is best done in the dark. Judgement about the suitability of the weather and the ability of the party to succeed in the conditions of the day is essential, as cloud and mist can make the crossing of the Dôme difficult to find if there is no track, and confusing even when tracks exist. They can head off in different directions to that of the summit, either towards the old ascent route via the Grandes Mulets, or more hazardously to the W and the Ridge of the Aiguilles du Bionnassay. This last is made more likely by the usual tendency to avoid the summit of the Dôme on its west slope to reach the Col du Dôme (4,237 m) and the Vallot Hut (4,263 m). In all this usually takes about 2½ hours from the Goûter Hut. The final ridge, with its Grande Bosse and Petite Bosse ends in a narrowing ridge below the summit prior to a widening in the last section and the top itself. In all this is likely to take perhaps 4 or 5 hours in good conditions and good weather.

Early starts at least provide a less tiring climb, leave time to enjoy the summit and to make a safe and more pleasant descent. With Mont Blanc this is especially important. Many parties go down the same way, or descend via the Grandes Mulets Hut. The latter route may be better if there is a high wind on the ridge, or a desire to vary the route, though in thick mist and snow it may be more difficult to find. From the Col du Dôme one goes acutely right onto the Grand Plateau and through a crevassed slope to the narrow shelf of the Petites Plateau at 3,650 m. Below is a second steep slope which is descended before crossing to the Grandes Mulets Hut (3,051 m). On this section there are a good number of big crevasses and sometimes the guides bridge them with ladders. There is also danger from sérac fall, particularly near the east side of the Dôme du Goûter (6½ hours ascent, 3–4 hours descent).

From the Grandes Mulets Hut the descent now usual is to follow a diagonal line to Plan d'Aiguille téléphérique station. At first one continues down the crevassed glacier to La Jonction and the flat section of the Bossons Glacier to the E. This is traversed to the Gare du Glaciers (2,414 m) from which a good path leads to the Pélerins Glacier and Plan d'Aiguille. In all this descent can be made in about 2 hours in good conditions, in bad, about 3 hours. From Plan d'Aiguille many take the cable car, or there is a path through the woods to Chamonix.

Overall this ascent is one of the finest mountaineering excursions in Europe, not belittled by its low technical standard. It is long and tiring, and there is often the risk of storm. Parties trying it should be reasonably fit in a conventional sense, well equipped, and preferably somewhat acclimatized by going before to close to 4,000 metres, spending some time at altitude then, or taking the ascent of Mont Blanc gently by staying an extra night on the way. The pace of ascent which is customary fails to observe the now well-known conventions of safe acclimatization, and many people either fail in the attempt, or become ill and a few may even die from altitude-related sickness as a result.

The mountain's attractions are so great that few healthy people should be discouraged by this. By taking reasonable precautions, an adequate tactical approach to the plan of the climb, and respecting the weather and the real abilities of the party, this is an experience to be delighted in, and an introduction to a mountain so multi-faceted that it can be a pleasure to mountaineers of many levels of ability. Few tire of Mont Blanc, for the mountain always has some new face or ridge, new mood or season to offer, and the attractions seem too numerous for most individuals to begin to exhaust them. Thus an ascent of the Bosses Arête is often an *hors-d'oeuvre*, a delicious beginning to a lifelong acquaintance with the vast range of climbing there.

CASCADE RANGE, USA
Mount Rainier (4,470 m)

Route:	Ingraham Glacier. Disappointment Cleaver Route
Grade:	1–2 (European PD)
First ascent:	Hazard Stevens and Philemon B Van Trump 17 August 1870, after being guided to the mountain by James Longmire and to the start of the climbing by an Indian, Sluiskin. Edward Coleman also accompanied them but was separated when he lost his pack. It is uncertain who made the first ascent of the route described, though in 1885 or 6 Allison L Brown climbed, with a party of 6 or 7 Yakima Indians, to a point high on the glacier.
Map:	Forest Maps-Mount Rainier National Park.
Approach:	Take the route from Paradise, Mount Rainier National Park, following the Skyline trail and snowfield route to Camp Muir.

Mount Rainier forms a huge massif and is the fountain head of more than twenty glaciers. Known by Indians as Tahoma, its sheer bulk justifies their meaning 'The mountain that was God'. It is also an active volcano. The whole area is designated as a National Park. Climbers must register with the Park service on entering and leaving the Park, and strictly observe various rules. When formalities are completed the Skyline trail and Snowfield route lead to the stone cabins at Camp Muir in 4–7 hours. These are often overcrowded, so be prepared to sleep out.

The objective of the Disappoint-

Mount Assiniboine.

ment Cleaver Route is the Ingraham Glacier which descends from the summit icefields. The upper part of this glacier can be crevassed heavily, particularly later in the summer season, and this may require the party to take to the rocks of Disappointment Cleaver.

Starting very early, cross the upper basin of the Coulitz Glacier from Camp Muir to the Cathedral Rocks Ridge, which allows a crossing at any of three points. The middle one at about 3,166 m is usual. From it climb up scree to the ridge crest and attain the Ingraham Glacier, and either go up the ice direct, or make a horizontal traverse across the glacier to the right onto the rocks of Disappointment Cleaver. Ledge systems of bad rock lead from its base through to the snowfield on the Cleaver's top. Go up to the top of this (3,670 m) and climb direct towards the crater rim, taking care with crevasses. In total the summit should be reached in 5-8 hours from Camp Muir. The late season route allows access to the summit plateau if the route to the Disappointment Cleaver proves too crevassed. It is possible to cross the Ingraham Glacier from near Cathedral Rocks and skirt under the rocks of Disappointment Cleaver, and to follow the Emmons Glacier on its true right side, just north of the Cleaver, and thereby reach the summit plateau.

The Cascades are serious mountains, and storms can occur at any time. Watch out for thickening cirrus, and the formation of cloud caps on the high summits. Volcanic peaks are even more susceptible to 'capping' than others making route finding on complex glacial routes difficult. Winds usually come from the SW in bad conditions with NW winds prevailing in the spring and summer. Summer storms are usually short but in spring and fall storms are often severe, with low temperatures, driving snow and nil visibility lasting sometimes for several days.

ROCKY MOUNTAINS, CANADA
Mount Assiniboine (3,618 m)

Route:	SW Face
Grade:	AD (alpine)
First ascent:	J Outram, C Bohren, C Hasler September 1901.
Map:	Canadian Department of Mines and Technical Surveys. Special Map Mount Assiniboine 1:50,000
Approach:	By road to the head of Spray Lake. One day of walking up Bryant Creek on good trails leads to Magog Lake, via either Assiniboine Pass or the higher Wonder Pass. Trails split at the Bryant Creek ranger station and converge near Strom's Lodge (19 km). There is a longer scenic north approach via Brewster Creek and the Allenby Pass or Healy Creek and the Valley of the Rooks. There is a hut above Lake Magog (Alpine Club of Canada), but many people camp.

This mountain is extremely scenic, but all the routes can be dangerous from avalanches. From Lake Magog ascend slopes and a rocky section onto the north glacier and cross it to Outram's first pass between Assiniboine and Strom (2,850 m). Descend a little on the other side to the glacier and cross to the Assiniboine – Sturdee pass, Outram's second pass (3,033 m) below the W ridge. Traverse ledges across the SW face to the S ridge at 3,000 m level. Ascend scree ledges to the base of a 21 m cliff at 3,279 m and gain a snow couloir just W. This is crossed diagonally to a point where the cliff disappears into the SW face. Go up diagonally over ledges and escarpments in mixed ground to the south arête, which is reached 100 m below the summit. The remainder is easy snow. In all this is likely to take about ten hours. The peak is extremely elegant, but the rock is loose and the snow very variable. It is usual to descend by the N arête, and the most popular route is now the NW face done by Tom Longstaff and R Aemmer in July 1910 following the route above to the SW arête Assiniboine-Sturdee Col and traversing up into the middle of the face. The route is almost entirely ice except for two short steep rock bands. Above these bands the route remains steep to the summit, with verglassed rocks (9 hours from Lake Magog).

```
CAUCASUS, USSR
Elbrus West (5,633 m), Elbrus East (5,621 m)
Description by Des Rubens
Route:          W Peak only and E and W Peaks traverse.
Grade:          Facile
First ascent:   The W summit was reached by Freshfield, Moore
                and Tucker in 1868, the E by Moore, Gardiner,
                Grove and Walker in 1874.
Map:            Russian maps are unobtainable. Austrian Alpine
                Club Kammkarte – 2 sheets on the Central
                Caucasus.
Approach:       Mineralyre Vodi in the Baksan Valley can be
                reached by air from Moscow. A system of cable
                cars and a chairlift (now being upgraded) lead up
                the mountain from the roadhead at Azan. From
                the top lift it is an easy walk to the Pruit Hut
                (4,100 m). The last time to start the upward
                journey by cable car is about 1 pm.
```

The Caucasus offers a full range of alpine mountaineering of all standards, and there remain possibilities of doing little-frequented climbs. Elbrus, the highest peak in Europe, is very popular. It is an extinct volcano. Des Rubens records: 'The slopes of Elbrus, which from a distant summit had seemed gentle, are deceptive. From the Pruit Hut (about 4,100 m) the mountain rears up sharply forming a double summitted graceful peak of immense dimensions. We left the hut at 2.40 a.m. and almost immediately climbed above the cloud into the magical glare of the full moon. For several hours we plodded upwards, stopping only to don crampons. There was a fair amount of soft snow, making going tiring, but we had for company the great peaks of the Caucasus in the silver light, Dongus-Orun, Ushba, even Koshtan -Tau and Dykh-Tau over thirty miles away. As the night wore on the air became cooler and cooler and despite double boots and overgaiters, my toes became numb. I longed for dawn, for an end to this alien nightscape. At about 4.30 a.m. as we approached the steep slopes of the cone of the eastern summit, a faint lightening appeared in the eastern sky. It was another hour before it came to anything, but as the moon finally set, a

greyness, a truly ghastly pallor stole over the peaks. At dawn this dispersed at a stroke as a rosy flush accompanied the sun's appearance. The light on our faces gave the appearance of warmth, but as we ascended the final slopes of the East Summit, we climbed into a strengthening wind. This became a gale on the top, forcing us to lie prone to make an obligatory radio call. My little thermometer registered 5 degrees F.

A quick run down to the col between the east and west summits brought fingers, thumbs and toes back to life. We dumped our sacs at the col and made our way up steep, icy and finally windslabbed slopes to the final few hundred yards of ridge to the higher west summit. Here at over 18000 feet, we were feeling the altitude a little.

Now, just after 9 a.m, the wind had dropped to a fresh breeze and we were able to enjoy the 360 degrees view. We first photographed the tattered red flag, then looked around. South were the secret green valleys of Svanetia with fresh snow covered Alps. North the land fell away to brown green steppe, indefinitely. East and west ran the spine of the Caucasus, a thousand jagged ridges punctuated by the great icy triangles of the principal peaks.

Nearly back at the hut the wind

had died and the heat was exhausting. Yun (the Soviet adviser) came up to greet us and gave a great spontaneous hug of welcome and delight at our success. No one else had made the ascent that day. We trailed back for endless coffees and to watch the tourists burning in the sun.'

Practicalities

1. One must apply early to Directorate of International Mountaineering Camps
   8 Luzhnezkaja Quay
   Moscow 119270
   USSR.
   Lists are available annually through national and alpine associations, listing terms and conditions, dates of meets etc, both in the Caucasus and in the Pamir mountains of Asia.

2. *or* be invited by an individual or Trade Union.

3. *or* Contact Intourist who only show limited interest in mountaineering.
   In method one, which most climbers would probably wish to adopt, all accommodation, food, transport, rescue arrangements etc are taken care of, including the provision of route briefings and details. Maps and guides are hard to obtain. An adviser is attached to a group and can be most helpful.

   Camps last about three weeks and cost $800 in 1984. This seems quite expensive, but covers everything once a group arrives in Moscow, including the hotel there and the flight to the south and back.

Routes

W Peak only. From Pruit ascend the E peak slopes until they begin to steepen. Make a traverse around the E peak and up to the col between the E and W peaks. Ascend steep slopes for about 200 metres, then follow an easy level ridge for a few hundred metres to the summit.
E and W Peaks traverse. From Pruit climb directly up the slopes to the summit of the E Peak, go easily down to the col, then continue as above.

Above: The Elbrus Peak, Central USSR.

Below: Soviet climbers at the German bivouac near Ushba.

Time. Pruit depart   2.40 a.m.
East Peak top   7.30
West Peak top   9.00
return Pruit   11.30

Technically easy (alpine 'facile') the ascent is nevertheless serious. The slope from the col to the west peak is steep and icy requiring crampons, and in many cases they may be advisable throughout the traverse. There is no shelter and high winds are common. Good clothing is absolutely essential.

The times given are for a fit and acclimatized party after two weeks' climbing on lower peaks. Though it is usual for parties to try the peak early in a visit, and the Soviet adviser may encourage this, it is not entirely advisable, given the altitude of the mountain. No weather forecasts are available though Soviet mountaineers are very friendly.

The Transition to Alpine Climbing: the Rockclimber

Traditionally rock climbing and mountaineering were not regarded as in any sense separate, but in this last decade some have sought to distinguish 'technical rock climbing' as a separate sport. This is justified by the specialized nature of modern extreme rock climbing practice, and the degree of concentration, fitness and training required to attain the highest standards. The contrast is most emphasized in countries where rock climbing is practised in different centres from the mountains proper, as in the forcing grounds of Yosemite or the Elbe sandstone of East Germany. Another factor has been the exaggerated conservatism of traditional mountaineering establishments, who have, in West Germany for example, tended to condemn aid reductions and whole emphasis of modern rock climbing as being a 'bastardization' of 'true' mountaineering. Either way this seems wrong headed, and a loss to most people involved in both aspects of climbing. The feats of 'technical rock climbing' are outstanding, and have much relevance in mountains as well as on small crags, as the recent outburst of high quality modern style rock climbs in the Chamonix Aiguilles illustrates, whilst those rock climbers who never apply their skills in a mountain environment may not regret missing the long walks and bad weather, but sacrifice much good rock and the possibility of applying their skills in the mountain environment. That in turn means that the small environments in which some 'technical rock climbers' muster are ludicrously overcrowded. Any real innovation there is increasingly the monopoly of the very few utterly outstanding practitioners.

In France many of the best rock climbers have managed to perform well technically but retain an interest in mountaineering, or rock climbing in the alpine environ-

Easier rock climbing on the Eichhorn (grade V) in the Wetterstein.

ment. For them it works well, for it contributes to a less atomized climbing culture, and provides more opportunities, choices and a form of profession. Where the two activities are more divorced, as is true in Britain since about 1975 and since the 1960s in the USA, there appears to be less scope for variation of activity by young pure rock climbers, more eventual bore-

dom and a degree of frustration of opportunities. An extraordinary degree of conformism has emerged, quite alien to the maverick innovatory traditions of mountaineering. There is a tendency for rock climbing to become a 'risk free' activity as protection is improved, so that elegance and style *per se* rather than the sheer imagination, effort, risk and innovatory nature of ascent predominate as criteria of excellence. The 'new' Anglo-Saxon model of the highly individual rock climbing leader thus leaves too little scope for the development of co-operative experiences by people climbing together to a common purpose, frequently in the face of adverse external circumstances. In bad weather modern technical rock climbers less often push on for that day's harsh but sometimes rewarding joint experience, retreating instead to the gym. Whereas peak performance in 'technical climbing' can last for a few years at most, mountaineering covers a wide range of climbing games and leaves an individual with freedom to participate in them as suits his or her personality, age and interests.

Rock climbers coming into mountaineering have many advantages. The steepness of mountains hold little fear, rope techniques and use of protection are familiar, the psychology of dealing with difficult obstacles is established and usually there are other rock climbers who wish to make the transition. Unlike the walker attempting 'mountaineering' for the first time, rock experts can enter mountaineering at any of a number of technical levels, with a bewildering but provocative range of options. There is still much to learn, especially about snow conditions and techniques, weather and route finding, but that ought to be stimulating when other technical hurdles to enjoyment are removed. Thus the range of climbs recommended is wide both in size and technical standard. This seems appropriate as a reflection of reality, where good rock climbers have frequently done major alpine ascents in their very first season of alpine climbing, seemingly with few qualms. Rock climbers will initially continue to favour alpine climbs where their skills are put to use, but will seek increasing competence on ice, snow and mixed ground.

CENTRAL SWITZERLAND
Salbitschijen (2,981 m)

Route:	S Ridge
Grade:	IV+
First ascent:	Alfred and Otto Amstad and Guido Masetto 16 August 1935
Map:	Swiss Landkarte 255
Approach:	From the village of Göschenen, between Andermatt and Wassen. From Göschenen go up the Göschener Tal. There are paths to the Salbit Hut (2,105 m) from Abfrutt or just past Ulmi. Both paths are signposted and lead to the hut in about 3 hours.

Salbitschijen S Ridge. The granite provides delightful climbing.

The ridge is of very fine granite, and surrounded by magnificent scenery, with views of the impressive and difficult West Ridge. It is a good introduction, like the North Ridge of the Piz Badile, to rock climbing in an alpine setting, without snow or other difficulties, but with gendarmes and an alpine character. The descent is very straightforward, which removes a major worry for the first timer. For the modern rock climber the rocks of Handegg and Grimsel with high standard technical climbing are only a few kilometres away.

From the hut go west on a path under the south ridge and up a gully to a col on the ridge (2,585 m). From a Point on the right start up the face for 15 m and go up to a corner leading to the ridge. There are a variety of routes to the top of the first tower (2,731 m). Abseil into the gap (25 m).

Go up left under the ridge edge, or direct to a chimney and up it to another gap below a smooth slab, the 'Elephantenauch'. Go direct for 6 m then up right to a corner and ledge, with a belay above, in very good position and on generally good holds. Another slab follows, and an obstacle is passed on the left to a corner running up just left of the edge. Go up this and the arête above to a slab and up this to a gap before another slabby section. This is climbed for a short distance and followed by thin cracks leading left until the arête can be attained. Climb the arête, with deviations on the left for a couple of rope lengths until reaching a ledge. From there go part way up the pinnacle above then traverse it to the left into a small col. The Plattenturm above is climbed straight up, or the upper section avoided by a few moves left and a diagonal back right and up the back. From the Plattenturm continue to the next tower, the Zwillingsturm (2,920 m) and continue to the main summit going round a tower *en route* on the left. This last section is not difficult in normal conditions (6–8 hours).

The descent lies down the East Ridge to the second little col, and by climbing down an easy gully leading left (north) towards the Salbit Glacier. Make a detour across the top of the glacier instead of heading straight down, and get into a couloir leading east towards the Salbit Hut. There are no great difficulties so long as the way is followed carefully and there are no crevasses (1½ hours). On our visit a very old guide took a non-climbing girl member of the party up the descent route as a half day outing, for the fun of it. There are a number of harder excellent rock climbs in the group, including the West Ridge (V+ −VI) the SE Wall of the Zwillingsturm (convenient V+) and the East Pillar (VI+), so an enjoyable few days are possible here.

WETTERSTEIN, AUSTRIA/GERMANY
Schüsselkarspitze (2,537 m)

Route:	S E Face
Grade:	VI −
First ascent:	R Peters, R Haringer 25–6 June 1934.
Map:	DAV 1:25,000 German Alpine Club, Wetterstein East
Approach:	From the main Garmisch-Partenkirchen to Innsbruck road, take the fork W to Ober Leutasch. From the Gaistal Inn walk to the Wetterstein Hut (1,660 m) in 2 hours. Alternatively from Garmisch (Germany) walk to the Oberreintal hut (1,525 m) – 4 hours. From the Wetterstein Hut take a path up to just below the Eastern Wangscharte and traverse E under the wall to the lowest point, beyond the fall line from the summit (1½ hours). From Oberreintal make a rather tedious ascent to the East Wangscharte and descend onto the S side by rappels past a multitude of memorial plaques, then follow the same route to the start (2½ hours).

The south face of the Schüsselkarspitze occupies an historic place in the history of rock climbing in the Eastern Alps. Its generally solid limestone is not as massive or elegant as the Verdon climbing, but it is nevertheless good, and the aspect of the face makes it quick to dry after rain. Nor does the face remain snowed up or verglas-ridden for long in the summer. Though the SE Face contains many pitons, it was mostly free climbed even in its original form, and is usually done that way today. It followed in the tradition of the Fiechtl-Herzog route, first done in 1913 on the same face a few hundred metres to the west. Though now only graded V+, or VI if the bottom cracks are taken direct, this was one of the most difficult rock climbs accomplished anywhere before the First World War, as the 'Sud-Ost' was to be in the 1930s. Since the 1970s this wall has gone through further transitions, with a number of modern technical free climbs at a very high standard, and the free climbing of aid sections on the established routes.

The 'Sud-Ost' begins just left of a small rock island below the face and at first there is little difficulty in reaching a crack system. This steepens, and contains a number of pitons. It is climbed with difficulty for several rope lengths (VI−) until an easier diagonal break heads off left. This is followed in its entirety, with odd steps of III and IV and at least one section of grade V climbing before easier ground leads past a snow patch to the summit. The descent lies down the West Ridge. At the saddle before the tower on the West Ridge go onto the north west face and find an abseil point, this leading in two

short overhanging abseils to ledges and a traverse which in turn leads down the ridge to the East Wangscharte ($1\frac{1}{2}$ hours). From there descend either by abseil again to the south side and the Wetterstein Hut or down to Oberreintal on the north. Both descents take about 1 hour from the East Wangscharte.

The ascent that Oliver Woolcock and I made in 1965 took about 5 hours. The weather had been wet, and some water streaks were still to be found on the face, so that the South Face Direct had looked too wet to try. The Sud-Ost had been enough sun to be in condition quickly, and gave sustained VI climbing though there was no truly outstanding difficulty. It seemed slightly less difficult than the Schöber route on the Unterer Schüsselkarturm which we had done a few days before. We were amused to see not only Hermann Buhl's name in the summit book, but Don Whillans' as one of the very few British climbers of the South Face routes. At the time

locals looked at us askance when we climbed with PAs and nut protection, and this was still the case in 1969, but it has now become common practice.

Peters and Haringer were to go on to make other important first ascents in the Eastern Alps and in 1935 Peters succeeded with M Maier in making the first ascent of the Croz Spur of the Grandes Jorasses, arguably the hardest big north wall climb of its day. For modern rock climbers the Sud-Ost poses few problems in good conditions, but it involves a confrontation with a previous highly developed culture of hard rock climbing in a mountain environment which flowered in the Eastern Alps from before 1914 until the Second World War, to revive only slowly after it. There is no doubt that its best free climbers were extremely capable, leading to the level of modern French grade VIa or British E1 with primitive equipment which was nevertheless the most advanced in use in their own time.

Other climbs in the same tra-

Chris Woodall in the Gonda Groove of Oberreintaldom, a classic grade VI.

dition abound in the Wetterstein, and there are some for example on Oberreintaldom, which were first done with aid but which have been substantially free climbed in a great wave of 'cleaning up' in recent years. This parallels developments in British and French rock climbing, but seems less well known outside German speaking circles. Some of the new climbs which have come from this movement should keep the 'rock climber turning to alpinism' interested during the transition, like the Heisse Nummer (Hot Number) on Oberreintaldom (VII) or the Knapp-Kochler Route on the South Face of the Schüsselkarspitze (VII−). All of these and many more hard rock climbs in the modern idiom are products of a 1980s renaissance in free climbing in the Eastern Alps which is built upon strong but ruptured indigenous traditions as well as developments elsewhere.

VERCORS, FRANCE
Rocher d'Archiane

Route:	S E Pillar and S Face
Grade:	V or VI 400m overall
First ascent:	First half 16-17 May 1959 G & M Livanos, R Lepage, M Vacher; Second half 31 May 1959 R Lepage, G Livanos, M Vacher
Map:	Swiss Landkarte 1,296 Sciora 1:25,000
Approach:	From the Route Napoleon S of Grenoble take the D7 from Clelles in the direction of Die, over the Col de Menée to Menée, then turn right to Archiane village.

The South East Pillar

Follow a path from the village east of the cliffs up the valley. After about 2 km go up left steeply to below a steep gully, with the main precipice of the Rocher D'Archiane to the left. Follow the path back under the precipice to the left to the prominent arête, which in detail takes the form of a big wall with spurs to each side. Start to the right of the left edge of this wall. Go up ramps and a chimney to the top of a flake then right into a crack and up it to ledges (3 pitches). Move round to the right and up a crack followed by a dièdre and slabbier section to the right. Climb cracks and walls to the enormous traversing terrace, which can be used as a means of escape to the right, leading into the descent couloir (3/4 pitches). From the top of the terrace take an obvious crack line with some small bushes sprouting from it, and climb a series of corners until an escape to the plateau by couloirs on the right. In summer this route can be very hot and debilitating as it gets the sun (4 pitches) for much of the day. It is desirable to wear suitable clothing and to carry drinks.

The terrace at mid-height also offers access to the following more difficult route on the impressive red walls to the left. Either begin via the Livanos or traverse in from the steep gully to the east, circumnavigating the buttress and crossing the Livanos at the terrace. To reach the 'Paroi Rouge' that way takes about 1½–2 hours from Archiane.

The Paroi Rouge

This is a climb of about 270 m, grade VI, very steep with a few aid points and some rock of dubious quality. It has an air of great seriousness as it overhangs big steep lower walls from the outset. From a cave in the terrace scramble up onto the terrace continuation and climb a wall of about 30 m to a higher ledge. Go left for a pitch to a

The Rocher d'Archiane, Vercors, France.

crack. Follow a series of cracks up into a most impressive diédre system, which is climbed, passing a whole series of overhangs and bulges. Eventually the diédre fades after about four pitches and the route takes to very exposed walls, with one hanging belay. Fortunately there are a good number of pitons for protection which many climbers may use for aid, as was done originally. The route eventually emerges on the plateau, but with very little 'let up' before the last few metres.

The Paroi Rouge has an atmosphere of seriousness and commitment akin to that of some bigger alpine climbs. On the descent from the summit plateau head for a wide grassy col north of the top, and a big steep gully. One goes round the head of this and out to the right (east) seeking a big tree down on a lower ledge which is festooned with abseil slings once it can be found. The abseil goes very steeply down a hanging chimney to a small change-over point and a further shorter abseil into the descent gully. That is then followed to the path back to Archiane.

The multitude of routes in the Vercors and the longer climbs of the Pre-Alps in general can be an admirable way of applying skills acquired on equipped or much climbed small crags in an environment which is big and serious yet not so badly affected by altitude and weather as the bigger peaks. The climbing season tends to be a little longer than on the highest alpine routes, with possibilities of ascent from May to October in good conditions, and the climbs are long enough to enforce an alpine pace if bivouacs are to be avoided. This is ideal physical and psychological preparation for more strenuous alpine climbs.

BREGAGLIA, SWISS-ITALIAN BORDER
Piz Badile (3,308 m)

Route:	NE Face and N Ridge
Grade:	NE Face V+ A+ 800 m sustained N Face V 750 m
First ascent:	R Cassin, G Esposito, V Ratti, M Molteni, G Valsecchi 14–16 July 1937.
Map:	Swiss Landkarte Val Bregaglia 1:25,000
Approach:	From Bondo in the valley between Chiavenna and the Maloja Pass it is usually possible to drive up a small lane and forestry road into the Sciora valley, though one is not supposed to leave a car there. This saves about two hours of walking up through the lower woods. It is possible to reach the Piz Badile from either of the Swiss Alpine Huts in the valley, with very little to choose between them. The Sciora Hut (2,118 m) is reached in about 2½ hours from the road end, following a signposted path up the left side of the valley. The Sass-Fura Hut, also 2½ hours from the road end, is reached by another signposted path crossing the river by a bridge and climbing steeply up the opposite (S) side of the valley, and again is signposted. Both huts are extremely pleasantly situated, and there are many bivouacs and boulder problems near the Sciora Hut.

The Piz Badile is one of the finest mountains in the Alps, a huge monolith to its NE and NW, of smooth slabs of granite. It is the more impressive for its position, dominating the Sciora cirque of granite peaks, several of which would predominate in a less rugged setting. Its position also makes it notably subject to violent summer storms, for it is close to the point where the hot air from the plains sweeps up daily to meet the cooler atmosphere of the Engadine and the Bernina peaks. Its thunder storms are notorious, and lives have been lost to lightning in this region. The NE face is one of the classic north face climbs in the Alps, not too difficult technically and congenial to the rock climber in good weather, it was soloed by Hermann Buhl, and later by a number of other good climbers, in 4–6 hours. However, it is a storm trap, has some loose rock high up and has some loose rock high up and dangers from stone fall or quick frosts which verglas the rock making it much more difficult. It was just such a sudden storm which slowed the first ascent and led to the deaths of the Como climbers Molteni and Valsecchi on the descent in 1937. There is considerable risk from stone fall on the face and in the upper couloir.

It was barely light as we climbed up the little glacier south of the rock rognon which cuts into it. This seems easier than the north fork, which has more crevasses and in any case is not a quick route to the North-East face. From the Point 2,420 m just right of the fall line of the couloir in the upper centre of the face, we soloed up ledges and short walls to the right with little difficulty, avoiding hanging around in a place exposed to stonefall. It was 1962, my second and Alan's first time in the Alps. We were climbing well on rock and confident of our ability, but awed by the size of the face, its reputation and by fear of stonefall or storms.

Soon we reached a fine open book diédre requiring the rope. This is where the ledge from the North Ridge and the route from the Sass Fura Hut comes in.

The corner went easily, (V) and the route led diagonally to another diédre. There was a need to take care with route finding on the big slabs, because technically it seemed possible to climb almost

Martin Boysen, with the north east face of the Piz Badile behind.

anywhere, but occasional pitons sprouted to point the way. The only problem was that some of these went the wrong way. After the second dièdre (V +) we loped at speed up more compact slabs, and reached the snowpatch in the middle of the face. There was no stonefall that day, perhaps because the face seemed dry but also the weather was relatively cool, so that there was not much melting of

snow lying in the upper couloir. Somewhere in this vicinity one of my early climbing partners Alan MacHardy found an anorak on a ledge, and since it was better than his took it with him. It had on it some dark stains. He later found that its owner had been killed by stonefall.

Above the snowpatch the rock steepens, but the cracks were festooned with pitons so that protection was no problem and progress was not too difficult even where the cracks were wet. A series of V and

V + pitches led enjoyably up the face, never causing us much delay after our short rest, a bite to eat, and a fag for Al at the Snowpatch. All the time in my mind was not only the epic of the first ascent, which nearly came to grief here, but also another fraught passage of the same section a year or two before our visit by Ian Clough, Mike James, Nev Crowther and Sid Clarke, who had somehow got roped up with the Italian Claudio Corti in a storm. (Storms seem to have been Corti's *métier*: in 1957, he was plucked from the North Face of the Eiger in desperate conditions after a difficult international rescue operation, the sole survivor of four men who set off to climb the mountain a week earlier.) As clouds of late morning rolled up from Italy we neared the ridge, and rather than taking to the great central couloir on the left we tiptoed direct up the slabs in a couple of delicate ropelengths onto the fine arete of the North Ridge. It had taken about 7 hours.

After going to the summit we had intended to descend the North Ridge, as is done often to avoid the long trek back over the Passo Bondo or even longer one via the Trubenasca Pass. But after a short distance down clouds closed in, so we decided to get off the ridges as quickly as possible, going back over the summit and looking for the descent in the mist. A storm was brewing.

Here a mistake was made, and we went off the summit a little too far to the right, missing the relatively easy and well marked descent and climbing a long way down into a couloir system. Now there is a summit bivouac hut. However by scrambling and one or two abseils we got down to a large snowpatch and easy terrain leading to a CAI Gianetti Hut at 2,534 m., but not before we were soaked as thunder roared and lightning rippled on the ridges. Next day we re-crossed to the Sciora via the Passo Bondo, a complicated and crevassed route, which involved abseiling and glacier bridges on a short but very crevassed descent.

MONT BLANC RANGE, FRANCE
Petit Dru (3,733 m)

Route:	W Face Direct
Grade:	ED 1,000 m
First ascent:	G Hemming, R Robbins 24–6 July 1962
Map:	Carte Vallot 1:50,000
Approach:	Take the Grands Montets Téléphérique from Argentière
Route:	The N Face
Grade:	V + 850 m
Abseil descent:	R Gréloz and A Roch 1932
First ascent:	P Allain and R Leininger 31 September – 1 August 1935

The stunning rock needle of the Petit Dru dominates the Chamonix Valley and cannot fail to inspire any climber. The tower is laced with hard climbs most of which are equipped with protection pitons, but that should not lead rock climbers to underestimate the true nature of its climbing. The Dru is a mountain Aiguille, an outlier of the Aiguille Verte, itself one of the most difficult of the 4,000 m peaks in the Mont Blanc Range. Thus the Petit Dru provides a whole range of magnificent rock pitches, but also the hazards of areas of unstable granite, stonefall danger, extreme length of the climbs and risk of bad weather. It is high enough to become very snowy in bad weather and can be beset by verglas near the summit when conditions are fair below. The approaches to the Bonatti Pillar, and the North Face Route require competence on ice. Few climbers complete the climbs without at least one bivouac, so take the necessary equipment.

The Petit Dru used to be approached from Montenvers, after taking the railway from Chamonix. This involved crossing the Mer de Glace and ascending a steep moraine gully under the Drus, taking a terrace on the top left of the first steep moraine slope and from it finding a minute path which led onto a narrow moraine ridge. This in turn led pleasantly to the rognon under the West Face, where there are good bivouac sites (3 hours from Montenvers). Though the impecunious might still prefer this, most people now come via the Grandes Montets Téléphérique from Argentière, descending by a little couloir from the big snowfield behind the Grandes Montets top station onto the glacier under the Nant Blanc Face of the Verte, and making their way across the glacier to the base of the face. This is almost entirely downhill. It is usual to bivouac at the rognon.

The **West Face Direct** has the advantage of being relatively

The north face of Les Drus, France.

stonefall free, though sometimes the lower slabs are peppered with rocks from high on the North Face route. A more serious problem tends to be other climbing parties, though one hopes that as more hard rock climbs are done around Chamonix the pressure may be reduced upon this magnificent classic. An early start allows parties to bivouac quite high on the West Face, or if they are very fast on the North Face or even in descent. It also allows ascent of the Direct to the junction with the Original Route and a rappel descent back down. The latter, usually done carrying little equipment, has been very popular for the last fifteen years.

The route starts right of the centre of the bottom buttress of the West Face. In 1975 Bob Toogood and myself reached this point about mid-day and descended before the snow on the glacier softened. The aim was to do this as a sequel to the Gouffre Berger, which we had just descended to the bottom. The unconventional starting time was a ploy to avoid the inevitable other parties. As we began we could see some climbers on the difficult cracks above the first terrace.

After scrambling up right on terraces an obvious line goes up more directly through the lower slabs, which in general are not too steep. The first few rope lengths went very quickly to the first terrace, though they were V or V+ in places. By then we were only about two rope lengths behind the climbers who had started earlier, and we could tell by their accents that they were East Europeans.

The big 40 m layback above (VI − VI +) proved strenuous, but there was plenty of protection equipment in it, though we used a few nuts too. There followed a series of steep but very beautiful pitches (VI and Vs), with good protection in place and scope for further nuts (or Friends.). In the middle of this section the climbers above agreed to let us pass and we pressed on to just below the big corner which comes from the

Niche des Drus, and bivouacked on a square ledge with very steep walls behind which effectively protected us from anything falling from above.

Early next morning, after one more pitch in the corner above (V) a ledge led us to the junction with the Original West Face Route. A couple of steep pitches were recognizable from my attempt on the Original West Face Route in 1962, which ended hereabouts when Les Brown injured his stomach. This was sweet revenge. Bob led the 90 m dièdre, using the antiquated points of aid, ancient wedges and pitons. At its top the old bolts, relics of the re-entry onto the face by Berardini's party in 1952, could be seen coming in across a blank wall on the left. A delapidated loop of ancient perlon ropes dangled to the right leading towards the upper dièdre. Belaying even more carefully than usual on our own gear, we just clipped into the sheathless mass of cord and slid across in an outrageously exposed position. Though we could hear voices below no one was to be seen, and clouds on Mont Blanc heralded worsening conditions. The climbing remained strenuous, but interesting all the way through steep rock to the sudden emergence onto a square ledge on the North Face. It was about 16.00 hours, and the West Face was complete.

It is not the end of the route. As there was some light left and cloud swept in I led a pitch above on the North Face and left the rope ready for the next morning. It began to snow heavily so we fled into our sleeping bags in the bivvy sheet. As darkness fell we could hear shouts somewhere below on the North Face, but there was nothing to be seen.

Next morning's weather dawned none too good, so we headed up post-haste. The rocks were covered in floury snow and verglas. I led and Bob followed. After a few rope lengths and a few hours we reached the hole which connects with the top of the Bonatti Pillar. Though there was a brief clearance we were in no mood to go to the

summit, so we traversed the quartz ledges to the descent route and began to abseil towards the Flammes des Pierres. Intermittent showers stopped and the sun even shone through the clouds a little.

I had been down here before, after the North Face in 1969, and roughly knew the way. First a series of abseils down chimneys and cracks just left, looking downwards, of the little ridge of spikes known as the Flammes des Pierres. Then down a less steep area of slabs, scrambling and abseiling with occasional steep steps and dangers from stone-fall. It was there that we heard the ominous roar above in the thick mist. I was just feeding the rope down to Bob across easy angled slabby ground. Two very small one metre rock walls were the only shelter, and we flattened ourselves against them. The rocks roared all around, then stopped. It was truly amazing, and we nipped off down, seeking out the abseil line down slabs which complete the rock descent and allow escape from that terrible trap of a couloir. The Charpoua Glacier was crossed high, but not too difficult, and we went right to the valley, just missing the last train and running through the woods in driving rain.

The earlier party went back down the West Face Direct, and a number of parties of the North Face joined together to battle their way out. Among them was the redoubtable Chef Patrick Green. Despite atrocious weather they succeeded – though it took them another two or three days to extricate themselves from the storm blasted mountain.

In many ways the **North Face** of the Petit Dru is the most alpine of the routes described. The sunless aspect of much of the lower part of the face, the icy condition of many of the cracks and the crossing of the Niche all make it feel a true north wall climb, as can the tricky nature of the final rope lengths in bad conditions. Usually it is possible climbing in boots with one pair of crampons per pair of climbers and one axe and ice hammer, though in bad conditions full equipment is needed. It can be done fast, but parties often bivouac, either low on the face to give a head start in the morning (some danger of stonefall in the late approach) or in its upper reaches. There are ample bivouac sites, near the Niche, at the junction of the West and North faces and at the Quartz Band high up.

In 1969 we began from the Rognon. With several climbs already completed we were already very fit and hoped to do the route in a day, not least because the weather forecast was for a fine morning but worse weather later. It was Jack Street's only real alpine season, but as one of Britain's best rock climbers of the day he had done the Walker Spur before I had even arrived in Chamonix, after climbing the North Spur of the Aiguille du Chardonnet for ice familiarization and acclimatization training. His companion Brian Shirley on these routes had climbed in the Alps for only one previous season, and had been with us on the Bonatti Pillar then. Leaving about 2.45 a.m. from the Rognon we soon reached the Nant Blanc Glacier and the Ryan Lochmatter Couloir, and soloed up it and across the first snow shelf to the start of the difficulties. Here we found our friends, Mo Anthoine and Alan Hunt debating a little after a cold bivouac, perhaps doubting the weather. Martin Boysen and Nick Estcourt had just set off and were a couple of rope lengths above in the cracks leading towards the Niche.

We steamed up the chimneys and cracks, though Jack was a little surprised by the standard of the Lambert Crack (VI or aid). Characteristically he did it free, pulling over the overhang very quickly carrying his sac, and heading up to the belay. Here we could see the other pair, already setting off up the snow in the Niche. Their steps, which probably followed others from previous days, made the Niche snow easy to climb to the steep series of grooves on the edge overlooking the West Face. Here there is a choice of two difficult cracks, the Martinelli (V+) and

the Allain (free VI). Jack launched off up the latter, dropping in one or two nut runners and clipping the odd peg as protection. He finished with great speed passing the Martinelli crack, and the rope ran out. I jammed and laybacked up the crack.

There was one other steep little section (V) before us and we reached the junction with the West Face by about 11 a.m. With Martin and Nick just ahead and the rocks in good condition, we were very soon at the Quartz ledges. The clouds rolled up and the afternoon storm brewed. Then we crossed to the descent, as the summit is an obvious lightning conductor. The abseils we fixed in turns, one pair setting up an abseil, the others going down with their ropes and finding and fixing the next. It was fast, but the rain soon started.

Martin and Nick had gone down an abseil and we had pulled down the ropes from above and were waiting to follow, when there was a long delay in the shout to indicate that the rope was free. Thunder banged all around, and there were occasional lightning flashes. Eventually Jack went down anyway, and I followed. Nick and Martin were sitting in the back of a chimney on a ledge. A lightning charge had come down the rope or gully or both and given both of them an awful shock, though they were not harmed in any obvious physical way. We set

off again, but soon afterwards made the mistake of trying to go left onto slabs too early. Perhaps shaken by the lightning Martin abseiled too hastily down a steep wall, not seeing in the mist that one of the two ropes had snagged on a flake dangling precariously a short distance down. As a result he ended up caught below it, unable to continue down or easily to disengage the rope but he managed eventually to extricate both himself and the rope. Below we traversed back a little towards the Flammes des Pierres, and continued down the main couloir line. The rain, hail, lightning and thunder continued.

Some of the descent here is easy, loose rock climbing which we soloed between abseils, and in one such place I heard a shout from the Flammes des Pierres which proved to be Sheffield climbers Don Morrison and Dave Marshall, bivouacking rather than going on after several days on the Bonatti Pillar as a first route of the season.

We pressed on, and eventually got onto the slabs leading to the escape to the Charpoua Glacier. With thunder still cracking we traversed a narrow ice ridge between two big crevasses across the top of the glacier. At last the glacier opened up before us and we ran down to the hut.

Les Drus from the west in winter.

MONT BLANC RANGE, FRANCE/ITALY	
Grand Capucin (3,838 m)	
Description by Michel Piola	
Route:	Voyage Selon Gulliver
Grade:	V11a–V11b
First ascent:	Pierre-Alain Steiner and Michel Piola
	21–22 May 1982 and 18–19 July 1982
Map:	Mont Blanc Range Vallot Map
Approach:	From the Midi Tap Station or Torino Hut

Pierre-Alain Steiner and I were convinced that modern technical rock climbing could be translated to big mountains even though new lines would clearly be much harder than existing routes. There were unavoidable blank slabs which could only be protected whilst leading provided we 'adapted' some aid techniques.

We felt ready for the *grand problem* of the Grand Cap: the bulging, not very pronounced spur separating the south and east faces that the Lecco (1968) and Volger (1981) routes avoided by passing diagonally on either side.

Between two snow falls on the 21st and 2nd May 1982, accompanied by Patrick Steiner, we climbed the first four pitches utilizing for protection the strange knobs which peppered the granite of the large red slabs. We returned from completing the fourth pitch deeply impressed by the exposure and the uncertainty of the protection—especially on the second pitch. This is a smooth slab on which the placing of expansion pegs (for protection) whilst perched precariously on lead remained a painful memory.

Pierre-Alain and I returned on the 18/19th July of the same year, to complete this astonishingly sustained route this time with the added piquancy of a hammock bivouac at the fifth stance.

Repeated twice during the same summer, the route was to become a classic and received many ascents in 1983. I would just like to state at this point, that the first 'free' ascent shouldn't be credited to a subsequent French team: we are not ashamed to admit to having taken a number of rests after the knackering effort of placing bolts whilst in the lead (often taking more than half an hour to drill a single hole standing on the same tiny protuberance), and I consider that we had already made the first 'free' ascent whilst creating it, apart from the aid of the three pendulums.

The only pendulum having been 'freed' after the ascent had been the work of Marco Pedrini a short time before the ascent (by first descending on abseil in this instance), the logical exit variation over the nine foot horizontal roof named *Panoramix*. This is a VIIa/VIIb at high altitude (3,800 m) that to date awaits a first on-sight free ascent, Marco having climbed it with a number of resting points.

The Grand Capucin and Tour Ronde north face.

Integrated Alpinism

The highest form of alpinism involves rock and ice climbing skills in a big mountain environment where choice of party, route and tactics on the day are matters of careful judgement. Essentially it is an integrative process, and ideally many of the actions taken should amount to reflex responses to the situations involved. When an experienced alpine climber meets a sudden risk, it is usual to have to take quick action in which correct technique combines with cool judgement to avoid the problem for oneself and one's companions. Here one should perhaps distinguish between preventative judgements which allow a party to avoid possible dangers from the outset, and crisis responses to dangers once they occur. Survival and success in alpine climbing require both, but probably the first in its application to choice of route as a whole, party, weather etc. is most vital. With a well-thought out plan of action, a suitable party and preparations, one is far less likely to face unexpected hazards, and more likely to be able to cope with those met than otherwise. At the same time one ought not to be surprised by the degree of uncertainty involved even in fulfilling a well planned route. This is one of the main attractions of big mountain climbing, and one of its main differences from 'école d'escalade' style rock climbing.

There can be little doubt that it is the snow and ice environment, and the problems of size, time and bad weather, which maximize uncertainty. In face of this, the climber requires a certain cautious optimism to enable him to look the immediate problems in the eye, attempt their solution and remain encouraged to go on to the next difficulty. Given the serious nature of the dangers, many people, including virtuoso rock climbers, are not cut out for it. They find the combination of different types of adversity alien as compared to the 'concentration' of high quality rock, and find it unsatisfying to have to make endless numbers of judgements of different types. Each person should make a careful appraisal of himself and those nervous of the mountaineering situation might be best to go gently, to choose routes which fit their interests, or even to decide not to do more alpine climbing. There is no disgrace in this—in relation to danger everyone has a cracking point. Ultimately in all climbing, as T Edward Howard said long ago, 'You've just go to want to do it.'

In mountaineering the maintenance of that motivation usually also means that it is best if the climbers respect Robin Campbell's dictum 'Love the mountains.' This applies not only to the preservation of a precious environment, but also to the preservation of self. It is not so

The north face of Monte Disgrazia, Bregaglia.

much that mountains have ways of dealing with the thoughtless or the over-ambitious, it is rather that such people tend to over-reach, and suffer the consequences.

Snow and ice and mixed climbs of intermediate levels of difficulty

Most alpine peaks can be climbed by routes which are predominantly snow climbs, but which involve some rock climbing of modest difficulty. A reason for rock climbing developing relatively late as an alpine skill was that many peaks could be climbed with moderate rock climbing techniques and with primitive methods of protection. At the same time considerable skills on snow and ice, albeit using now outmoded step-cutting methods, were to be found among the greatest guides and amateurs late in the nineteenth century.

The combination of ability to lead rock up to about grade V (Severe-mild VS – 5.7 in the USA) and experience and steadiness in glacier travel and snow and ice climbing will allow a party to climb the ordinary routes of almost all alpine mountains in Europe, and most of those in mountains under 5,940 m. The intermediate routes mentioned or described in this section are intended to indicate a possible progression from the easier snow routes described in pp.146–155 to the next more ambitious stage, where snow and ice skills and alpine style rope management are combined with modest rock ability in the ascent of some of the best climbs on the European continent.

Many of these, like the Whymper couloir on the Aiguille Verte or the Frontier Ridge of Mont Blanc, require fitness, competence and speed if the party is to complete the ascent in a day, as is usual. Precise timing and avoidance of delays are critical, as is the ability to climb together roped on ground which is not technically difficulty but where a slip might be dangerous to the party as a whole. This, a skill little used on small rock climbs, is a key to safe and fast progress on bigger climbs because there is simply not always the time to proceed in pitches. There are a range of ways of making such techniques safer, including the use of running belays between leader and second even when no fixed belay is taken, and the careful use of spikes and projections on ridges to afford a measure of protection even when climbing together. Such methods require care on the part of the whole party, and a degree of slickness in rope management to avoid snagging or tangling the rope. Most important is the trust and knowledge between members of the party, so that they can anticipate each others' movements and also possible falls or slips and be ready to attempt action to limit their effects. This situation anticipation is very difficult to teach, but develops with practice particularly between people who climb a lot together.

Safety hints for potentially serious mountain situations

- Leader or second falls into crevasse – other person or person's anchorage and action to aid rescue.
- Slip by leader or second when climbing together – check any intermediate anchors or other means of preventing the other climber or climbers being dislodged.
- Avalanche or stonefall – decide whether or not a particular slope is avalanche prone. Check for any shelter, and ensure that chosen route is the best to avoid these possibilities. On many alpine routes helmets remain strongly recommended.
- Safety of previously rigged belays and other anchors for abseils – this is one of the commonest causes of alpine accidents. Ensure that there is back up if an anchor fails, either itself, the slings attached to it, or the rock or ice into which it is inserted.
- Know the key rescue signals for a helicopter or other rescue party, and how to indicate that it is not required.
- Know the main precautions to take when traversing a corniced ridge.
- Deploy your equipment properly – check that crampon straps are fastened so that the crampons remain attached and the straps cannot be snagged by the points from the other foot. Check that the harness is properly fastened, the knots are tight, the rucsac buckles are fastened in properly to avoid loss during ascent. In alpinism climbers get extremely fatigued and minor errors creep in even with the most experienced people, especially on multi-day climbs or extremely long day routes. Do not hesitate to keep an eye on your partner, and do not object to your partner watching out for you—a mistake can be fatal.

The Peuterey Ridge of Mont Blanc.

MONT BLANC RANGE, FRANCE/ITALY
Aiguille de Chardonnet (3,824 m)

Route:	The Forbes Ridge and the North Spur
Grade:	Forbes Ridge PD sup North Spur difficile
First ascent of Forbes Ridge:	L H and A Aubert, M Crettez 30 July 1899
First ascent of North Spur:	A Migot and C Dévouassoux 28 July 1929
Map:	Carte Vallot 1:50,000, École Versant Français 1:20,000 (French side only), Carte d'Italie 1:25,000 Monte Bianco
Approach:	From Le Tour in the Chamonix Valley walk up to the Albert Premier Hut (2,702 m) up the true right moraine of the glacier (i.e. left facing uphill), or go up the Col de Balme path. At the Charamillon Inn go up right and pass below the lake, then traverse round a big shoulder until the direct path is joined. The direct is very steep, taking $2\frac{1}{2}$ hours, the other way more pleasant, taking $3\frac{1}{4}$ hours. Alternatively take the téléphérique to the Col de Balme and follow a traversing path to the ordinary way near the lake ($1\frac{3}{4}$ hours).

The Forbes Ridge and the North Spur both provide excellent snow and ice climbs. The Forbes is quite long, with a glacial approach and some tricky short sections on the climb, and a fairly steep descent to the Col Superieur Adams Reilly and the Épaule Glacier. Overall it is a fine expedition at reasonably high altitude, which is often found to be both testing and rewarding to inexperienced parties, or even experienced groups wanting a high scenic route. It is a good route to do for acclimatization before climbing on Mont Blanc. The North Spur gives a short, steeper ice climb. This is a useful route for good rock climbers making the transition to ice and mixed climbing, who often do this as a preparation.

From the hut for either climbing route it is best to make a detour towards the Col du Tour to avoid the rather crevassed lower section of the Tor Glacier. From the Trient Hut, the Col is crossed to join this detour path. The path leads into the glacial valley under the Forbes Ridge and the North Face. Climb the snowy basin under the Aiguille Forbes, keeping to the left to avoid crevasses, to a plateau. Above, the arête is more defined, with a large ice boss which is a key feature of the route. Cross the small plateau to the right under some séracs, then climb the arête to the Boss. The Boss itself is steep for about 50 m and requires care. Go by easier ground towards the main eastern arête of the mountain, pass a bergschrund and reach the arête just right of gendarme 3,703 m ($4\frac{1}{2}$ hours). Cross the first tower on the ridge or by a slope to the left (III) and then several others with good snow arêtes and cornices between. A last gendarme is passed on the left, leading to a chimney and the top ($6\frac{1}{2}$ hours from the Albert Premier or Trient Hut).

From the summit go along the West Ridge until it steepens. Go left a little and take a steep slope of rock, snow and ice which leads eventually to a snowy shoulder. There are some abseil points which may be useful in bad conditions in the afternoon, or storm. The snowy shoulder leads to the Col Superièur Adams Reilly. Go down a steep slope to a big bergschrund, on the north side. It is usual to jump this if the snow is suitable, or to abseil from an anchor (ice screw) in the slope above, if it is icy. Go down the crevassed glacier and rejoin the route of approach via the Tour Glacier, keeping well right to avoid many crevasses directly in the line of the Albert Premier Hut. Descend to the Hut by the same path as in ascent or return across the Col du Tour to the Trient Hut ($2\frac{1}{2}$ hours to Albert Premier from summit, or the Trient Hut $3\frac{1}{2}$ hours.).

The North Spur is a classic 'difficile' ice climb but at 500 m is not too long and exhausting for it to be done as a first route of the season by competent people. Approached from the Trient or Albert Premier Huts by the same route as the Forbes Ridge, one then descends into the basin below the face. Turn a lower rock pillar by steepening glacier slopes on the right, avoiding big crevasses. Cut up left towards the ridge just before the first buttress and continue up the snow ridge to a second buttress. Climb it passing séracs on the right and take the final steep slope in a fairly direct line to the summit, taking care if it is bare ice in particular (5–6 hours, but can be done much faster). There are many variant, including a detour left on the upper slope and the ascent of a steep couloir on the right low down (TD). Descend by the same route as the Forbes Ridge.

These and many similar climbs are serious undertakings, long, arduous and requiring a mixture of mountaineering skill and steadiness in all the party. Modest grades are only one factor, for in the mountain environment they can become epic if the weather is poor. Some are in condition only in the summer season, or early in that, becoming bare ice in high summer or early autumn. A spell of bad weather in summer can put them back in condition in its aftermath, a point often missed. Stone and sérac fall is often most dangerous in very hot dry summers. All tend to be feasible in winter, so long as conditions are judged correctly.

The Grandes Courses and the North Walls

Since the 1920s the focus of higher standard alpine climbing has been upon the long serious and technically difficult climbs opened up on the steepest and most forbidding walls. In the European Alps and in North America many of these are the ice bound north faces where past glaciation and aspect combine to give very high steep walls with much snow and ice. In general north wall climbing is mixed, involving all the skills and judgement of the accomplished alpinist. Traditionally in Europe by the late 1950s accomplishment tended to be measured in terms of how many Grandes Courses and/or North Walls a person had climbed, as well as by the invention of new routes and demonstrable technical skill.

There are six big North Walls in the Alps: the north faces of the Cima Grande, the Petit Dru, the Matterhorn, and the Eiger; the north east face of the Piz Badile; and the Walker Spur on the Grandes Jorasses. Though these are the most famous north walls, in fact there are many others which are comparable, and not a few that are a good deal harder in the Alps. It is for this reason that the two following climbs have been dealt with as advanced intermediate possibilites, for already acomplished rock climbers. Routes such as these are never likely to be easy. Good conditions in some respects, like the dry rock associated with a long period of good weather, make them difficult in other ways – like the stonefalls, waterfalls by day and verglas and hazards caused by other climbers. The technical standard of the rock climbing, or the steepness of ice, is no longer exceptional on these routes, but their general position, exposure to bad weather and length make them undertakings of great seriousness. Very few climbers will avoid a bivouac on the latter two, despite the feats of high speed climbers like Christophe Profit or Eric Escoffier, who have each soloed at this standard, Profit completing the Eiger North Wall in one day in March 1985 and thereby coping with winter conditions as well.

Most climbers will be unable to emulate this, but some hints at better performance can be given.

1 Get to know the route you want to do well before you start. Famous climbs have been described to death, but often impressionistically. This may not help much when it comes to finding the way in detail. Study the diagrams and photographs, in guides and other accounts. Look at alternatives. Different conditions may force you onto a different variant than that given in the standard description. Watch out for difficulties and ploys which might arise if you have to go down because of injury or bad weather. Are there 'short cuts' to use in an abseil descent? Look out for anchor points and key landmarks which might be recognized even in a storm.

2 Before undertaking a Grand Course in an area, do some shorter or easier climbs. Get to know about the local weather, other local lore and ideas about your intended route. Whilst avoiding being put-off by 'Prophets of Doom' who always abound in alpine centres, watch out for the good advice amongst the dross. Acclimatize by going as high as possible before the big route, and get fitter as well in doing so, and used to the habits of your climbing partners. Ordinary routes up peaks you intend to do later by the hard way can be an excellent investment.

3 Such familiarization should also allow you to make a few mistakes with your gear in places where it is of little moment. Ill-fitting boots, uncomfortable or ill-manufactured rucsacs and clothing, fragile sunglasses belying their smart appearance, gloves which wear out in a day of ice climbing or which restrict circulation unexpectedly, crampons which disintegrate after a few hours, or crampon straps that break, ice-axe picks which simply snap off under pressure and ice screws which blunt or break on first use—all of these and more potential horrors can be suffered. On lesser climbs they can often be sorted out or laughed off. On a Grande Course they can make the difference between success or failure, or even life and death.

4 Do not attempt the route with too heavy a load. Try to plan for a quick ascent while being realistic about your own and your companions' abilities. Be realistic but efficient.

5 Eat well *before* departing to climb, even taking more big meals than usual the day before. Take good food, while trying to keep weight down. Once underway, try to eat often.

6 Make an early start, and on ice routes even a super early start, following a route spied out the day before if it is complicated. That in turn sometimes means getting up to the hut or bivouac site early on the day before. Anyway that gives you a longer rest and makes the next day's early start easier to achieve.

7 On many climbs ropes of 50 m are useful. On some it may be desirable to use one 'light' 7 mm rope and a 10 mm climbing rope to reduce weight below that of two 9 mm.

8 Only stop and belay on snow and ice when it is really needed, but try to get good anchors when this occurs, using rock, or a combination of ice and snow anchors if the climbing is technically difficult. Axe belays are not very effective at best.

The north face of the Eiger, the most notorious of Grande Course climbs.

9 Do not linger unnecessarily in couloirs and stone chutes. Watch out for climbers above you as they are perhaps THE major hazard. Remember that descent routes which may be safe in a morning can be lethal by the afternoon, and plan accordingly. Snow gullies often have to be rappelled by nearby rocks when possible once they have been softened in the sun.

10 A rope of three can be sociable but is slow unless very well organized, though on multi-day routes where a stove etc is carried it *can* allow each person to carry less, as the same rack of climbing equipment, stove, pan and other joint equipment can serve three as easily as two. Three can rarely be as fast as two, but if all climbers are capable, it can be a strong unit.

MONT BLANC RANGE, FRANCE/ITALY
Grandes Jorasses (4,208 m)
Description by Nick Kekus

Route:	Gervasutti Route, E Face
Grade:	ED (750 m)
First ascent:	G Gervasutti, G Gagliardone 16–17 August 1942 (rarely repeated)
Map:	Carte Vallot 1:50,000
Approach:	Via the Frebouze glacier

The East Face is very much a tactical climb; it has all the awe, I guess, of the Eiger Nordwand. The main problem is getting established above the 'Y', out of the line of fire from the stonefall. Secondly, the major difficulties take at least ten hours but, as the guide book says, 'the last decent bivvy is at one third height'. We did find suitable sites higher, their disadvantage being the lack of water. Consequently a balance has to be struck between speed and caution.

The approach via the Frebouze glacier has some tricky sections, made even more so when approached in darkness. Although we were following tracks, on many occasions our way appeared blocked by enormous crevasses, making long tedious diversions necessary to pass them.

From the Hirondelles col a fairly straightforward line led underneath the 'Y'. We wisely took a line well to the left, which went in a big loop to the easy terrace which forms the top of the 'Y'. This terrace and the gully that descends from it, so-called because of its shape, is usually well covered with snow, but we found it very bare and extremely loose. We experienced considerable stonefall and were at the mercy of fate as we crossed the worst sections. As part of our 'pre-route planning' we reached the bivvy site mentioned in the guide and settled down to a comfortable afternoon sleep.

Unfortunately our ascent was not made in a spell of settled weather as we had been led to believe. The weather man in Chamonix promised us 'good weather until Thursday' and even a 'beau temps' for the Monday – how wrong he was. Our days were shrouded in swirling cloud – occasionally the sun would manage an appearance; and the nights were plagued by thunderstorms. The first night's storm was so intense a good ten inches of hailstone covered our tiny ledge by the morning.

This storm caused problems the following day. Once the sun melted the hail, streams of water poured down the wall, gushing in grooves, fanning slabs and creating all but easy conditions.

The climbing was very steep and the route difficult to follow. On more than one occasion did we

The north face of the Grandes Jorasses.

believe we were off route. It took much commitment to convince ourselves the guide book was right and follow apparently blindly up impending arêtes and blank-looking walls. The attitude 'Oh just follow the pegs and we'll be alright' didn't wash here; we only found ten pegs in place and all but two of them were in the aid pitch. The aid pitch worried us; it is described as needing blade-pegs. We imagined a horrific overhanging crack which would be tentatively climbed on tied-off knife blades. It was a great relief to find the pitch straightforward, very tame compared to some of the earlier free pitches.

Above, the route took on a totally different character, for two rope lengths we climbed thin slabs which streamed with water. I remember thinking at the time how reminiscent of Etive slab in Scotland the climbing was, wet and no runners. The slabs marked the end of the difficulties, after which we found a spacious ledge for our second bivvy. All that remained were three easy pitches to the Tronchey ridge and scrambling to the summit.

We ventured rather slowly to the summit the next morning, the new snow hindering our progress, but also because we were now quite tired. For a change the weather was clear and on reaching Pt. Walker we felt well pleased with our efforts, quite happy to sit in the warm sun and admire the scenery.

The evening's thunderstorm arrived with renewed energy, in the thick of which we were both struck by lightning.

On our return to Chamonix we were eager to tell all of our unique experience, only to find that everbody who had been on the hill had a similar tale to tell.

ROCKY MOUNTAINS, CANADA
Mount Temple (3,878 m) (Description by Dave Cheesmond)
Route: N Face
First ascent: George and Jeff Lowe 1971
Map: Canadian Department of Mines and Technical
             Surveys 82 N8 1:50,000

The trend that is still prominent in the Rockies, that of tackling ever more difficult and larger mixed faces, perhaps started way back in 1966 when three local lads gained the central snow couloir of Mt Temple's North Face. Starting in the early hours of the morning in order to avoid rockfall on the lower sections, Brian Greenwood, Charlie Locke and Heinz Kahl were soon kicking steps up the snow of the 'Dolphin'. This couloir, showing up from the Lake Louise townsite as a huge creature from the sea eternally caught in mid-flight, is the key to rapid progress on the side of Mt Temple. A short while after starting Kahl became ill, a portent of his eventual death from cancer, and while he descended Greenwood and Locke continued unroped to the top of the 'Dolphin'. Reaching the rocks they found the way straight ahead barred by blank, slabby rock, and were slowly forced to the right hand side of the rockband. From their bivouac that night they had a grandstand view of the sérac fall that raked the entire central portion of the face. A convincing argument that they had chosen the safest line! Next morning they climbed some more free and aid rock pitches before making the summit slopes in the early afternoon. They had made the first ascent of the North Face, but the problem of a direct route still remained unsolved. In 1971 cousins George and Jeff Lowe took up the challenge. Approaching directly up the central rock rib, they forced a way through the prominent sérac barrier, using aid from ice screws. Their route has become popular due to its aesthetic line, but climbers on it are exposed to ice falling from the sérac barrier. No one has yet been on the face when the barrier calves, but the chances of anyone surviving such an occurrence would be minimal. A sobering thought for those wanting to climb a route on one of the classic North Faces of the world.

The N face of Mount Temple.

The Alpine Winter

Description by Al Rouse

'One day alpine winter climbing will come to surpass alpine summer climbing in importance.' So wrote Marcel Kurz nearly sixty years ago. His prophecy is in the process of becoming true as now the leading exponents of European alpinism turn their attention away from the overcrowded classics of the summer. Summer climbing is not of course worked out but it has become a less fertile field for pushing the present frontiers of difficulty. Winter climbing in the Alps has often been compared to Himalyan climbing: snow conditions, the more serious nature of a winter expedition and its often prolonged nature demand a commitment of an order seldom encountered outside the world's greater ranges.

An alpine winter climb is officially recognized only if it is carried out between two distinct dates. The winter starts on December 21 and finishes on March 21. Woe betide anyone who climbs outside their period. They will only be credited with an autumn or spring ascent or perhaps at best a 'quasi hivernal'. For many newcomers the definition seems arbitrary and unfair. In Scotland the conditions rather than the date decide whether the ascent is a winter or summer one. With the all year round ice of the Alps a definition relating to snow and ice conditions is clearly inappropriate and so to avoid confusion and a blurring of the distinction between summer and winter the precise dates mentioned above have been generally accepted as a suitable definition. If you visit the Alps in winter the differences will become apparent enough; the snow two metres thick on the roofs of the houses, the temperatures often dropping to minus thirty centigrade on the icy north faces, the hordes of affluent skiers and the desolate mountains themselves with scarcely a climber in sight. The complete silence of a perfect winter's day is a beautiful

and inspiring experience. The clatter of stonefall has long since ceased and the powder snow deadens all sounds. The fury of a winter storm is not usually a short lived affair as are the violent thunderstorms of summer. The wind and the cold make the survival of a winter storm a prolonged and sometimes deadly struggle. The approaches and the descents become major expeditions in themselves and a day's summer climb might occupy a week in winter. The answer to the question, why climb in winter when the conditions are more difficult, is of course the same as the question of, why climb at all?

Some faces, like the north faces of the Peigne and Pélerins, are transformed in Scottish fashion from mainly rock to steep ice runnels. The ice on these faces is soft and a delight to climb. Most of the low-lying north faces and northwest faces are changed like this. Sunny south-facing slopes and crags are quite different. Sometimes they are plastered in impossibly time-consuming powder snow yet a week of good weather later they will scarcely be different to summer. Some unlikely lines become attractive in winter, but take care because major avalanches can occur at any time, particularly on south-facing slopes. The big unclimbed gully line on the south side of the Grandes Jorasses looks brilliant in winter but the heat of the sun makes it a dodgy proposition because of avalanches and stonefall.

The French guidebooks record winter ascents but give no clue about their difficulty which can vary greatly from summer. Big snow couloirs, eg Couturier Couloir on the Verte, can be virtually the same as in summer but easy rock climbs can be much harder. It is the north faces which offer the best winter climbing and the hardest and most enjoyable mixed climbing imaginable.

The valley
The huts are all open in winter and in general free. It is important not to abuse their hospitality because it would be a disaster if these unguarded huts were to be locked up for the winter. Above the level of the huts there is somtimes surprisingly little snow because of high winds and cold temperatures.

Camping is out, except for the really impoverished. It is impossible to dry out in a tent and also uncomfortably cold. The most practical solution is to stay in

dormitory-type accommodation or rent an apartment for two and put six people in it. The cost of an apartment varies greatly, depending on size, length of hire and season. Everything seems to cost a bit more in winter. Skiing is expensive, even assuming you already have the gear, but because of the variable weather it is a useful adjunct to climbing.

Equipment
Equipment has improved a lot just over the period that I have been going to the Alps in winter. Boots are a major area of change; plastic boots have completely replaced double leather boots. They are warmer, do not freeze and are much lighter in weight. A Koflach Ultra is the most popular choice and can be used with skis. A normal inner will be found adequate although the alveolite inner could be considered for a prolonged excursion. For pure ice climbs, especially those accessible on skis, many climbers are now enjoying the support offered by rigid

The north east ridge of the Mönch during a winter ascent.

skiing-type boots. Something like a yeti gaiter completes the footwear.

Sleeping is very important in the long winter nights and I always go for maximum luxury with the warmest sleeping bag that I can get. For single bivouac routes a lighter sleeping bag will be found adequate. The problem for multi-day routes is that despite the useful Goretex cover the sleeping bag will get damper each night. Bivvy bags are of limited use because of the scarcity of ledges. It is rare on a steep route to be able to sleep next to your partner and I sometimes carry a belay seat for those awkward moments when there is no ledge to sit on.

Down clothing is not practical for climbing but an insulated Goretex jacket that is not too bulky like Thinsulate is ideal. Lined salopettes are excellent for the legs but all the body clothing really de-

pends on the aspect of the climb. Temperatures can drop to minus thirty five on cold north faces but fortunately things nearly always warm up considerably in stormy weather.

Gloves are particularly important and I would strongly recommend three pairs of big gloves. The gloves get covered in snow from spindrift and clearing of holds and so sometimes need to be changed each day.

Hardware is very much up to the

individual but be prepared for hard winter ice which is very brittle and heavily snowed up rock. Small snow shoes(raquettes) can be purchased out there and can be essential for the non-skiing climber after heavy snowfalls. For anyone who dares make the effort and is lucky with the weather, they will be rewarded with nearly deserted mountains and huts as well as superb climbing.

The Argentière in winter.

MONT BLANC RANGE, FRANCE/ITALY
Les Droites (4,000 m)
(Described by Laura O'Brien)

Route: Shea Jackson Route, N Face
Grade: ED
Map: Carte Vallot 1:50,000
Approach: From the Grandes Montets Téléphérique (Argentière) top station 2–3 hours up the Argentière Glacier

5.30 a.m. and the piercing 'beep-beep' of our digital alarm wakes us. The sky is incredibly clear, the cold intense as Andy sets off, balancing precariously on the lower lip of the bergschrund. An overhanging spacey exit from our hole and

we're out and up and the climbing begins. Strange and yet good to be getting again the feel of tools and balance. Perfect front point nevé. and I think that if we have to do 2,000 ft of this today at least it is nice stuff. The pleasure is short-

lived and we find ourselves on horrible black rock-hard winter ice. I follow Andy's runnerless lead feeling unsure of myself and knowing that I must now do the same. I balk at the beginning—there is so much space. I prefer the confines and security of a couloir or the false security of mixed ground when at least there is a protruding rock every now and then to perpetuate the illusion of security.

Finally I move, but the apprehension is still there and the ice still dinnerplates from under my feet. It takes two or three blows with my axe before it sticks in an airy and insecure position. Luckily my conidence returns and the ice begins to flow by. I am still glad when my three pitches are finished and Andy takes the lead again.

The rock-band broken by thin runnels of ice looms overhead, always close but never any nearer. Time passes and pitch after pitch is put behind us 11, 13, 16. Finally, the rock (and our bivvy I think) are actually closer, but a new familiar feeling has set in. I am tired. My calves ache and I have to stop a couple of times each pitch.

We eventually stop at the foot of the rock and procure a rather sloping bivouac on a two-feet square piece of granite.

I awake with a start (for the twentieth time that night) and struggle out of my bag to the sight of a sunlit valley below. 'Oh Jesus! Andy, wake up quick, the bloody alarm didn't go off! It's morning, we've go to get going – what time is it?'

Almost 8.00 a.m. and it doesn't seem fair. If we really push it we just might make the summit by dark. Having no particular interest in another night like the last one we quickly (if that is possible with numb fingers and limbs in two feet of space and a sleep-fogged mind) shove things in our sacks, gulp a brew of tea and set off.

I traverse nervously and reluctantly across 140 ft of the black, iron-hard ice, struggling to find a rhythm. I try not to think of the space, falling, protection, or other dumb things. I manage to fix a runner on a small spike and finally I arrive at a belay (ah-ah, I find my first peg) at the base of an incredibly silly thin-looking two feet wide runnel of ice. Well, there is no ice to the right and only a big overhanging mass to the left, so this is it. Wasn't I clever to take this lead and leave this improbable-looking pitch for Andy? My spirits lift a little when mutterings from the other end of the rope announce that Andy is also finding the traverse shaky and airy. About time, it must be boring feeling secure all the time.

The ice is so thin I try to use the ready-made holes for my own

placements. Fear releases my adrenalin and all my concentration is focused on to the two picks and the four points of my crampons. The ice seems to creep by but in the midst of it I realise that I am really enjoying it. THIS is climbing; where the mind is working all the time, where the body is so tense but in tune with the tension, where you are picking and choosing everything so carefully, you feel the balance, self-confidence grows, rhythm comes, man, THIS is what it's all about!

Les Droites: the north east ridge and north face.

I begin to traverse a thin sheet of ice beneath an overhang on top and at the opposite end of which, Andy is belayed (I do not allow myself to wonder how he got there). The ice is so thin I can see every crystal of granite beneath it and find myself traversing with my knees at chest level, Andy has already removed the lower half of what little ice there was. I feel the pounding in my temples but I do not stop to think in case the whole thing decides to take leave of the rock. My heart races but time stands still. Then I'm across and with the adrenalin still coursing through me manage to swing out into space and over the lump above me and I'm there. Yahoo!

We have no hope of reaching the summit that night so we allow ourselves to relax and take pleasure in the climbing. I lead off again, confident now, finding the route technical enough to be interesting and interesting enough to be hard. We inch upwards and then it's nearly dusk and pleasure disappears as I turn my thoughts to a bivvy. The prospect of a comfortable one seems almost good as we find a patch of snow, the only one on the whole face. The reasons for it being there are obvious, but we realize this when it's too late. After much chopping, tramping and laboured breathing we have a ledge which is like a king-sized bed in comparison with last night's balance-beam affair. We crawl (literally) into our bags actually lying side-by-side and thinking that maybe alpine winter climbing isn't so bad. The last thing I remember before fading out is the howl of the wind.

Whoomph! The shock to my system as I struggle coughing and choking out of my deep reverie, is too much for me. I can't seem to get my bearings – realizing only that I am buried under a lead weight and what was once a dry, almost warm nest, is rapidly turning into a freezing wet mass of down. A voice comes floating across asking if I'm alright, I fight to clear my mind to think. Although my mind is muddled, my senses are all too sharp and I realize that I'm not alright, I'm freezing and wet and what happened to paradise? I know that I've got to drag myself out of my bag and empty it of snow, but the incessant wind keeps blowing more off the tops, dumping it down my neck and I am so cold that maybe if I go to sleep it will all go away. I don't go to sleep and it doesn't go away. I manage to force myself out and rid myself of most of the congealed mess and only just

On the north face of Les Droites.

manage to crawl back in before the next onslaught. Andy is holding a Karrimat over my head trying to shield me from the worst of it. We vainly try to arrange ourselves in sitting positions as our ledge is now almost uniform with the rest of the slope, and lying down is a luxury to be dreamed of only. I take the Karrimat from Andy and with numb fingers try to canopy myself (I regret being lazy and not putting a drawcord on my bivvy sac). Looking out I realize with a shock that the night is beautifully clear with thousands of stars and even a full moon. I wonder why, of all the places I could be in, I am actually here.

I survive, though at times I wondered if dawn would ever come. For once we've no need for an alarm. We stuff our sacks with the wet ice-encrusted gear – we just want to move. No food, one precious sip of water and we are off, at least that's what we like to think, but we are faced with 150 ft of near vertical thin ice. For the first pitch of the morning this is hard to face

nonchalantly. We tune our minds out and our limbs in, in attacking the pitch with the enthusiasm (or is it desperation?) of people who just want out. It seems so cold with the wind continually tearing at us trying to pluck us from the ice. I feel damp, frozen and out of touch with it all.

As I climb the warmth seeps back in, I loosen up and enthusiasm returns. We suddenly emerge into the final couloir and there is the top. It is there and it is for real. I start to lead off but decide to dispense with belays. Andy had better climb with me and just as fast as me because I just want to get there. Motivation for this turn of speed is the summit and the sun.

The sun hits me with such force that I stand for a moment stunned. Then Andy is there next to me on the summit and after a while we rush to get out of the wind, descending rapidly to the hut where we are greeted by friends with pots of sweet tea.

FRONT RANGE ROCKY MOUNTAIN NATIONAL PARK, USA
Longs Peak (4,334 m)
Description of solo ascent 13–17 January 1983 by Mark Wilford

Route:	Grey Pillar and D7 (Diamond 7)
Grade:	Grey Pillar 5.9 AIV
	D7 section 5.7 AII
First ascent:	D Rearick and Bob Kamps 1–3 August 1960
Map:	US Geological Surveys Quadrangle 1:24,000 Longs Peak
Approach:	Leave Colorado Highway 7 10 miles S of Estes Park. Turn L to Longs Peak Ranger Station. 4 miles trail to Chasm Lake. Go up screes (or talus) to the Mills Glacier and the start of the pillar.

The first pitch was moderate except for the initial moves. Getting established on the rock was more akin to swimming than climbing. Every time I tried to exit from the steep snow slope onto the rock, the miserable white stuff would collapse. After much plunging, I resorted to a graceless dog-paddling technique. It worked. The remaining climbing followed a vertical crack via free moves and easy aid moves.

From my bolt-anchored stance, I leaned out precariously. The first placement was a blindly slotted knifeblade. The hammer's tone indicated a solid pin, and so I high-stepped in my aiders. The next few placements were thin but solid. Gradually the hairline crack arched up and joined a suspect, horizontal expanding flake. I placed one good angle and then turned to my supply of Friends in order to avoid finding out just how expanding the flake really was. After 20 feet of horizontal leap-frogging, I found the flake made a right-angled vertical rise. Back in

the top steps of my aiders, I probed around for my next placement. Using both hands I attempted to place a nut high up in the crack above. Wrong-sized nut! I leaned back down on my last piece. As I stooped down, I waited for my daisy chain of karabiners to take my weight. Cruising at 32 feet per second squared, I realized they had not. Fifteen feet down, I stopped. My heart was lodged in my throat. My mind quickly found a positive side to the flight: the belay system worked. Recomposed, I continued. The flake soon ended at a blank face. From here a pendulum would be necessary to gain a ledge system 15 feet to the left.

After letting out the necessary slack for a pendulum. I lowered myself into shooting range. A few short swings later I latched onto a flake system just below the ledge I wanted. From there I had to free-climb the ice-filled flake until I reached a stance 20 horizontal feet

The East Face of Long's Peak, the Diamond, in winter.

from my pendulum point. The search for protection was on. With one hand I let out more slack and edged my way along the snow-packed ledge. With grim consequences for failure. I left the ledge system and face-climbed to a thin crack above. The crack recognized my position and offered me a small pocket. Giving thanks, I overdrove a bugaboo pin. The remaining climbing followed the crack system upwards and ended at the base of a large, overhanging dihedral.

Jümaring the 8 mm and then the 9 mm lines was strenuous and awkward at first. Gradually I fell into a slow but efficient routine. The continual movement warmed my body and raised my morale. Back at my high point, I was faced with the task of retracking gear and arranging ropes. From this point on, I would lead with a small pack containing food, water, camera and wind gear. While cleaning a pitch, I would wear a larger pack with the remainder of my bivvy gear. The 8 mm rope would be used only to rappel down pitches. Having double and triple checked everything, I started the ominous pitch up the overhanging dihedral. The climbing started out as easy, thin-crack nailing. After 30 feet in the corner I was forced onto the overhanging left wall.

After a short break I investigated the somewhat rotten flaring cracks above my stance. After 50 feet these cracks reached a short roof and made a decaying path out of it. This obstacle was the most intimidating of the climb so far. Hanging from upward-driven pins, I reached the lip. Rotten flakes and ice stuffed the crack above. Trusting Friends in the expanding mess, I moved over the lip onto a slightly less than vertical face.

The start of the sixth pitch offered a deceptive view of the remaining climb onto the large ledges of Broadway. Easy slab climbing appeared to be all that was left. After 130 feet of moderate free-climbing, the icy tongues of the Broadway snowfield licked down on me. The verglas-coated, boiler-plated rock offered few cracks. What cracks there were had been infested with ice. At 150 feet I found myself nowhere. My lead line had run out and I had at least 20 feet to go, or 100 feet if I fell. I tied the 8 mm trail rope onto the lead line and gave myself the extra 20 feet. The belay stance finally showed itself at a large block, precariously frozen to the slope. Light was waning. After collecting all my equipment, I began to work my way up the frozen slope in search of a bivouac. One hundred feet later I found a suitable ledge.

With cargo loaded and feet cramponed, I left my tiny sanctuary and began the 300-foot traverse across Broadway to the base of the Diamond. After 150 feet of steep snow, I stopped at the beginning of a narrow ledge system. I roped up and left my large pack. Initially the ledge was about a foot wide and covered with frozen snow. As I neared the start of D7, my proposed route, the ledge narrowed and protection became scant. Looking at 40-foot pendulums, I front-pointed across the glazed edges. Just as rope and nerves were running out, I arrived at a stance with fixed protection. The good anchors were heaven to my tiny, tired mind.

D7 offers little resistance but requires persistence and attention. It is basically a vertical line, intersected by many large hand- and footholds. I clipped about every third piece, economizing with A1 protection. Gradually I replaced the gear I had lost lower down from the abundant fixed protection.

The day's climbing melted into the early dusk. Chasing the last photons up the wall, I finally reached an adequate bivouac site. The bivy consisted of a bolt set out on a face, blank save for a small ledge three feet below it. This ledge was the most valuable feature of the site; it lodged the elusive water-bearing snow. After retrieving gear, I set to melting snow while sitting on my hammock and dining on variously flavored hot sugar water.

My luck was holding. In the morning I awoke again to the sun. The previous day's easy aid and free climbing mixture continued. I leap-frogged placements, free climbed out from protection and practised other gear-saving moves. Although I was generally warm, my fingers began to show the toll of climbing gloveless in the icy cold. Beside the cuts and bruises from bashing about iron and stone, my fingernails had begun to separate at the tips.

As the day finally yawned, I reached the exit pitch onto Table Ledge. My belay was on 20 feet below it, but it would take three desperate attempts to reach it. The obvious route was straight up, but after 12 feet I backed down because of 5.9 climbing and an utter lack of protection. I turned my attention 15 feet to the right. Standing on the top steps of my aiders, I was able to gaze upon someone's poor idea of a joke, Table Ledge. Only a most modest dinner could be laid on the ten-inch ice-and-snow-packed ledge. With no crack above it, there was little chance of leaving my aiders. I retreated again. Dusk was on me. A desperate third possibility loomed out to the left.

I traversed and down-climbed for 15 feet to the base of the final option. Above was a short flake ending, ten feet below salvation, at a blank-looking face. With my rope running horizontal to the belay anchors, I nailed the flake. My last piece was doubtful but I high-stepped onto it anyway. The face wasn't quite blank. I forced a blade placement. The pin put me at chest level with another horror. The ledge had widened at this point to coffee-table size but was veneered with ice. Darkness dared me on. With ten feet on slack I left my aiders and high-steeped onto the narrow skating rink. Cramponless, I kicked and scratched my way leftwards. Not until I had given myself ten more feet of slack did I find the sedation of protection. There was no time to enjoy it. Night was setting in. Gradually, the passage widened and I gently laced my way through large blocks. Finally, with rope running out, I reached the southern shoulder of the Diamond.

Extending the field

Following the premise that the Alps still provide an ideal school for alpinists, the greatest number of examples have been chosen from European alpinism. Climbing has developed following the alpine pattern throughout the world, providing opportunities for peak bagging, face climbing, large scale mixed climbing and winter ascents on a global scale. Alaska, the Andes and Patagonia, the Arctic and Antarctic, the Himalayas, Pamir and Tienshan, the Pyrenees, New Zealand—these are just some of the areas for the adventurous to consider. The following accounts give a taste of what is available.

CUMBERLAND PENINSULAR, BAFFIN ISLAND, CANADA
Mt Asgard (2,011 m)

Route:	SE Ridge of N Peak
Grade:	ED 1,130 m. The summit cracks are V10 (USA)
First ascent:	As described, P Braithwaite, D Henneck, P Nunn and D Scott July 1972
First solo:	C Porter September 1975 W Face Dihedral
Map:	Canadian Department of Mines and Technical Surveys Baffin Island 1:250,000. (They also supply aerial photographs.)
Approach:	By air to Pangnurtung via Frobisher Bay. Skiddoo or boat to the head of Pangnurtung Fiord. On foot to Summit Lake, and via either Turner Glacier or Caribou Glacier to Asgard. It is also possible, but difficult, to walk in as well as back. Some parties have been helicoptered to the Summit Lake area. The area is now Auyuittuq National Park.

We assembled in Hudson Heights near Montreal, where Mrs P Baird entertained us royally. Dennis proved to be anything but the lean, rock-drilling technocrat that I had half expected. Instead he was a muscular, blond, fun-and-pleasure-loving character who seemed to enjoy the occasional discipline of climbing, and who was prepared to take great pains to do it well.

On July 3rd, we flew to Pangnurtung, a dusty Eskimo settlement across the Cumberland Sound. Blue skies, after a murky journey, boded well.

From the beginning there was a sense of unreality in this land of myth and magic enjoying its brief summer. On July 4th, Jok Polliollok and another Eskimo took us by sledge and skidoo 35 km down the fjord ice towards the mountains. There was a gala atmosphere, even when a sledge broke under the weight of five people and a boat. The Eskimos played at shooting imaginary seals and we golloped food and brews together when we arrived under the great face of Mount Overlord. It was a light-hearted and fortunate start, for the sea-ice was late, and we were saved at least two days.

Then we conned one another. None of us had ever carried such monstrous loads as we assembled. Food for nearly three weeks, tents, big-wall gear, fuel; the pack frames bent and creaked under the load, and so did we. Somehow, tottering upright, we trekked off from the dump at the fjord head into Weasel Valley's pebble flats. After two

Traversing bad snow on Mt. Asgard, Baffin Island.

days of wandering up these flats and through moraines which disappeared into soaring granite walls and a grey snow-laden sky, we camped to rest for a day by the frozen waste of Summit Lake.

Again the ice was useful. On consecutive days we tramped on snow shoes 10 km over the lake-ice, taking half-loads to the Turner Glacier and a camp below Asgard. On July 9th, we stamped out tent sites by a glacier lagoon. It was snowing quite heavily, but we were all pleased—the carry was over.

Snow shoes were essential to get far on the glaciers in 1972. Crevasses were deeply covered, making unroped wanderings hazardous, though we sometimes indulged ourselves. It froze for only a short time at night, leaving a weak crust. The camp was idyllic, on the snow at the junction of two glaciers, by the blue lake, with the plumb-vertical walls of Freyr Peak opposite and Asgard behind. Rocks trundled from an outlying minor summit, but we were adequately distant from their path. Moreover, we were well fed and well equipped, and on July 10th

the weather began a lasting good spell.

Our first objective, the main cause of our weight crucifixion coming in, was the West Dihedral of Asgard. Doug and I broke a track on the 10th, and dug a trench up deep insecure snow on the lower slopes. The dihedral is a real siren, drawing the eye up its clean-cut features for over 500 m. On a sparkling morning, we snow-shoed over the light crust to the base of the face again. Cloud rolled in dazzling furls over the ice cap to the north. Doug and I carried gear, while Tut led up the initial 500 m of snow and mixed ground. It was unsafe and avalanche-prone, with little security. A last lead of over 120 m led to the dihedral base.

Doug set off up an iced chimney with Dennis seconding, while we cut a large platform. It seemed that the donkey-work was over. For today, tomorrow, maybe the day after, we would swing and dangle, hammer away, and sleep in our hammocks in the relative safety of the vertical. This opinion seemed confirmed when the 120 m slope avalanched in a sea of slops, although it was modified by ice lumps falling from far above and blowing in a keen wind to the dihedral.

But our confidence was premature, however well-equipped physically and mentally we might have been. Apart from the cold on this side of the mountain, which could have been a problem in a really prolonged attack, the dièdre was not a pegging fault but a closed granite joint with aberrant, unlinked cracks. Dennis found himself faced with a painful choice at 60 m—the first of several long bolt ladders or nothing. The bolting seemed premature, and perhaps ultimately undesirable. In the early hours of July 12th we reached camp after about twenty hours' absence.

Snoozing re-appraisal led to a quick decision. Late on the 12th, Tut and Doug broke tracks to the North-East Ridge of Asgard North

Mount Asgard.

Peak. Next day, lightly equipped, we all set off in relentless sun. For me, the route had immense appeal; it was a smooth pillar of slabby and near-perfect granite, about 1,500 m high from the glacier. It was to be an alpine-style push with no provision for stopping.

Doug and Dennis led through up the magnificent lower slabs, while for a time Tut and I suffered the divorcing experience of prusiking. Then, about mid-day, we led on. It was a flood of pleasure to me, with corners, jamming cracks, delicate slabs, and a gradual steepening of angle as the upper pillar came nearer. We stopped once for food, and then followed a crack system of escalating difficulty, deeply reminiscent of all the best alpine granite climbs I have experienced. We used few pegs, nut protection being usual. In the late evening, a cold mist flung a grey cloak over us. At midnight, after about ten hours of leading, Tut and I relegated ourselves to the rear for the headwall.

The red granite, compact but split by a crack system, reared up towards the summit. There were four hard pitches for Doug and Dennis, and airy swinging prusiks on lightly frozen ropes for us. Dennis did the all-star lead on a Curbar-style 55 m crack. It took at least two hours of real struggle and was extremely difficult, especially coming as the penultimate pitch of a hard climb. Doug finished it off up a gritstone jamming crack at Hard VS, straight to the summit. During the sojourns we dozed in our duvets, waiting for the sun to re-appear. At 6.00 on the 14th we were on the table-top summit in brilliant sun.

The aftermath was deflating. The glacier lagoon had flooded and the tents were threatened if not awash, fifty-five miles out from Pang. Good weather has its costs. Attempts at a quick descent of the original route were defeated by obnoxious, deep, wet snow, which reduced us to a commando crawl, ludicrous and deadly serious as we sank into crevasses. It was easy to see how people fail to make it under

Dawn at the summit of Asgard after 24 hours' climbing.

such circumstances. Fortunately the lower glacier was better, and we reached the snowshoes and the camp thirty-three hours after departure. With battered feet and still heavy loads, our retreat became a ramble. Time was taken up with peering at flowers and wildlife, and snoozing and eating food remnants.

We took the best part of a week to cover the 80 km or so to Pang. By then the mosquitoes were coming to life, the pack-ice was breaking rapidly, the arctic summer was weakening enough to allow a little night, the food was eaten and it was time to go.

As an exercise in logistics, and as an intensely personal experience, the expedition was gratifyingly complete. Amazingly, it was a product of motivation which was less 'achievement-' or 'summit-orientated' than most such excursions. Perhaps therein lies its variation.

CENTRAL CAUCASUS, USSR
Pik Schurovskl (4,259 m)

Route:	N Face
Grade:	ED (Russian 5b)
	1,000 m of mainly steep mixed climbing
First alpine	As described, Hamish MacInnes, Chris Woodall
style ascent:	and Paul Nunn 24–26 July 1970
Map:	Austrian Alpine Club Kammkarte 2 sheets on
	Central Caucasus
Approach:	See Mount Elbrus (p. 154)

The Elbrus-Ushba region is the Mont Blanc of the range, unmatched for altitude and for quality and variety of climbing. Here are the Soviet Trades Union Camps to which climbers come in the summer. Before long the area will become a major European ski resort. I was glad to be there before it all happened.

We were pushed too hard for time by a month-long visa which covered a 2,400 km drive in each direction. The testing journey left us understandably lethargic, and negotiations with regard to objectives, together with some bad weather, strained our luck in the first couple of weeks. Frustratingly, our first objective, the North Face of Nakra Tau by the Abalakov route, never came into tolerable condition. This rather ambitious first objective (about one and half times the length of the Matterhorn North Face and of similar seriousness and overall altitude) was subject to bad weather, soft and dangerous snow conditions, and potentially lethal sérac avalanches. A near miss in bad conditions and continuing bad weather forced us to abandon the project.

Our attention shifted to the Ushba region. But new snow fell at 300 m on July 20th. The inexorable scissors of time now made us give up our plans for a new climb on Ushba, which seemed unlikely to come into condition quickly enough. Instead, we grabbed at an objective which suggested itself overwhelmingly from the German or Skelda Bivouac—a new climb on the North Face of Pic Schurovski. With some head sha-

king but much sympathy, Paul Rotatiev, Vice President of the Soviet Mountaineering Federation, agreed to our plans.

We aimed to storm it, without tents, sleeping bags, or large sacks full of food. We worked off our frustration in a brutally simple plan which placed a massive premium upon a small quantity of high quality gear, the use of Terrordactyl axes to eliminate step cutting and, above all, upon experience and speed.

On July 24th the dawn was frosty. Moving solo, Hamish, Chris and I crossed the glacier and ascended the runneled ice above the bergschrund. In the gloom a party of friendly Russian instructors paused, lights twinkling, to observe our eccentric individualistic progress.

A steep couloir necessitated the rope. Hamish led, Chris followed and I prusiked, taking pictures. After a few rope lengths we escaped on to rock as ice particles and small stone began to bespatter the lower cliffs. Rocks (IV–V) and perfect snow followed to the base of the first rock barrier. A beautiful traverse on perfect ice led out right to a granite rib and a patch of sun.

The rib was steep and a little loose, and gave way to typical Nevis mixed ground (V+ rock). The lower barrier passed with remarkably little incident, and we emerged at the foot of the Central Icefield. Luckily the sun passed away again behind the mountain, leaving the ice firm. We did not see it on the wall again that day.

At 12.00, after several rope lengths on ice, we reached a small exposed shoulder (a possible

bivouac site). Probably we were nearly half way up the face. Confidence overtook us as we scrunched through our staple diet of Mapleton bar. Hamish, with his Lawrence of Arabia neck-shield flopping, led up the short and very steep ice field below the Central Rock Barrier. He had to cut a few steps in the approach to the only feasible-looking weakness, a gully-like depression between the icicle festooned walls. It became apparent that Rotatiev had been right in stressing the steepness of the face and of the Central Barrier in particular. Upon close inspection the rock went a little beyond the vertical everywhere but in our depression. Even there it was extremely steep and required devious route finding.

Hamish led the pitches in about three hours. The first was extremely difficult mixed climbing on steep insecure ice and loose rock for about 25 m, while the second was an easier groove (Scottish 3–4) to a horizontal rock traverse and a good small ledge. The climbing, typical of harder British winter routes, was an admirable lead in any conditions. Half way up a Caucasian face it was remarkable.

To reach the upper ice field was the next pressing problem. Above were ice-decorated walls for several hundred feet. Binocular study had revealed an ice chimney and possible traverse to the lowerlip of the plunging upper slopes. Chris grated round the arête in crampons, carrying the large sac which he preferred. The chimney, again far steeper than we had anticipated, involved an athletic spur of dynamic bridging. A gloomy traverse in the gathering storm and failing light led to the edge of the ice. A small buttress of rock seemed the only feasible bivouac site.

Thunder crashed round the summit and sheets of hail swept down the ice fields as Chris and I excavated for an hour. Hamish engineered a brew in his slot. Pitons and tiny wire slings secured our position, while my antique bivouac sheet hung down as a curtain. It

seemed that we would probably be able to mange the ascent but, with four or five pitons left, we certainly would not be able to retreat.

5.00 a.m. Hamish sets out in rapid moves across the encrusted ice to the lower outlet of the steep upper ice field. The storm has given way to a fierce frost, but white wind-torn streaks threaten its return. The upper ice field is steep but not too difficult, and the gradual fading of the sun prevents the development of avalanche danger. It is very long.

12.00. At the base of the summit pyramid there is perhaps 230 m to go. On my lead the clouds mass and the wind rises. The rock is much worse than we expected and the snow had seen too much of the morning sun. Chris takes the lead from a horrible stance on steep

mush, just in time for the full blast of the snow to begin. As he ploughs up the deep snow, avalanches of powder drown his yellow cagoule. Seconding involves swimming up a trough of horrible, insecure snow. At one point Hamish and I inhabit a small ledge while Chris is totally lost in the maelstrom above. Eventually we follow tightening ropes up.

16.00. The Traverse of the Screws avoids the final impossibly steep 30 m of avalanche snow by an escape to the last few metres of the North West Ridge. A great mass of soft snow is removed; screws protect leader and second alike. On the ridge in a brief clearance Hamish swarms up the last rocks and flails up the final insecure mound to a stormy summit.

20.00. The second bivouac is a

Hamish MacInnes leading off after the storm on the first bivouac on the British route of the north face of Pic Schurovski (1970).

collapsible snow cave on the Ushba plateau, after a plodding descent through deep snow which is threatened by avalanches and punctuated by apocalyptic visions of the huge ice walls of Bezingi to the east. Mist cheats us of respite at a food dump at the head of the Ushba ice-fall. The limitations of alpine tactics in the Caucasus become apparent as we shudder through to morning in a pile of powder snow on a steep slope, with a cold wind blowing.

July 26th. The mist clears briefly to reveal Ushba towering over us. Hamish's camera is frozen as we descend to the food dump. After twenty-four hours without drink, eating is difficult. Hycal renders one completely speechless. The Ushba ice-fall provides the sting in the tail—a nasty 25 m abseil from ice screws into a yawning green hole, followed by a run in balled-up crampons below a monster serac in the mist. Something falls, but it is too thick to see. After a moment peering up into the gloom of yet another storm, the crashing noises descend to our left. Towards mid-morning we skirt the last large crevasses and slide down soaking snow on to the upper Skelda Glacier. Schurovski is plastered, and streams of snow run down the lower slabs out of the mist. Ushba is hidden in mist and snow above the crumbling ice-fall. Richard waits to help us down at the German bivouac, while Tut assists in the rescue of an unfortunate Bulgar in a deep crevasse. Our toes are uncomfortable: Ushba will have to wait.

Mountain Experience

The immense scope of alpine climbing in all its forms should be apparent from this short survey. There are few real limits which are absolute, and the various climbing games merge in different ways according to the desires of the climber and the nature of his objectives. In this spirit climbing easily survives as a lifelong source of inspiration, backed by deepening experience. Long commitment to the mountains will generally be marked by many successes and a feeling of elation at times which it is a great privilege to enjoy. To share that with others creates bonds of friendship which can last a lifetime, even when physical abilities slip away, and for many of us past climbing has left a legacy of shared experience and friendship which transcends all specific

Ushba, the jewel of the Caucasus.

'feats'. Whatever the intensity of a particular experience, memories fade and perceptions after the event are highly selective. Of course, everyone is ready to exaggerate, re-reading the past to enliven the present and showing old photographs of scenes which can look far more dramatic than perhaps they originally were when seen after a few beers in the warmth of home.

Rifts between climbers can occur when both written accounts and publicized photographs can distort the overall impression of an ascent, sometimes to the detriment of less well-known personalities. In their day Edward Whymper, Sir Martin Conway (the explorer mountaineer), Frank Smythe and T Graham Brown, Heinrich Harrer and, more recently, Césare Maestri, René Desmasion and Reinhold Messner have all been controversial in their ambitions and 'achievement'. Some were belligerent and self-advertising to a level unjustified by their real talent. Others fell into bitter dispute over so-called ethics and tactics, sometimes in the defence of old traditions, and sometimes in the creation of new ones, frequently adopting an iconoclasm against their elders which was guaranteed to provoke intolerant reactions.

Things are easier for the host of mountaineers who can find little reason to imitate the antics of the supposed élite – most get far too much from their climbing to sully it with exaggerated claims of past events. Generally climbers adopt a kind of self regulation: those who are too pushing or egotistical have their feuds, but tend to get marginalized by their commonsensical contemporaries; those who feud for too long are either humoured or ignored.

Remember, too, that the biggest or hardest climbs are not necessarily the most important or the best. Ascent of the biggest mountains can seem unadulterated masochism at the time, as they are enormous, inhuman and unyielding. The great pleasures often creep upon us unawares, when we are not forcing ourselves too much.

Overreaching oneself and seeking to dominate the mountain can often lead to failure and accident. By making provisional, flexible plans for ascents within your capabilities, you can increase your enjoyment beyond the alpine environment and share the exhilaration of success, however limited, with your companions and friends long after the event.

European Alpine 4,000 m peaks

	Mountain	Height	Area	Difficulty	Approach and ridge
1	Mont Blanc	4,807 m	Chamonix-Courmayeur	PD –	Goûter Ridge
2	Monte Rosa – Durfourspitze	4,634 m	Zermatt-Macugnaga	F +	NW flank and west ridge
3	Monte Rosa – Nordend	4,609 m	Zermatt-Macugnaga	PD	SSW Ridge or via above
4	Monte Rosa – Zümsteinspitze	4,563 m	Zermatt-Macugnaga	PD	Usually climbed en route to Dufourspitze or on traverse
5	Monte Rose – Signalkuppe	4,556 m	Zermatt-Macugnaga	PD or AD –	NW flank or east ridge Crest Signal
6	Dom	4,545 m	Zermatt-Saas	F or PD –	North Flank or NW Ridge
7	Lyskamm	4,527 m	Zermatt-Macugnaga	PD +	Traverse of both summits. E or WSE Ridge to East summit. SW Ridge to West summit.
8	Weisshorn	4,505 m	Zermatt	PD +	East Ridge
9	Taschhorn	4,491 m	Zermatt	PD +	SE Ridge
10	Matterhorn	4,477 m	Zermatt-Cervinia	PD or AD	Hörnli Ridge or SW (Italian) Ridge
11	Mont Maudit	4,465 m	Chamonix-Courmayeur	PD	Traverse from Mont Blanc to Col du Midi
12	Dent Blanche	4,357 m	Zermatt-Evolene	PD +	South Ridge – Wandflüh Route
13	Nadelhorn	4,357 m	Zermatt-Saas	PD +	NE Ridge or traverse.
14	Grand Combin de Grafeneire	4,314 m		PD	North Flank Mur de la Côte.
15	Dome De Goûter	4,304 m	Chamonix	PD	Best done during ascent of Mont Blanc.
16	Lenzspitze	4,294 m	Zermatt-Saas	PD	South Ridge Lenzjoch.
17	Finestaarhorn	4,274 m	Grindelwald/Fiesch	F + /PD – or	SW Flank – NW ridge or SE ridge.
18	Mont Blanc du Tacul	4,248 m	Chamonix-Courmayeur	PD +	North Face from Col du Midi or traverse from Mont Blanc
19	Aiguille du Croissant	4,243 m		PD	Subsidiary summit of Grand Combin.
20	Stecknadelhorn	4,241 m	Zermatt-Saas	PD	Subsidiary summit on Nadelhorn traverse.
21	Castor	4,226 m	Zermatt	PD	Traverse with Pollux from Mont Rosa Huta.
22	Zinalrothorn	4,221 m	Zermatt	PD +	SE Ridge or SW ridge (AD) or N Ridge (PD +)

23	Hohbeghorn	4,219 m	Zermatt	PD −	Subsidiary of Nadelhorn reaches by W flank.
24	Pyramide Vincent – Monte Rosa	4,215 m	Zermatt-Macugnaga	PD	SW Ridge.
25	Grandes Jorasses – Pointe Walker	4,208 m	Courmayeur	PD +	SW Flank direct.
26	Grandes Jorasses – Pointe Whymper	4,184 m	Courmayeur		
27	Grandes Jorasses – Pointe Croz	4.110 m			
28	Grandes Jorasses – Pointe Marguerite	4,066 m			
29	Grande Jorasses – Pointe Hélène	4,045 m			
30	Alphubel	4,206 m	Zermatt-Saas	PD	West Ridge – Rotgrat.
31	Rimpfischhorn	4,199 m	Zermatt-Saas	PD −	WSW Ridge Rimpfischwange
32	Aletschorn	4,195 m	Grindelwald	PD	SE Ridge or SW rib. From Jungfraujoch NE
33	Strahlhorn	4,190 m	Zermatt-Saas	PD	WNW Ridge or WSW Ridge.
34	Grand Combin de Valsorey	4,184 m		PD	SW ridge or W ridge
35	Dent d'Herens	4,171 m	Zermatt-Valpelline	PD −	SW Flank and W Ridge (Italy)
36	Breithorn	4,165 m	Zermatt-Cervinia	F	SSW Flank; North Spur (AD −)
37	Jungfrau	4,158 m	Grindelwald	PD −	SE ridge
38	Bishorn	4,153 m	Zermatt	F	NW Flank
39	Aiguille Verte	4,122 m	Chamonix	AD	Whymper Couloir. Serious.
40	Aiguille du Diable – L'Isolée	4,114 m	Chamonix-Courmayeur	D +	Diables Ridge (SE) of Mont Blanc du Tacul.
41	Aiguille du Diable – Pointe Cramen	4,109 m	Chamonix-Courmayeur	D +	Diables Ridge (SE) of Mont Blanc du Tacul.
42	Aiguille Blanche de Peuterey	4,107 m	Mont Blanc.	D +	Usually done as part of Peuterey Arête.
43	Grande Rocheuse	4,102 m	Chamonix	AD	Grande Rocheuse Buttress, subsidiary of Aiguille Verte.
44	Barre des Ecrins	4,101 m	La Berarde/Valloise	PD	North Face
45	Mönch	4,099 m	Grindelwald	F − PD	SE Ridge.
46	Pollux	4,091 m	Zermatt		see above.
47	Schreckhorn	4,078 m	Grindelwald	PD + ESE	Ridge from Schrecksattel. SW Ridge (AD −)
48	Breithorn – Roccia Nera	4,075 m	Zermatt-Cervinia	PD −	South flank.
49	Mont Brouillard	4,069 m	Chamonix	AD +	Via the Brouillard Ridge or the Col Emile Rey. It is rarely climbed and is remote and dangerous.
50	Obergabelhorn	4,063 m	Zermatt	PD + or AD	ENE ridge or WSW ridge often traversed.
51	Gran Paradiso	4,061 m	Pont Valsavaranche	F	West flank
52	Aiguille de Bionnassay	4,052 m	Chamonix	PD +	South Ridge; East ridge (AD)
53	Gross Fiescherhorn	4,049 m	Grindelwald	PD	NW Ridge
54	Piz Bernina	4,049 m	Pontresina/Tschierva	PD	SE Ridge Spallagrat; E Ridge (PD) to traverse mountain; North ridge (AD +)
55	Gross Grünhorn	4,043 m	Grindelwald	F + to PD +	SW ridge – many variants
56	Lauteraarhorn	4,042 m	Grindelwald-Grimsel	PD	South Couloir and SE Ridge.
57	Durrenhorn	4,035 m	Zermatt-Saas	PD +	Hohbergjoch, or traverse Hohberghorn
58	Aiguille du Jardin	4,035 m	Chamonix	AD +	Jardin Arête. Outlier of Aiguille Verte.
59	Allaninhorn	4,027 m	Zermatt-Saas	F +	Feekopf traverse of SW Ridge
60	Hinter Fiescherhorn	4,025 m	Grindelwald	PD	SSE Ridge
61	Weissmies	4,023 m	Saas Fee	F + or AD	SW Ridge or North Ridge.
62	Dôme de Rochefort	4,015 m	Chamonix-Courmayeur	PD	SW Ridge, or as part of Rochefort ride traverse (D serious)
63	Dôme de Neige des Ecrins	4,015 m	Dauphiné	F +	West Ridge
64	Aiguille du Géant	4,013 m	Chamonix-Courmayeur	AD	SW face
65	Lagginhorn	4,010 m	Saas Fee	PD	WSW flank
66	Aiguille de Rochefort	4,001 m	Chamonix-Courmayeur	AD	West Ridge
67	Les Droites	4,000 m		PD or AD	West ridge, west summit or traverse.

Expeditions

The experience of an expedition is far removed from a sporting competition. It is an adventure—a complete way of living for perhaps months on end, demanding total commitment and involvement from the participants. Fortunately the rewards are commensurate with the effort put in to the expedition. Ask those who have already been and you will find few that regret the experience, in spite of the hardship and sometimes pain which they may have endured. As the other fields of climbing already described become increasingly squeezed into well defined avenues, expedition climbing remains closest to the fundamental spirit of adventure. The rules which climbers feel obliged to impose upon themselves in other areas are largely absent. Every climber has an expedition within him, however modest its objectives. It is an opportunity to become privy to that rather secret world of those who know what it is like to be very close to raw nature.

K2, the world's second highest mountain, seen from the summit of Broad Peak. K2 is probably the hardest mountain in the world to climb.

Expeditions and You

Many climbers feel an indefinable barrier preventing them from going on an expedition. They read in books of well-known super-climbers on the heights and assume that the experiences described are beyond their reach. Tales of bureaucracy, hassles with porters, endless snow slopes, sickness and heroism all combine to deter the average climber in a most unfortunate way. Nonetheless every year more expeditions leave for the world's highest mountains. Each year the process becomes easier and things are changing fast. The big army-style expeditions are becoming outmoded and replaced by the idea of a small group of friends having an extended holiday in the mountains. Unless you are unusually skilled and experienced you will not be setting off with one friend to climb Everest on your first expedition, but you can have very similar experiences on a much smaller mountain. Principles of climbing learnt in the Alps can be applied directly to the world's greater ranges. As the mountains become more and more accessible, climbing in them has begun to resemble what climbing was in the Alps several decades ago. It is the same sport with the same techniques by and large. More organization is required of course but it is not really that difficult.

In the following pages I hope to use my experience to help you through the system and enable you to enjoy the pleasures of climbing in remote places. You will probably find that once you start the ball rolling a momentum will develop which will carry you through the whole process. One moment you are idly thumbing through photographs of mountains, then six months later you are standing under some enormous mountain, rather bewildered as to just how it all happened. An unexpected phone call from a friend inviting you on an expedition can change your life instantly. Whatever the experience, you will remember it always.

A Brief History

Three threads have consistently run through expedition climbing from Victorian times to the present day: scientific enquiry, exploration and sport. At the turn of the century the first two factors were predominant, but by the twenties and thirties expeditions were being launched for the achievement and enjoyment of climbing itself. Often they retained a nominal scientific content to ensure respectability and more importantly to secure funds. Now climbers need no such excuses unless perhaps they are a university party after lucrative scientific grants.

Height Records

In 1892 Martin Conway led the first full scale mountaineering expedition in the world's highest mountains. They explored the Baltoro, Hispar and Biafo glaciers and climbed, amongst other peaks, the first ascent of Pioneer Peak (6,890 m). Conway's idea was to explore and this is exemplified by the fact that he did not take Mummery (who was at the time a leading climber in the Alps) because 'He wanted all the time to be given to finding a few big mountains and climbing them'. In 1907 Tom Longstaff and the two Brocherel brothers climbed the fine peak of Trisul (7,125 m) setting a world altitude record which was to stand for twenty years. They climbed the last 1,830 m in a twelve hour push and they were more or less climbing in the same way a modern climber would approach things.

The Duke of Abruzzi set a new height record in 1909 of 7,500 m but this was not a summit. He had taken a massive well-organized party to the Baltoro glacier and after placing fourteen camps on Bride Peak, he failed just 156 m from the summit. In 1921 the first Everest expedition was launched, led by Colonel Howard-Bury. It was necessary to trek 725 km from Darjeeling to the mountain and good organization was absolutely essential. The following year another party set off. They were carrying oxygen and equipment, and with it G Finch and G Bruce reached 8,235 m, but the weight of the equipment all but cancelled out the help it gave. Two years later Mallory and Irvine disappeared

A lantern slide of Longstaff in the Karakorum in 1909.

high on the north ridge of Everest, in what has subsequently become a great mountaineering mystery. There is still speculation that they may have reached the top, but it seems unlikely. Numerous further attempts were launched in the thirties but the final stretch proved elusive until 1953.

There was a strong element of national pride involved in the British expeditions to Everest in the twenties and thirties and the German expeditions to Nanga Parbat in the same period. The projects were not entirely sporting ones. However at the same time people like Eric Shipton, Bill Tilman and Erwin Schneider were climbing mountains with far less publicity and organization. The Anglo-American ascent of Nanda Devi, the highest peak in India was achieved in 1936. By the fifties the climbers who believed that Himalayan climbing should be carried on much as in the Alps were usurped by the scramble to bag the first ascents of the world's 8,000 m giants. An army-style logistical pyramid offered a greater chance of success and so competitive reasons dictated these tactics on a large number of ascents.

The Eight-thousanders

There are fourteen major peaks above 8,000 m in the world and by 1950 none of them had been climbed despite numerous attempts. Annapurna (8,091 m) was the first to be climbed in 1950 by a very strong French team with an excellent record of climbing in the Alps. Through the next decade all the eight-thousanders were climbed except for Shisma Pangma which was not climbed until 1964 for largely political reasons. The whole history of climbing in the great ranges of Asia has been considerably affected by politics. The highest mountains lie in border areas and even to this day mountains remain unclimbed purely because no one is allowed to go and attempt them. Everest was climbed in 1953 and the following year the hardest of all, K2, was climbed by an Italian party. These expeditions

Lawrence Wager (left) and Percy Wyn Harris (right) on Everest, 1933

had all but given up the pretence of exploration and science. They were sporting and competitive with the prime idea of getting to the top (and planting the flag) by any means necessary. Often armies of sherpas, ladders to get through icefalls, bottles of oxygen and numerous fixed camps were employed as the only means possible of climbing the mountains at the time. It was a far cry from the Alps and many climbers felt that in some way it was not even climbing.

One noticeable exception to the general pattern of heavy expeditions to bag the first ascents of the eight-thousanders was when Schmuck, Wintersteller, Diem-

berger and Buhl climbed Broad Peak (8,047 m) in 1957 as a four man team, without sherpa assistance or oxygen.

Recent History

During the sixties and seventies there has been a mopping up of the three hundred odd 7,000 m peaks and now nearly all of them have been climbed. At the beginning of the seventies attention turned to the steep faces of the high mountains and climbs like the South Face of Annapurna, the West Face of Makalu and the Rupal Face of

Roger Baxter-Jones and Brian Hall returning from the summit of Jannu after making the first alpine style ascent in 1978.

that almost anything could be climbed if enough resources were applied to the problem. Significantly it also took place in 1975. In 1985 Wojciech Kurtyka and Robert Schauer climbed the West Face of Gasherbrum IV, probably the hardest climb yet achieved in the high ranges. They climbed for nine days in pure alpine style. They have proved that if you are good enough anything can be climbed in good style. Expeditions are continuing to climb in the traditional way but really they are no longer the sharp edge of high altitude climbing. Although even now only a small minority of expeditions to very high mountains use alpine tactics the balance will shift in the future. Throughout climbing history those who have probably got the most pleasure out of expedition climbing are those small groups who have always been out there doing their own thing and keeping out of the limelight. The lightweight philosophy of people like Eric Shipton in the thirties has come to be seen as the mainstream of climbing consciousness and in the future big expeditions will be a sideshow.

A Personal View

My first expedition was a disaster from a climbing point of view. Six of us went to New York and made our way overland to Patagonia but it took so long to get there and we were beset with so many difficulties that we only climbed for one day in a total of nine months. We did have fun however and we learnt from our mistakes. Three years later in 1976 we set off on a nine month tour of South America. We climbed in three pairs on different routes from Patagonia to Peru, completing seventeen first ascents. We climbed exactly as we had done in Chamonix and this expedition became my model for future trips. In 1978 we climbed Jannu (7,710 m) in two pairs with minimal gear and no support. Again we climbed exactly as we had done in the Alps without camps or fixed ropes, which to us seemed against the spirit of climbing itself.

Nanga Parbat were achieved. They brought alpine standards of difficulty to the Himalaya but they used traditional Himalayan siege tactics to climb them. It was generally felt at the time that to use alpine tactics was more or less impossible. Younger climbers felt no such inhibitions. For them the Alps had become a playground and they needed to go farther afield to

find adventure and test themselves. Sweeping aside all preconceived notions Reinhold Messner and Peter Habeler made a pure alpine style ascent of a new route on Hidden Peak (8,068 m) in 1975. This was rightly seen as an important achievement because of its style, a factor which had largely been ignored in the quest for harder and harder climbs at any cost.

Subsequently a small but growing number of climbers decided to opt for an alpine style of climbing. In a way the British ascent of the South West Face of Everest proved

I have participated in all kinds of expeditions but the most enjoyable have always been with a small group of equals. Even after fourteen expeditions I am still learning. Alpine climbing on the heights is still finding its feet. Acclimatization is the bugbear because you cannot just walk up to an 8,000 m peak and climb it. You need up to a month to get suitably acclimatized. It was no problem on old style fixed rope expeditions, where you got used to the altitude by carrying loads and fixing camps. One interesting way around the problem is to climb a series of mountains of increasing height. I was on a Doug Scott expedition to the Baltoro in 1983 where we used this approach. After making several first ascents on the rocky spires of the Lobsang Group, which were under 6,000 m, we went on to climb Broad Peak (8,047 m) and then attempt K2 (8,611 m). There is less problem of acclimatization with very technical climbs as progress is slow and so altitude is gained relatively slowly and you can acclimatize on the way up the route. I have always found it far more satisfactory to climb an easier route than to fail on a harder route and have always tried to keep some relatively easy options in the plan, in case the main objective proves impossible.

Choice of Team

If possible your team should be chosen from amongst friends. You are going to live in tight proximity to each other, often under stress for a long period of time, so it is useful to have some idea in advance of each others' personalities. Usually a few people get together and a plan emerges. They then sit down and agree a few more possible members. Never invite people casually —it is very hard to undo the invitation later.

Number of Members
Although a two-man expedition sounds simple and appealing there are considerable disadvantages to take into account. If one person is

ill the other person will have to solo or give up the expedition, and the cost per head will usually be higher than with a larger party because some overheads, for example the Peak Fee and Liaison Officer, are fixed and independent of the number of members. Four is a convenient number for a small expedition and has worked well for me. We have usually approached the climbing plan by regarding the four man team as two ropes of two. Before leaving home we have already sorted out who will climb with who on the mountain. This

High on the unclimbed East Face of Jannu. Climbing as a four man team divided into two ropes of two is very efficient.

can always be changed during the course of the expedition if necessary of course. It allows pairs to sort out their tentage, climbing hardware, cooking gear etc. before setting off, and has the useful side effect of minimizing the amount of gear taken.

Two pairs climbing together on a big mountain are efficient and speedy. In an emergency they can

Pete Boardman, Joe Tasker and Chris Bonington at 7,000 m on the first ascent of Mount Kongur (7,719 m) in China.

pool resources but otherwise they maintain independent food and equipment. This allows each pair to go at its own optimum pace and also allows one pair to retreat and another to continue, if that becomes necessary. This removes pressure from, say, a climber who feels ill and wants to go down but does not want to ruin everyone else's chances. He can retreat with his partner. There is also no awkwardness over who descends with the ill climber as his partner automatically goes with him. This pairbonding provides a framework which climbers seem to work well in. They care mainly about their partner. It is hard to really be in tune with more than one other climber at the same time. It avoids the awful three: one split, which can occur in a four man team.

Three pairs are a good idea if the mountain is very high or serious or you are operating in a remote area. The same principles apply as with two pairs. Usually you can reasonably expect at least one in four of your team to be incapacitated due to local bugs, altitude sickness or freaking-out at the difficulty and commitment. Therefore, for really big projects you need a kind of built-in reserve of climbers. Four pairs would be the maximum size party in which I would personally care to participate.

The Leader
The pair system I have described above may be regarded as the heart of the expedition but for various reasons a more extended party may be considered and various nonclimbing roles need to be allocated. A leader is traditional and makes sense. The authorities need a leader to deal with in the bureaucracy and so at least a nominal leader is essential in most countries. Also the expedition will need a co-ordinator in the home country and it may as well be the leader. The semantics of the title can be argued about, particularly as the word leader affronts the entrenched anarchy of the climbing world, but in the end a leader will emerge anyway out of the anarchy. The leader should reflect the views of the consensus of the members when the trip is basically a group of friends. On the mountain a leader is irrelevant unless ropes are being fixed and the mountain sieged. On the mountain the strongest climbers automatically become the leaders in decision-making. Most of the foregoing comments apply to a group of friends of similar ability, which for me is an ideal kind of expedition. On many occasions this position will be compromised however and the structure of the expedition becomes more complicated immediately.

Personalities
Personality clashes are frequently a major problem on an expedition, particularly if things start to go wrong. Old fashioned virtues such as reliability, honesty and straightforwardness should be looked for.

There is a lot of hard work to be done and if you have a lazy person this will cause resentment from the hardworking members of the team. The biggest problem in picking people for a trip comes when you need to go outside your immediate circle of friends. It is then essential to assess the personality of the newcomer and how he will fit in with the rest of the group. It is sound sense to have a mixture of cautious people and 'go-for-it' types. If all the members are cautious you will never climb anything, but if all the people are pushy and necky then you may all end up dead. Of course everyone should be suitably skilled and experienced and be able to do the necessary when it comes to the crunch. In my experience the biggest problems on expeditions revolve around ego, so be careful of *prima donna* type characters, especially if you have more than one of them on the same team.

On Jannu we knew each others' strengths and weaknesses and we formed a well balanced team. Although it was our first Himalayan trip we had already climbed extensively in the Andes and the European Alps in winter.

Choice of Objective

The greatest difficulty for many parties is in finding a suitable objective to climb. Asia has the vast bulk of the world's interesting mountaineering objectives but South America also has a varied choice—from the spires of windswept Patagonia to the volcanoes of Ecuador in the north. North America has plenty of objectives in the arctic latitudes, while Africa, although it has relatively little to interest the serious climber, can offer a fun trip. The first priority is to decide when you can have holidays. This will be the primary limiting factor in the choice of area to visit. Every area has definite climbing seasons and it may well prove a waste of time to climb outside them (see the table on page 205).

The Cost Factor

The second priority for most people is cost. As a very rough guide the following costs per head can be expected with a four man team on a two month expedition, assuming costs are cut wherever possible and assuming that most of the necessary equipment is already possessed by the team.

on which they make final decisions on arrival. This makes a lot of sense for experienced climbers but it is easier on your first trip to select a defined objective even if on arrival you find it necessary to modify your plans. Surprisingly many expeditions fail to appreciate that big mountains always prove to be much harder in reality than they appear from photographs. This is the main explanation for the very high failure rate on expeditions. If I were to offer one single piece of advice for newcomers to expeditioning, it would be to choose an easier objective than you think you are capable of. There are always so many more obstacles between your home town the summit than you can ever dream of, that you want to give yourself a decent chance of succeeding by picking a not-over-ambitious objective. Four out of five Himalayan expeditions fail in their main objective and after all it is actually rather nice to stand on top.

The Experience Factor

Look hard at the experience of the team, particularly in terms of alpine experience. If none of the

Approximate costs per person

	£	$
Pakistan under 6,000 m (19,686 ft)	1,000	1,400
Pakistan over 6,000 m (19,686 ft)	1,500–3,000	2,100– 4,200
China	4,000–8,000	5,600–11,200
India	800–1,500	1,120– 2,100
Indian Karakorum	1,500–3,000	2,100– 4,200
Nepal trekking peaks	900–1,300	1,260– 1,820
Nepal climbing peaks	1,400–2,500	1,960– 3,500
Bhutan	5,000–7,000	7,000– 9,800
Africa	600–1,000	840– 1,400
Patagonia	1,000	1,400
Peru/Bolivia	800–1,000	1,120– 1,400
Alaska	700–1,000	980– 1,400

These costs are return from Europe at 1985 prices and the costs in US $ in this and the following tables are based on an exchange rate of 1.4 $ to the £1.

The Mountain Itself

The next consideration is the actual objective to be climbed. Quite a few trips these days go out to an area with only a loose series of ideas

The north-west summit of Nuptse (7,789 m) has only been climbed once, by the ridge on the left. The right hand ridge remains unclimbed.

team have climbed in the Alps and experienced glaciers and snow climbing then you should seriously consider going to the Alps to get some experience. The Himalayas is not a place to learn techniques—it is a place to practise techniques already well-learnt in other areas. As a very rough guide on mountains up to around 6,000 m the team should be going for an objective at least one grade easier than climbs they have all done in the Alps. For example climbers capable of Walker Spur-type climbs should look for climbs of Route Major-type difficulty in the Himalaya. The gap can be narrowed on subsequent climbs as the problems become more comprehensible. Many climbers actually go for harder routes in big mountains than they have ever done in Europe or comparable areas. This is clearly a big mistake which may have very serious consequences. Climbers with little alpine experience should really go for 'walking' type mountains if they want to stand a decent chance of success.

The Tactics Factor
While selecting a route an actual plan should be borne in mind. It is popular to pick an objective, say you are going to climb it in alpine style, and then forget all about a climbing plan until arriving at base camp. This approach is not good enough. A more careful plan will pay dividends even though it will undoubtedly need some modification on arrival. Where will base camp be? Is the foot of the climb a long way from base camp, necessitating an advance base camp? In this case extra tentage will be needed for the advance base camp. Will there be ledges big enough for tents on the route, places to dig snow holes or just miserable little ledges like many alpine climbs? How many days do you expect to take? A question I frequently ask is how many successive bivouacs has the party had before? Many climbers who have only bivouacked for single nights happily plan a six bivouac route, unaware of the problems of successive bivouacs and

their drain on strength. Any climb involving more than five nights out on the hill is extremely problematic. The sacs will be very heavy, probably necessitating hauling over steep ground. Yosemite-style big wall tactics may be appropriate. These questions of the precise form of style are frequently overlooked at the cost of a potential success.

Areas to go to
The best countries for a first expedition are India, Pakistan, Nepal,

The west side of Kang Taiga (6,809 m) in the popular Everest area of Nepal. It has three separate summits with a total of only two different routes so there are still plenty of new routes to try. All the new routes to be done would be harder than they look from the photos.

and Peru. They all have a wide choice of interesting mountains, unclimbed routes and marvellous scenery. Few people would be disappointed whatever their aspirations.

Peru

In Peru the Cordillera Blanca offers a cross between climbing in Chamonix and a full expedition. After arrival in Lima you can catch a regular bus service to Huaraz and check into a hotel. Basic acclimatization can be had in the swimming pools and night clubs, since Huaraz is at over 3,000 m! After a few days a taxi will take you to within one or two days' walk of a base camp. After completing a few climbs you can return to the fleshpots for a break, but beware, since you will lose a lot of your hard-earned acclimatization very quickly.

Peru's highest mountain, Huascaran (6,768 m) is in the Cordillera Blanca, which is the most extensive of the mountain ranges in Peru. Information is readily obtainable, particularly from *Yuraq Janka*, Ricker's excellent guidebook to the Blanca, published by the American Alpine Club in 1977. This has good maps, photos and local information. More up-to-date information about which climbs have

been done since 1977 can be obtained from the American Alpine Club Journals.

Just to the south of the Blanca lies the Cordillera Huayhuash, a compact but very interesting collection of beautiful mountains. This is usually approached by getting a bus from Lima to Chiquian, followed by a fascinating two day approach march. Peru's second highest mountain Yerupaja (6,634 m) is here. The best source of information is an article in *Mountain* Number 90. Down in the south of Peru near Cuzco lies the other major mountain group. There are many smaller mountain groups like the Huagaruncho or Raura which offer more modest objectives and still a number of easier unclimbed peaks for those interested in more unusual places. The mountains of Bolivia are similarly accessible to those in Peru and are of comparable scale.

Some features of Peruvian climbing are unique. Many of the faces have massive flutings of unconsolidated snow. They look very

beautiful but can be problematic to climb. The ridges, heavily decorated with cornices and precariously balanced towers of rotten snow, are much harder than they look. Generally they are best avoided. The faces offer better climbing. The daytime heat is quite an enemy in the Andes. The south faces are similar to alpine north faces. If they are easy angled you may encounter deep powder snow, but if they are very steep then usually excellent névé will be found. I have found it useful to carry snow stakes for climbing with when the snow is too unconsolidated to use an ice-axe.

Nepal

Nepal is a mecca for mountaineers and indeed anyone who enjoys mountain scenery. Eight of the fourteen eight-thousand-metre peaks lie in Nepal, but there are

From left to right Tsacra Grande (5,774 m), Rasac (6,040 m) and Yerupaja (6,634 m) in the Cordillera Huayhuash, Peru.

also appealing snowy mountains right across the country. For many people the biggest disadvantage is the monsoon, which falls in the middle of summer, when a lot of people are obliged to take their holidays. Climbing is impossible from June until the end of August in all areas, except for a few very high mountains, like Everest, which avoid the worst of the monsoon and can be climbed in August. Even September is not a good month for climbing on most of the Nepalese mountains.

The economy of Nepal is largely based on tourism, of which moun-taineering and trekking play a vital part. Consequently the system here is highly organized. There are many trekking agencies who can help you with expedition arrangements or even run the whole trip for you. There is an established system of using sirdars who organize the porters for you. There also plenty of good cooks and other staff. The country is very beautiful and the approach march to the mountain will usually be very enjoyable, especially if you hire good staff to deal with any problems that may arise.

One big disadvantage is that all the permitted peaks have already been climbed and climbing peaks that are not on the official list is not allowed under any circumstances. There is a wealth of attractive unclimbed mountains between 6,000 and 7,000 m but when they are finally permitted there will be a terrible scramble to get permissions.

Pakistan

The Karakorum offers the greatest concentration of attractive high mountains of anywhere in the world. Expeditions have concentrated on the bigger mountains up to now and there is a fantastic

choice of unclimbed peaks and new routes of all difficulties just waiting to be done. The big plus for a first expedition is that you can climb any peak below 6,000 m without specific permission so long as it lies in a permitted area. No Liaison Officer is required for peaks under 6,000 m so costs can be cut to the bone. This is the place if you want to do rock climbing on good solid granite. The whole of the Karakorum is littered with granite spires up to now ignored by climbers apart from such very dramatic towers as Trango on the Baltoro glacier.

The foothills and the approach marches are very dull when compared with Nepal and also arduous and dangerous in parts. The area is a giant desert with occasional villages surviving by artificial irrigation. If you like wild and remote places the Karakorum will appeal to you. Nearly all the peaks are permitted, apart from a few reserved for Pakistani expeditions only. This gives you plenty of room to be imaginative about your objective. If you wish you can choose a mountain which no one has even attempted before. Access used to be extremely difficult but since the construction of the Karakorum highway, which links the plains of Pakistan to China, a twenty-four hour drive will take you to Skardu or Gilgit.

India
Delhi is the cheapest place to fly to and this helps to make India one of the cheapest places in which to launch a modest expedition. For those with short holidays, India is a first choice because many of the mountains can be reached within a few days of leaving the home country. The granite peaks of the Gangotri offer superb climbing on excellent granite rock. In most cases peaks will need to be applied for and a Liaison Officer will acompany your party to the mountains. There are plenty of beautiful areas like Kishtwar, Kulu or Barnaj which offer interesting peaks of up to 7,000 m with a minimum of fuss and expense. Recently the Indians have been allowing parties to visit the Indian part of the Karakorum but the rules and the costs make it a difficult business.

Research
Picking your precise objective is very hard. First of all you should narrow your search down to an area which has suitable seasons and which you can afford. If you select an area in which permission is required you will need to pick more than one objective in case your first choice is unavailable. Having decided provisionally on an area it is a good idea to consult maps to get an idea of the topography, while at the same time trying to relate the map to any photos you may have obtained of the area. Photos are the key to picking an objective, although knowledgeable friends can also be invaluable. Many

Two unnamed, unclimbed peaks to the south of Jannu, in Eastern Nepal. They are each about 6,500 m high and would make ideal objectives for a first expedition if they were permitted by the authorities.

The photo on the right is taken from 6,500 m on Broad Peak looking back towards Concordia, the meeting place of the Baltoro and Goodwin Austen glaciers. The Karakorum is a sea of mountains, containing the greatest reserve of interesting unclimbed routes of any mountain area in the world.

mountaineering publications are littered with useful pictures of all the world's mountain areas (see Bibliography). You should be very wary when your sole source of information is a single photo. Mountains are usually topographically far more complex than any one picture would indicate. Previous expedition reports and books can provide masses of useful facts about an area. Local climatic variations, particular problems with the approach, snow conditions and the type of rock for climbing can only be found out about by careful scrutiny of previous reports. Nearly every area has been visited and photographed by climbers and with luck you should manage to find someone who has already seen your objective first hand and can offer an informed opinion about its specific characteristics.

Permission to Climb

It seems a little strange that you need to apply for permission to climb, but that is the system in most of Asia. It is in part a legacy of British rule in India, when visitors to remote frontier provinces had to be accompanied by a Liaison Officer. The system has been carried on in some areas for genuine security reasons as many of the climbing areas have disputed frontiers. In other places it is purely a way of seeing that the expedition only does what it is permitted to do for reasons of maximizing income. The allocation of a Liaison Officer which usually accompanies a permission system can be very useful in remote areas, particularly in Pakistan, but in some places it is unnecessary and is enforced largely because it always has been. Broadly speaking although permissions are sometimes necessary outside Asia, obtaining them will always be more or less a formality. Getting permission in a country like Nepal can be a very frustrating business as some mountains are booked up for many years to come. Everest is now booked for ten years in advance. Until you are familiar with the system you may as well forget about applying for any of the 8,000 m peaks or any of the very popular lower peaks.

Filling in the Forms

Usually a detailed form will need to be filled in and you must answer all the questions, otherwise the form will be treated as incomplete and therefore not be dealt with at all. Nobody will inform you if this happens so you need to take great care in the initial application. Despite dire warnings to the contrary most countries are rather more flexible than the rules and regulations would suggest (except for China where the letter of the rules is applied rigorously). However they are never flexible in writing, so expect no concessions until you arrive in the country you intend to climb in. Changes of team and route are sometimes permitted if there are good reasons to justify them. In every country it is useful to have an agent on the spot to help your application through the system. There are plenty of trekking agencies which can offer such assistance. Make sure you send them a duplicate copy of the application to avoid contradictory stories.

Do not expect to hear the results of your application for a long time. Bureaucracy is slow moving and the best way to find out if you are likely to get the permission is to get your agent to go along in person to enquire on your behalf.

The two obvious mountains are Lingtren and Khumbutse, not at present permitted by the Nepalese authorities.

	January	February	March	April	May	June	July	August	September	October	November	December
Nepal			▓	■	■			■	▓	■	▓	
Bhutan		░	▓	■	■				▓	■	▓	░
India			▓	■	■	▓	░	▓	■	■		
Pakistan				░	▓	■	■	▓	░			
Pamirs/ Northern Tibet						■	■	■				
Africa	■	■				■	■					
Peru				░	■	■	■	▓				
Bolivia				▓	■	■	■	■	░			
Central Andes (Aconcagua area)	■	■	■									▓
Patagonia	■	■	■								▓	■
Alaska and Arctic Canada			░	▓	■	■	■					

Legend: ■ Best time   ▓ Reasonable time   ░ Poor time   □ Not recommended or not known

NOTES
The times for India vary from those of the Karakorum to those of Nepal depending upon the exact area.

Seasons

Climbing seasons around the world are based on dry and wet seasons rather than summer and winter in most cases. In Asia the monsoon dictates when you can climb. The further east you go along the Himalayas the longer and wetter the monsoon becomes. In Bhutan for instance you can expect very poor weather from the beginning of June to the end of September, whereas at the far western extremity in the Karakorum you can climb throughout the monsoon season. There are anomalies, particularly in the case of Everest which seems to create its own high pressure system keeping off the worst of the monsoon weather, particularly in August, towards the end of the monsoon. This effect is very localized however and even mountains as close as Ama Dablam, which is only a few kilometres south, do not benefit from the presence of Everest. On an expedition in the autumn of 1979 we encountered snow every day just 15 km south of Everest on KangTaiga, but when we later arrived at Everest base camp at the beginning of October we found to our amazement that they had just enjoyed five weeks of nearly perfect weather.

It is extremely unwise to plan an expedition outside the established climbing seasons for a particular area. In general there is a very good reason for these traditions. The only noticeable exception is during the months of July and August, when because so many climbers have holidays, some areas of the world have become very popular during those months even though it is not the optimum time. A good example is Peru, where in my experience May and June are the best months, despite July and August being the most popular. A similar effect occurs in the Karakorum, where June and July offer perhaps the most reliable weather conditions but many teams are only in a position to go for the summit by August.

This table only gives a rough idea of the best times to climb in an area. Researching the experience of previous parties is sensible.

Pre-Monsoon and Post-Monsoon

These are the two main climbing seasons in Nepal, although recently climbers have started to experiment with the winter season, partly for an added challenge and partly because they have been unable to obtain permission for the mountain they wish to climb in any other

Doug Scott on the first ascent of the north face of Nuptse (7,789 m) in the cold post monsoon season, wearing a full down suit.

season. The pre-monsoon season extends from March to the end of May and generally the weather improves as the season goes on. You should plan to leave your home country so as to be in a position to go for the summit during the last three weeks of May. Quite a few expeditions arrive in Nepal very early and actually get fed up with waiting round for good weather and leave before the best climbing season. Of course mountain weather is fickle in every part of the world and these comments can only be taken as a very rough guide. The pre-monsoon season has the advantage of a pleasant approach march, relatively high temperatures and few storms of any great severity. It has the disadvantages of retreating in the monsoon, which is never pleasant, avalanche danger greater than after the monsoon because of the warmer temperatures and frequent minor afternoon snowfall. The expedition has a well defined limit on the time it can stay which might be an advantage or a disadvantage.

The post-monsoon season is much colder, particularly at high altitude and is also much windier. On the other hand a very stable couple of weeks of weather often occurs during the last three weeks of October, giving an excellent opportunity for an alpine style ascent. The cold temperatures minimize, but of course do not eliminate, avalanche danger. For a high mountain you will need to set off at the beginning of September in order to have sufficient time to become acclimatized. This is a horrible time for an approach march because of frequent rainstorms and the accompanying leeches. For mountains of up to 7,000 m it is becoming more popular to climb from the beginning of October to mid-November. The weather is usually quite good throughout and the approach and return are pleasant at this time of year. Temperatures akin to the Alps in winter will be encountered and probably strong winds, although neither of these facts should prevent an ascent so long as the mountain is not too high. Over 7,000 m it is a different story with winds frequently making climbing impossible for weeks on end. It is the winds which make winter the worst of the seasons for climbing. Throughout January it can be completely impossible to climb because of their severity.

The monsoon affects most of the Indian Himalaya but to a lesser extent than in Nepal. Each area has a different climate and in some places it is perfectly feasible to climb during the monsoon. Tradition has it that the monsoon does not affect climbing in the Karakorum but it is my experience that when the monsoon breaks on the plains of Pakistan the weather often becomes more than usually unreliable in the mountains, particularly in the Nanga Parbat area which lies a little to the south of the main mountain massif.

Above: Joe Tasker jumaring on fixed ropes at 7,200 m on the West Ridge of Everest in winter. He is wearing specially made clothes to combat the intense cold of the Himalayan winter. Very strong winds are the factor which stops most winter excursions at high altitude but the season can be useful for lower mountains.

Left: Climbing to the Lho La col on the same expedition as above. Strangely enough there is less snow in winter on Everest than at any other season because of the strong winds and cold temperatures, which never allow the snow to consolidate.

Experience

The experience of the team must be equal to the project planned. It is very difficult to gauge your experience and that of your fellow team members. It is not just climbing experience that is important because all sorts of other talents come in useful on an expedition. As a very rough guide you should be dropping at least one technical grade from the standard you climb in the Alps for mountains up to 7,000 m and two grades for higher mountains. If you can climb a Grande Course route in the Alps you should not be looking for a route like that in the Himalaya but rather something like the Route Major or Peuterey Ridge. This is because you will need to apply techniques in an unthinking automatic manner, and so they must be second nature, not something at the limits of your powers and experience. Many climbers when planning in the comfort of their own living room ignore the enormous difference in seriousness between the Alps and even the simplest of Himalayan or Andean peaks. Glacier approaches can be long and complex, snow conditions

infinitely variable and of course there is no rescue service if things go wrong.

A climber should never consider going on an expedition unless he already has snow and ice experience. This should have been in a wide variety of circumstances and include travel on snow-covered glaciers and survival in severe conditions. It is often too late to start learning once bad weather closes in on a big mountain. The Alps is of course an ideal training ground, particularly if winter excursions are undertaken. Big routes in the Alps in winter are the nearest thing to a Himalayan climb that you can get in Europe and they have provided myself and many friends with the necessary background experience to attempt major Himalayan climbs confidently. Unfortunately the modern climber, even in the Alps, will spend very little time bivouacking and yet this is one of the most crucial skills on expeditions. At the very least a spell of camping high in snowy conditions should be undertaken if you do not have the required alpine background. In essence the climb-

er should be familiar with all the techniques described in the first three sections of the book because he may have to use any of them at any time.

Altitude Experience
If none of your party has been to altitude before then you should restrict your choice of peaks to those under 6,500 m. With a proper period of acclimatization most people can manage this sort of height without any particular difficulty. On peaks above 7,000 m the altitude can severely affect your progress even when acclimatized and so previous altitude experience is invaluable in anticipating what will happen and formulating a realistic plan. There is evidence to suggest that climbers become physiologically better adapted to altitude and acclimatize more quickly when they have regularly been to altitude. Scientific evidence to support this is largely inconclusive, but my personal observation of many different climbers on different expeditions suggests very strongly that this is the case. Of course it is hard to disentangle the psychological and physiological factors because familiarity with the feelings that high altitude produces must help cope with the problems and give a great deal of confidence. Despite the foregoing opinions there are occasional climbers who have climbed to very high altitude on the first expedition, but they have usually acted within the framework of a much more experienced party. Do not be too daunted by the altitude question – the average climber is perfectly capable of reaching altitudes up to 7,000 m without any serious difficulty or danger, so long as he takes the precautions which are discussed in the medical section later on.

Climbing in the Alps in winter is ideal expedition training, technically, psychologically and physically. On the Croz Spur at Christmas.

Some climbers have come to me complaining that they have suffered from altitude headaches and sickness even in the Alps at 4,000 m so how can they possibly manage any higher altitudes in the Himalayas. This is nothing to worry about—it is perfectly normal to feel like that if you are not acclimatized. On nearly every expedition I go on I have a couple of days feeling rough because of altitude. This nearly always happens at around 4,000 m and after that I have no problems for the rest of the trip. Everyone reacts in a different way but most of the problems seem to occur in the first stages of acclimatization; after that it usually plain sailing, except for much higher altitudes when unpredictable oedema problems can occur even when all the rules have been followed.

Training for an Expedition
It is hard to train for miserable conditions and hard work without indulging in some rather masochistic activities. Mind training and physical training are equally important. Running round a track is great for mountaineering fitness but this is only a small, though important, part of the qualities needed to get to the top of a mountain. The best training without any shadow of doubt is to go out and climb. Climb on rock, climb on ice, walk in the hills, do anything in the mountain environment. Familiarity with this environment is crucial and every day you spend in the mountains you will learn something new and get fitter as well. Do not spend time in the gym unless you really have to, get out and do something adventurous. It will be more enjoyable and put you in a much better position to climb your mountain. An activity like caving can be physically demanding and adventurous and is far more appropriate training than running or gym work. For those who already have a great experience of the mountains straightforward fitness training, like running, might be just the thing, but this book is not really written for them.

Carrying heavy sacs is a basic part of an expedition and for the newcomer may prove to be its most gruelling aspect.

My personal favourite for training is to go on long arduous walks, carrying as heavy a rucsac as I can manage. Most people find that carrying a heavy sac and climbing with it are the hardest part of expedition climbing. Therefore it makes sense to train for this aspect of the trip. After all if you get used to carrying 30 kilos then when you set out on the mountain your sac will feel light. It is the one thing that you do not normally encounter in the usual climbing year and so a special effort should be made. Like all new exercises the process should build up gradually to avoid injury. Although I am not an expert on the physical benefits of such training I believe that doing stints of at least six hours is best because it closely simulates one day's expedition work. It will hurt and you will get used to carrying on when your body tells you to stop—an important psychological benefit.

General fitness can be obtained in many ways and nowadays most people are fully aware of the health and fitness questions. Alpine climbing is extremely good but things like Scottish winter climbing come a close second for all round preparation. If you are very busy with little time to train or climb before an expedition then the walk-in can be used to get fit but you must be careful to eat well and avoid such hazards as heat stroke. I often carry a 30 kilo load to base camp as a method of training. If there is a two or three week approach then you will get more or less as fit as you need to be during the course of the expedition, although of course training at home will not do you any harm. People who run regularly and become very thin because of it should be particularly careful on an expedition. One dose of diarrhoea can mean the body taking in no food for several days and muscle loss will occur if you are very thin. It is always a good idea to eat plenty of food for the last few weeks before an expedition because you are sure to lose weight and you do not want to lose strength.

Doug Scott with a full load on his way to climb Nuptse. He will be a lot thinner on the return.

Chris Bonington ferrying a load in China. His books such as *Everest the Hard Way* provide useful appendices for expedition planners.

Planning at Home

Dividing the Jobs

As soon as you decide to go on an expedition you should divide up the tasks to be completed at home and also consider what roles each member will play subsequently. An expedition can be divided into the following organizational areas, each of which should be allocated to a particular individual.

members know well in advance how much money they are likely to have to find. Although it goes against the grain for many people it is a good idea to circularize a kind of bulletin on progress to date. This keeps people informed and encourages them to get on with their jobs. At times even the keenest have doubts about going.

Leader	General co-ordination, dealing with permits and general finance.
Equipment	Writing a list of what is required by the team and by each individual and then buying it, or trying to obtain it by writing to manufacturers.
Food	Deciding what food should be brought from the home country and obtaining it, bearing in mind availability in the country that you are visiting.
Fund Raising	Dealing with the media if appropriate and writing for sponsorship and grants.
Medical	If you have a doctor he will obviously do this, but if not you must consult with a doctor for advice.
Travel	Arranging air travel and freight.

Assistance in Planning

In most countries there are national mountaineering bodies which can offer some general guidelines to mountaineering parties. They will have lists of where to apply for permits and where to get a set of current regulations about climbing in the countries you wish to visit. In Britain the BMC can offer a certain amount of assistance and in America local mountaineering groups can put you in touch with climbers who have already visited the areas you are going to visit. The embassies of your chosen country may be able to help in some ways. In the planning states your bank manager will be able to advise and it is a good idea to open an expedition account at your bank. Occasionally expedition seminars are held by various bodies and they are advertised in the mountaineering press. Magazines also run up-to-

Joe Tasker jumaring at 7,000 m on Everest in January 1981. Fixed rope expeditions are an expensive and complicated business.

If anyone has a particular skill then obviously he can be used in his speciality but otherwise the jobs need to be allocated by the leader with the agreement of the members. The leader must make sure that the respective jobs are done in time and making a schedule with dates by which certain tasks should be completed is a sound idea. During the whole organizational process at home one eye should always be kept on factors which will come into play once you have left home. For instance if porterage is particularly expensive then food should be planned to be as light in weight as you can make it. The same obviously goes for gear. In many places you will need to supply members of your staff with equipment and this must be obtained according to the prevailing rules of the country you are visiting. An overall budget must be prepared as soon as possible so that

date features about particular areas so it is worth scouring through them.

If you write to a fellow mountaineer for information try to be as specific as possible on what information you require. It is no use just saying 'I am going to Peru this summer please tell me a suitable objective, how to get there, etc.'. This would need a book to answer the question fully. Do as much research as you can before asking for help about points that you cannot find out about yourself.

Raising Money

This is a frequently asked topic. People have the idea that they will send off some letters to a few firms and then they will have a free expedition. This has never happened and will not happen in the future. Out of fourteen expeditions that I have been on, I have personally met over seventy per cent of my costs on all but three trips. Therefore you should pick an objective which you can afford out of your own pocket. That said, you can probably raise a little money from grants and various other sources. You will find there is a point at which you can spend an immense amount of time trying to raise funds when if you had spent the time doing something you were better at, you would have earned the money anyway and be under no external obligations.

You can raise money in two distinct ways and they cannot be mixed up: either you can pretend to be a charitable cause to which people should donate money because they believe what you are doing is worthwhile and worthy of support; or you can put your expedition together as a commercial package, to which people give money because they will get a sound commercial return. In each case the features which appeal to one type of sponsor will put off the other type of sponsor. A slick brochure and a commitment to a professional attitude will appeal to those seeking a commercial deal but will put off those who wish to help on a charitable basis. If you

Mike Shrimpton filming on Everest at 6,000 m for YTV. Making films can be a good way to raise money but is very expensive.

are a fully grown, employed person then there is no real reason why anyone should help pay for your holiday. On the other hand such groups of people as students have potential access to all sorts of charitable funds, which the crafty climber might be able to channel in his direction with a bit of lateral thinking.

The Amateur Approach

If you do not want to get involved with publicity for your expedition, then there a few ways of raising money other than grants from educational and research federations and societies. You can indulge in the usual fund-raising exercises like raffles, discos, etc. but do not expect to find more than ten per cent of your costs this way, otherwise you are likely to be disappointed. There is little point in going to the expense of producing a glossy brochure about your expedition, but it is a good idea to have a duplicated sheet about the trip so as to save repeating yourself endlessly. Any fund-raising you attempt is best done on a local level, particularly if you have friends with good local contacts. The national media and consequently the national companies are unlikely to have any interest in your project unless you have a curious angle like attempting to take a dog to the summit or performing some circus-like stunt which might be

eligible for the Guinness Book of Records.

The grants you might get in Britain would total about £1,000 if your project was an interesting one of some difficulty. This would come roughly half-and-half from the Mount Everest Foundation and the BMC. Their grants are dependent purely on the team and its objectives. Other countries have similar awards for comparable amounts, again depending on the project. In America funds are generally raised through sponsorship or by climbers themselves, although some awards are given for scientific or youth projects.

The Professional Approach

The soundest way to raise a large proportion of the cost is to offer a good chance of publicity for a sponsor, and if this is a real possibility then go ahead. There are of course disadvantages with publicity—it takes up a lot of time and tends to be divisive between team members. Your expedition may be of local or national interest but you will need to promote it like a soap brand: a process which is not one relished by any real climbers because of the way it can redirect your energy and objectives. The overall cost of the expedition is the key factor. If you wish to go and climb in China for instance it will cost at least £5,000 per head—a figure well beyond the reach of most young people. Thus you will need to generate publicity and find a sponsor. If however your expedition is only costing £1,000 per head you are probably better to go out and earn it because your fundraising efforts may anyway prove fruitless. Because the large expeditions led by public figures like Chris Bonington tend to be free trips for the participants, novice climbers imagine that that is how the whole thing works. In fact the vast bulk of trips from any country are financed by the participants.

The media do have large sums of money floating around but it is hard to lay your hands on it. Making a film is the core of a commercial success but newspapers have an important role to play. The whole business is complex and time-consuming but if you can pull it off then good luck. A strong 'human interest' will tip the balance if your expedition is not to a famous objective or full of famous

Chris Bonington sending news reports back to the media at home in order to satisfy sponsors.

names. Realistically this means an expedition with women participating or an expedition consisting wholly of women. This is for the straightforward reason that people are well aware of men doing adventurous things like going on an expedition but do not realize that women do these things as well. In fact more women are climbing and participating in expeditions every year but the general public are not yet aware of the fact. Doubtless the novelty will wear off as it becomes commonplace. Speaking rather cynically, the difficulty of your objective or the strength of your team is essentially irrelevant to the public at large and you stand the same chance of raising money for walking up a pimple as climbing an unknown objective of great difficulty with an unknown team.

Sponsors in Kind
After the rather dismal news on the money front I am happy to say the situation is far more cheerful when it comes to gear and food and other

Paul Nunn, Brian Hall and Andy Parkin on a four man expedition to Ogre 2 (6,960 m) in the Karakorum. A typical self financed low cost trip.

forms of non-monetary assistance. Many firms will give food to expeditions on a purely charitable basis, asking for no return, although you should always send them a card and an expedition report, in which their assistance is acknowledged. The free food will come from a general public relations budget and so you should write accordingly. It helps firms considerably if you specify exactly what you require in your first letter to them. If you ask for sponsorship without specifying what it is you require they will be very loath to say yes, thereby entering into an open-ended commitment. If you say what you require they can say yes or no on the spot and avoid time-consuming communications for both sides. You should always start a begging letter with what you can offer the firm, however insignificant that might be. Even if you say that you will send them a photo of their product in use and mention it in any publicity, it at least shows that you are going to do what you can in return for their help. For a large firm any photos you send are most unlikely to be of any use to them for advertising but they will be of personal interest to the department that helped you.

Climbing equipment manufacturers are inundated with requests for assistance and most of them are relatively small concerns that cannot possibly afford to help everyone who asks. They will often offer trade price or a similar deal but will usually only donate gear to teams that will give a good feedback in terms of genuine testing of new gear and good publicity in the climbing media. Taking good advertising shots on an expedition requires considerable effort and a degree of expertise, so firms tend to go with known quantities in this area. If a firm does give you any help then make sure you do everything you can for them on your return. A lot of parties never even correspond with their sponsors after the end of the expedition and this messes things up for other expeditions as well as any expeditions that they might like to go on

in the future. On the other hand, if you do mention their name in articles and provide good advertising photos you can be sure of a warm response in the future to any requests for gear. Remember to ask a long time in advance for what you need and be specific about what you require, including sizes, colours etc. Detail any publicity you expect to receive and how they could benefit from it. A professional sort of approach is always the one to take with climbing equipment manufacturers. Good equipment reports detailing positive and negative aspects as well as specific problems and suggestions for the future are very valuable to progressive companies and will be welcomed. This is the way that much of the well-designed modern gear has come about because expeditions provide an excellent accelerated test ground for new items.

Patrons

To give credibility to your expedition you can enlist a patron who can write letters of support where appropriate and add his or her name to your expedition stationery. This is some help when your team is unknown to the people you are dealing with but your patron's name is known to them. When

applying for permission I have found that the systems are quite fair and that external influence from such bodies as embassies is minimal so do not expect your patron to affect things on that front. Sometimes you will find a patron who will actively help you contact people and raise money so it is an idea well worth considering.

Schedule

Most people decide to go on an expedition a year in advance. For many Himalayan countries this is a bare minimum. If you want to climb Everest for instance you will have to think many years in advance because it is more or less booked up for the next ten years from Nepal, or else go from the Chinese side where the enormous cost discourages most parties, though permission is easier to obtain. Some places like Peru can be decided on just a few weeks beforehand. A general guideline is permissions a year in advance, sponsorship at least six months, and flights, equipment and food three months in advance.

From left to right Tasker, Bonington, Boardman and Rouse after making the first ascent of Mount Kongur (7,719 m). Logos on clothing help sponsors.

Costs

The total expedition cost is difficult to assess. The main areas of expenditure are travel, equipment and food if the trip takes place in Peru or Patagonia. If you are going to Nepal then you need to add the following major items as well: peak fees, staff wages, staff equipment and porters' wages. On top of these there are other areas of expenditure which need not be great if you want to keep the costs down to a bare minimum but could be increased considerably if you were an accountant wishing to offset the amounts against a tax bill. These are: administration, hotel and food bills in cities, taxis to and from endless offices and banks while dealing with bureaucracy, purchase of cookware, miscellaneous hardware connected with transport of loads, customs dues which can be very large if things go wrong, film, cameras, agents fees, insurance, and mail.

Your first expenditure if you are going to Asia will be the Peak Fee (these are listed at 1985 rates on pages 216–17). Often this will have to be found long before you start raising money so you can get all the expedition members to make an equal contribution at this stage. This has the big advantage of committing people to the project from an early date. Asking for a little more than is needed for the peak fee makes sense because the surplus can be used for administrative costs at home. The next major expenditure will be on travel but this is not normally required until two or three months beforehand.

When you leave the home country you will need to take quite large sums of money. I find that it is best to take mainly travellers cheques of a well-known brand in a major world currency plus a reasonable quantity of money—perhaps ten per cent in dollars or pounds. A wide variety of denominations of travellers cheques should be carried so that it is possible to change more or less exactly what you want. It is often very difficult to change money back from a local currency to an internationally accepted currency so you do not want to be left with a massive surplus of local money. In a country like Nepal, for instance, you can change back a maximum of ten per cent of the amount you originally changed, providing you have bank receipts for the original transactions. As each year passes more use can be made of Eurocheques and credit cards but it will be quite some time before your average Balti porter accepts American Express!

A good insurance policy is essential unless you are a sufficiently large group to act effectively as your own insurers. Loss of baggage

On a remote glacier in Xinjiang, perhaps the most expensive part of Asia to visit for climbing, after Bhutan.

in transit and in the cities should be covered as well as the usual risks covered in a policy for travel. Medical insurance may need to be via a special policy because of the special circumstances of an expedition. In most areas there is no real rescue service but nonetheless special costs might be incurred in getting an injured person back to the city and these should be covered. In Pakistan there is a helicopter bond which can either be guaranteed by your embassy or deposited in a Pakistani bank nominated by the Ministry of Tourism. The bond is at present US $2,000 and covers possible special use of a helicopter for evacuation from the mountains. The system came about because several expeditions never paid their rescue helicopter bills. You can insure in your home country against the bond being used but this policy alone will not satisfy the authorities. You actually need to hand over the money to them for the duration of the trip and it is returned to you at the end of the expedition.

Most parties want to keep costs to a bare minimum and main areas where costs can be cut are: shopping around for the best travel deal, minimum purchases of new equipment and minimizing the total weight of food and equipment taken to base camp. In some places, particularly China and Bhutan, there is no way round having a very expensive expedition no matter how careful you are but most other places can be done on the cheap if you are prepared to make the effort.

An Expedition to Peru

For a four man expedition to the Cordillera Huayhuash for seven weeks away from home the following costs can be reasonably expected, assuming that each climber already has his own equipment and that the team is climbing without fixed ropes.

An expedition to Nepal

	£	$
Peak Fee	1,000	1,400
Travel London—Kathmandu return	2,500	3,500
Agent's Fee	150	210
Costs in Kathmandu	200	280
Porter and Staff Insurance (arranged in Kathmandu)	200	280
Personal Insurance (arranged at home)	250	350
Local Travel (to the end of the road in Jiri)	80	112
Porters' wages for approach from Jiri to base camp (25 porters)	600	840
Flights from Lukla to Kathmandu with baggage	200	280
Porters' wages from base camp to Lukla (10 porters)	100	140
Staff wages (cook and sirdar)	250	350
Liaison Officer's wages	130	180
Staff Equipment (at wholesale prices)	500	700
Cooking gear and fuel	80	112
Food	500	700
Incidental costs on approach	100	140
Miscellaneous	200	280
Contingency	400	560
Total	7,440	10,416

The cost per person is £1,860 ($2,604). In this case the cost is not directly proportional to the number of participants because approximately £1,500 ($3,500) of costs are fixed independently of numbers. These are staff costs in terms of wages and food for the porters, agent's and peak fee, Liaison Officer, etc. Roughly speaking an eight man team would work out at £1,550 ($2,170) per head or a six man team at £1,650 ($2,310) per head. Obviously a two man expedition can work out particularly expensive in these circumstances, although one member of staff could probably be dispensed with. £2,000 ($2,800) is probably a bare minimum per head for a two man team.

An expedition to Peru

	£	$
Air Travel return from London (bucket shop prices with 40 kilo/88 lbs baggage allowance)	2,000	2,800
Three days in Lima—living costs	100	140
Purchase of food in Peru	180	252
Travel in bus to Chiquian	80	112
Hire of donkeys for two days to and from base camp	200	280
Insurance	200	280
Miscellaneous (fuel, stoves, airport taxes, etc.)	200	280
Contingency	400	560
Total	3,360	4,704

Split four ways this comes to £830 ($1,176). The cost in this case is directly proportional to the number of participants.

An Expedition to Nepal

The following costs are for a four man party going to climb Ama Dablam (6,856 m) in the post-monsoon, leaving home on 15 September, arriving at base camp on 4 October, leaving base camp on 1 November and returning home on 14 November. This assumes walking all the way to base camp but only walking down to Lukla and then flying back to Kathmandu on the return. The bare minimum of staff is a Liaison Officer, sirdar and cook with twenty-five porters for this duration of trip.

An Expedition to Pakistan

As an example I have chosen a four man party to Baintha Brakk 2 (6,960 m) near the Biafo glacier in the Karakorum. This involves a drive from Islamabad to Skardu, a further jeep ride to Dassu, three days' walk to Askole and then a further four days' approach march on the Biafo glacier. You will need a Liaison Officer and a cook. The time scale of the expedition is to arrive in Islamabad on 1 June, arrive Skardu on 7 June and base camp on 15 June. Assuming one month of climbing and leaving base camp in the middle of July you will arrive back home on say 25 July. Apart from the fees and costs below you will need to take a refundable helicopter bond of US $2,000.

An Expedition to a peak of less than 6,000 m in Pakistan

A four man party going to climb a rock spire below 6,000 m in the lower Baltoro area, near the Trango Towers. The cost is considerably less than a full scale expedition. The assumed timescale is the same as the previous example as the walk is about the same length, perhaps one or two days longer.

An expedition to Pakistan

	£	$
Peak Fee	1,000	1,400
Travel London—Islamabad return (including element for freight)	2,000	2,800
Agents' fees (optional, but saves time and effort)	150	210
Costs in Islamabad	200	280
Porter and staff insurance	200	280
Personal Insurance	250	350
Hire of minibus to Skardu	200	280
Travel to Dassu and return to Skardu	200	280
Bus back from Skardu to Islamabad	50	70
Porters' wages for approach (22 porters)	1,250	1,750
Porters' wages on return (8 porters)	450	630
Liaison Officer's costs (food, equipment)	350	490
Cook's costs (food, wages and equipment)	450	630
Cooking gear and fuel	80	112
Food	500	700
Miscellaneous	300	420
Contingency	400	560
Total	8,030	11,242

The costs are approximately £2,000 ($2,800) per head with about £2,300 ($3,220) of the costs being independent of the number of team members. With a six man team the cost would be about £1,800 ($2,520) per head and about £1,700 ($2,380) with an eight man team.

An expedition to Pakistan (below 6,000 m)

	£	$
Fees (agents and permits)	350	490
Travel London—Islamabad return	1,950	2,730
Costs in Islamabad (shorter stay needed)	150	210
Porter and staff insurance	150	210
Personal Insurance	250	350
Hire of minibus to Skardu and other travel as before	400	560
Porters' wages (estimated at 18 porters for nine days)	1,200	1,680
Mountain Guide costs (food, wages and equipment)	550	770
Cooking gear and fuel	70	98
Food	450	630
Miscellaneous	250	350
Contingency	400	560
Total	6,170	8,638

The cost per head is therefore £1,540 ($2,156) and this cost is more or less proportional to the number of climbers. The contrast with an expedition peak is most marked for a two man team which would cost about £2,500 ($3,500) per head in the previous case, but only about £1,700 ($2,380) in this case.

All costs are based on 1985 prices at an exchange rate of $1.4 to the £1.

Travel

Most parties are working on a tight budget and air travel is one of the biggest single costs. Sometimes an airline will help you out but in general they will not. Expeditions optimistically write for free seats, offering some publicity in return, but really the level of publicity offered is in general of no interest to the airlines. The best bet is to get married to an air hostess and then get tickets at vastly reduced prices but this has other consequences which are outside the scope of this book! Thus most parties shop around the bucket shops. Air tickets are cheaper now than they have ever been relative to the cost of living. Bookings need to be made a long time in advance as local circumstances often produce full planes. For instance flights that go via the Middle East are very full around the time of Hadje when pilgrims from all over the world visit Mecca. The beginning and end of school holidays are also key periods for air travel. If you have a job to go back to it is worth making a definite return booking, as getting home without a reservation is notoriously difficult.

It is worth finding out which days are public holidays in the country you are visiting. Many expeditions arrive only to find that all the offices are shut for three days and so they cannot get on with the necessary bureaucracy. On the return journey it is common to encounter overbooking which the airlines indulge in because of the very high 'no-show' rate in some countries. One way or another they will get you back but you need to be forceful with airline officials if you are not to be pushed to the back of the queue.

Freight of Baggage

This is a perennial problem for expeditions and my first piece of advice is to avoid freighting at all costs. If your baggage is unaccompanied, then it will be subject to a bewildering variety of customs regulations which do not apply to accompanied baggage. It is also frequently subject to delay and occasionally lost in transit, particularly if a change of planes is involved such as when flying to Kathmandu. In most countries you will need to either pay customs duties, which are considerable, or pay a bond which is partly returnable on the re-export of the goods involved. The exception to this is Pakistan which has a system for the duty free importation of goods pertaining to an expedition. It is my experience that this system works in Pakistan so long as gear is freighted direct to Islamabad by air, where the customs authorities are now familiar with the special rules governing mountaineering expeditions. It is still necessary to traipse round endless offices obtaining about a dozen stamps of authorization before the gear will be released, but there are agents on the spot who will assist you in this process—for a fee of course. In other countries the system is more difficult to deal with, and in all countries gear shipped to a port will become a nightmare to extract from the docks.

It should be possible for small expeditions to carry all their gear as accompanied baggage thereby avoiding any real problems with customs. The weight limit for international air travel is 20 kilos but judicious use of hand luggage can effectively extend this to nearly double. Often an airline will officially offer some assistance with your baggage limits if you are flying with them but the normal excess baggage rates, at one per cent of first class air fare per kilo, are prohibitively expensive and must be avoided. With prior agreement from the cargo manager you can arrange for extra baggage to be sent on the same plane as you are travelling on but at freight rates which seem to average out at about a quarter of excess baggage rates. The gear will need to be taken to the airport at least twenty-four hours before your flight. There is also an internationally agreed reduced sporting goods rate for baggage which should be investigated.

Initially it may seem impossible to get all your food and equipment inside the weight limit, but remember that it is probably cheaper to buy extra gear in the country you are visiting than to buy it at home and then transport it over. Expedition food and equipment are readily available in Kathmandu at reasonable prices and can be resold at the end of the expedition. It is quite feasible to arrive in Kathmandu with just money and a passport and acquire everything you need on the spot. In other Asian countries it will be more difficult, and perhaps impossible, but food of sorts is available everywhere at a price, even if climbing gear is not.

A light plane arriving at Shyanboche airstrip in the Everest area.

Food

The key to food planning is to find out what food will be available locally. Find someone who has already been to get some idea. If you can drive yourself then it may make sense to bring all your food from home, but normally you will be flying and the cost of air freightage is prohibitive for most expeditions. Accompanied excess baggage can be as much as £12 per kilo from the UK to the Indian sub-continent, or $122 per piece from the US. Air freight will probably be around £1.20–3.00 per kilo ($8.5–$9.8 from the US).

Whatever is not available locally you will need to transport from home, but this is difficult in the case of shipping, where customs will probably throw a spanner in the works, or expensive by plane. Consequently a change of diet to largely local fare makes sense. In Pakistan it makes sense to buy plenty of atta (flour) to make chappatis, whereas in Nepal rice is the staple fare. If you have a local cook, which is compulsory if you have a Liaison Officer in most countries, then he will only be able to cook certain types of food well.

Most regular expeditioners have developed a profound preference for fresh food, and a simultaneous dislike of dried food. There is no really concrete reason, just a gut feeling. On the approach march a small party will find it easy to buy local supplies, except in the Karakorum. It seems best to live off these, supplemented perhaps by some goodies to eat during the day's walk. There is some problem in adjusting to a different diet from our western one but during the course of the trip your system should settle down. While still at home you can get in practice by going to cheap curry houses, which offer a toned down version of the food you can find in a third world country. Those who have been brought up in countries with strict food and health regulations tend to have a lot of problems when they arrive in third world countries as

they have built up relatively little immunity to stomach bugs. They should take extra care and make frequent use of water sterilizing tablets until they get to base camp.

Availability

On your travels you will almost certainly pass through the capital city and all kinds of food will be available, including processed foreign food, although that will be more expensive than at home. The biggest exception is in India where regulations effectively exclude

Above: A local market in Huaraz, Peru. Eating fresh food as much as you possibly can makes sense for your health and your pocket. Local availability should be checked out in advance and the team should always be prepared to modify normal eating habits to suit local circumstances.

Below: Chillies drying at Dharan Bazaar in Nepal. Heavily spiced food can have a useful antiseptic affect.

Cooking with petrol or paraffin is usual at base on most expeditions. Our cook and sirdar at Jannu Base Camp (c 5,000 m).

most foreign processed food. The same is true in China although better quality locally processed food is available there. Tinned meat of any quality is the hardest thing to get hold of. In India the best you will find is tins of unspecified meat canned in Calcutta with a rather appropriate green label on the outside. Tinned fish is usually OK throughout the world although beware the fable on the label. We bought tins of fish in Peru that had pictures of a salmon on the front but contained sardines inside. In fact we discovered that every type of tin in Peru with fish on the cover had sardines inside. Local trade descriptions acts seem to vary considerably. Obviously if you are travelling to Patagonia or Alaska you can buy everything in the country you are visiting. In Nepal you have the bonus of surplus food sold off from previous expeditions. Much of this food is high quality East European stuff which the Poles or Czechoslovaks have brought with the idea of selling to raise hard-to-come-by hard currency. This can be bought in Kathmandu but also at numerous tea houses. Namche Bazaar, on the way to the Everest area, sells large quantities of expedition surplus

food at quite high prices. However the prices are still less than it would cost you to buy, and then transport the food from Kathmandu.

In the lush areas of India and Nepal food can be bought in small quantities at towns on your approach march, but it is best not to rely completely on this source as a poor crop of rice, for instance, may mean supplies are short. In Pakistan you need take nothing from home. You can buy all your food in Islamabad or wait to buy staples in Skardu or Gilgit.

What to Bring From Home

Rations for use above base camp will need to be planned before leaving as these sorts of supplies are rarely available on the spot. Most parties take far too much of this type of food. For various reasons explained elsewhere you will not need to take more than one kilo per day per man above base camp and on the average trip you are most unlikely to spend more than fourteen days above base camp per person, unless you are sieging the mountain and living in high camps. If the latter is the case then weight is less critical anyway and you can take up a proportion of local food to your high camps. In conclusion, for the average four man expedition a total weight of hill food brought from home should not exceed about 50 kilos. Realistically 20 kilos will be enough for the vast

bulk of small parties. The following items should be considered for import:

Drinks Herbal teas, instant coffee, powdered fruit drinks, soup sachets

Goodies Chocolate, sweets, grain bars, dried fruit and nuts

Cold Food Salami, tinned pate, cheese, Crispbread, tinned fish, sachets of jam or honey, muesli-type grain mixes

Hot Food Boil in the bag meals, dried and freeze-dried meals, potato powder, freeze-dried rice, freeze-dried noodles

Within each of these categories you should invest in as wide a variety as possible so as to tempt the palate on the bivouacs.

How much you will need

As a very rough rule your food will weigh one kilo per man per day, assuming a certain amount of dried food and periods of time on the hill when less will be consumed. If you have any less than an average of a kilo per man per day you may well run out. If you will be spending a lot of time at base camp and are taking fresh foods such as potatoes and odd luxuries such as tinned fruit then your rations may come to more like 2 kilos per day per man.

Certain items of food, like sugar, tend to be used faster than you might think. A lot depends on local habits. In Nepal for instance your local cook will add vast quantities of milk and sugar to a pot of tea and even those who do not take sugar at home will tend to consume a lot on an expedition. A local can eat vastly more rice in one sitting than we could dream of and it is absolutely essential not to run out of staple foods. Fortunately in many mountain areas you can send a runner down for more basic supplies if they look like running out at any time. On one expedition to Nuptse we employed a full time vegetable runner who journeyed to and from the nearest source of fresh vegetables.

Cooking the Food

Although some base camps have wood, in most areas you will need to carry fuel—petrol or paraffin. Primus stoves can be bought locally in most countries but they are often of inferior quality, so either buy more than you need in anticipation of breakdowns, or else bring good quality stoves from Europe. For a four man team with Liaison Officer and cook you will need about a litre of fuel per day on average at base camp, assuming that quite a few days will be spent away from base camp on the hill. In cold places you will need more fuel, particularly if tin cans freeze up and there is no running water.

The quality of fuel is very important. Poor quality fuel soon ruins the stoves, all of which become more temperamental with the rise in altitude. A useful tip is to try and get helicopter fuel from an airport (or propeller plane fuel, but not jet fuel which is very low quality). White gas, which is a high quality unleaded petrol, is unobtainable in my experience in third world countries, so forget stoves that need it.

A pressure cooker is essential for all expeditions and can always be bought out there. It saves on fuel and also avoids the problems of the low boiling point experienced as the altitude rises. Cheap, lightweight aluminium pans can always be obtained on the spot and they are ideally suited for expedition use. A kettle is useful for brewing up. All aluminium ware is frequently sold by weight in the bazaar, independent of what shape it is! Good plastic cups may be difficult to obtain but basically all of your cooking and eating utensils are best bought in the country you are going to. They will be cheaper and also lighter in weight than comparable items brought from home. Solar cookers can save on fuel, particularly if snow needs to be melted to get water, but they can only supplement more usual forms of cooking for obvious reasons.

How it will be carried

All food should be extremely well packaged in order to survive porterage through monsoons, rivers, and rough terrain. Good quality plastic bags are hard to obtain in most places and I would strongly recommend taking a large quantity of plastic bags of various sizes from home. Jute sacs can be used to make up porter loads. With a particularly sensitive item which must not get wet, like flour, we put it inside double polythene bags, then a jute sack, more polythene and another jute sack. It is a good idea to paint a number on the sacs and make a list of the contents. You never know when you will need some unanticipated item.

Dietary Requirements

Most people are now overinformed about human dietary needs and there is little that I could add. Some expedition climbers are confirmed vegetarians, but having lived off a vegetarian diet myself on some expeditions I find I lose too much weight. Most people experience some loss of appetite at altitude and it is a problem to eat enough food to maintain strength. A balanced diet is of course essential and it is probably a good idea to supplement your diet with vitamin pills, in case you are missing out. Each climber has personal preferences and these must be taken into consideration when planning.

Cooking in the relative comfort of a snow cave using a petrol-based MSR stove at 6,000 m.

Equipment

Clothing

In the past ten years there has been a revolution in protective clothing and there is now a wide choice of well-made garments which do the job that they are intended for. The outer layers are the most critical and here Goretex has had a big impact. Originally developed for artificial arteries, it is now laminated onto nylon to form a waterproof but breathable fabric. Despite imitations and various competitive fabrics, Goretex is still much the best material for expedition work. The biggest drawback is its high cost: a basic cagoule costs a minimum of about £60 ($200) in the shops. Goretex salopettes, lined for cold places and unlined for others are highly recommended. Overtrousers are a very poor second to salopettes for all serious mountaineering because of the gap that an be formed around the waist.

For extremely cold temperatures with strong winds such as encountered on Everest in winter I wore the following clothing; a one-piece Goretex suit, lined with Thinsulate and then with down, a one-piece fibre pile suit, and underwear. This was adequate in winds of 130 km per hour and temperatures down to −45°C. The one-piece outer garment is not commercially available but can be made up by special request to firms such as Mountain Equipment. One-piece garments are much warmer than a comparable weight of garment in two pieces because most of heat loss in a well-insulated garment is through the pumping of hot air out of the clothing by movement. In a one-piece suit warm air is just moved from one area of the body to another when movement takes place. These suits do have the disadvantage of inflexibility as you need to wear the whole garment or none of it.

For mountains above 7,500 m a one-piece Goretex and down suit is good for the same reasons as before. It is a very light item for the warmth it gives. All one-piece suits

should be designed with suitable zips for going to the toilet, and clothing underneath must be designed to coincide with the zips. It is not always feasible to take off clothing when going to the toilet. For less severe conditions and in fact those encountered on most expeditions salopettes and an insulated jacket are more suitable. Thinsulate is good for actually climbing in but the jacket must be cut to allow freedom of movement in the arms. Underneath fibre pile is very good. It is warm and light and does not absorb lots of water like its

Modern clothing, such as Chris Bonington is wearing here, has made a big difference to comfort and survival on the mountain. His clothes are made of Goretex, which is waterproof but still breathes.

more natural counterparts. Thermal underwear and perhaps a pullover complete the rig out.

A balaclava of wool or fibre pile prevents excessive heat loss from the head—a key area of concern in keeping warm. Hands need to be covered most of the time and I have found gloves of Goretex lined with fibre pile to be the best all round. Mitts are much warmer than gloves and really I have never come across gloves that are adequate for mountain conditions. Thin gloves can be worn inside and used for delicate operations like cooking on the bivouac.

Many mountain areas of the world experience searing heat from the sun in the middle of the day and a wide-brimmed hat is pleasant to wear and makes one feel rather traditional. To combat burning of the skin good quality sun creams and blocking creams should be carried and used at all times. Sunglasses must be worn nearly all the time, even when it is misty as the damaging ultra-violet rays still penetrate well through mist. A spare pair of sunglasses should also be carried. I carry a lightweight fold up pair as my spares.

Sacs

Modern sacs are much better than old-fashioned ones for carrying heavy loads. Most have an internal frame design which allows a good degree of weight transfer to the hips. Straps are well padded and the sacs are very stable. Many companies have sacs designed specifically with expeditions in mind, particularly Berghaus and Lowe.

Climbing Hardware

Personal

Certain items should be possessed and looked after by individual members of the team. A harness is essential for climbing or operating on glaciers. There are many different models but the traditional Whillans harness is still very popular as it gives freedom of movement in the legs. Remember to check that it will still fit over all your clothes. On glaciers a pair of jumars or prusik loops should always be carried and also you must know how to use them in case you fall into a crevasse. I find it convenient and weight-saving to carry one jumar and one prusik loop permanently on my harness throughout the expedition.

A pair of rock shoes may be useful in case hard rock climbing is necessary but remember to get a big size to avoid the risk of frostbite. They are also great for bouldering at base camp.

Ice-axes and ice hammers are largely a matter for personal preference but a long ice-axe can be much more useful than the short model used for technical climbing. 65 cm is a useful sort of length for general, less technical climbing and about 55 cm if hard ice climbing is going to be undertaken. A helmet will protect you from falling chips of ice when a climber is above you and to some extent from stonefall. Because of weight considerations climbers usually opt for a lightweight helmet, which offers little protection in the case of a fall.

A headtorch is essential and the Petzl model is light and very reliable. Some climbers convert their torches to take the highly efficient

Modern sacs have made load carrying much more comfortable. On an alpine push of several days each climber will be carrying more than 20 kilos.

Georges Bettembourg coiling our shortened rope, used for glacier travel in the Western Cwm of Everest.

Lithium batteries, which can last for up to fifty hours, giving an excellent weight saving. A figure of eight descendeur is ideal for abseil descents, particularly when there are fixed ropes with knots that need to be crossed. It can also be usefully employed for belaying.

Climbing Hardware

Communal
There are two totally different cases to consider, depending upon the style of the expedition. On an alpine-style expedition you may find it convenient to pre-group into pairs so that each pair looks after its own gear requirements: ropes, tentage, cooking gear, etc.—in fact everything needed on the hill. This is a system I have often used to advantage, rather than arriving at base camp with a big pile of gear, for which no one has responsibility. If you are fixing camps and/or ropes then you need equipment which belongs to the whole expedition. You also need one person to be in charge of it.

First of all the basic pair will need the same sort of equipment as in the Alps. If your climb is relatively straightforward and mainly on snow I would plump for 45 or 50 m of 9 mm rope and the same length of 7 mm rope which is basically kept in the sac and only used for abseiling. Spare rope at base camp is always important because rope can get damaged so easily in an alpine environment. If you are on steep rock, on which jumaring is needed to second pitches, then an 11 mm rope is essential, with a 9 mm rope as well for sac hauling. The 9 mm is substantial enough to be used for climbing if the 11 mm gets seriously damaged. The actual hardware of pitons, nuts and ice screws depends entirely on the nature of the climb undertaken but remember the possibility of losing a lot of gear in a big abseil descent. Extras not normally carried in the Alps include a snow shovel for digging snow holes if the terrain looks suitable for them and a tent for bivouacs if there are ledges on the climb. If you are doing a very steep climb without bivouac ledges then an American-style porta ledge should be considered.

Certain aspects of equipment needed above base camp are dealt with in the section 'survival on the mountain' (p 230), where their specific use is simultaneously described.

Base Camp Equipment
Polythene and string are invaluable on an expedition. While walking in the porter can use big polythene sheets for shelter at night, particularly on the desolate glaciers of the Karakorum. On arrival at base camp the polythene can be used to help make a shelter for eating in and offer storage facilities for gear and food. Large sheets preferably reinforced to form tarpaulins are ideal but smaller pieces can also be invaluable. This is something you must bring from the home country in most cases. There are usually plenty of rocks around to make walls and the tarpaulins can be used for the roof. If you are going for a long period of time to a desolate place then a family-type frame tent is good news for the feeling of homeliness it brings. You can sit around playing cards, drinking tea or reading when the rain is lashing down outside. Having a covered area where everyone can get together is important for morale and the unity of the team. Entertainment is very important to help get through prolonged periods of bad weather. Plenty of good books are *de rigueur*, cards and chess very useful. A good radio which picks up short wave can usually tune into the BBC world service and keep you in touch with the outside world. Your own radio communications are frowned on in most countries and obstructed by an unbelieveable amount of bureaucracy. Only the very big expeditions with sponsors hungry for immediate news go to the trouble of fixing up an external radio link.

Walkie-talkie sets are great for fixed rope expeditions but of minimal use when climbing in alpine style. Check the local regulations if you plan to take them—normally it will be a complicated business. Most expeditions will employ an occasional mail runner to maintain contact with the outside world. Some of the big Japanese expeditions have computers at base camp, linked by satellite with Tokyo so they can get the news and weather. Some expeditions have generators for lighting and video equipment. This sort of paraphenalia is of course outside the scope of this book.

Alternative sources of energy

may be worthwhile: a solar cooker can save fuel, particularly for melting snow but even something as simple as a black polythene sheet can be used to good effect to melt snow on hot days. If you have rechargeable batteries, particularly for movie cameras, then solar cells can be used effectively to recharge them. There is of course very intense light at high altitude and so solar cells are particularly effective.

If you are away for a few months most climbers prefer the privacy of a tent apiece. Most base camps are relatively sheltered from bad weather and very strong winds so the type of tentage is not critical: dome-type-tents or A-frames are both fine. A good sleeping mat is essential—closed cell foam is indispensible—but on glacial base camps where the underneath of the tent is constantly changing an open cell foam mattress about 5 cm thick

adds considerably to the comfort of the climber. Also effective and increasingly popular are Thermarest-type sleeping mats which are inflatable but contain open cell foam inside.

Batteries are expensive for lighting and a tilly lamp is handy along with some candles. Individual stereos are popular, although a bit antisocial on occasions. When I was on a K2 expedition in 1983 we were all sitting around at base camp in murky weather when we heard the massive roar of an avalanche. It seemed to be coming straight for us so I shouted and everyone ran out of their tents and went into a sheltered place a few hundred metres from the campsite. Everything was soon enveloped in a swirling cloud of snow and then a few minutes later as the snow cleared we realized one person, Steve Sustad, was missing. We

went back over to the tents which had in the end only received a sprinkling of powder snow. We opened Steve's tent to find him inside listening to his Walkman stereo, oblivious to the avalanche that had just occurred!

Two sleeping bags are a good idea so that one sleeping bag can be left dry at base camp and the other can be used on the hill and perhaps left at an advance base camp. With a fixed rope expedition at least two sleeping bags per head are necessary to avoid a lot of unnecessary movement of weight up and down the mountain.

A family type frame tent is great for base camp as a communal tent, particularly if your base camp is in a hostile glaciated environment, as here below Everest West Ridge in February.

Medical

My advice is based on personal experience and should be supplemented by information from a doctor. Within the scope of this book there is only space to discuss the special medical problems associated with expeditions. These fall into three main categories: stomach and intestine problems, high altitude illnesses, and physical injuries. If you have not got a doctor in the party then one member should make it his business to learn enough first aid to act as medical officer. Apart from treating expedition members you will be pestered to give medical assistance to local people. If you have a doctor this is obviously no problem and medical supplies should be geared up for it, but if you do not, amateur treatment can be a dodgy business. We have taken large supplies of Vitamin C tablets to dole out to locals on the basis that they cannot do any harm. If we were sure what the problem was we have tried to treat it, but you must always take great care with pills because they may give them subsequently to young babies, whatever instructions you give them. A lot of locals believe that a pill good for one malaise will be equally effective for another and so they will come up to you faking an illness so as to get a supply of pills for future illnesses. Any pills given out should be consumed in front of you for these reasons.

Before leaving home a full range of inoculations should be undertaken: typhoid, paratyphoid, tetanus, polio, cholera and any other recommended by your health authority for the countries you are visiting. Check with the embassies of the countries you are visiting as you may need a formal certificate of inoculation in order to enter the country. Gammaglobulin is used to reduce the chance of getting hepatitis and is probably worthwhile particularly in the Andes. In malarial areas, which includes most of the Indian sub-continent, you should take anti-malarial tablets. The weekly tablet, maloprim, is convenient and fairly effective. It should be taken for a few weeks before and after entering and leaving a malarial area. Although there is no danger of malaria at base camp you are well advised to take the tablets throughout the trip as you will pass through dangerous areas on the way in and the way out.

In my own experience gastroenteritis of various forms is a major expedition problem. If it reaches base camp it is very difficult to get rid of and tends to recur amongst the team members. Take particular care with any staff you have as they are sometimes carriers of local stomach bugs. On one expedition to Everest we finally traced our recurrent cases of guardia to our mail runner, who came once a week and reinfected the camp with the disease. Getting your cook to be meticulous about cleanliness is essen-

The author (on the right!) with a broken ankle, a long way from the nearest hospital. Basic first aid knowledge should be acquired by all expeditioners to be able to cope with the odd emergency.

tial. This is particularly difficult if all water has to be melted from snow because there is not much water for washing up. Cities are prime places for stomach problems. Even expensive restaurants and hotels are not immune from them. Avoiding uncooked food, particularly salad stuffs is a sensible precaution, particularly before the approach march. In Nepal you will find numerous tea houses on the walk in and most of these are not bad from the health point of view so long as you stick to simple food. In Pakistan there are no tea houses and you will be preparing all your own food so the only thing you need to be particularly careful with is the water. Wherever you go you will occasionally be obliged to drink water of dubious origins so always carry water purifying tablets and use them until you are well above all habitation. Most dysentery clears up of its own accord but if it persists for more than forty-eight hours then a cure should be instituted. Amoebic dysentry and guardia are both common and the only effective way to treat them is to take large doses of the powerful drug Flagyl. Bacilliary dysentry can be alleviated by Lomotil, the standard dysentry drug. The actual details of these drugs and diseases should be researched beforehand as they are highly likely to be relevant.

There are other conditions which do not frequently occur in normal medicine. Snow blindness can occur even in cloudy conditions and sunglasses should be worn nearly all day at high altitudes. It is an extremely painful condition and appropriate treatments must be carried. Lasix is a diuretic which will help oedema, although a cure must be affected by a reduction of altitude. A full range of bandages, pain killers etc. should be carried in case of injury. A range of antibiotics should be carried for injuries, infections and frostbite.

Frostbite
Frostbite occurs when tissue at the bodies extremities is frozen. For-

tunately it is not as prevalent as it used to be due to better clothing, particularly the extensive use of plastic boots rather than leather. As the tissue thaws out it is prone to infection and antibiotics need to be taken. The skin must not be broken as that will allow infection in, so generally the patient will have to rest up. In severe cases the damage may not recover and amputations of fingers or toes will be necessary. It is therefore best avoided by taking sensible precautions like always carrying spare gloves.

Altitude Sickness
If anyone was whisked from sea level to 8,000 m they would quickly

At 7,300 m on Everest. This is the maximum sort of height which can be reached safely on expeditions of less than six weeks.

die from lack of oxygen. To reach high altitude safely a period of acclimatization must be gone through. Everyone needs to go through this process no matter how many times they have previously been to altitude. Most people will suffer some symptoms from the process but nearly everyone can acclimatize given sufficient time.

If you employ a local cook, which is standard procedure in a country like Nepal, you must make sure he sticks to basic rules of hygiene.

The tables opposite show some typical examples of acclimatization programmes in the Andes and in the Karakorum which can be followed as rough guides.

The top table shows a sensible sort of minimum time scale to climb an easy mountain of under 6,000 m. It can be done quicker but it will be painful and perhaps dangerous. Basically two weeks is needed to reach 6,000 m and at least a month to reach 7,000 m or higher, at least from a physiological point of view (bottom table).

Obviously these time scales are a very rough and ready guide. They are based on my personal experiences with a wide variety of climbers.

During the process of acclimatization headaches and sickness frequently occur but will usually pass away after a couple of days. If the symptoms are severe then altitude should be lost immediately in case pulmonary or cerebral oedema has begun to set in. Once oedema has started it will be fatal unless altitude is lost. There is no other cure, although Lasix will alleviate symptoms, helping the patient to descend. Oedema of this kind is aggravated by exercise according to several scientific studies. The fluid balances in the body are disturbed by lack of oxygen and water goes from inside cells to outside them. If this occurs in the lungs drowning results eventually. Extra pressure will build up from this water inside the head causing headaches and ultimately death. Pulmonary and cerebral oedema seem to affect young active people more frequently than older climbers. Why this is so is not entirely clear but young climbers tend to rush acclimatization and also exert more energy each day, unlike the more relaxed and craftier older men who conserve energy whenever possible.

There are certain well established rules for avoiding serious complications with the mysterious and not fully understood process of acclimatization:

1) Do not gain more than about 600 m per day in altitude.

Schedule to reach 6,000 m		M	Ft
Day One	Arrive Huaraz valley in Peru	c 3,500	c 11,500
Day Four	Leave Huaraz valley and drive to end of the road	c 4,000	c 13,100
Day Five	Walk to base camp	c 4,400	c 14,400
Days Six to Ten	Walk around base camp to heights of (but returning to base camp to sleep)	c 4,400	c 14,400
Day Eleven	Move to advance base camp	c 5,300	c 17,400
Day Twelve	Rest in advance base camp	c 5,300	c 17,400
Day Thirteen	Climb to summit, returning the same day	c 6,000	c 19,700

Schedule to reach 7,000 m			
Day One	Arrive Skardu (Karakorum)	c 2,000	c 6,500
Day Seven	Arrive base camp after a gradual height rise on the approach march	c 4,000	c 13,100
Days Eight to Twelve	Walks around base camp returning each evening	c 4,000	c 13,124
Days Thirteen to Twenty	Climbing at heights of up to spending the night up to	c 6,000 c 5,700	c 19,700 c 18,700
Days Twenty One to Thirty	Climbing at heights of up to spending nights at around	c 6,600 c 6,000	c 21,650 c 19,700
After Day Thirty	Ready for push to the summit	c 7,000	c 23,000

2) When acclimatizing climb high then return to sleep low.
3) Avoid unnecessary exercise until fully acclimatized.
4) Drink plenty of fluids at all times.
5) Descend for a couple of days if you feel particularly ill.

Beware of taking tablets which suppress symptoms to the extent that you feel able to carry on and ignore them. Diamox is a drug which appears to help the process of acclimatization, but research is still continuing and caution should be exercised in its use. A well-known effect of altitude is the increase in the red blood cell count due to the hormone erythropoietin. This high number of red cells predisposes to thrombosis, which has affected a number of mountaineers. From my own experience I have encountered cases of severe oedema most frequently at around 4–5,000 m in the initial stages of acclimatization and again at very high altitudes around 7,500 m or

above. This is perhaps because physically it is very easy to rush the first stage and the final stage is often completed in a prolonged push, gaining heights rapidly which have not been previously reached. Evidence suggests that there is some long term deterioration above 5,500 m and base camps at this sort of height do not offer adequate recovery potential.

When you descend again to sea level your hard won acclimatization is lost in a few days and it seems from anecdotal evidence that it is particularly dangerous to reascend rapidly to altitude. On one occasion in California a climber went to San Francisco for the weekend, having spent most of the summer living and climbing at 3–4,000 m in the Palisades. On his return at the end of the weekend he came straight back to 3,700 m and developed pulmonary oedema so seriously that we had to carry him down during the night. He immediately recovered once he had lost sufficient altitude.

Bureaucracy Abroad

One of the big headaches of all expeditioning is the customs. Tradition has accorded them a great deal of power, which is wielded from numerous similar offices and governed by complex and incomprehensible rules. The problems have already been mentioned in the travel section but on arrival you will find that the official rules do not always bear a direct relationship with reality. A couple of days of shuffling around dusty offices clutching fragile pieces of official paper and collecting indecipherable rubber stamps will usually suffice. The process cannot be rushed so do not be impatient. Your agent's help will be invaluable here.

In countries needing a permit you will need to visit the Ministry of Tourism for an official briefing. The information from them and your agent will enable you to make the necessary insurance arrangements for porters and staff as well as deciding wages and other terms of employment.

Liaison Officer
In Pakistan, India, Nepal and China you will be allocated a Liaison Officer and you will have to comply with various rules about the equipment you supply him with as well as other terms of reference. It is important to treat the LO as an expedition member rather than an encumberance. You are then far more likely to get his assistance and cooperation when you need it. The role of the LO varies between the different countries. In Pakistan or China the LO will usually play a major role in organizing local facilities and porters. In Nepal the Sirdar undertakes these tasks and the LO does not usually concern himself with day-to-day matters unless major problems arise. In India the situation lies somewhere between the two extremes. In each country a list of gear the expedition needs to supply to the LO will be available and it will often need to be com-

plied with to the letter, unlike with other members of staff who will frequently strike a deal loosely based on the official requirements.

Other Staff
I am often asked whether expeditions really have to hire so many other staff. The answer is that each country has a well established system and if you buck against it you will be in for a rough ride. A cook is normally essential as in nearly every case your LO will require one even if you feel you can do without. When you are tired from a long spell on the mountain it is good to be waited on at base camp. You tend to eat better food if you have a cook because he will take the trouble to cook time-consuming real food, rather than instant packet meals. In Nepal a sirdar is *de rigeur* but in other areas optional. Nepalese staff are in general superb as they have got accustomed to the whims of fastidious trekkers and their impossible de-

mands. On occasion they seem to work miracles, producing superb food from nothing.

Once your staff have been hired they can help you with such tasks as food buying, packing the food and equipment for porterage and of course the hire of suitable porters. If it is your first time then take careful notice of the advice of your staff even if it seems illogical to you at the time. They usually have a very good idea of food quantities and necessary cooking equipment for instance.

A mail runner should be considered for letters and information and lines of communication should be set up so that letters can get to and from the home country. Often the mail runner can be shared with a nearby expedition. Choose someone fit and do not pay him until the end of his work for the expedition. Rab Carrington on his first day in India, leafing through his file, which will start to grow considerably.

The Walk In

The Loads

Making up loads should be done with great care. Try to anticipate the worst things happening, such as total immersion in water, getting covered in snow, rubbing against sharp rocks, being thrown on the ground or dragged across a rough boulder field. All these things will probably happen and there is always the greater danger of something being stolen. Here are a few guidelines based on practical experience:

1. Numerous polythene bags should line the loads. Key loads like flour, which must not get wet, should be in polythene, covered by a soft bag, then polythene again, then another soft bag, more polythene and finally a hessian sac. Some expeditions manage to get hold of plastic drums at home and obviously these are very good, though difficult for porters to carry.

2. Paint a number on each load and have a list of contents. Checking in loads at night is easy by calling consecutive numbers. Also if a load goes missing you know straight away which one it was and what it contained.

3. Spread out absolutely critical equipment between various loads in case of loss by theft or accident. For instance do not put all the expedition crampons in a single load.

4. Keep the number of loads which might need to be opened on the approach to a bare minimum by carefully choosing where everything is put.

5. I have found a good system is to enclose every load in a hessian sac which is then sewn up and numbered with red paint. This reduces the temptation for a porter to have a look inside, particularly if it is sewn well with nylon thread of a colour unobtainable locally.

6. Keep loads manageable in size and shape as after all people will be carrying them.

7. Never carry anything else in a

fuel load as leakage will undoubtedly occur. The actual weight of loads depends on local regulations but if you have a heavier than normal load you can usually get it carried by individual negotiation on wages.

The Porters

Pick the healthiest porters you can and try to give a quick medical examination if at all possible. In Pakistan you will need to supply certain items of equipment but elsewhere you just pay a wage. The approach marches in many parts of the Karakorum involve long glacier walks and the porters are ill-equipped to deal with such conditions. You need to supply sunglasses (essential to prevent snow blindness), basic shoes and rudimentary shelter. Large polythene sheets are best for shelter, or else tarpaulins. All these items can be obtained over there. Also in parts of the Karakorum you will need to provide the porters with food and cooking facilities. This becomes very complex and expensive. In every country the amount you finally pay for porters will not neces-

In Nepal each porter carries 30 kg to base camp, using a basket and headband. This particular porter was delegated as an assistant to our cook, so he ate with us on the Jannu approach.

sarily be what you expect. Certain traditions will be adhered to, such as a walk which takes three days being counted by the porters as a four day walk, from the point of view of pay. There is nothing you can do about this, so it is advisable to consult all the sources you can, to find out what your porterage bill will actually be.

Deciding on the number of porters is always difficult until all the loads are actually packed and weighed. As a very rough guide a four man team with LO, cook and sirdar going away from the road for a total of six weeks would need about 25 porters, assuming each carries 30 kg, as they do in Nepal. As another example an eight man expedition to the upper Baltoro with a cook and LO leaving the road for two months would need 75 porters carrying 25 kg each. They would also need a further 25 por-

ters to carry food for the first 75 porters. These figures are based on a bare minimum of food and equipment.

The Approach

Again most areas have an established routine and you just go with the flow. Most places are hot so early starts are the order of the day, with the bulk of the walking being completed before mid-day. A few tips for the walk in are as follows:

1. Keep a rope or two immediately available, in case of crevasses or accidents.
2. Enquire about the state of rivers and carry gear to do Tyrolean traverses if necessary.
3. Be available to help porters over difficult sections.
4. Have one expedition member bringing up the rear in case of stragglers, particularly on dangerous terrain.
5. Count the loads every night and be seen to be counting them. This will help deter any potential thief.
6. Do not make unreasonable de-

mands on your porters such as forcing them to walk in a situation where a rest day is usually taken. On the other hand make sure they are not taking you for a ride. A strike can occur in which case more forceful methods of dealing with the porters will need to be taken and it is in this situation that your LO can be invaluable.

Above: Two expeditions passing on the Baltoro glacier. Because of the desolate nature of the long Karakorum glacier, there has been a history of strikes and other troubles with porters. Fortunately the system now works better.
Below: Paying off porters at the Ogre base camp, after a seven day walk from Dassu, near Skardu in Pakistan.

Techniques and Plan of Action

Base Camp

In many areas of the world the base camp is more or less decided for you by established tradition. The last bit of greenery makes a lot of sense for a base camp but occasionally, as on Everest or K2, it is still too far to the climbing if you pick the last grassy moraine. Psychologically, living greenery provides a welcome environment after a hard spell on the hill. Spending months on a deserted glacier, surrounded only by stones and ice, only appeals to a very few people of masochistic inclination. In most mountain areas of the world you will find an alpine type transition zone on the sides of glaciers. Small meadows with streams and flowers are often found tucked away in the most inhospitable environments. Your plan probably included a site for base camp and if the local porters cannot find you a suitable place it is worth sending a couple of people in advance to select a campsite which will suit your requirements. Some

key points to look for in a base camp are as follows:

Safety

The base camp must not be threatened by avalanches. Even distant seracs can fall an awfully long way in the right circumstances. If you are camping on a snow-covered glacier make sure it is not a crevassed area—you do not want to have to walk around the camp roped up because of crevasses. Often crevasses will appear as the season wears on and the innocuous flat snow will melt to reveal gaping holes where you have happily been walking.

Places to pitch the tents

Flat ground can be hard to find and it is time-consuming to dig out or construct platforms. If you are camped on a dry glacier the ice will move and melt so tents will need to be repitched from time to time otherwise the ground below will become very uneven to sleep on.

Water

A stream is invaluable because it saves fuel and is convenient. The stream should be no more than fifty metres from your base camp Stagnant pools might be the only alternative in some areas but they should be avoided if at all possible. Melting snow is extremely expensive on fuel costs and inconvenient but fortunately it is rarely necessary at base camp itself. If it is a commonly used base camp, be very careful with water supplies. A place like Everest Base Camp is notoriously bad for picking up diseases from the water supply, because of all the debris left by previous parties.

Our 1983 expedition to Lobsang Spires, Broad Peak and K2. The idea was to climb mountains of increasing height in alpine style. From left to right; Greg Child, Roger Baxter-Jones, Don Whillans, Jean Afanasieff, Goah Shah, Doug Scott and Steve Sustad.

Proximity to the Mountain

In general a base camp should not be more than two or three hours' walk from the start of the climbing. If it is further than this then you will probably need an advance base camp as well. This point is not so important if you are climbing super-lightweight. For instance in Peru I have sometimes climbed routes that were twenty hours' walk away from base camp, crossing several cols to get to a different part of the mountain chain, just to make a change.

Aspect

A camp with a view and one that gets plenty of sun is psychologically valuable. I like a camp with plenty of bouldering to pass the time when resting at base camp.

Living at Base Camp

A central cooking and eating tent is very useful. Sometimes we have made shelters from rocks, sheets of polythene or tarpaulins and string, on other occasions we have had the luxury of a family-type frame tent. In a place like Patagonia it is easy to construct a fine wooden hut and this gives you something to occupy yourselves during the frequent periods of bad weather. In my experience you will always spend considerable periods of time at base camp, usually because of the bad weather. If the trip is longer than a few weeks then it is usual to have separate tents for each individual expedition member at base camp. Having one's own territory is important and it is also possible to sleep better if completely undisturbed. With the often daunting prospect of climbing the mountain it is essential to feel relaxed at base camp and to be able to rest fully, both physically and mentally. If the base camp is above 5,000 m then a slight long term deterioration sets in but, fortunately most base camps are below this.

A good selection of books provides hours of pleasure and a good chance to catch up on reading. Cards and chess provide a useful social interaction as well as relieving boredom.

The Climbing Plan

Although you will have made a climbing plan back home you will inevitably find that it will need to be modified considerably as you learn more about what you are up against. Do not be afraid to make drastic changes of plan if the terrain dictates it. You may have planned on climbing a lovely safe ridge which looked an ideal route from photos in Britain but on arrival you find that out of sight from your photograph is a horrendously dangerous icefall which is the only way to reach your chosen route. Heavy snow might make your route extremely dangerous from avalanches, something which is hard to discern without immediate contact with the mountain.

After arrival at base camp you should rest for a day or two, spending the time making your camp site pleasant, particularly if you have been involved in a rapid height gain on the approach march. Then a series of reconnaissances is usually called for. It will be necessary to start acclimatizing further, and climbing easy mountains in the vicinity of base camp is a pleasant and rewarding way of achieving this, particularly if the ascents lead to further insights about your proposed route. Finding the way to the base of your climb, and also marking it out if it involves complex terrain, makes sense. Cairns can be used or marker flags which are

At most times of the year it will be pleasantly warm at base camp when the sun shines. The climbing plan can be openly discussed and gear endlessly sorted and overhauled.

often better if a complicated glacier needs to be crossed frequently.

After these initial stages plans will diverge depending on your proposed style of climb. Ferrying loads and establishing advanced camps is the order of the day if you plan to fix a line of camps on the mountain but if you plan to climb in alpine style then you will need to look for other methods of acclimatization. The height of your objective is a crucial factor in an alpine-style climb. For peaks of up to about 6,700 m, a week around base camp doing short excursions will probably allow you to become sufficiently acclimatized for your main objective. For peaks of up to about 7,500 m you will almost certainly need to spend some time at around at least 6,000 m. Three weeks around and above base camp is probably a sensible sort of time to aim for on mountains of this kind of height. For peaks above this height it is unlikely that you would be reading this book as you will have already climbed on lower mountains and formed your own ideas and opinions about tactics.

Always be prepared to modify your plans depending on circum-

Following sharp corniced ridges, like this one at 6,500 m on Jannu, is usually very time-consuming and precarious.

stances. There are many compromises between expedition style and alpine style so do not feel tied by other people's ideology.

Choice of Route

Although you will have made some preliminary decisions about the route at home and you may be limited in your choice by the terms of the permission, there is always a lot to think about when you see the route in the flesh for the first time. Three main factors should be weighed up: technical difficulty, length, and danger from rock or icefall. Other considerations are aspect of route with regard to prevailing winds, availability of campsites or other ledges, dangerous snow slopes that might avalanche, difficulty of retreat, length of approach from base camp and prevailing weather conditions. All of the factors mentioned are important and any one of them could completely prevent an ascent.

Technical Difficulty

This is notoriously difficult to assess but normally the route will be technically harder than you imagined sitting in your living room at home. Very technical climbing is extremely slow: if sac hauling and aid climbing are involved your pace may drop as low as three pitches per day at altitudes above 6,000 m. For alpine terrain of a TD grade on mixed or rock ten pitches per day is a respectable figure to aim for. Ice or easy rock is much faster and alpine AD to D terrain can be tackled at a rate of 20 to 30 pitches a day. In many cases your route will involve little more than steep snow walking, on which 600 m to 1,000 m of vertical progress can be made each day. The actual rates of progress depend heavily on the amount of gear and food you need to carry and the altitude the climbing takes place at. Technical climbing involving rock above 7,500 m for instance is unbelievably slow. If possible choose a route where the technical difficulties are low down, especially if your summit is more than 7,000 m.

Length of Route

Complex routes, involving large horizontal distances, will be difficult to retreat back down in bad weather. Fresh snow will make high altitude plateaus a real grind to cross and marker wands should be taken if there is a chance of making a mistake in route finding on the descent. Long knife-edge ridges are a nightmare for climbers because they are so time-consuming. Peru is notorious for elegant ridges that prove well nigh impossible to climb because of the rotten and precarious nature of the snow adorning them. Faces tend to be a much better bet unless the ridge is of a broad whale-back type, because they are more direct. As far as possible pick a route which ends directly at your summit because otherwise you may be involved in desperate ridge traverses at high altitude.

Danger

Ridges do have one plus point in that they tend to be relatively free from avalanche or stonefall danger. Séracs litter many faces in the greater ranges and sometimes you will be obliged to climb under them. Try to ensure your route avoids them as far as possible and if you do need to climb under them go as quickly as possible. Contrary to popular opinion, séracs are not most likely to fall at the hottest time of the day—they fall most often when the ambient temperature is changing most rapidly, whether freezing or thawing. Early morning and evening are the commonest times for major avalanches. They are rare at night so that is the best time to climb under them. Stonefall danger depends on the month you are there. When faces are heavily snowed up there is little stonefall danger but as spring strips the temporary snow cover of winter, loose rocks again emerge to clatter down couloirs and provide a considerable hazard. The stonefall only eases again when all the snow

has melted, such as happens on some of the lower rock peaks of the Karakorum, or when heavy snowfall reflects much of the heat of the sun away.

Having selected a suitable line you will need to wait for the right conditions. Weather is the main factor as with all mountaineering and in your initial excursions you

Above: Climbing through a complicated icefall below the north face of Nuptse.
Below: Séracs present a constant danger in all mountain areas. The avalanche in the centre of the picture has come from the ice cliffs above on an unclimbed and unnamed peak in the Biafo area of Pakistan.

will have started to get a feel for just what sort of cloud and wind conditions will presage good weather. Waiting for the right weather is very frustrating and sometimes it never comes. When the weather finally dawns clear it may well be after a big storm which has left the mountain pregnant with fresh snow. You should never climb on dangerous slopes the day after a big fall of snow because of the avalanche danger.

Grouping on the Mountain

As previously mentioned operating in pairs works well on the mountain. It is a suitable grouping for camping or bivouacking as well as cooking and eating. Also most climbers have done nearly all their previous climbing in pairs so they are familiar with how the system will work, regarding ropework on pitched climbing and moving together. The exception is big wall climbing when three is perhaps the optimum number, one person leading, one jumaring and de-pegging and the other sac hauling. Rather than swing alternate leads I have found it better to lead six pitches on the run before handing over the lead to my partner. Otherwise it is too tiring to second 50 m then immediately lead a similar distance without a break.

Pairs can work together in various ways. The first pair can leave a rope for the second pair to jumar

on if the terrain is particularly difficult. This reduces the strain of leading and pairs can lead on alternate days or half days. Otherwise they can climb as if the other pair were not on the mountain, only combining resources in bad weather or on the descent. Sometimes it is practical for the first pair just to leave odd pieces of hardware in place to assist the second pair but this means the second rope will have to catch up with the first from time to time to hand over gear accumulated and this can involve wasting time. Each pair should be self sufficient at all times in case the pairs get separated. This is particularly important with food, cooking and camping equipment.

Aid Burgess reaching the Lho La on the Nepalese–Tibetan border at 6,000 m. Even on a fixed rope it makes sense to work in pairs.

Timescale

It is rarely possible or desirable to climb all day, unless the route is a very slow, highly technical one. A straightforward slog on snow can only be sustained for about eight hours as an absolute maximum and this is best done when the route is in the shade, perhaps the early morning. This also gives plenty of time for brewing up and making a good place to sleep the night. Climbing in the great heat of midday is often counter productive because of the massive sweat loss it entails with consequent exhaustion. At some stage you will be in striking distance of the summit and a big decision will need to be made, whether to abandon all unnecessary gear and go for the top without bivi gear, or to plod on fully laden. Once most of the gear has been left behind you can make much faster progress, however you will be burning your boats, because if you fail to make the summit by a certain time, you will need to turn round and come down. The chance of a second summit attempt would be

Joe Tasker and Pete Boardman on the upper Kok Sel glacier basin on Mount Kongur on a hot afternoon.

virtually nil without a descent right back down to base camp for a rest.

Personal Relationships

Hard decisions will need to be made on the hill which affect not just your chances of success but your survival. Inevitably they need to be made by a consensus of opinion at the time. The strongest person physically will be found a far more potent force in decision making high on the mountain than the strongest person mentally. If there is some doubt about continuing but you decide to carry on the physically strongest person is the one who will be carrying the largest burden and that gives him an ultimate power. That power should only be exercised with careful consideration of the rest of the group. If at any time someone wants to go down then you have little choice but to turn back. These difficult decisions cause conflict even in the best balanced of teams so try and anticipate some of them, and talk them out beforehand. Despite these problems the shared experience is an extremely valuable one and if your friendship survives it then it will be all the stronger.

Communications

On a fixed rope expedition walkie-talkies are invaluable to find out who is doing what, whether there is food at camp two or whether the lead pair is about to run out of rope for fixing. On an alpine ascent this form of communication is redundant. The team left at base camp would rarely be in a position to help, and weight factors mean that the walkie-talkie is one of the first items to be chucked out. What the team on the mountain should do is give a clear idea of their plan and its accompanying timescale. They should also imagine all the possible outcomes and agree a course of action for each contingency. It is not unknown for an expedition to return to base camp after being delayed unexpectedly on the mountain, only to find that the rest of their team has given them up as dead and gone home!

A successful climb requires close co-operation and understanding between the members of the team. The descent from the summit can often prove the most taxing part of the climb.

Descent

When climbing you should always remember things which will help you on the descent. Surprisingly the descent is usually far less problematic in reality than you imagine it to be, particularly because you feel so much better as you lose altitude and also at the same time the mountain becomes friendlier. Winds and bad weather diminish as you drop and terrain laboriously slogged up on the ascent goes quickly and easily. Nonetheless it is a serious business, particularly in bad weather.

If you plan to descend your route of ascent you can leave stashes of food and equipment on the way up. Long abseil descents need lots of gear and careful rationing of what you do have. On snow you can do 100 m abseils if you are two pairs with a 100 m rope each pair. This is quick and efficient but not recommended if the terrain is rocky or hard to reclimb if the ropes to hap-pen to jam while retrieving them. Abseil anchors of snow and ice bollards should have been practised at home because they can prove life savers when you are low on gear.

A good rhythm will help to ensure a smooth descent by abseils. One person goes first, finds a new anchor then the second person descends. One person pulls the rope down while the other feeds it through the belay sling. If you have one rope of smaller diameter than the other then the knot must be on the side of the thicker rope in relation to the belay sling. Otherwise the greater stretch factor in the thinner rope will produce creep and can entangle the knot joining the two ropes in the belay sling.

Survival on the Mountain

Out for the Night

You have three basic options for spending the night out: a tent, a snow hole or a straight bivouac. Until you are very experienced I would strongly recommend one of the first two options unless the terrain makes those choices impossible, such as on a steep rock wall, where there is no room to pitch a tent. One bivouac is not so bad but a series of bivouacs over several days can be very demanding. Each night will be damper and colder than the last, even with modern gear. Sleep will be intermittent, particularly in a big storm with snow pouring down your neck. Cooking can take many hours and sometimes conditions can be too foul to even make tea. Before contemplating a prolonged series of bivouacs in such serious circumstances you must have obtained comparable experience in other slightly less committing conditions, such as the Alps in winter.

Tents

Camping high on an exposed mountain is a far cry from the boy scout camp. Fierce winds may tear at the tent during the night. Think ahead and expect the worst when you find a place for the tent. Finding a suitable place is the first consideration. It is rare indeed to find flat ground once you leave base camp so you will need to dig into the snow to make a suitable platform. The primary factor is whether the snow is deep enough to dig into and eventually provide a more or less flat platform for the night.

On steep snow and ice slopes, without features, finding snow deep enough will probably be impossible as the snow will rarely be as much as a metre deep. On steep terrain you need to find a natural feature to assist you. Sometimes where the snow abuts against a rock wall you will find soft snow and suitable conditions to erect your tent after an hour or so of work. In general you will only find a decent expanse of soft snow if the rock wall above is substantially overhanging. If the rock above is quite easy angled then it will be hopeless to look for a campsite at the junction of the snow and rock as you will encounter ice or rock just below the surface. The junction of arêtes can offer a suitable platform under certain conditions but this is rather a second choice because of the exposed position. Crevasses and séracs can prove ideal areas to find a safe flat piece of ground for your tent but remember that you are in an area of ice movement and blocks may fall off or crevasses get wider.

This brings in the other equally important factor in selecting a

Where large areas of easy angled ground exist then tents are ideal for surviving the night in relative comfort.

campsite—that of safety. It seems strange to mention this as a second requirement but the first requirement really is finding a place where it is physically possible to place a tent, a feat which is never as easy as it sounds on high mountains. Safety is paramount in a sense; that of always doing things in as safe a way as you can given the circumstances, but total safety is not possible—if you need total safety you should stay at home. Often your selection of a campsite is a Hobson's choice.

The mountains change constantly and you need to anticipate what can happen when you select your campsite. Innocent safe slopes may be a death trap after heavy snowfalls, when they are

Right: Bad weather is the one common factor between all mountain areas. A complete ascent in good weather is rare.

Below: This tent was at the site of camp two on the West Ridge direct of Everest at 7,000 m.

pregnant with fresh snow. Danger may threaten from a long way off, perhaps some séracs out of sight around the corner. Shelter from wind is a desirable asset but frequently is unattainable. One thing to watch for and avoid is a place where spindrift will build up between your tent and the slope behind, eventually forcing the tent off its platform. Ridges tend to be safer than open faces but are of course more exposed to the elements.

Tent pegs are a waste of time once the grass line is left behind.

Anchors are extremely important and cunning is essential in preventing your tent floating off into the night. On snow, ice axes, snow stakes and deadmen are usually good anchors for the guys. However, a good tip is to bury a polythene bag full of snow with the guy rope wrapped around it. This has the great advantage of involving hardly any extra weight at all, whereas snow stakes are heavy to carry up. In very soft snow burying the axe sideways will make a more secure anchor. Normally a mixture of rock pegs, boulders, ice screws

etc. will provide a solid foundation against the snow and wind.

The most common form of high mountain tent is a free-standing type. This has a considerable advantage over tents which require guys to maintain their shape. They will maintain a reasonable shape even on very uneven ground and you have more choice in ways of anchoring the tent to the surrounding terrain. Free-standing tents basically come in two forms; the box shape with rigid poles, or a dome or tunnel tent with flexible poles which maintain their shape through tension. If you intend to leave a fixed camp a strong tent is imperative and a heavy duty box tent has been popular, particularly in severe conditions. This type of tent is however totally unsuitable for lightweight pushes when the weight is prohibitively high. One big problem with dome tents is that snow tends to build up on them if left *in situ*. The weight of snow may finally crush the tent, breaking the poles. If you choose a dome tent for a fixed camp it must be of the highest quality, since cheaper tents tend to have poles which deform and break under severe conditions. Another advantage of free-standing tents is that they need a relatively small platform for their volume and so less time will need to be spent digging a ledge. For base camp any sturdy tent will do as weight is less critical because porters will in general be the only people carrying it.

Under most circumstances you will be obliged to cook in the tent. For this an extended flysheet is useful, particularly if you are cooking with petrol or paraffin. Many otherwise excellent American designs fall down on this point. Staying dry is a bit of an art on the hill. Every design of tent will suffer some condensation because the air inside will have more or less a hundred per cent humidity and be warmer than the tent walls.

Although we climbed alpine style on Mount Kongur, we still pitched tents each evening for the night's bivouac.

breatheable fabric such as Goretex will still see condensation on the inside because the fabric itself will be cold at night. Once condensation starts it will usually freeze therefore forming an impermeable layer of ice on the inside of the fabric. Thus ice will rapidly build up and then be shaken off in windy conditions, landing on the sleeping bags. Inevitably your sleeping bags will become damp, although I have found a Goretex outer minimizes the problem, particularly for a prolonged stay.

On an alpine push a bivouac tent may be the most suitable shelter, especially if the climb is steep and suitable tent platforms are unlikely to be found. There are not many commercially made bags which are suitable for high mountains so you should consider making your own, designing it with a particular climb in mind. My favourite design is of triangular cross section with lots of attachment points so as to make use of various anchors and lift the fabric away from your body. It is also worth having a sewn through loop to belay yourself with, otherwise you will need to bring a belay through the entrance. The tent should work for a sitting or lying down position and take two or three people, depending on your climbing unit. For very steep rock climbs individual porta ledges are useful. They are rigid frame ledges which can be erected from smaller pieces and provide a flat horizontal sleeping place for one. They have a single point of suspension and a covering sheet of nylon. They were developed for 'big wall' climbing in North America and their use can be extended to prolonged big wall climbing in the Himalayas, when sac hauling tactics are employed. They are far too heavy to be carried if straight alpine-style tactics are used.

If your camps on the hill are in constant use then obviously they should be left up all the time, but if they are to be abandoned for more than a day or two then you should seriously consider taking the tents down to avoid storm damage. Remember to use marker wands or similar devices to indicate the site of your camp. It is not unknown for an expedition to completely lose their camp after a massive snowfall.

Snow Holes

Undoubtedly the best means of survival on the mountain is in a snow hole. Sheltered completely from the elements, a snow hole makes an ideal home for a mountain man. Winds will not affect you and avalanches should with luck just slide over the top of the cave. It is far warmer than a tent at night but pleasantly cooler in the heat of the midday sun. There are just two disadvantages; it is not always possible to find soft snow deep enough to dig into, and the process of digging is time-consuming and also gets you thoroughly wet.

The criteria for a location to dig are similar to that for pitching a tent. Finding snow sufficiently deep isn't that easy, and it is always worth investigating natural features, particularly in the vicinity of crevasses and bergschrunds. If there is a steep slope above a bergschrund then the snow sloughing off can build up at the lower lip of the bergschrund. This is an ideal place to try and dig. It will take about four or five hours to dig a hole. There is little difference with two or four people because although the hole needs to be twice as big with four there are twice as many people to dig.

Common sense will suffice for digging a snow hole—there are no special techniques, but a shovel is very handy as with most hole digging. Certain models of ice-axe, particularly one made by Grivel, have a detachable shovel attachment. The pick of an aluminium shovel can be screwed onto the adze to form an entrenching tool which is ideal for working in the close confines of a tunnel. You will need to take turns at the snowface as the work becomes intolerable after twenty minutes or so. Removing snow from the face is the hardest work in most circumstances.

Although snow holes are primarily used on a fixed rope expeditions, their use should by no means be dismissed for alpine ascents. Despite the time and effort involved in digging there are some major plus factors: if a spell of bad weather moves in you can ride it out comfortably in a cave. There is a big psychological plus in escaping so completely from the environment. There is also a genuine element of security—it is possible to survive for a long time in a snow

The author emerging from the comfort of a snow hole at 6,000 m on Everest in winter. Temperatures outside were down to −35°C during the small hours but the cave was at least 10° warmer.

Above: At the site of camp three on Everest in winter we were lucky enough to find a natural snow cave in a crevasse.

Below: This super luxury snow hole took days to dig because of the hard snow. When finished it was used for nearly two months.

cave. They also offer a convenient place to spend the night on your descent and are good places to aim for in a storm.

Bivouacking
The third option for spending the night out is the least comfortable. If a bivouac tent can be pitched then things will be similar to living in a tent, but often you may not have brought the bivi tent so as to save on weight or perhaps the disposition of the available ledges has meant that the team is scattered and cannot share the bivi tent. In these cases a good sleeping bag is absolutely essential. Although climbers for many years managed without it, now Goretex is available it is a must for the outside of sleeping bags when bivouacking without any other shelter.

A very large hood is a useful addition so that tea can be drunk inside it without snow pouring down you neck. I have a very large hood which I can comfortably do things inside. It can be zipped down to make a reasonably weatherproof seal but can also be rolled back during good weather conditions.

Belaying is usually essential on a bivouac in case you slip off the ledge during the night. It is always difficult to do this in any convenient way as it entails a rope or sling disappearing into your sleeping bag. Spindrift is an enormous problem on bivouacs. It seems to

get everywhere, particularly behind your back gradually forcing you off the ledge as it builds up.

Cooking on the Hill

Cooking above base camp will be time-consuming and problematic. You have a choice of gas or liquid fuel. Gas is safe and convenient but very slow. Petrol and paraffin are fast but can be dangerous and are usually unreliable. All stoves are designed for sea level conditions and as you go up in altitude you will notice increasing problems. In a fast burning stove the flame seems to have difficulty getting sufficient oxygen, particularly above about 6,500 m. This effect is scarcely noticeable in a gas stove. Cold temperatures are the biggest enemy of the gas stove. The vapour pressure of butane becomes almost negligible at temperatures below about −15°C so either you need a propane–butane mix or some way of feeding back the heat of the flame to the gas cylinder. Even with the mixed gases a system of heat feedback will help cooking times.

I have used gas stoves extensively but if I am bivouacking out then I have used a specially modified stove to provide the flame with shelter from the wind. This tower cooker system is popular but you will need to make your own out of

Above: A traditional bivouac on the first alpine style ascent of Jannu. We had no tents and, out of naïvety at the time, no snow shovel.

Below: Cooking is a time-consuming and laborious process on all bivouacs, but it does pass the time.

Cooking in the middle of the day can save fuel and also a good liquid intake will speed the afternoon's progress.

an aluminium tube, into which you can fit a small pan or cup. The system has the enormous advantage in tricky situations of being capable of being hung from a piton. Because of weight I always carry a minimum of cooking gear on an alpine push. For one pair that consists of two plastic cups, two spoons and one pan. If you are

extremely careful you can just manage on one gas cylinder for every two days for a pair but at this spartan ration you will need to do the bulk of cooking and water-producing while the sun is out. If you brew up more or less whenever you like then one cylinder each day is about right using cylinders of 200 g.

Familiarity with a petrol or paraffin stove is a prerequisite for using it on an expedition. All stoves are temperamental, particularly when fed a diet of local fuel.

One stove stands out in my experience: the MSR stove which can run off most fuels, seems very safe and is highly convenient. The fuel can be carried in aluminium Sigg bottles which are just screwed on to the stove when needed. The fuel is separated from the burner so even when petrol is used it seems pretty safe. Weight-for-weight, liquid fuel is almost identical to gas in terms of how much water you can melt from it.

Food for the Hill
The actual choice of food has already been dealt with but there are a few special tips in using the food. The usual system on the mountain is to eat a meagre breakfast, then set off early to make use of good snow conditions. During the day only foods with immediate energy should be consumed—there is scarcely enough oxygen for living and working at altitude without the extra needed to digest food. If, as is often the case, you have finished climbing very early, you can spend the rest of the day brewing up and eating. You will probably never want to eat a lot in one sitting and anyway cooking arrangements would usually preclude this.

If the cooking process purely involves bringing something to boiling point then it is more efficient in practice to cook small quantities consecutively rather than cook a large quantity. As you approach boiling point the heat loss from the pan becomes similar to the heat input from the flame and with a large quantity of water you can reach a point where heat in and heat out are equal so the water gets no hotter. Thus small pans and small quantities seem the best option. Cold drinks will save considerable fuel and of course they will be welcome in the heat of the day. All food will need more cooking than the sea level instructions will indicate, because the boiling point of water lowers as the pressure drops.

A system we have used to good effect is to climb for a few hours in the morning then stop in the heat of the midday sun for several

Gear and food report from 1978 Jannu expedition

Equipment:

On our final ascent we climbed the mountain with the following equipment. (The list includes the gear in the sac and the things we were wearing)

Equipment carried by each pair

Food 6 kilos
Gas stove with three spare cylinders.
Small pan for cooking, 2 spoons and 2 plastic cups
Cigarette lighter and matches.
Bivouac bag (weight 800 g).
Toothbrush for clearing snow from boots in the evening.

Hardware
150 ft 9 mm rope.
2 Salewa drive in ice pegs
1 Salewa ice screw
1 Chouinard ice screw
1 Snow stake (between all four of us)
4 Nuts on slings
3 Small nuts on wire
4 Rock pitons

Equipment carried by each individual:

1 Whillans harness (or swami belt)
1 Ice hammer
1 Ice axe
1 Pair crampons with straps
1 Pair Scarpa double boots (with built in gaiters)
1 Pair socks
1 Pullover, 1 Vest, 1 Complete set fibre pile, 1 Shirt
1 Whillans suit (full down suit)
1 Goretex cagoule
1 Pair Rohan salopettes

1 Balaclava
1 Head torch (with two U2 mercury cells)
3 Pairs of heavy mitts
2 Pairs light gloves
1 Pair down boots
1 Goretex covered Everest Sleeping bag
1 Spider rucksack
1 Pair prusik loops
1 Full length closed cell foam sleeping pad.
1 Camera and three or four films
1 pair sunglasses, suncream for lips and face
1 Descendeur

General (carried between us)

1 Altimeter
British and Nepalese flags (very small and light)
Extremely basic medical kit,
2 Penknifes

Food on the Mountain

As always this was problematic. Weight is critical yet dried food has the major disadvantage that it needs to be cooked, a big problem in itself. We compromised and an average one man day of food on the hill consisted of the following:

50 g Muesli, 75 g Sugar, 120 g Fudge, 50 g Sardines, 10 g Dried Veg., 25 g Dried Meat (freeze dried), 25 g Soup powder, 20 g Kendal Mint Cake, 15 g Nougat, 20 g Nuts and Dried Fruit, 1 Small Chocolate egg, 15 g Boiled Sweets, 4 Tea Bags, 8 g Milk powder, 30 g Potato Powder.

The total comes to half a kilo per person per day. In practice these rations are often stretched for

somewhat longer than intended. Small quantities of other items were also taken e.g. jelly crystals, which are useful for cold drinks as they are not too acidic. As a substitute for potato powder we tried out freeze-dried rice. This proved very good and we regretted not having brought more than a sample. The freeze dried meat was very good and became edible even after the pathetic temperatures that our stoves managed to achieve at very high altitude. Liquids are always craved at altitudes, and as the water needs to be obtained from melted snow the proper functioning of the stove is absolutely essential. Our paraffin stoves did not function properly above about six thousand metres and so for our major efforts we employed the use of modified gaz stoves. We were unable to establish the root cause of our problems with the half pint paraffin stoves despite considerable thought. The gaz stoves, built into a tower cooker system for heat feedback and protection from the wind, always worked but became highly inefficient as the temperatures dropped and the air became thinner with the higher altitude. At night we took the stoves into our sleeping bags (along with books) to keep them warm for the morning.

With careful usage we managed to get our consumption down to one cylinder for two people every two days. This we achieved by often having cold rather than hot drinks and by cooking in the relative warmth of the midday sun, if a suitable place was to be found.

---

hours to have a brewing and eating session when the stoves are at their most efficient. Then we climb again for a few hours in the afternoon.

Clothing

Clothing depends very much on the environment: the high Himalaya in winter will need the very best clothing of the day, and lots of it, but a pre-monsoon climb up to 6,000 m will need only the sort of clothing you would use in the Alps

in summer. A few general guidelines of what to take when you actually set out from base camp are as follows: a waterproof outer layer for at least the top half of your body, any waterproof system on the legs tends to be unsatisfactory to some extent although I have found Goretex salopettes to be very useful so long as they are wearable all the time. Selecting clothes which will suit all temperature conditions is difficult, especially because the temperature

changes will occur during the course of the climbing day and it is very difficult to remove inner layers of clothing. Basically the outer layer will be on most of the time and so will the inner layer. It is the central layers which are flexible. Clothing should be added when the temperature drops but really nothing should be removed. Certain rules should always be observed whatever style you are climbing in. A spare pair of gloves should be carried at all times because although it is possible to minimize the risk of loss by tying them to your wrists a lost glove is extremely serious if you have no spare. I never carry spare socks because I never take my socks off on the climb. Carrying crampon spares is advisable if you have crampons that might fall apart—I know of more than one climb which has had to be abandoned because of lost crampon screws.

A reliable headtorch is essential along with at least two spare bulbs. If you can find them Lithium cells are ideal, providing up to fifty hours of light from one 2.7 volt U2 sized battery. Normally your headtorch will need modifying to use such batteries. When these run down and no longer produce light they should be removed from the equipment. Over-discharge can cause the cells to produce gas.

Coming Home

Many expeditions end up in some disarray on their return from the mountains. Promises made to sponsors in the initial flush of enthusiasm are long forgotten. Often no contact at all is made with sponsors on the return to the home country. This spoils your chances of future sponsorship deals as well as that of others. Although another expedition may seem a remote thought when you are fresh back to the welcoming comfort of home, it is surprising how time mellows and enhances the experience. We have all come back from some expeditions thinking never again.

Even if you did not climb to any summits you should write an expedition report so that other people can benefit from your experience. This need not be elaborate unless you have major sponsors to satisfy. The report can be sent to all the people who helped you as well as other climbers who may be interested. Equipment reports written specifically for the respective manufacturers are invaluable, particularly if you have found any problems with the gear.

Do not expect to be quite the same person when you return: an expedition experience away from the influences of modern society can change your perspectives and values profoundly. So long as you do not have an accident or contract some exotic disease it might be said that expeditions are good for you. Certainly you will always remember them.

Below: On the summit of Mount Kongur (7,719 m) battered by the winds which are the permanent accompaniment of high altitude. **Opposite**: The summit of the Ogre.

Bibliography

Acknowledgements

Fred Beckey *Mountains of North America* (1982)
Stephen Bezruchka *A guide to Trekking in Nepal* (1986)
Alan Blackshaw *Mountaineering, From Hill Walking to Alpine Climbing* (1965)
Walter Bonatti *On the Heights (1964)*
Christian Bonington *I Chose to Climb* (1966)
Joe Brown *The Hard Years* (1967)
T. Graham Brown *Brenva* (1944)
C.G. Bruce *Himalayan Wanderer* (1934)
Hermann Buhl *Nanga Parbat Pilgrimage* (1956)
Riccardo Cassin *Fifty Years of Alpinism* (1981)
Charles Clarke and Audrey Salkeld *Lightweight Expeditions to the Great Ranges* (1984)
John Cleare *Collins Guide to Mountains and Mountaineering* (1979)
Kurt Diemburger *Summits and Secrets* (1971)
Claire-Eliane Engel *A History of Mountaineering in the Alps* (1950)
Douglas Freshfield *The Exploration of the Caucasus* (1896)
Giusto Gervasutti *Gervasutti's Climbs* (1957, 1978)
Peter Gillman and Dougal Haston *Eiger Direct* (1966)
Heinrich Harrer *The White Spider* (1959)
Dougal Haston *In High Places* (1973)
Charles Houston *Going High, the Story of Man and Altitude* (1980), and *Going Higher* (1984)
Chris Jones *Climbing in North America* (1976)
Francis Keenleyside *Peaks and Pioneers, the Story of Mountaineering* (1975)
Layton Kor *Beyond the Vertical* (1983)
Ed LaChapelle *The ABC of Avalanche Safety* (1961)
Karl Lukan *The Alps and Alpinism* (1968)
Hamish MacInnes *International Mountain Rescue Handbook* (Revised 1986)
Reinhold Messner *The Seventh Grade* (1974)
Randy Morse *The Mountains of Canada* (1978)
Mountain Magazine *World Climbing*, introduced by Terry King (1980)
A.F. Mummery *My Climbs in the Alps and Caucasus* (1895)
Wilfred Noyce *The Alps* (1964)
Wilfred Noyce and Ian McMorrin *World Atlas of Mountaineering* (1969)
Tom Patey *One Man's Mountains* (1971)
Walter Pause and Jurgen Winkler *Extreme Alpine Rock* (1979)
Jim Perrin (ed) *Mirrors in the Cliffs* (1983)
Gaston Rebuffat *Starlight and Storm* (1954)
Gaston Rebuffat *The Mont Blanc Massif. The 100 Finest Routes* (1974)
Peter Robson *Mountains of Kenya* (1971)
Steve Roper and Allen Steck *Fifty Classic Climbs of North America* (1982)
Doug Scott *Big Wall Climbing* (1974)
Franck Smythe *Climbs in the Canadian Rockies* (1951)
Leslie Stephen *The Playground of Europe* (1871)
Lionel Terray *Conquistadors of the Useless* (1963)
Walt Unsworth *Everest* (1981)
Michael Ward (ed) *The Mountaineer's Companion* (1966)
Don Whillans and Alec Ormerod *Don Whillans, Portrait of a Mountaineer* (1971)
Edward Whymper *Scrambles Amongst the Alps in the Years 1860–69* (1871)
James Wilkerson *Medicine for Mountaineering* (1967, Revised 1985)
Ken Wilson (ed) *The Games Climbers Play* (1978)
Geoffrey Winthrop Young *On High Hills* (1934)

The authors and publishers would like to thank the following people for photographs and illustrations used in the book. Alpine Club of Great Britain, 21, 81, 136, 137, 192; Steve Ashton 39 above and below centre and right, 48 below; John Beatty 14/15, 16, 17, 18, 18/19, 19, 26, 28, 30 above, centre and below, 33, 34, 35 above right and left, below, 36 left, centre, right, 37 above left and right, below left and right, 39 below left, 41 all photographs, 42/3, 43, 45 above and below, 46/7, 48 above, 50, 52, 53 left and right, 54, 55, 56 left and right, 57 left and right, 58 left and right, 59 left and right, 60 all photographs, 61 above left and right, below, 62 above left, centre and right, below centre and right, 63, 65 above left and right, below, 66, 68 above and below, 69, 70, 71, 73, 74; © Chris Bonington/photo Rouse 213 above; David Breashears 126; George Brewer 123; John Cleare/Mountain Camera 6, 20, 23, 24, 173; D.R. Climbing Walls 25; Ron and Gill Fawcett 31; Duncan Ferguson 119; Photo Homberger 11, 147, 149, 171, 174/5; Roger Baxter Jones 243 above; Alli Kellas 153; Mike Kennedy 129; reproduced by courtesy of Kern Knotts Fell and Rock Climbing Club 22; W.C. King 133; ©The Ladd Company 140; Jeff Lowe 27, 51, 80, 82, 88, 90, 91, 96, 97, 102, 103, 104 above, 105, 107, 110, 111, 116, 118, 120, 121, 122, 124, 128, 130, 131; Greg Lowe 104 below; Mike Lowe 85; P. Ben Masterson 67; D. Morrison 168; Chris Noble 78/9; Paul Nunn 134/5, 139, 142, 145, 151, 155 above and below, 159, 160, 162, 163, 165, 166, 167, 176, 181, 182, 183, 185, 186/7; Charly Oliver 89; Oxford Illustrators front endpaper; Glen Randall 84, 93 left and right, 94, 95; Dolf Reist 150, 157; Bill Roos 86; Alan Rouse 190/1, 194, 195, 196, 197 above and below, 198/9, 200, 201, 202/3, 203, 204, 206, 207, above and below, 208, 209, 210 above and below, 211, 214, 215, 218, 219 above and below, 220, 221, 222, 223, 224, 225, 226, 227, 229, 230, 231 above and below, 232, 233, 234, 235 above and below, 236 above and below, 237, 238, 239 above and below, 240, 242 above, 243 below, 244, 246, 246/7; Stephanie Rowlands 148; John Ruger 99; Frank Sarnquist 117; J. Simpson 177, 178; Thexton 241; Mark Twight 83, 87; Karel Vlcek 32, 76; Mark Wilford 49, 98, 100, 101, 112, 113, 114, 115.

Index

Italic entries refer to captions and illustrations

Alpine Associations

ANDORRA
Club Pirineng Andorra
Carrer de la Unio 2, 20
Andorra-la-Vella

ARGENTINA
Federacion Argentina de Ski y Andismo
Viamonte 1560
1055 Buenos Aires

AUSTRIA
Verband Alpiner Vereine Osterreichs
Backerstrasse 16 (11)
1010 Wien 1

Österreichischer Alpenverein
Wilhelm-Greil-Strasse 15
6010 Innsbruck

BELGIUM
Club Alpin Belge/Belgischer Alpen Club
Rue de l'Aurore 19
1050 Bruxelles

BOLIVIA
Club Andino Boliviano
Avenida 16 de Julio 1473
Casilla 1345
La Paz

BULGARIA
Federation Bulgare D'Alpinisme
Boulevard Tolboukhine 18
Sofia 1

CANADA
Alpine Club of Canada
P O Box 1026
Banff
Alberta TOL OCO

Federation Quebecoise de la Montagne
1415 East Jarry Street
Montréal
Quebec H2E 2Z7

CHILE
Federacion de Andinismo de Chile
Vicuna Mackenna 44
Casilia 2239
Santiago

CHINA
Alpine Association, R O C
30 Lanchou St
Tapai
Taiwan

CZECHOSLOVAKIA
Ceskoslovensky Horolezecky Svaz
Na Porici 12
11530 Praha 1

DENMARK
Dansk Bjergklub
c/o N.O. Coops Olsen
Fuglesangvej 42
DK-3460 Birkeroed

ECUADOR
Associacion de Excursionismo Y
Andinismo de Pichincha
Casilla 8288
Officina de correo american Y mazosca
Quito

FINLAND
Suomen Alppikerho
c/o Veikko Korhùmäki
Juholankatu 11 D
04400 Järvenpää

FRANCE
Federation Française de la Montagne
20 bis,
rue La Boétie
75008 Paris

Club Française
7 rue La Boétie
75008 Paris

GERMANY
Deutscher Alpenverein
Praterinsel 5
8 München 22

GREAT BRITAIN
British Mountaineering Council
Crawford House
Precinct Centre
Booth Street
Manchester
M13 9RZ

GREECE
Federation Hellenique D'Alpinisme et de
Ski
Karageorgi Servias 7
Athènes 126

GUATEMALA
Federacion Nacional De Andinismo
Palacio de los Deportes
2° nivel zona 4
Guatemala City

HOLLAND
Koninklijke Nederlandse Alpen
Vereniging
Lange Voorhout 16
2514 EE-s-Gravenhage

HUNGARY
Magyar Hegymaszo Klub
Bajcsy Zsilinszky ut 31. 11
1065 Budapest 6

INDIA
Indian Mountaineering Foundation
Benito Juarez Road
New Deli 110021

IRAN
Iran Mountaineering Federation
P. O. Box 11–1642
Tehran
Islamic Republic of Iran

IRELAND
Federation of Mountaineering Clubs of
Ireland
Sorbonne 7
Ardilea Estate
Dublin 14

ISRAEL
Club Alpin Israelien
P.O. Box 53
Ramat-Hasharon 47100

ITALY
Club Alpino Italiano
Via Ugo Foscolo 3
20121 Milano

Federazione Italiana Sport Invernali
Via Piranesi 44
20137 Milano

Alpenverein Sudtirol
Sernesiplatz 34/1
39100 Bolzano

JAPAN
Japanese Mountaineering Association
c/o Japan Amateur Sports Association
1 1-1 Jinnan
Shibuya-Ku
Tokyo
150

KOREA
Korean Alpine Federation
29-1 Myoungryun-Dong 4GA
Chongro-Ku
C.P.O. Box 6528
Seoul

Korean Alpine Club
New Pagoda Building
Room 506
39, 2-Ga Jongro
Jongro-Ku
Seoul

LIECHTENSTEIN
Liechtenstein Alpenverein
FL 9496Balzers

LUXEMBOURG
Groupe Alpin Luxembourgeois
Place d'Armes 18
Boite Postale 363
Luxembourg

MEXICO
Federacion Mexicana de Excursionismo Y
Montanismo
Eje Central Lazaro Cardenas 80
Desp. 408
Deleg Cuauhtemoc
08090
Mexico D.P.

NEPAL
Nepal Mountaineering Association
16/53 Ran Shah Path
P.O. Box 1435
Kathmandu

NEW ZEALAND
New Zealand Alpine Club
P.O. Box 41-038
Eastbourne

NORWAY
Norsk Tindeklub
P.O. Boks 1727
Vika
Oslo 1

PAKISTAN
Alpine Club of Pakistan
228 Peshawar Road
Rawalpindi

PERU
Club Andiano Peruano
Casilla Postal 5360
Lima 18 (Miraflores)

POLAND
Polski Zwiazek Alpinizmu
U1 Sienkiewicza 12/439
00-010 Warszawa

PORTUGAL
Club Nacional de Montanhismo
Rue Formosa 303-2°
Porto

SPAIN
Federacion Espanola de Montanismo
Alberto Aguilera 3-4°
Madrid 15

SWEDEN
Svenska Klatterforbundet
P.O. Box 1245
75142 Uppsala

SWITZERLAND
Club Alpin Suisse
Geschäftsstelle SAC
Helvetiaplatz 4
3005 Bern

Rendez-Vous Haute Montagne
Postfach 15
6390 Engelberg

TURKEY
Turkiye Daggilik Federasyonu
Beden Terbiyesi Genel Müdürlügü
Ulius Ishani A Blok
Ankara

U.S.A
American Alpine Club
113 East 90th Street
New York
N.Y. 10028

U.S.S.R.
Federation D'Alpinisme D'URSS
Lushnetzkaja Kai 8
119270 Moskau

YUGOSLAVIA
Planinarski Savez Jugoslavije
Dobrinjska 10/1
Beograd